Corrections and Clarifications

Black Dog Publishing, Arnolfini and Michael Snow regret the errors and omissions listed below. Unfortunately, during the preparation of the book, Michael Snow was unable to supply complete information.

PAGE 11: *Wavelength*, 1966-1967
Right: film still, not a production still

PAGE 13: *Presents*, 1981
16mm film, not 35mm

PAGE 14: *That/Cela/Dat*, 2000
Video installation
Left: individual frames
Top right: installation view, Palais de Beaux Arts, Bruxelles
Bottom right: first page of score showing timings of words

PAGE 17: *Press*, 1969
C camps not G clamps

PAGE 18: *Rameau's Nephew by Diderot (thanx to Dennis Young) by Wilma Schoen*, 1974
Top: production still
Bottom: two film stills

PAGE 19: ↔ *(Back and Forth)*, 1968-1969

PAGE 33: *Fish Story*, 1979
Colour photographs on acrylic painted cardboard with wood frame
Sheep, 2001
Video installation, 15 min, colour, silent, shown looped

PAGE 35: *Couple*, 2000
Video installation, 3 min, colour, silent, shown looped
Not *Corpus Callosum, work in progress, 16mm film, colour, sound but excerpted from *Corpus Callosum

PAGE 37: *Michael Snow/A Survey*, 1970
Bookwork, 128 pages, illustrated, 21.7 x 20.5 x 0.8cm
Published by the Isaacs Gallery, Toronto, and the Art Gallery of Ontario, Toronto
Trade edition of 1000, plus edition of 125, annotated, signed and number by the artist

PAGE 53: Collection of the Art Gallery of Ontario, Toronto

PAGE 54 & 56: *Plus Tard*, 1977
25 Ektacolour photographs in painted wood frames with clear plastic

PAGE 58: *Sighting*, 1982, has been positioned wrongly. The top of the image is the left-hand edge.
Seating Sculpture, 1982, Steel, 140 x 53 x 234 cm, Art Gallery of Ontario, Toronto

PAGE 63: not containers, but container

PAGE 65: *Blind*, 1967
Shown being installed, Poindexter Gallery New York 1969

PAGE 71: *Transformer*, 1982
Collection of the Art Gallery of Ontario, Toronto

PAGE 77: *Rameau's Nephew by Diderot (thanx to Dennis Young) by Wilma Schoen*, 1974
Right: film stills, not production stills

PAGE 83: ↔ *(Back and Forth)*, 1968-1969
Left: production still

PAGE 84: *La Région Centrale*, 1970-1971
Right: two production stills

PAGE 104: *Imposition*, 1976, in case you're wondering, is correct but *Red*[5], 1974, is wrongly positioned, upside down

PAGE 117: *Wavelength*, 1966-1967
cropped film still, not production still

PAGE 136: *Immediate Delivery*, 1998
(detail: frame cropped out)
Back-lit transparency, 116.2 x 200 x 16.5 cm, Art Gallery of Ontario, Toronto

THE
STRUGGLE
FOR
MODERNISM

THE STRUGGLE FOR MODERNISM

Architecture, Landscape Architecture, and City Planning at HARVARD

ANTHONY ALOFSIN

W. W. NORTON & COMPANY

New York • London

For information about permission to reproduce
selections from this book, write to Permissions,
W. W. Norton & Company, Inc., 500 Fifth Avenue,
New York, NY 10110

The text of this book is composed in Optima
With display set in Impact
Manufacturing by Friesens
Book design and composition by Abigail Sturges,
Sturges Design, New York
Production manager: Diane O'Connor

Library of Congress Cataloging-in-Publication Data

Alofsin, Anthony.
The struggle for modernism: architecture, landscape
architecture, and city planning at Harvard / Anthony
Alofsin
p. cm.
Includes bibliographical references and index.
ISBN 0-393-73048-4
1. Modern movement (Architecture)—United States.
2. Harvard University. Graduate School of Design—
History. I. Title.

NA712.5.M63 A45 2002   2001030683

ISBN 0-393-73048-4

W. W. Norton & Company, Inc.,
500 Fifth Avenue, New York, N.Y. 10110
www.wwnorton.com

W. W. Norton & Company Ltd.,
Castle House, 75/76 Wells Street, London W1T 3QT
0 9 8 7 6 5 4 3 2 1

To the guardians and critics of memory

CONTENTS

ACKNOWLEDGMENTS

For assistance in this project, I thank Peter G. Rowe, successor to Gerald McCue as dean of the GSD, and two generations of Harvard staff and administrators: Polly Price, Larry Watson, Anne LeRoyer, Margaret Reeve; and Sean Conlon, Lynn Holstein, William Saunders, and Nancy Levinson. This project would have been impossible without the assistance of the former and current staff and librarians of the Frances Loeb Library: Christopher Hail, Janet Hatch, Kathryn Poole, Angela Giral, James Hodgson, Hinda Sklar, Mary F. Daniels, and Martha Mahard. The staff of the Harvard University Archives facilitated my research, particularly Harley Pierce Holden, curator of the archives, and Rodney Dennis, curator of manuscripts at Houghton Library. Joe Wrinn, director of Harvard's Office of News and Public Affairs, generously provided information about the university. I sincerely thank the alumni, faculty, and friends of the GSD who contributed their time in interviews, illustrations of their student work, and their insights. Too numerous to mention here, their names throughout the text give insufficient thanks to people who taught me what the school has meant to them.

The text was revised at the University of Texas at Austin upon the advice of wise counsel. Anonymous readers of an early version of the manuscript provided serious criticism, for which I am most thankful. The subject brought forth strong opinions about how it should be treated and its scope, and the text was substantially revised in light of their insights and thoughtful suggestions.

At the University of Texas at Austin I received a Faculty Research Award from the University Research Institute and a Research Internship Fellowship from the graduate school. At the School of Architecture, I was also fortunate to receive endowed support from the Sid Richardson, Martin Kermacy, and Roland Roessner Professorships. Colleagues, staff, and students provided assistance and support: Janine Henri, Chris Livingston, Christopher Long, Cynthia Merritt, Kevin Milstead, Dana Norman, Charlotte Pickett, and Elizabeth Schaub.

I owe special thanks to Edward L. Richmond and Elizabeth Deviney for information about the last testament of Joseph Hudnut, and to several friends and colleagues who provided advice and material: Anne Engel, Richard Filipowski, Alexander Tzonis, Liane Lefaivre, Eleanor McPeck, Peter Reed, Joseph Rykwert, Melanie Simo, Eduard Sekler, Patricia May Sekler, and Carter Wiseman. Betty Sue Flowers provided inestimable insight and guidance in her reading of the manuscript. Kathryn Holliday assisted this project first as research intern and then as a doctoral candidate. She helped in preparing the manuscript, cast a critical eye over the text, and organized the illustrations. Finally, I thank Patricia Tierney Alofsin for the gift of her laughter.

PREFACE

This book has a long and unusual history that began when I attended Harvard College in 1967 and graduated in the first class of the new Department of Visual and Environmental Studies in 1971. José Luis Sert was the dean of Harvard's Graduate School of Design (GSD), and Walter Gropius was a much revered presence on the scene. Like my peers I shuttled between Robinson Hall, home of the GSD, and the Carpenter Center for the Visual Arts. Foremost among my teachers was Eduard Sekler, the architectural historian who directed the center, taught the major courses on the history of architecture, and indelibly impressed upon me the permanent validity of historical inquiry. James Ackerman, lecturing in the Department of Fine Arts at the Fogg Museum, was the first art historian I encountered who understood the art, science, and politics of architecture. Those years in Cambridge were exciting, challenging, and, in political terms, occasionally tragic times.

I left Cambridge after graduation, but when I returned to study architecture at the GSD in 1978, I found a different world. The arena of polemics had shifted from radical liberalism to conservative postmodernism. The reuse of history was now valid—"Look to Rome for the answers," I was told by my new teachers— and anyone interested in the structural systems or craft of building was seen as a *retardataire* modernist. I began to wonder where these positions originated within the school. Much to my amazement, no one had answers. The GSD was oblivious

to its own history and its own traditions. Virtually no one knew who had founded the school, what it stood for in its early years, how it had evolved in the modernist era, or the origins of its pedagogical program. Among the few interested in those questions was Richard Wesley, who had graduated from the GSD in 1975 and was teaching architectural theory and design. Wesley was the first person to encourage my interest in the history of the school, the sources of its pedagogical program, and the history of architectural history itself. His encouragement was augmented by Henry N. Cobb, a graduate of Harvard College and a student at the GSD in the late 1940s. A partner of I. M. Pei, Cobb had returned to the GSD as chairman of the architecture department. His devotion to architecture and his insights helped inspire this book. He knew the value of history and encouraged this work over a period of years. Eduard Sekler continued to widen my horizons, while Alexander Tzonis, a Yale graduate teaching at the GSD, opened my eyes to critical theory. With their support and encouragement, I began to dig for the sources of Harvard's modernist agenda in the archives scattered throughout the university, including Gropius's correspondence, housed at the Houghton Library, and to interview some of the witnesses to the school's history, such as Kenneth Conant, retired professor of architectural history. At Harvard my obsession with history was balanced by my study of design under some contemporary masters—Jorge Silvetti, Gerhard Kallmann, and Michael McKinnell. After graduation in 1981 I continued to investigate the gestation of modernism, while also studying the history of art and architecture at Columbia University.

In 1986 Gerald McCue, then dean of the GSD, invited me to return during Harvard's three hundred and fiftieth anniversary year to write a definitive history of the school for its fiftieth anniversary. My perspective was that of an outsider enjoying distance from his subject and benefiting from the critical assessments of modernism allowed by postmodernism. The GSD provided funds throughout the 1985–86 academic year for my appointment as visiting scholar, as well as for a research assistant and typist. This support was given with full assurance of intellectual freedom; the material and opinions expressed here are those of the author, and do not necessarily represent the views of the Graduate School of Design or any of its programs or faculty.

More important than marking anniversaries, a history of the school was needed because no study had carefully documented and analyzed the history of design education at Harvard, and many views of events were inaccurate and incomplete. With Dean McCue's generous support and the assistance of Polly Price and Larry Watson, a small cottage industry was created to investigate the school's history. Julia Bloomfield, a renowned editor in the world of architectural publishing, came to Cambridge to manage and edit the volumes of manuscript I produced. She brought a brilliance and precision to the whole enterprise,

edited the endless drafts, arranged illustrations, and provided insight into the issues under investigation. We were joined by Andrea Greenwood, then a capable research assistant and now the Reverend Greenwood. She unearthed facts with meager leads and had the patience, tenacity, and insight to help steer this project. During one year of intensive research and writing, over six hundred pages of documentation were produced—enough material for several other books. Our efforts were assisted by numerous alumni, faculty, and former faculty, who generously provided their insights, recollections, and, in several cases, examples of their work from their student years. Several submitted to numerous recorded interviews.

Throughout the research and writing of the text, Walter Littlefield Creese played a particularly important role. After graduating from Brown University in 1941, Creese pursued a Ph.D. degree at Harvard University, which he received in 1950; his dissertation topic was American architecture from 1918 to 1933. He subsequently became a distinguished architectural historian, teaching at several universities, and he brought his Harvard experience to his work in the public domain. I was fortunate enough to benefit from his experience through an exchange of letters, interviews, and conversations over the project's entire history. He constantly supported this work and encouraged its completion when its author's courage waned. To his insights and generosity, I owe an inestimable debt.

After I finished the initial research and drafting of the text, I became so involved with other projects over the next several years that I had little time to revise the manuscript into a single volume. By the time I concluded those projects, I realized that the story of modernism in architecture, landscape architecture, and planning still needed telling, as the late 1990s were marked by a modernist revival.

The final result of this long gestation is a book that uses the education of designers at Harvard to reconstruct the efforts exerted to create an American modernism and how those American efforts were fundamentally altered at Harvard. This book differs from traditional school histories, which limit their focus to narrative accounts of events and people, because it explores both institutional history and the evolution of modernism in three fields at one university: architecture, landscape architecture, and city planning. At Harvard, the developments in one discipline cannot be fully understood without looking at all three. Also, the complexity of the interaction between people and events requires different modes of discussion at different points in time.

While the book is not intended to be a conventional school history or a general history of design education, it does provide a historical account of an academic institution from its formation through its halcyon years. My reasons for this approach are several: the seminal events at the GSD have never been fully described; their accounting is complex and requires sufficient detail to make

them understandable; and the story needs to speak not only to students and scholars interested in the history of architectural education and the history of architecture, but also to a larger public.

Not included here is an extensive investigation of the ripple effect of Harvard's modernist curriculum, which was widely emulated as a model in the United States and elsewhere, and its influence through the generations of GSD graduates who became teachers and leaders of other schools. Their stories will provide a further history of modernism. Also not explored in detail are the years after the GSD's fiftieth anniversary—events too recent to allow historical perspective. Similarly, the current faculty, students, and their work are not the subject here; their efforts, positions, accomplishments, and frustrations await the assessment of a future historian.

This book is based largely on archival documents and primary sources, supplemented with numerous recorded interviews and correspondence assembled from 1978 to the present. When I began this research, there were only a few general studies in addition to a small group of school histories.[1] In the interim, several important publications have provided a context for this investigation. Reginald Isaacs' official biography of Walter Gropius appeared in German and English editions and was complemented by Winfried Nerdinger's indispensable catalog of Gropius's architecture.[2] The relationship between American modernism and the architectural profession from 1910 to the

early 1930s was the subject of Paul Bentel's brilliant dissertation.[3] Eric Mumford's documentary history of CIAM (Congrés Internationaux d'Architecture Moderne) provided much needed background for understanding some of the conflicts within the modern movement in Europe and its transfer to the United States; his study filled several gaps in my knowledge of the 1940s and 1950s.[4] Numerous books by alumni and former faculty have added to an understanding of the period, particularly for the 1940s.[5] Scholarly research on American modernism in the 1950s is expanding.[6] Just as the editing of this book was completed, Melanie L. Simo's *History of Landscape Architecture at Harvard 1900–1999* appeared.[7] It provides an excellent historical narrative of one part of the GSD and fleshes out many of the details absent here. Curious readers will learn much about the personalities and historical events in landscape architecture from her study—and about the history of the field itself. Simo's book complements this book, which puts the teaching of landscape architecture into a broader context of architecture and city planning and shows the complex interactions between these fields as they played out at Harvard.

CHAPTER 1

THE HARVARD EXPERIENCE OF MODERNISM

A vibrant form of modernism in architecture existed in America at the end of the nineteenth century. It drew on multiple sources: the arts and crafts reform movement, innovations in technology, the history of architecture as a source of contemporary forms, and, in some circles, a rejection of that history in a search for a new language of expression that broke with the past. That these sources provided contradictory impulses is not surprising: Americans wanted to express themselves but were still tethered to Europe. An intense American self-consciousness fueled the search for modern expression by calling for the creation of a national architecture that somehow distinguished a young America from its aged European roots. The skyscraper was one building type that particularly embodied the effort to create forms of national identity by expressing American ambition and technology.

The development of nineteen university programs in architecture between the end of the Civil War in 1865 and the turn of the century testified to the desire to create an appropriate atmosphere for the practice of architecture in the industrial modern era. By the end of World War I, Americans were concerned that the country's technological prowess was outstripping its cultural independence. National identity became a major sociological issue in the 1920s; it was an issue to which the profession of architecture accorded significant attention. The American Institute of Architects (AIA) debated the means of creating an American culture through build-

ing design and, at the same time, considered the social implications of rapid technological change. During this time period, Americans were increasingly aware of the new architecture of modernity that was emerging in Europe. The AIA's professional journal became a platform for discourse about the European and American scenes, publishing the work of Ludwig Mies van der Rohe and Le Corbusier as early as 1923 and 1924.[1]

But the momentum of American modernism was severely sapped in the late 1930s and 1940s: the combined effects of the Depression, global war, and the increasing pace of technology profoundly disabled the earlier efforts to create American identity through design. By the late 1930s American intellectuals were viewing European modernism as a vital force that could be used on their own continent to rejuvenate the beleaguered practices and ideas associated with the Depression. By the end of World War II American modernism had all but vanished, and the effort to define an American identity through architecture had given way to a belief that European ideas would fill a deep cultural void. This loss of confidence affected American identity in ways we can recognize only now.

The thrust forward towards an American modernism and its eventual deflation was mirrored in the history of Harvard University's Graduate School of Design (GSD). Investigating the GSD at Harvard also illuminates the history of modernism, the American movement toward fashioning a national identity, and the education

of architects, landscape architects, and city planners. A study of the GSD is particularly useful in understanding modernism because its programs became models for other institutions, its graduates became the teachers and founders of schools that disseminated modernist ideas throughout the United States, and its practitioners became successful and sometimes famous advocates of modernism.

Harvard founded its architecture school in 1895—twenty-seven years after MIT had done so. After Harvard's late start, it moved forward quickly by creating the first graduate school of landscape architecture in America (1900) that put design before gardening or horticulture. It also established the School of City Planning (1929), the first school in the world dedicated

exclusively to the study and teaching of city, state, regional, and national planning. In the late 1960s, this graduate school pioneered the academic study of urban design as a field of postgraduate training.

The story of the GSD serves as an excellent case study of the collision between American and European identities. At Harvard, radical European modernist attitudes overwhelmed a nascent American modernism peeking out from progressive efforts at reform. This collision took place at the GSD from the late 1930s through the 1940s, when the school became the center of modern design education in America. But it was the European version of the modernist agenda—long associated with Walter Gropius, the German founder of the Bauhaus who

Redevelopment of downtown Providence, Rhode Island. General view of model showing the proposed cylindrical office towers, vertical mechanical parking garages, spiral department store, and shopping courts. Collaborative thesis by William Conklin, Robert Geddes, Ian L. McHarg, and Marvin Sevely, 1950. Photo by James K. Ufford.

came to Harvard in 1937—that reverberated through generations, ultimately producing the office buildings, housing projects, and urban renewal projects of modernism into the 1970s.

Threaded throughout these developments was the issue of collaboration. From the turn of the twentieth century, the Harvard design programs had responded to the complexities of modern life with an interdisciplinary approach that joined art and science. At this time, the old separation of disciplines in academia appeared artificial and inadequate. Design professionals, it was thought, would be in a better position to collaborate after graduation if they were taught to work together while still students. This objective could be realized only by training architects, landscape architects, and city planners together and having them work in teams on joint projects as they matured. Collaboration was the major innovation at Harvard's design schools even before the arrival of European modernism in the 1930s.

It is often assumed that Harvard's history is well known and that the story of teamwork at the Graduate School of Design has long been recorded. The following evaluation, made in the mid-1960s, shows a commonly held misconception: "Harvard led an architectural revolution in the 1930s under the direction of Walter Gropius as dean of the graduate school, that was virtually responsible in this country for the breakthrough for modern architecture."[2] Gropius, in fact, was never the dean of the GSD.

This view of Gropius's role and his "Bauhaus architecture" received widespread notice in Tom Wolfe's popular book *From Bauhaus to Our House*, which wittily characterized the ethos of the modernist agenda as an almost totalitarian war waged against comfort and pleasure in architecture.[3] Major figures of modern architecture, such as Walter Gropius, Mies van der Rohe, and Philip Johnson, appeared as dictators who routinely suppressed the simple desires of their clients. From his teaching pulpit at the GSD, Gropius spread the gospel of a reductive functionalism. The resulting "white cube" or "glass box" of modern architecture, termed the "International Style" by the Museum of Modern Art in New York in 1932, infiltrated American cities with disastrous results. Wolfe articulated a healthy skepticism for a whole generation of people who questioned the context of the cultural events around them. However, his broadly brushed view of Harvard and Gropius missed the nuances that only a careful historical reconstruction can provide. Wolfe, in particular, failed to recognize the American roots of the modernist agenda at Harvard.

A more careful view of modernism in the design arts at the GSD corrects popular views and other misconceptions that the modernist program at Harvard was Gropius's accomplishment. In fact, it was actually developed at Harvard prior to his arrival—and as a distinctly American effort. Though the very conditions that allowed the modernist agenda to flourish were embedded in its origins in the

Schools of Architecture, Landscape Architecture, and City Planning, the history of these efforts was forgotten or ignored. Even the contribution of the original founder of the School of Architecture, Herbert Langford Warren, a man who dedicated much of his energy and life to the school, has been lost.[4] An indefatigable champion for the professional training of architects and landscape architects at Harvard, Warren was one of the leading American architectural historians of his time. Except for a few landmark dates and important names, it seemed as if the forty years preceding the GSD had not existed.

Denial of a past that does not fit a convenient explanation is a common polemical strategy. From the radical modernist perspective, innovation is good, tradition is bad, and whatever had preceded the GSD was either irrelevant or *retardataire*. However, at the core of the predecessor schools of the GSD was the idea of collaboration, for which the GSD—and, particularly, Walter Gropius—received credit. From their beginnings, the Schools of Architecture, Landscape Architecture, and City Planning had espoused collaboration among the fields, an essentially modernist idea. These efforts often produced tension and conflict, however, which ultimately divided the schools. Each of these three schools has its own history of the struggle to create an agenda for dealing with the modern world, and these histories are complexly intertwined.

From the American perspective at Harvard, collaboration meant cooperation between architects, landscape architects, and city planners, with all efforts directed towards complete design. This was an evolving ideal that was not always held in balance and that changed over time. The European perspective, particularly among the avant garde, viewed collaboration as a process that should occur between architects and artists, with architects fulfilling multiple roles—the city planners and landscape architects seemed irrelevant. Both positions reflected what appear to be similar responses to the broad phenomenon of modernism with its demands for change.

When these two visions of collaboration collided at Harvard in the 1940s, friction resulted. From Gropius's perspective the term *collaboration* was rightly replaced by *teamwork,* and though the team would involve other disciplines, professionals, and artists at times, its core members tended to be architects working with other architects. Harvard's original emphasis on the integral role of landscape architects and specially trained city planners waned considerably. The modernist position increasingly became one in which the architect dominated all other design fields—the antithesis of Harvard's original ideal. The nuances in meaning that had given birth to the ideal of American collaboration were lost amid the vague and global associations of collaboration with modernism. The ideal actually reflected a complex historic response to modern conditions.

The creation of the Graduate School of Design in 1936, which amalgamated the three earlier schools, was actually the accomplishment of a forgotten American genius, Joseph Fairman Hudnut, the first dean of the GSD. It was Hudnut who, with the assistance of Harvard's president, James Bryant Conant, brought Gropius to Harvard. The central idea of collaboration that was present from the beginnings in 1895 became distant in the 1920s, but it was reformulated with vigor in the 1930s.[5] The ebb and flow of the search for a collaborative design education characterized the history of the GSD in the succeeding decades, as it continually redefined itself in light of changing perceptions of modernism.

Uncovering the nuances of the history of modernism at Harvard refutes some of the conventional assumptions about how modernism evolved in America. The history of these ideas and events chronicles a progressive modernism with American roots confronting a radical version that originated in Europe. The confluence of these forces, both searching for solutions to the modern dilemma, was central to the scene at Harvard.

The idea that modernists eliminated the study of architectural history from professional education and practice has gained the character of a myth: architecture students in the 1990s have all heard the stories about how Gropius got rid of all the history books while at Harvard. But this was not true. The revision and removal of history courses from graduate design education began during the 1920s under George Harold Edgell, the second dean of the Schools of Architecture, Landscape Architecture, and City Planning.

Even then, an art historian like Edgell could see that the increased complexity of modern life demanded more than an artistic approach to design; he eliminated history courses to make room for improved design courses. The conventional view holds that modernists rejected history as a viable element in the development of a new ideology. But the situation was far more complex than history simply being jettisoned by modernists. The importance of architectural history over the last one hundred years at Harvard has flowed in cycles, mirroring the culture around it.

Another widely held notion is that the traditionalists trained in Beaux-Arts techniques before the 1930s were not concerned with the social purpose of design. This view of the past is, again, inaccurate. The students and professors at Harvard were not exclusively fixated on designing estates for the elite. Concerns for the betterment of society emerged emphatically in 1909 with the establishment at Harvard of the first course in America on city planning, a course specifically intended to address how designers could contribute to creating a better future for urban America.

Criticism from radical modernists further holds that designers educated in the "old schools" were "paper architects" who designed unbuildable projects and knew nothing about technology and construction. This is another unfounded view. At least at Harvard, students in the 1920s and early 1930s were trained with a rigor in construction technology that equaled and usually surpassed the level of expertise attained by students trained under the modernists of the GSD. The fundamental difference is that modernists saw technology as an end in itself, worthy of celebration, and as a source of inspiration, while the progressives of the 1920s and earlier saw technology as an essential, though often concealed, component of the contemporary building system. For the radical modernists, technology was a symbol of modernism; for the progressives, technology was a means to an end, and styles were chosen for their appropriateness to a building's program and the client's preferences.

Tracking the details and following the flux of ideas within one intellectual circle—the design fields at Harvard—reveal the "big picture" of how American modernism emerged, struggled, grew, changed, and was ultimately eclipsed. The early efforts to deal with modern conditions and the origins of collaboration as an organizing principle are cloaked in questions that concern American national identity and how that identity was framed in terms of an evolving modernism. Harvard's first design schools were traditional but not hidebound. Sensing the modern world emerging, their leaders responded with their greatest innovation: the search for a collaborative ideal. In order to recognize the legacy the GSD inherited from these earlier pioneers and to identify the points from which it departed to form its own version of the modern agenda, we need to explore its early years.

For practitioners at Harvard at the turn of century, joining the programs in archi-

tecture and landscape architecture immediately led beyond considerations of buildings and gardens to cities themselves. Designing cities required a training that did not exist at the time. Harvard responded to this vacuum by creating the first course on city planning in 1907 and the first School of City Planning in 1929.

From the late 1930s to the early 1950s intense efforts were exerted toward finding the ideal format for collaboration as the means of propagating the evolving agenda of modernism. The university's presidents, deans, professors, and students spent a great deal of energy analyzing and constructing curricula and formats they all hoped would result in the ideal design professional. The most obvious result was the amalgamation of the separate schools into one: the Graduate School of Design.

The joint efforts of Hudnut and Gropius to make collaborative training the basis of a modern design education finally reached an apogee immediately after World War II. Returning GIs filled the GSD, and though they brought maturity, energy, and enthusiasm to the study of architecture, the unitary vision of modernism so powerfully articulated by its European proponents was daunting to most American architects; efforts to link modernism and national identity rapidly dissipated. American architects thoroughly and quickly jettisoned their own modernist experiments in favor of European models.

The close partnership between Hudnut and Gropius started to disintegrate in the

mid-1940s and culminated in open tension and conflict in the early 1950s, when the once-stellar school began to be seen as the locus of "decadent design." Understanding the demise of the Hudnut-Gropius era requires a consideration of the deep-seated ideals and problems embedded in their originally shared vision for the GSD, and their differing views of history and modernism itself.

Events from the 1950s to the present have served to fracture a unitary vision of modernism into reactions and revisions. With the departure of Hudnut and Gropius, the functionalist sector of modernism was seriously splintered, creating offshoots that led either nowhere or to the present. The past fifty years have hosted a complex flux of ideas: Le Corbusier's, followed by an ethos of pluralism, then social activism, environmentalism, scientism, the reactions of postmodernism, and, ultimately, a revival of modernism. Because many events are too fresh to evaluate, the recent past is presented only as an outline of bare facts. But even that outline points to important observations and questions. The challenges of collaboration among the fields of design and the interplay between American and European perspectives, paralleling national and international interests, persist into the present. The twenty-first century begins with more questions than answers: for one, is the goal of design to define an American identity, or is defining identity itself the question?

Looking at events at Harvard confirms that no single ideology defines mod-

ernism, contrary to what the early historians of the modern movement wanted us
to believe. Many different kinds of modernism developed in Europe and America
from the late nineteenth through the mid-
twentieth centuries. Just as moments identified as distinctly modern in the broad
contexts of culture, science, and politics
did not occur simultaneously or with
equal intensity and impact, modern
moments in architecture also appear as
increasingly diverse expressions.

Modern design is so often associated
with agendas for political and cultural
changes, which I identify under the
broad rubric of *social intention*, that
Harvard's activity in this arena can be
helpful in gaining an understanding of
this important aspect of the field. Within
any creative individual it may be impossible to distinguish between motivations
that arise from the self and serve art, and
those that come in response to the outer
world and are directed towards society
in some way. I associate the term *social
intention* with a generalized desire to
improve the conditions under which the
masses of people live. Such intentions,
which first emerged during the Industrial
Revolution, were expounded with a particular fervor by reformers in the late
nineteenth and early twentieth centuries.
If Europeans seemed more radical than
Americans in their cries for reform, it
was because their cries came in response
to particularly oppressive political and
economic conditions. Judging the effectiveness of social intention is extremely
difficult, but that difficulty does not

mean social purpose does not exist or,
even if incompletely grasped, is not a
valid concept.

Most of the events discussed here took
place in a small school that appears to have
little in common with the large and powerful institution that is today's Graduate
School of Design, located in George Gund
Hall at Harvard. In part, this is due to the
simple fact that for thirty-six years the GSD
was located principally in Robinson and
Hunt Halls in Harvard Yard, the historic
core of Harvard College that contains fresh-
man dormitories, classroom buildings,
administrative offices, major libraries, and a
chapel. The school's student body was
much smaller, its programs far fewer, and its
administration limited to two or three individuals. With the move in 1972 to Gund
Hall, nearby but outside Harvard Yard, the
student body, programs, and staff expanded
dramatically, losing the intimate—and
argumentative—atmosphere that existed
during the school's residence in Harvard
Yard. After thirty years of growth, enrollment in the 1960s hovered around 280 in
all its programs; by the year 2000 enrollment had reached 577 degree candidates.[6]

The story of the struggle for modernism
in this particular context extends far
beyond the circumscribed history of a single school. It is the story of how modernism became imbedded in the design
education of generations of Americans
and others around the world. And it
shows what happened when an American
modernism confronted its European
counterpart within the process of searching for a modern national identity.

CHAPTER TWO

THE ORIGINS OF DESIGN COLLABORATION, 1895–1917

Before the American Civil War, young men who wished to become architects had no certain path to follow to achieve their goals. No university programs existed to train design professionals. Instead, individuals pursued a number of different paths: university training in art and engineering, professional apprenticeships, and/or study in the esteemed design schools of France and Germany. This plethora of training possibilities created a highly varied mix of skilled designers and builders to serve the burgeoning growth of American cities and industry. At Harvard, for example, Henry Hobson Richardson studied at the university's Lawrence Scientific School (founded in 1847 as Harvard's undergraduate school of engineering and applied sciences) as an undergraduate, received a bachelor's degree in 1859, and then went to the École des Beaux-Arts in Paris. William Le Baron Jenney also studied at the Lawrence Scientific School in 1853, but transferred to the École Centrale des Arts et Manufactures, also in Paris, finding the instruction at Harvard inadequate. Only after the Civil War did Americans begin to seriously address the need for a means to create truly American architects. Richard Morris Hunt, America's first graduate of the École des Beaux-Arts, opened an atelier in New York in 1855 to provide systematic training to young would-be architects; in 1868 the first university-based school of architecture opened its doors at the Massachusetts Institute of Technology (MIT) under the guidance of William R. Ware.[1]

Rapid change in America during the preceding fifty years—the result of astronomical growth in population, the spread of railroads finally connecting the coasts in 1869, the increasingly urban character of the young nation, and the expanding international prowess of its industrial economy—had created a world of opportunity for architects, engineers, and builders. But despite the breakneck pace of physical expansion of American cities, architecture as a profession in America barely existed. When Europeans confronted the common problems of modern life—industrialization, urban growth, and social dislocation—they could call on architects trained at well-established academies and the relatively new polytechnic schools throughout the Continent. But Americans still searched for a proper means of creating a new generation of architects equipped to deal with the needs of a rapidly modernizing America.[2]

Ware was himself a product of the system of education that had served the previous generations of American architects: he graduated from Harvard College, class of 1852, and studied at the Lawrence Scientific School. Ware and many others followed in the footsteps of Charles Bulfinch, the first American-born architect, who studied mathematics and perspective at the university and graduated in 1781. Fifty years before Ware's student days, Bulfinch had proposed that Harvard give instruction in architecture, but the president and fellows, Harvard's

governing board, had informed him that this "ornamental and useful art" had not yet gained sufficient character to admit it to the company of scholars.[3] By 1890, Harvard had still not established an official program of architectural study, though several other universities had followed Ware's example at MIT. By 1894—the year before the official beginning of architectural study at Harvard—eight professional schools existed within universities and institutes: MIT (1868); the University of Illinois at Urbana-Champaign (1870); Cornell University, Ithaca, New York (1871); Syracuse University, Syracuse, New York (1873); Columbia University, New York City (1881); Pratt Institute, Brooklyn (1888); the University of Pennsylvania, Philadelphia (1890); and the Armour Institute, Chicago (1893). The founding of these schools helped propel the number of architects in America from 2,000 in 1870 to 3,300 in 1880.[4]

The Beginnings of Architecture Education at Harvard

The story of the establishment of architecture as a viable course of study at Harvard offers a unique perspective on the growth of the profession in America. Though Harvard was not the first to begin an architecture program, it was fortunate in its early leadership to have men of great vision shape its content and perspective. For most nineteenth-century American schools of architecture, the École des Beaux-Arts provided the principal model for architectural education. Roman and Renaissance architecture were the paragons of the past and guide to the future. Ware, in establishing programs at MIT and then at Columbia University, used the École as a model but tried to steer American training along its own path, independent of Europe. He was, however, uncertain how to achieve a distinct American character, and his

programs at MIT and Columbia remained heavily influenced by the École's tradition.

In Boston, local practitioners with a penchant for the arts and crafts movement and the ideas of John Ruskin tended to prefer Gothic and Romanesque styles to counter their competitors in New York and Philadelphia, who adhered more closely to the Roman, Renaissance, and French methods. Ralph Adams Cram, the Boston architect and America's most important proponent of the neo-Gothic style, led the charge against the École.[5] Not every school followed the Beaux-Arts model exclusively and not all practitioners idolized Roman and Renaissance architecture. At the University of Illinois, for instance, Nathan Clifford Ricker modeled his program on the structured curriculum of German education where practical and scientific attitudes were paramount but where the importance of history was also emphasized. Ricker even translated the principal German language texts, such as Otto Wagner's *Moderne Architecture*, for the teaching of architecture.[6]

At Harvard, Herbert Langford Warren was finally able to establish a Department of Architecture in 1895 (Fig. 2.1).[7] He was a cultural hybrid, the son of an American father and an English mother. Born in 1857 in Manchester, England, Warren studied in a German gymnasium, where he learned rigor and rationalism, and at Owens College in Manchester, where he was greatly influenced by Ruskin. Warren came to America to study architecture at

2.2 Professor Herbert Langford Warren.

MIT, where he absorbed Ware's ideas and teaching format. Next he went to work for H. H. Richardson in 1879, became his chief draftsman, and developed a sensitivity to Romanesque architecture. Charles Allerton Coolidge, senior partner of Richardson's successor firm Shepley, Rutan & Coolidge, noted that when they both worked at Richardson's office, Warren was a "Goth at heart, and yet the work at Richardson's office was Romanesque."[8]

Once Warren arrived at Harvard, he applied Ware's principles for architectural education: it would be based on high standards of scholarship in the liberal arts; the study of ancient buildings (and the cultures that produced them); the scientific study of construction and materials; and the study of historic examples to learn the practice and the theory of design (Fig. 2.2).

Warren's program, though situated within Harvard's walls, hallowed by its conservative puritan origins, was filled with a progressive vision for the future of the architectural profession. He began the architecture program not just as a response to the practical need for architectural training but also for the lofty purpose of helping to fulfill the cultural and social destiny of America.[9] Under Warren's protective wing, the official study of landscape architecture and the beginnings of the academic study of town planning were inaugurated in America.

Warren viewed architecture as ideally representing a synthesis of art and science in the service of the new American society. He recognized America's special circumstances—the young country lacked its own cultural traditions, and architecture needed to address this absence: "In our day and country we are almost without traditions, and, however much we deplore the fact, we cannot change our circumstances. We must take our birthright as we find it. . . . There is only one thing which can be substituted for tradition and prevent our architecture from running, as it so often has, into parrot-like imitation of bygone styles or hopeless and vulgar extravagance, and that is Scholarship."[10]

In the *Official Register* that described Harvard's academic programs, Warren further pointed out that "modern conditions" demanded a broad expertise from the architect; the skills of artist, scholar, builder, and businessman, and knowledge of the science of construction were necessary for professional practice. Architecture was a unique profession because it not only was an exalted fine art but also had to provide habitable and stable spaces that responded to the practical and exacting demands of everyday life. In addition, Warren wrote: "Architecture is essentially a Fine Art, the practice of which must be based on a thorough knowledge of Construction. Great stress has therefore been laid on continued practice in design and drawing and thorough instruction in the history and principles of the Fine Art of Architecture and arts allied to it."[11] *Scholarship*, the study of the conditions under which design came into being, was the means of understanding and absorbing culture and the only way to avoid slavish imitation and vulgarity. An appreciation of the beauty of culture and the societies that produced it was essential to scholarship and to professional training. Science and engineering would provide the practical realities necessary for architects to wield their art successfully in the real world.

In connecting art and science, culture and architecture, Warren established the framework for Harvard's responses to the design needs of modern life: the joining of different faculties in the conviction that collaboration could produce better trained professionals. This was an American answer to modern problems, inchoate at this point. But over time it would define Harvard's uniqueness.

Uniting art and science was easier said than done. Between 1893 and his death in 1917, Warren hired faculty, secured a building for classes, found funds, and administered their use. As he perfected his philosophy of teaching, he also published in journals and lectured at professional meetings. He oversaw the translation of Vitruvius's *The Ten Books of Architecture* by Morris H. Morgan, published in 1914, a standard reference for decades.[12] Though his lectures were only published posthumously (as *The Foundations of Classic Architecture*), Warren became known as one of the leading architectural historians in America.[13]

Before launching the program at Harvard, Warren first sought advice from Ware, then the leading American educator in architecture at Columbia, as well as from the appropriate parties at Harvard: Nathaniel Shaler, professor of geology

and dean of the Lawrence Scientific School where technical courses would be taught; Charles Eliot Norton, the most eminent art historian in the country and Harvard's first chair in Fine Arts[14]; and Charles Herbert Moore, Assistant Professor of Fine Arts, a consummate draftsman, watercolorist, and art historian, who, like Norton, was a colleague and friend of the great English aesthetician John Ruskin. These men represented the fields that lay at the core of the new program; collaboration between the Lawrence Scientific School and the Department of Fine Arts was crucial for the new program in architecture.

In 1893, with the support of Norton, Moore, and Shaler, Warren taught the first courses at Harvard devoted exclusively to the history of architecture, focusing on Greek and Roman traditions with additional courses the following year.[15] He also began to search for a professor of design, and wrote John Merven Carrère of Carrère & Hastings in New York to obtain a list of Americans who had studied at the École des Beaux-Arts.[16] Finally, in the academic year 1895–96, Harvard offered its first official curriculum in architecture, becoming the ninth school of architecture in the United States. The program was offered to undergraduates in the Lawrence Scientific School and led to the degree of Bachelor of Science (S.B.). The Lawrence Scientific School at Harvard was under control of the Faculty of Arts and Sciences but functioned with almost autonomous independence.[17] The broad intent of the pro-

gram was to prepare practitioners with preliminary and technical training in architecture that would be supplemented by practical experience in an architect's office during summer vacations.

If architecture was a science and an art, then balancing the two—in terms of either training or practice—was no simple matter. Despite the fact that the study of architecture started within the classrooms of the Lawrence Scientific School, the scales tipped toward art at the outset. Norton, in his esteemed position in the Department of Fine Arts, had already catalyzed the intellectual association of architecture and fine arts; he had been Warren's teacher. Norton's department actually considered taking on the new architecture program as one of its own programs because, according to Moore, positioning the new architecture program under engineering "would be very undesirable and even harmful."[18] Clearly, their goal was to get architecture out of engineering and into art, a discipline closer to its own heart. Reinforcing the Harvard connection with Ruskin and, indirectly, with the Gothicizing and rational principles of Eugène Viollet-le-Duc, Moore continued the principle and practice of collaboration. As the first director of Harvard's Fogg Museum in 1895, Moore promoted architecture at the university as a fine art and taught courses for architecture students. The Departments of Fine Arts and Architecture shared resources, including casts and models (their core of study materials), and developed a bond that lasted until the late 1930s.

2.3 Hunt Hall, Richard Morris Hunt, 1893.

2.4 Hunt Hall, Richard Morris Hunt, 1893. Interior view showing collection of casts.

In this early period from 1895 to World War I, the teaching of architecture, fine art, and the history of art and architecture was a highly collaborative effort. The faculties of the Departments of Fine Arts and Architecture cooperated in teaching drawing and modeling, forming a single, integrated enterprise that recognized no division between the practice and study of art and architecture. This joint effort was convenient, too: after bouncing around in a number of buildings, the new courses in architecture were now given in Richard Morris Hunt Hall, opened in 1895 and named for the great architect, originally the home of the William Hayes Fogg Museum (which Hunt had designed), and snug within the walls of Harvard Yard (Figs. 2.3, 2.4).[19]

Though establishing the Department of Architecture consumed Warren as an administrator and a teacher, he also retained an outside professional practice, making clear that the practitioner-teacher had a viable place in a university setting. Warren designed schools and houses, often in a murky Gothic mode. Participating in Harvard's first collaborative project between engineering and architecture, he designed the Carey Cage (1897), a gymnasium, with L. J. Johnson, professor of civil engineering.[20] Warren also adapted the plans of German Bestelmeyer and became supervising architect for the Germanic Museum, later called the Busch-Reisinger Museum, at Harvard. It was devoted to furthering an awareness of German culture. The Church of the New Jerusalem (1901) in Cambridge, Massa-

chusetts, a Swedenborg chapel (next door to the future site of Gund Hall, current home of the Graduate School of Design), clearly expresses Warren's design aesthetic and skills (Fig. 2.5).

The Beginnings of Landscape Architecture Education at Harvard

Warren's efforts to find an American response to modern conditions through architectural training were further propelled by a unique mix of personal tragedies, great philanthropy, and the emergence of a new professional field, landscape architecture. The new key figure was Charles Eliot, Jr., son of Harvard's president, Charles William Eliot (Fig. 2.6). The young Eliot had developed a passionate interest in landscape architecture through his uncle, Robert Swain Peabody, confidante of Langford Warren and partner in Peabody & Stearns, designers of several Harvard buildings.[21] Getting an education in landscape architecture, however, was problematic. The usual means were through the study of agriculture and horticulture or by apprenticeship and travel. At Harvard, Eliot could study plants and trees at the Bussey Institution, a "museum" of trees that supported scientific research in arboriculture, forestry, and dendrology. Located five miles southwest of the center of Boston at the outer edge of Jamaica Plain, it was operated by Harvard and provided a training ground for farmers, gardeners, landscape gardeners, and managers of estates, parks, public institutions, towns, and highways.

2.5 Swedenborg Church of the New Jerusalem, corner of Kirkland and Quincy Streets. Herbert Langford Warren, 1903.

2.6 Charles Eliot, Jr., at age 33.

In addition, there was the Arnold Arboretum, founded in 1872 on a portion of the Bussey Farm in West Roxbury. The arboretum represented a shift after the Civil War from the romantic vocabulary of horticulture to serious landscape architecture. The Botanic Garden, founded in 1807 on a seven-acre tract at the corner of Linnean and Garden Streets in Cambridge (later built over as the Botanic Gardens Apartments), had over 5,000 species of plants cultivated for scientific and educational purposes. It also contained the Gray Herbarium, a gift to the University from Professor Asa Gray, which housed mounted specimens for the study of botany. But Harvard offered no program in which to study landscape architecture as a distinct professional discipline. Eliot argued the case for making a special field to Charles Francis Adams II, a member of the Harvard Board of Overseers and the treasurer of the university:

> As to Landscape Architecture, I believe that such instruction as might be formally offered by the University ought by rights to be associated with the courses in Architecture given at the Lawrence School, rather than with courses in Agriculture, Horticulture (and Forestry) given at the Bussey. The popular notion that my profession is chiefly concerned with gardens and gardening is utterly mistaken. Landscape Architecture is an art of design, and in a very true sense covers agriculture, forestry, gardening, engineering, and even architecture (as ordinarily defined) itself. . . . If you will recall our metropolitan park reports (to mention none of Mr. Olmsted's), I think you will

perceive how far my profession has advanced beyond landscape gardening; and why I think it would be best to give the proposed instruction in a School of Design rather than in a School of Horticulture.[22]

Here was the first call for a collaboration between architecture and landscape architecture, even foreshadowing the name the school would ultimately take: *School of Design*. The liberation of landscape architecture from the Bussey Institute, and eventually the Lawrence Scientific School, directly contrasted with the policies of institutions such as Cornell, where courses in landscape architecture were offered through a separate department within the College of Agriculture.[23]

Eliot made the best of the available opportunities. In 1883 he began a two-year apprenticeship in the office of Frederick Law Olmsted, the preeminent landscape architect in America, who maintained a firm with his two sons in Brookline, Massachusetts. Eliot then left for a year of travel, returning to Cambridge in 1886 to set up his own practice. In 1893 Henry Codman, the newest partner of the Olmsted firm, died and the Olmsteds invited Eliot to become a partner. He accepted and the firm's name was changed to Olmsted, Olmsted & Eliot. In the fall of that year, the firm was appointed as landscape architects to the Metropolitan Park Commission in Boston, with Eliot as their representative. For the next four years Eliot devoted himself to the development of the park system while continuing his general duties as a partner.

The pace was exhausting, and he died from meningitis on 25 March 1897 at the age of thirty-seven.

Eliot's grief-stricken father decided to carry out his son's dream of creating a professional program in landscape architecture. He began corresponding with Frederick Law Olmsted, Jr., about establishing a department of landscape architecture that would both honor the memory of his son and support the profession to which he had been dedicated.[24] Olmsted, Jr., had been educated at Harvard (AB 1894); he worked in the Olmsted office until 1898, three years after the retirement of his father, when he and his half-brother created a partnership called Olmsted Brothers. Olmsted's practice involved large-scale projects, including efforts to complete the Pierre L'Enfant plan for Washington as well as the creation of the Great Mall, with the assistance of Daniel H. Burnham. The practice kept Olmsted too busy to begin teaching immediately, but over the next two years he planned a detailed curriculum for the new department.[25]

In 1900 Harvard announced a program in landscape architecture, headed by the thirty-one-year-old Olmsted, "to provide instruction in the elements of technical knowledge and the training in the principles of design which form together the proper basis for the professional practice of Landscape Architecture."[26] The four-year program in the Lawrence Scientific School would provide students with a Bachelor of Science degree. At the end of the program's sec-

ond year of operation, Olmsted reported to President Eliot that in his introductory course, thirty-seven students had enrolled.[27]

Faculty for landscape architecture courses were relatively easy to recruit; they came largely from the Olmsted firm in nearby Brookline. Olmsted's assistants in 1900 were Arthur Asahel Shurtleff, an MIT graduate who had also studied at Harvard and apprenticed in the Olmsted office in Brookline, and Benjamin Marston Watson, an instructor in horticulture from the Bussey Institution.[28] Olmsted and Shurtleff taught during the winter months, and for seven years, until Shurtleff's departure, they trained men—and only men—who received degrees in landscape architecture and subsequently became prominent practitioners and teachers at Harvard.

The Development of a Collaborative Curriculum

By the beginning of the twentieth century, two separate programs, in architecture and landscape architecture, existed at Harvard, but they shared a single curriculum, faculty, and resources, with specialized courses required of each field. Both programs prepared practitioners with preliminary and technical training in architecture, to be supplemented by practical experience in an architect's office during summer vacations; both programs maintained the same preprofessional objectives of providing knowledge and training that formed the basis for professional

practice by creating conditions that were "made to approximate those of actual office practice as close as possible."[29]

The curriculum in architecture was allied with the teaching of fine arts through joint courses and shared faculty but existed within the school of engineering, thus ensuring a grounding in both art and the physical sciences. Warren, with the help of assistants, taught almost every course offered: architectural history, design, and technology. He wove together these three main subjects, using the history of architecture as the primary tool for studying not only monuments but also design and the links between architecture and society.[30] A three-year history sequence was given under the rubric of "Technical and Historical Development." Warren's basic teaching approach was to establish a cultural-historical setting by discussing buildings as part of a tradition that either adhered to, or deviated from, models, and analyzing them in terms of construction, materials, and visual appropriateness. The mastering of classical detail and elements was emphasized both for historical significance and as a malleable addition to contemporary design vocabulary.

Ancient architecture, with an emphasis on Greek and Roman contributions, was the subject of the first-year history course, which started with instruction in elementary drawing techniques (perspective, projection, shades, and shadows). A summary of the architecture of Egypt, Assyria, and Persia led to a more detailed discussion of the Greek and Roman

2.7 Example of the Corinthian order, W. T. Littig, 1901. First-year problem, elementary architectural drawing.

2.8 Freehand drawing, T. B. Faye, 1901. Second-year problem, freehand drawing. Drawn from cast on gray paper and rendered with white shade and shadow of India ink and highlights of Chinese white.

2.9 Freehand drawing, Alexander E. Hoyle, 1902. Third-year problem, freehand drawing. Drawn from cast on white paper and rendered with India ink.

orders and their appropriate use. In addition to providing a base for studies in architectural design, the course on ancient history was foundation for the second-year "Technical and Historical Development of the Medieval Styles of Architecture" and the third-year "Technical and Historic Development of the Renaissance and Modern Styles."[31] The latter two courses were given in alternate years. In Warren's curriculum the Renaissance provided the last coherent style, while "Modern Styles" was the catch-all category for post-Renaissance architecture. From Warren's perspective, the eclecticism and revivals of the nineteenth century had no historical viability, and their diversity represented to him a deplorable fall from taste. Through the history sequence, Warren emphasized the relationship of decorative arts to architecture, stressing that beauty in architecture comes from the artistic expression of use and construction.

Architecture students studied drawing before they began learning to design, and then drawing and design courses continued in tandem over the four-year program, supplemented with a course in modeling in the fourth year. In addition to formal classwork, beginning students were required to draw careful renderings of building fragments or of the classical Corinthian, Ionic, and Doric orders that they could select with the approval of the instructor (Figs. 2.7–2.9). Assistant instructors in the Department of Architecture taught architectural drawing; Charles Herbert Moore taught delineation and freehand drawing in a combined theory and studio course in the Department of Fine Arts.[32]

When architecture students began the study of design in their second year with Warren and his assistant, they were asked to draw portions of buildings using their own measurements, which were sometimes made during the preceding summer (Fig. 2.10). They also began "design by dictation": a building description was read aloud and the students drew it from memory, a teaching practice originating with William Ware at MIT.[33] These "problems," which became increasingly complex over the four-year program, served the students in the dual goals of learning the principles and methods of their field while studying the history of the world's highest architectural achievements.

Intermediate design was taught in the third year and involved complex building projects that ranged from a dormitory for a boys' school to a hall for concerts and plays, to a public library for a country town, a city bank and church, and a museum (Fig. 2.11). Warren and his assistant gave the initial problems and members of the Visiting Committee posed the concluding problems. The Visiting Committee for architecture, appointed by the university in 1899, was intended to bring a professional perspective to students' education. The first such committee consisted of Boston practitioners Robert Swain Peabody, R. Clipston Sturgis, W. Wadsworth Longfellow, and Edmund M. Wheelwright, who were distinguished graduates of Harvard College or had

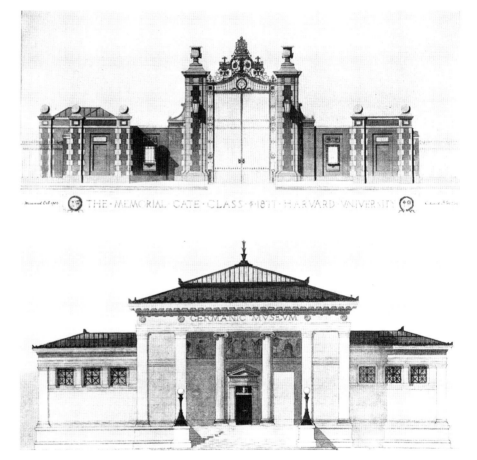

2.10 Memorial gate, Harvard University, E. B. McGirr, 1902. Second-year problem, measured drawing.

2.11 A museum and lecture hall, G. R. Ainsworth, 1902. Third-year problem, intermediate design.

2.12 An entrance to an apartment house. T. B. Faye, 1901. Arch. 4a, fourth-year problem, building design.

2.13 Palazzo, John A. Gade, 1897. Fourth year, thesis.

2.14 United States arsenal, N. G. Andres, 1902. Fourth year, thesis. Perspective by Oglesby Paul.

designed buildings for Harvard, or both. The visitors kept the students in touch with "ideals of the community" and allowed the committee members to gauge the progress of the school.[34]

Advanced design followed in the fourth year and consisted primarily of lectures, given by Warren, that explored problems in planning contemporary buildings, such as schools and other educational institutions, museums, public libraries, railroad stations, town halls, theaters, concert halls, and commercial and domestic buildings (Fig. 2.12). In addition, there were lectures on landscape gardening and its relationship to architecture. A thesis was required in the latter half of the fourth year with a choice of two kinds of topics: an original architectural design, or a series of drawings of an important historic monument (Figs. 2.13, 2.14). In both cases a written essay discussing the aesthetics of the original design or the history of the monument was required. Students who pursued an extra, fifth, year of study tackled additional design problems (Fig. 2.15).

The study of art history formed a sequence that began in the third year with ancient art and continued into the fourth year with the history of Romanesque and medieval art. Courses in the history of the fine arts helped students understand the relationship of architecture to the other arts, and the relationship of the art of different periods to social and political life—"a knowledge without which the architect is not likely to use the forms of his art in an intelligent and scholarly manner."[35]

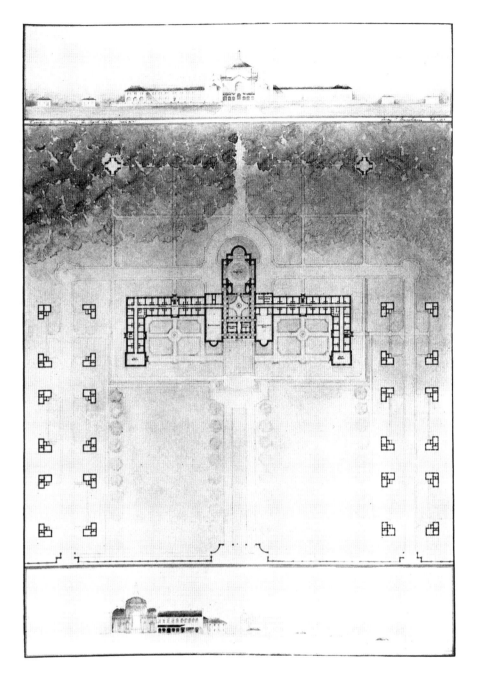

Hence, "Private Life of the Greeks as Illustrated by Works of Art" and "Private Life of the Romans as Illustrated by Works of Art" were offered during the third and fourth years. In addition, the Fogg Art Museum provided an important learning source with its Egyptian and Assyrian sculptures and its casts of Greek, Roman, and medieval sculpture, including works by Michelangelo.

Balancing history, drawing, design, and art were courses in the liberal arts, rhetoric, English composition, French, German, mathematics, and physics. The latter two prepared students for the study of mechanics and the strength of materials, which was followed by a study of building construction (Fig. 2.16). Learning general principles and their application to modern work was stressed more than learning the specifics. Students also took a course on the proper rendering of architectural drawings, descriptive geometry, shades and shadows, perspective, and stereotomy (cutting solids into figures or shapes). Technical courses taught by professors of engineering covered topics such as structural design and the theory of building construction. In the third and fourth years lectures in architectural practice, heating and ventilation, and sanitary engineering were given, as was a half-year course (in the fourth year) on geology and the mineralogy of building stones.

Students in landscape architecture took the same courses as architecture students, plus Olmsted's course on the history and principles of landscape design, which relied on an assessment of the

2.15 Home for aged people, L. P. Burnham, 1903. Fifth year, design problem 4.

2.16 Student work, 1901–03. Construction models for a Gothic vault.

2.17 Estate, Oglesby F. Paul, n.d., LA 3, fourth year, advanced design problem

2.18 Hall of Casts, Robinson Hall.

"highest developments" of landscape architecture and used plans, drawings, photographs, and references to examples in the Boston area whenever possible to demonstrate those developments.[36] Occasional lectures were given by Dean Nathaniel Shaler and by George L. Goodale, director of the Botanic Garden in Cambridge, one of the resources on which the program relied.[37]

In their third year, landscape students began to design in a two-year studio sequence. Making sketch plans, measured drawings, and reports of existing sites dominated the exercises given from 1901 to 1903 and resulted in the relative absence of original design. Documentation of existing parks and estates in the Cambridge and Boston areas, with an occasional redesign, was the focus of the studio course. At least one problem involved making a topographic survey, and detailed construction plans for the more important parts of the design were required. Subjects of theses, in the fourth year, ranged from site plans for public and private buildings to designs for private estates and parks (Fig. 2.17). Sketches and reports on existing sites, such as the Back Bay Fens or Franklin Park in Boston, dominated the programs.

More important for the future of the programs than the individual courses and curriculum was the goal of collaboration between practitioners of the distinct disciplines. With the creation of the Department of Landscape Architecture, the Department of Architecture now had a partner in its efforts to create a philosophy

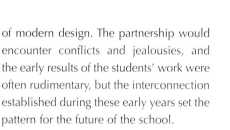

of modern design. The partnership would encounter conflicts and jealousies, and the early results of the students' work were often rudimentary, but the interconnection established during these early years set the pattern for the future of the school.

Expansion of the Architecture and Landscape Architecture Departments

Little progress would have been made towards expanding the two departments without the generosity of a mysterious benefactor, Nelson Robinson of Buffalo, New York. Like President and Mrs. Eliot, Robinson and his wife had lost their young son—skylarking, he fell off the top of a building at Harvard. Empathizing with the Eliots, the Robinsons offered to memorialize both young men. In 1899 they provided $100,000 for the construction of a new building for the Department of Architecture and the emerging program in landscape architecture. Over the next three years they funded an endowment of $300,000 to provide for the maintenance of the building, one or two traveling fellowships, a graduate scholarship, an addition to the salary offered for the position of professor of architecture "so as to procure the best talent," and the hiring of curators, assistants, and whomever else was needed. In addition, $5,000 was set aside for the purchase of equipment for the newly established Department of Landscape Architecture according to the wishes of Olmsted. Robinson amended the initial terms of his gift, adding another

2.19 Nelson Robinson, Jr. Portrait by Federico Carlos de Madrazo y Hahn, 1900. Loeb Library, Harvard University.

2.20 Hall of Casts, Robinson Hall.

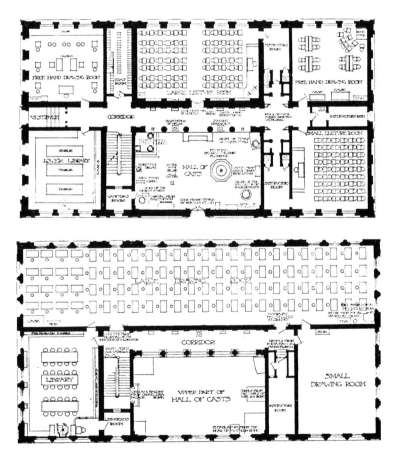

2.21 Nelson Robinson, Jr., Hall.
Photo showing tower of Memorial
Hall in background.

2.22 Robinson Hall. Plan,
upper floor (top) and lower floor.

$50,000, and stipulated that funds should be used to pay the professor of landscape architecture, and to help pay retirement allowances in the Department of Architecture or any other department.

Extremely private and modest, the Robinsons reluctantly allowed the university to name the building, Nelson Robinson, Jr., Hall, after their son (Fig. 2.19). Instead of providing extraneous cash, the Robinsons felt that their financial gift should be so large as to create a real financial burden for them and, consequently, represent a true memorial. Their endowed professorships became the Nelson Robinson Professorship in architecture and the Charles Eliot Professorship in landscape architecture, named for the president's son. Their subsequent gifts included the Charles Eliot Traveling Fellowship, established in 1914. Their gifts totaled over $450,000 and provided the young Departments of Architecture and Landscape Architecture with one of the largest endowments Harvard had ever received.[38]

Situated in the northwest sector of Harvard Yard near Sever and Hunt Halls, the new building for the architecture and landscape programs strengthened the departments' efforts at collaboration by giving them an official "home" of their own and allowing the consolidation of the fine arts collections in Gore Hall, reference materials in the Boston Public Library, and other materials in the Fogg Museum in Hunt Hall.[39] Langford Warren wanted his architecture department to design the new building, but the university selected Charles Follen McKim.

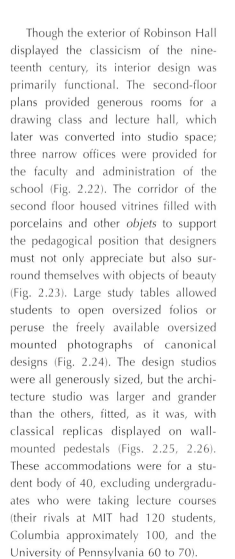

2.23 Second-floor corridor showing vitrines, view toward Architecture Library, Robinson Hall.

Charles Francis Adams II, treasurer of the university, opposed awarding the commission to Warren on the ground that if the department produced a poor design, it would reflect badly on the program. Furthermore, Adams felt that McKim had "the highest skills available," and, as a reticent person, he was a good match for the shy benefactor, Nelson Robinson.[40]

Despite his initial disappointment at not getting the commission, Warren became the client. First he examined the survey of the building's location in Harvard Yard; then he studied the rooms at Columbia's School of Architecture in Havermeyer Hall, which he considered to be "the best of any school of architecture in the country."[41] Warren subsequently wrote the detailed program for the building, which guaranteed his input and ensured the building's functional ties to the collaborative educational ideals of the design programs. Warren approved of McKim's early sketches, describing them as "an arrangement admirably adapted to our purpose and also a very beautiful building," though he later suggested modifications.[42] To equip the building, Warren specified drafting rooms with large windows, a library with tables and cases for photographs, a freehand-drawing room, a room for samples of building materials and small structural models, and two instructors' rooms. Pride of place went to the Great Hall, a space intended for the exhibition of original antique fragments and casts. Filled with artifacts and models of the monuments in the history of architecture, the Great Hall represented classi-

cal beauty, proportion, and form, and its proximity to the students of both architecture and landscape architecture was essential to their training. Warren maintained that simply being around these cultural artifacts elevated students' aesthetic sensitivity (Figs. 2.18, 2.20).

McKim's Beaux-Arts neoclassical building opened to occupancy in 1902, though its decoration continued for several years while casts arrived from Greece, Italy, and New York (Fig. 2.21). Every detail was considered important, including the Latin inscriptions on the bronze doors, designed by McKim to face the quadrangle in Harvard Yard. These doors, costing the then phenomenal sum of $3,000, created contention. Warren claimed they were "a nuisance and an extravagance," but McKim insisted that they reinforced the validity of classical culture—and he won the debate.[43]

Everyone agreed on the value of the sculptures and fragments, but not everyone was thrilled with the building itself. A classical building in Harvard's midst rankled the local Ruskinians, especially Charles Eliot Norton. He severely criticized the building as "not itself . . . a model of good architectural design. . . . The building has neither beauty nor impressiveness, and both without and within is open to legitimate criticism in the disregard which it here and there exhibits of established principles of good architecture. Moreover, in design, in material, and in color it is out of harmony with Sever Hall, to which it stands in close and subordinate relation."[44]

Though the exterior of Robinson Hall displayed the classicism of the nineteenth century, its interior design was primarily functional. The second-floor plans provided generous rooms for a drawing class and lecture hall, which later was converted into studio space; three narrow offices were provided for the faculty and administration of the school (Fig. 2.22). The corridor of the second floor housed vitrines filled with porcelains and other *objets* to support the pedagogical position that designers must not only appreciate but also surround themselves with objects of beauty (Fig. 2.23). Large study tables allowed students to open oversized folios or peruse the freely available oversized mounted photographs of canonical designs (Fig. 2.24). The design studios were all generously sized, but the architecture studio was larger and grander than the others, fitted, as it was, with classical replicas displayed on wall-mounted pedestals (Figs. 2.25, 2.26). These accommodations were for a student body of 40, excluding undergraduates who were taking lecture courses (their rivals at MIT had 120 students, Columbia approximately 100, and the University of Pennsylvania 60 to 70).

2.24 Architecture Library, second floor, Robinson Hall.

2.25 Architecture studio, Robinson Hall, second floor.

2.26 Landscape architecture drafting room, basement, Robinson Hall.

The faculty was expanded to accommodate the new programs and students in the new building. Olmsted, Jr., brought in James Sturgis Pray in 1902 as his assistant in the School of Landscape Architecture.[45] Pray had entered Harvard College in 1891, withdrawn in 1894 for two years, and graduated "as of 1895," having studied at the Lawrence Scientific School and Bussey Institution. By 1898 he had worked for the Olmsted Brothers in Brookline and, most significantly, under the late Charles Eliot, on the development of the Boston metropolitan park system. His career at Harvard lasted almost three decades.

The teaching of technology was bolstered by the arrival in 1908 of Charles Wilson Killam, a brilliant thirty-eight-year-old engineer formerly of the Boston firm Peabody & Stearns. Within a year of his arrival at Harvard, Killam was appointed assistant professor of architectural construction and began a long, active academic career that also spanned three decades. Killam served as chairman of the Faculty of Architecture briefly in 1917 and acting dean of the faculty from 1918 to 1922. He became associate professor of architecture in 1921, full professor in 1924, and his span as professor of architecture emeritus from 1937 to 1961 was the longest in the school's history. Despite Killam's lack of formal education—he began working at the age of sixteen—he became a prolific, assiduous writer of articles in professional journals and numerous texts on architectural construction. As a teacher, Killam strongly believed that modern methods of construction and new materials should be integrated into styles inherited from the past. In his course, "Resistance of Materials and Elementary Structural Design," he demanded that his students gain a sound knowledge of construction, that they learn how to derive formulae from theory, and that they even learn how to create their own tables and handbooks, if necessary. His required reading consisted of his mimeographed notes along with texts by Milo Ketchum, the author of widely used books on structural design. Students warned one another to be wary of "Catch'em and Kill'em." Kenneth John Conant, a student and later a teacher at Harvard, recalled that he and his peers created a mythical firm they named "Ketchum, Killam, and Burnham." According to Conant, when it came to the knowledge of building construction, "there never was a man who had a better idea of fabric than did Killam."[46]

In 1909 another young architect, Henry Atherton Frost, began a career at Harvard that extended to his retirement in 1949. Highly popular with students and particularly effective in teaching analytical drawing, he was a mainstay in the school. Like many of the early teachers of design at Harvard, Frost was himself a Harvard College graduate (1905) and began as an assistant to Langford Warren in his history courses. In 1910 Frost started teaching the drawing courses that became his specialty. On the first day of class he was reported to have drawn a large, perfect circle on the blackboard and then assured his students

that they, too, would be able to do the same. Over the next twenty years at Harvard he taught the required courses in architecture: "Elementary Architectural Drawing," a course on the orders that lasted until 1915; "Descriptive Geometry"; "Stereotomy, Shades, and Shadows"; and the "Theory of Perspective and Its Application to Architectural Subjects." Simultaneous with his teaching he pursued, under the tutelage of his colleagues, a Master of Architecture degree, which he received in 1918. From 1919 he practiced in partnership with Eleanor Raymond in Boston and later was president of Nichols & Frost in Fitchburg, Massachusetts. During World War I Henry Frost was connected with the U.S. Housing Corporation, the government's emergency organization for war workers' housing. In 1929–30 Frost was acting dean; from 1930 to 1940 he was associate professor of architecture; from 1940 to 1949, full professor; and from 1949 until his death in 1952, professor emeritus.

Other teachers supplemented this core faculty. From 1902 to 1910 Denman Waldo Ross, a sophisticated connoisseur and collector, taught the first theory course—"Theory of Design: Pure Design, Balance, Rhythm, Harmony"—which explored the abstract relationships of color and representation.[47] Ross had received his Ph.D. from Harvard in 1880 in economics and history but turned his attention to researching the practice and history of painting. His students explored color contrasts, particularly in the design of stained glass (Fig. 2.27). He taught that design the-

2.27 Stained-glass composition, C. A. Loring, 1900. Theory of design problem.

ory was relevant to stained glass because the decorative arts of furniture and sculpture were not alien to architectural design but an integral part of the process, worthy of study from both historical and contemporary perspectives. Empirical in approach, Ross's course anticipated the German-inspired teaching methods that swept art history at Harvard in the late 1930s. The course, however, was only part of the architecture training for four years. Ross and his protégé, Arthur Pope, then offered courses in the Department of Fine Arts, where they taught methods of sharpening the eye rather than making pictures per se—an analytic (and unemotional) approach vigorously pursued generally at Harvard. A contemporary writer pointed out that Warren and Ross, along with Charles Eliot Norton and Charles Herbert Moore, constituted "a really great tradition not without influence in civilizing the instincts of American life."[48] Ross's influence in the School of Architecture, however, is difficult to determine because after 1910 his course was not a requirement for architecture

2.28 Villa Lante, The Gardens, Janiculm Hill, Rome, C. R. Wait, 1901.

students. As a collector and painter, his exemplary aesthetic judgment is still reflected in the fine works of European and Asian art that are part of the Ross Collection at the Museum of Fine Arts in Boston.

Harvard's Search for a Modern American Identity Through Design

Civilizing the citizens of sprawling America was one thing, but did civilizing them mean making them receptive to modern ideas? From the American perspective, civilizing the populace was part of making it modern, which meant making Americans more American, attuned to technological and social change. From a European perspective, modernity jettisoned old identities in search of the new. But how could teachers and practitioners create a modern American architecture when no American style had emerged to combat the dominance of the ideas of the École des Beaux-Arts? Who or what would focus the challenges of modern design? H. H. Richardson had died in 1886, Adler & Sullivan had completed

Chicago's Auditorium Building in 1890, after which their commissions declined, and Frank Lloyd Wright only began his independent practice in 1893. Skyscrapers in Chicago and New York were unique modern American inventions, accompanied by a dramatic range of technological innovations in plumbing, heating, cooling, and electric lighting. But there was no unified image, no consensus of what real modern architecture looked like. Admiring American industrial efficiency, Europeans were on the verge of defining those images in the late 1890s and early 1900s as they pushed beyond the arts and crafts ethos of reform and art nouveau to various Secession movements in Germany and Austro-Hungary and, ultimately, to the "objective" design of the German Werkbund. Yet, architects in both Europe and America faced the same basic challenges in defining modern design: the use and meaning of architectural history for contemporary practice; the appropriate expression of new materials and technologies; and the defining of architecture's role as a force for social change.

Warren inherited a vocabulary of historical styles from which to fashion a modern language. His approach was to sift through the methods of the École to find what would work in practice and in teaching and to remain open to cultural precedent from the past while, at the same time, incorporating technological advances. This philosophical orientation meant that teachers and practitioners had to be willing to explore, open mindedly, the history of all styles. History thereby

became the tool for interpreting the past, winnowing its lessons, and transforming them for the future. Historical inquiry was an integral part of the design curricula and served as both a guide to students, by showing them precedents, and a critic, by offering age-old standards. In Warren's teaching, serious historical study demanded a critical attitude. He sanctioned no wholesale imitation of antique and Renaissance models as practiced at other schools modeled on the École des Beaux-Arts. Find what works in the École's methods, Warren wrote, but look also to the full range of history from the Gothic and Romanesque to the ancient world of the Middle East itself.

Judging from the earliest student work in the architecture department, studying history did little except show how far the department had to go simply to catch up with other institutions that followed the methods of the École. The student work was not impressive—scholarship had not yet taken hold—even though some of Warren's pupils were capable of exemplary work, as seen in C. R. Wait's study of the Villa Lante in Rome (Fig. 2.28). Intended in the tradition of the École des Beaux-Arts as an *envoi* (a study executed during travel abroad to be sent back to the school), Wait's drawing shows both a mastery of rendering technique and an appreciation of the integration of landscape in a Renaissance villa. Truly innovative designs, however, were rare, as seen in reproductions from the *Boston Architecture Club Yearbook* of 1897: a thesis project for a palazzo awkwardly assembled disparate forms, and

2.29 A House of Studies for a Community of Canons Regular, elevation, front tower. Kenneth J. Conant, 1919. Architecture, design thesis.

2.30 A House of Studies for a Community of Canons Regular, plan, first floor. Kenneth J. Conant, 1919. Architecture, design thesis.

a design for a Germanic museum, lecture hall, and palazzo was flat, stiff, and rigid (see Figs. 2.11, 2.13).[49] In general, in the early years, student work at MIT and the University of Pennsylvania surpassed that of Harvard students. The dilemma of adapting a historical language to contemporary needs was widespread. Designing an entrance to an apartment building using the Ionic order begged the question: why, in 1902, use a classical vocabulary for a building type that did not even exist in antiquity (see Fig. 2.12)?

If history were at the core of a modern training, then modern design would reflect history—but not a narrow slice of history. Warren and his colleagues taught precedents from the best examples of Greece, Rome, and the Italian Renaissance because "these comparatively simple forms are more readily apprehended and because these forms underlie most of our modern work." The students were encouraged to use these historic elements freely and thoughtfully, modifying them to fit the design circumstances. At the same time that they relied on classical prototypes, they also studied "planning and mass," as Warren termed it, using the principles of the École des Beaux-Arts. He also referred frequently to the finest achievements of French architecture and design, insisting, as was the practice at all "good" schools, that the plan of the building was the key to the study of architecture—even though Warren and his colleagues considered the plan not as an end in itself but as a means to produce "a convenient and beautiful building."[50]

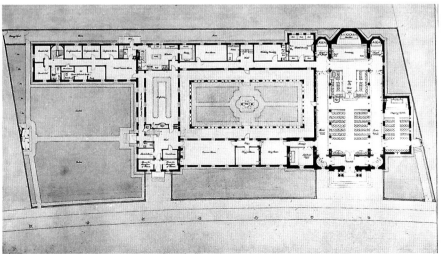

2.31 Handicraft establishment, Alexander E. Hoyle, 1906. Elevation.

2.32 Handicraft establishment, Alexander E. Hoyle, 1906. Plan.

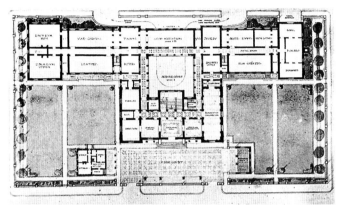

The scope of sources was wide and even exotic, including Egyptian architecture and much-neglected early Christian architecture. Kenneth Conant's thesis for a contemporary monastery, a house of studies for a community of canons regular, shows consummate skill in adapting Italian prototypes for an exquisitely drawn design (Figs. 2.29, 2.30). Conant would succeed Langford Warren as the school's professor of architectural history, pioneering studies in the field of Carolingian architecture and eventually offer the first American visual catalog of modern architecture.

For a small avant-garde in Europe, the modernist issue centered on the expression of technology as the guiding philosophy of modern design. For Americans, technology had its place but was not necessarily center stage. Many American practitioners already used every available technological advance in their buildings, from fireproofing to cast concrete, but they allowed the surface expressions to

vary with stylistic preference and urban context.[51] The appropriate vocabulary was a traditional one, which usually concealed modern technology in steel-frame construction and mechanical and sanitary innovations; the principal exceptions were some of the skyscrapers of Chicago and New York, in which the structure was abstractly expressed on the exterior.

The Harvard architecture program believed that the latest building practices should be incorporated into contemporary building, but it did not promote the experimental expression of structure or building technology arising out of the extensive use of steel, concrete, and glass. In providing instruction from an experienced architectural engineer—Walter Killam—the program gave a rigorous training in structural analysis and methods of building, and it also included extensive construction problems in the design studio. Students made both detailed calculations and models. Beginning in 1912 they

even took a course on architectural acoustics taught by Wallace Sabine, a physicist and a pioneer in the field of acoustics.[52] Having received a solid education in how buildings are made, the program's graduates were in demand within the profession.

The question of architecture's relationship to society—should it support the status quo or champion social transformation?—received different treatment in the United States than in Europe. From the later perspective of European modernists, American designers of the early 1900s lacked social consciousness. At Harvard, though, instead of pushing a socialist manifesto or drafting a political agenda, as contemporary Europeans did, the architecture faculty took the position that defining an American identity through architecture was a social responsibility itself. Furthermore, they responded to social concerns in ways that, while certainly not radical, would still have sur-

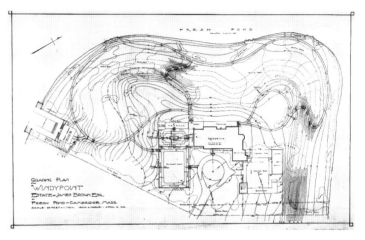

2.33 Estate on Fresh Pond, S. Herbert Hare, 1909. LA 2, problem 2.

2.34 Grading plan for Windy Point, Irwin J. McCray. 1912.

prised radical European designers. An awareness of a larger clientele than just the landed gentry appears even in the early design problems students tackled in their classes. A design for a home for aged people, for example, shows a simple arrangement of single rooms placed around open wings of a main building with detached houses; such a design acknowledges, in however a rudimentary way, the widely differing lifestyles of the aged (see Fig. 2.15). A project for a U.S. arsenal extended the repertory of design problems beyond the public to the governmental domain (see Fig. 2.14). Another student's interpretation of societal needs produced a place for the communal production of handcrafted objects—not so distant from the concerns of Europeans, particularly the return of British craft guilds. In proposing a building for a "Society of Useful Arts," the student gave men and women an opportunity to work in a variety of materials, from clay to iron

(Figs. 2.31, 2.32). With studios flanking a central hall and preceded by a forecourt, his design used the techniques of Beaux-Arts planning to create a straightforward, symmetrical plan.

Absent was any pressing sense that a new architectural style had to correspond to activities of those working in a handicraft establishment, nor was any rhetoric injected by the more self-conscious arts-and-crafts practitioners who might have pushed for architecture's contribution to social reform. Responding to social concerns of the middle class coexisted with designing for high society. Conspicuous wealth in the Gilded Age was impossible to avoid, and students received many projects for clubs and estates. After all, the students were surrounded by demonstrations of wealth and power. The founding of the architecture school, for example, coincided with the building of monuments to private wealth, such as "The Breakers" in Newport, Rhode Island

(1892–95), designed for Cornelius Vanderbilt by Richard Morris Hunt. And students at Harvard automatically became members of an elite.

In these initial years the landscape architecture program tended to focus on projects for the wealthy. Nearby Fresh Pond, in Cambridge, provided the general site for a variety of projects. It was here that as a student S. Herbert Hare, who later became a prolific town planner, designed an entire estate—including both landscaping and buildings—while his fellow student, Irwin McGary, worked the detailed grading changes for "Windpoint," an estate he designed in 1912 (Figs. 2.33, 2.34). By this date students clearly had become adept in the basics of providing plant plans and garden furniture details (Figs. 2.35, 2.36).

The education at Harvard produced landscape architects who were also adept in the design of buildings. A residential design in 1913 for an area of Weston,

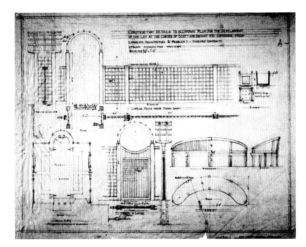

2.35 Planting plan; hen house, Samuel D. Zehrung, 1916. LA 8.

2.36 Construction details to accompany plan for the development of the lot at the corner of Scott and Bryant Streets, Cambridge, Mass., J. P. Blaney, 1916. LA 2, problem 1.

2.37 Design for a residential area in Weston, Mass., Faris Barton Smith, June 1913. LA master's thesis.

Massachusetts, shows their skill in laying out roads, siting buildings, and intervening minimally in an existing wooded landscape (Fig. 2.37). The future lay in these types of larger-scaled residential developments as designers became increasingly focused on serving a middle-class client base. Students mastered basic skills by creating planting plans for the Olmsted enclave itself in Brookline, a popular early assignment. Students' technical abilities improved over time, as seen in the manipulation of topography to provide suitable sites for tennis courts and boathouses (Fig. 2.38). Studying with architecture students had a noticeable impact on Frederick Kingsbury's design for an estate, which gives as much prominence to the house as it does to the grounds (Fig. 2.39). Future clients would need villa gardens and country clubs.[53]

However, landscape architecture increasingly addressed more public-minded projects, like Charles Eliot's metropolitan park system for Boston. Student schemes, though often awkwardly executed, demonstrated reformist attitudes that acknowledged the need for community facilities such as parks and playgrounds (Fig. 2.40). Their work reflected an increased interest in the subdivision of land and the already-established practices of eminent domain, which allowed the appropriation of property for public welfare (Figs. 2.41, 2.42). While the echelons of high society suffered no lack of competent designers, civic awareness entered the consciousness of the faculty and students at the Department of Landscape

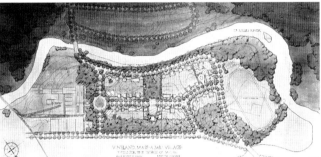

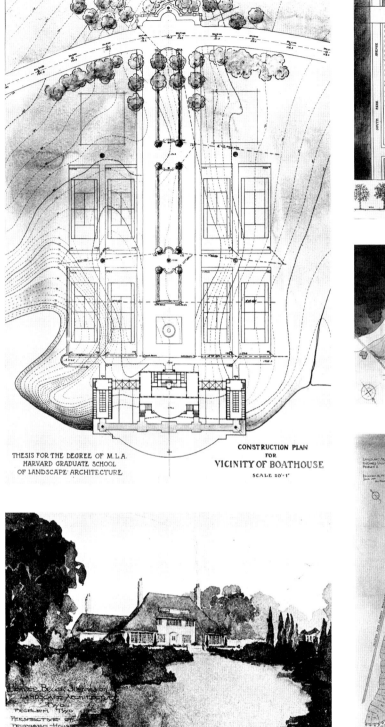

THESIS FOR THE DEGREE OF M.L.A.
HARVARD GRADUATE SCHOOL
OF LANDSCAPE ARCHITECTURE

CONSTRUCTION PLAN
FOR
VICINITY OF BOATHOUSE
SCALE 20'=1'

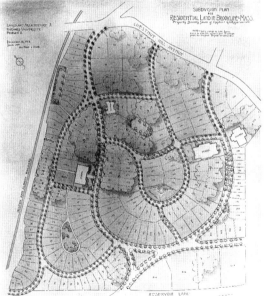

2.38 Construction plan for vicinity of boathouse, Marcus H. Dall, 1914. LA master's thesis.

2.39 Perspective of proposed house, Frederick Kingsbury, 1916.

2.40 Marcus H. Dall, n.d. South Park Commissioners, Chicago Ill. General plan for Park 18.

2.41 A mill village, Vineland, Mass., Robert Wheelwright, 1908. LA master's thesis.

2.42 Subdivision plan for residential land in Brookline, Mass., Raymond H[?], 1913. LA 3, problem 2.

Architecture; this new awareness stimulated new approaches to urban and regional problems that went beyond the scope and benefit of the individual.

The Development of Graduate Programs in Architecture and Landscape Architecture

During these early years, significant structural changes within the university affected the programs in architecture and landscape architecture. In 1906 Harvard scrapped the old Lawrence Scientific School and replaced it with the Graduate School of Applied Science, which allowed the granting of graduate degrees.[54] The programs in architecture and landscape architecture were moved, as components of the Division of Fine Arts, to the new Graduate School of Applied Science; both design programs now offered master's degrees exclusively for students who already had bachelor's degrees or the equivalent in four years of general education. This change had serious long-term repercussions. To enter the design programs at Harvard, students now needed a four-year bachelor's degree, which provided a broad general education. Graduate work implied advanced study dealing with complex professional issues.

Just a few years later, in 1912, the Graduate School of Applied Science, with its departments and faculty, was eliminated in favor of individual graduate schools, each with its own faculty. With the dissolution of the Faculty of Applied Science, a Faculty of Architecture was created to oversee and direct both schools of design. Warren served as the first dean of the Faculty of Architecture.

The conflict between these two enterprises with their similarities and differences lay at the core of design education at Harvard. Despite a new building and coursework uniting the education of architecture and landscape architecture students, collaboration—the cornerstone of the design philosophy—produced innate tensions. The need for distinct professional identities began to fracture the close relationship between the two schools. James Sturgis Pray, the landscape architect who continued the Olmsted lineage, led the effort to give landscape architecture an autonomous identity.

As Olmsted, Jr., grew increasingly busy with his practice, Pray assumed more responsibility in the landscape architecture program, becoming its chairman in 1907. Like Warren, Pray had a professional practice in Boston, opened four years earlier, under the name of Pray & Gallagher, but his principal contributions to Harvard and the profession came from his teaching. Over the next twenty years, Pray exerted a powerful influence over the landscape architecture program. His students called him "Big Daddy"—and Big Daddy's quest was to put landscape architecture on a par with architecture.

Pray's appointment coincided with significant and rapid changes. Beginning in 1906 the first graduate-degree program ever offered anywhere in landscape architecture was inaugurated; within one year the curriculum increased from five to twelve courses. Pray began to push for the autonomy of the program and for the recognition of the profession of landscape architecture as a fine art in which plant materials were subordinate to aesthetic principles. As part of his goal to define a distinct professional identity, he argued for the autonomy and separation of the Schools of Architecture and Landscape Architecture. As a result, in 1908, the Department of Landscape Architecture was officially created as a separate entity from the Department of Architecture. But when the two departments went under the rubric of the Division of Fine Arts in 1914, the teachers of landscape architecture belonged to Warren's Faculty of Architecture. Omitting "Landscape Architecture" from the name irritated Pray, for it smacked of inequality. As chairman, he continued to help the field seek its own definition as an art and a science not limited to the study of farming, trees, and plants.

Pray strengthened his position by hiring thirty-one-year-old Henry Vincent Hubbard, a graduate of Harvard College, class of 1897. After graduation, Hubbard completed two years of MIT's architecture program, then pursued a landscape architecture degree as an independent study. In 1901 he became the first recipient of a degree in landscape architecture from Harvard, receiving the Bachelor of Science in landscape architecture from the Lawrence Scientific School. Just as Olmsted, Jr., had brought in Pray as his professional associate, Pray hired Hubbard, his partner in professional practice, who in 1906 formed a partnership of Pray, Hubbard & White that continued until 1918. This kind of symbiotic relationship between teaching and practice—with teachers hiring their business partners—has persisted throughout the history of Harvard's schools of design. Hubbard's career at Harvard lasted for thirty-five years, during which time he became a leader in the field of city and regional planning.

After the architecture and landscape architecture programs became separate departments in 1908, the level of tension rose to internecine squabbling. Pray worried that landscape architecture would not get its share of the Robinson endowment. Consequently, he asked President Eliot to decide which department owned what equipment. Pray also complained that the landscape students were relegated to the status of "second-class citizens" by the selection of rooms allowed for their use in Robinson Hall, and that the overall arrangement of the "joint rights" between landscape and architecture was threatened.[55] He maintained that the degree in landscape architecture appeared "as a subordinate phase of architecture," and that the confluence between the architecture and the landscape architecture departments should exist primarily in the undergraduate years.[56]

Pray's campaign for increased autonomy continued under Harvard's next president, A. Lawrence Lowell, who succeeded Eliot in 1909. Lowell championed more structure and rigor in undergraduate education by instituting areas of concentration (known as "majors" in most colleges), course distribution requirements, and a program of tutorial instruction. He believed that "the best type of liberal education in our complex modern world aims at producing men who know a little of everything and something well."[57] While his predecessor, Eliot, had drawn on the German system of education, Lowell looked to Oxford and Cambridge for his models. He launched a new wave of building projects, ranging from the construction of Widener Library to the expansion of the Gray Herbarium. He involved himself with all aspects of college life, and set the stage for changes in the fields of applied science and engineering.

In 1914, when the two departments became schools, Pray wanted a separate faculty for his school.[58] President Lowell, however, persuaded him that there should be one faculty for which a dean would be required, with Langford Warren the obvious choice.[59] The two schools operated thereafter with one faculty and a dean, on the same basis as the Schools of Law, Medicine, and Divinity.

Typical of Pray's promotion of landscape architecture were his requests in 1916 asking Lowell for a share of income from a new gift to pay for equipment, instruction in freehand drawing, and instruction in architecture for landscape architects. Pray pointed out that architecture students had two instructors who taught drawing, whereas landscape students had to rely on instruction from the Division of Fine Arts. Though Pray certainly recognized that freehand drawing was required by both fields, he also wanted landscape students to participate in a special course in elementary architectural design. Despite all his efforts to make landscape architecture autonomous, he could not avoid acknowledging that teaching landscape students the basic concepts of architectural design dovetailed with the goals of those who espoused a collaborative relationship between the two programs—one of whom was President Lowell. Pray wrote to Lowell that the course would be "vital, in the interest of the mutual understanding and sympathy between Harvard Landscape Architects and Architects, which you have long had so much at heart, as well as for the later success of our students, and the maintenance of our prestige, that they should not graduate with any less knowledge of Architecture than they are now getting."[60]

The Birth of City Planning at Harvard

The internal conflicts between architecture and landscape architecture appeared, disappeared, and reappeared throughout the history of the two programs. Personal ambitions often played a role in this tension. For example, Pray's efforts to separate his department from architecture may have been fueled, in part, by his own ambitions. As early as 1908 Pray informed President Eliot that since he (Pray) had gradually assumed Olmsted's duties, he felt that he should assume the Charles Eliot Professorship as well—a desire realized only when Olmsted, upon resigning, designated Pray his successor in 1915.[61] But what could be seen at the most rudimentary level as an occasional academic turf war or an excess of egotism did not prevent the early schools from exploring a new area of professional training in 1909: the academic study of city planning.

The growth of the architecture and landscape architecture programs in Robinson Hall coincided with the emergence of the progressive movement, a turning point in American politics and social policy. After Theodore Roosevelt assumed the presidency in 1901, he involved the federal government in this important movement. Although differing in style and approach, Roosevelt and the presidents who followed him, William H. Taft and Woodrow Wilson, all agreed to curb the political and financial excesses and corruption that had arisen with the industrialization of America. Manufacturing, mining, and industry had shifted immense amounts of capital into the hands of a powerful oligarchy that exerted unprecedented control over government and individuals. Industrialization had not only created unbelievable wealth, it had also altered the social fabric of American life. From a country reliant on individuals' abilities to provide for themselves in the context of a social network they knew and recognized,

citizens had now become dependent on integrated systems of production to provide their bread and meat. Americans had become employees of the oligarchy—and vulnerable employees, at that.

Under Roosevelt the government began to wake up to what American society wanted and had already started to put into place. If the down side of the situation was corruption and greed, the up side was hope and idealism. As succinctly summarized by historian Samuel Eliot Morison, "Common to all Progressives was belief in the perfectibility of man, and in an open society where mankind was neither chained to the past nor condemned to a deterministic future; one in which people were capable of changing their condition for better or worse."[62]

The implications of this social philosophy for the design professions were highly significant: change *was* possible, the past could be reconsidered, the future could be better, social life could be enhanced, and the disenfranchisement induced by industrialization could be tempered by new social institutions. Reformers, municipal leagues, and social welfare institutions, like Jane Addams's Hull House in Chicago, attracted not only progressive citizens but also architects and landscape architects. The designers' reforms focused on individual buildings as well as on the fabric of the city. The urban center became the focus of needed change. Lincoln Steffens' series "The Shame of the Cities," in *McClure's* magazine, created a sensation, as did the work of other progressive writers like Ida Tarbell, who

exposed Standard Oil for questionable business practices, and Upton Sinclair.

Although the conditions that motivated the progressive movement in America provided the fuel for social change in a manner that paralleled conditions spurring the modern movement in Europe, the collective response on the two continents was necessarily different. European cities, like their American counterparts, needed to adapt to industrial pressures, but European governments had social and political structures of centralized control that differed from the intense individualism shaping comparable American structures. In the American context the moment had arrived for progressives to focus more scientifically on the city. To do that, they needed professionals who were properly trained, and from that social need grew the new field of city planning.

The efforts at Harvard to establish landscape architecture as an independent profession still intimately connected to architecture coincided with the growing momentum for the planning of cities that had been spurred by the 1893 World's Columbian Exposition held in Chicago. The Exposition had initiated the greatest experiment in professional teamwork within the building arts up to that time and produced, with its glistening temporary buildings, the start of what many called the White City movement, which expanded to the idea of the City Beautiful. This drive to render the city aesthetic and humane through the application of Beaux-Arts methods on an urban scale marked the birth of planning as a field in America.[63] Daniel Burnham's Chicago Plan of 1908–9 was a case in point. The Columbian Exposition also stimulated Charles Mulford Robinson, a young journalist from Rochester, New York, to take a deep interest in city planning. His series of articles, editorials, and books—the first American writings on city planning—coincided with the founding years of Harvard's Schools of Architecture and Landscape Architecture.[64] Robinson even went to Harvard in 1910 as a "special" research student, taking a break from his busy practice. His studies at Harvard resulted, in part, in his publication of *The Width and Arrangement of Streets* in 1911.

The Olmsted firm had been involved with city planning in its landscape practice, but Robinson focused his attention further afield on the visual appearance of the city, which took the form of "civic aesthetics." Harvard's direct link with the Olmsted tradition automatically propelled it towards larger issues of parks, roadways, infrastructures, and the dynamics of expanding cities. While never losing touch with the old tradition of making gardens, landscape architecture was poised to seize on a distinctly modern necessity: the design of cities.

Another figure stimulating interest in city planning was John Nolen, who, in 1903 while still a student of landscape architecture at Harvard, started a practice in Cambridge that was to gain national recognition. His presence helped Boston become a center of city planning efforts;

he also later taught at Harvard.[65] By 1909 the first National Conference of City Planning was formed with Olmsted and Nolen at its head. In 1910 an International Exhibition of City Planning was held in Boston at the Museum of Fine Arts then located in Copley Square.

In 1909 the students at Harvard demanded instruction in city planning, a field of study that did not yet exist in any school in the country. Pray responded to this groundswell of interest with a new offering: "Principles of City Planning, Illustrated by a Critical Study of Examples." Pray's assistant instructor was Bremer Whidden Pond, then a twenty-four-year-old graduate in botany from Dartmouth College.[66] Pond typified the Harvard teachers whose careers lasted decades and who saw the world change dramatically around them even as they retained their early philosophical roots. Before coming to Harvard, Pond had traveled in Europe, where he had become interested in landscape architecture. While he acted as assistant, he also studied landscape architecture and earned a master's degree in 1911. For the next three years Pond worked as secretary to Olmsted. Except for military service from 1917 to 1919, Pond was successively an instructor in landscape architecture, assistant professor (1926–28), associate professor (1928–30), and finally the Charles Eliot Professor of Landscape Architecture (1930–50), a professorship he held as an emeritus until his death in 1959.

Pray and Pond's course in city planning was a response not only to the

demands of the students but also to the needs of the new profession itself. It was the first American pedagogical effort to deal with the growing complexities of running and designing the modern, post-industrial city. The only comparable model was on the other side of the Atlantic Ocean: in the Department of Civic Design and Town Planning of the School of Architecture at the University of Liverpool (founded in 1909). Knowledge of the Liverpool school soon reached America. Pray and Pond both had copies of the original prospectus from the Department of Civic Design for 1909–10, and the school soon obtained additional materials from Liverpool.[67]

Pray's course topics examined the kind of basic problems intrinsic to the modern city that still preoccupy city designers today. He emphasized "the idea of the modern city as a living organism," whose efficiency required many separate services—which he categorized into activities extending from the construction of simple dwellings to civic architecture, and from waste disposal to traffic circulation.[68] The functions required of the "modern city" included the provision of shelter, especially "housing," air, light, food, water, and other necessities: disposal of wastes; circulation and transportation by land and water; roads, rivers, harbors, terminal facilities; open areas for public recreation (parks, playgrounds, boulevards); civic centers and spaces, civic monumental architecture; and architecture, in general, in its effect on the appearance of the city, with special reference to building regulations.

44

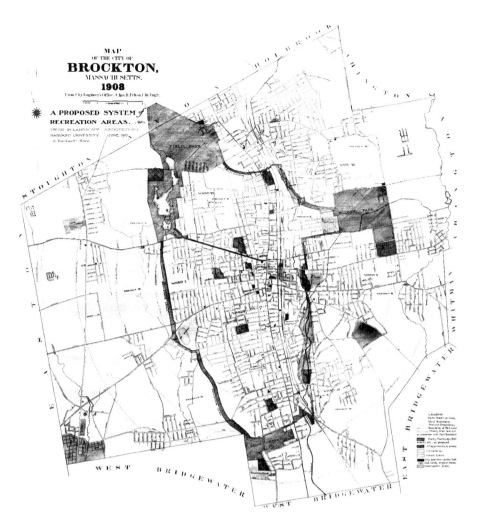

2.43 A proposed system of recreation areas, Brockton, Mass., S. Herbert Hare, June 1910, LA master's thesis.

The centers of small and medium-sized cities were also subjects of study: one student proposed a redesign of Winchester to create a common called Winchester Square; another student redesigned the center of Waltham, where he replaced factory buildings with a common that led down to the Charles River (Figs. 2.46, 2.47). The ultimate goal, of course, was the design of large cities, a daunting challenge. One ambitious student proposed a new city plan intended for presentation at the National Conference on City Planning in 1913, a convention that itself attested to widespread interest in city planning.[70]

In 1911–12, Pray toured principal cities throughout Europe to study city planning and to collect material for teaching. He visited England, France, Switzerland, Italy, Spain, Austria, Hungary, Germany, Norway, Sweden, Denmark, Belgium, and Holland. Returning with an immense collection of documents and illustrations for the school (they were valued at $12,000), he provided the basis for the creation of a library for landscape architecture and city planning, a separate collection from the School of Architecture's library, though physically connected in Robinson Hall.[71] In itself, the existence of two libraries for the study of design reflected and created a duality in the midst of efforts to create a unified education. Theodora Kimball became librarian of the landscape and planning collection in 1913, the same year she coauthored, with Pray, *City Planning: A Comprehensive Analysis of the Subject.*[72] It was so authoritative that the U.S.

By presenting the determinants of city form through the use of historical examples, Pray attempted to derive fundamental principles of planning that would be applicable to the problems of modern cities. As can be seen from his correspondence, he was quite aware of international developments; he particularly admired the work of the Viennese planner Camillo Sitte, whose publications Pray esteemed as the most important German-language contribution to the science of city planning. On March 27, 1913, Pray wrote to Sitte's son Siegfried on behalf of the American Society of Landscape Architects to ask for original plates: "I have already told you how much I admire the work, and indeed were it not that it seems to me the most important German [sic] contribution as yet to the Science of City

Planning, I could not afford to take the necessary time to translate it." Siegfried Sitte replied enthusiastically.[69]

Pray and Pond used nearby towns in Massachusetts for the sites of the design problems. Student projects captured the earliest days of this new field. One student proposed as his thesis a system of recreational areas—parks and playgrounds—for Brockton, which he related to the population distribution of the town (Fig. 2.43). A proposed general plan for a park between the towns of Riverside and Newton Lower Falls and a study for the residential development of the western section of Brighton show the increasingly large scale at which the students designed and the attention they gave to roadways, views, and a mix of amenities from meadows to sports facilities (Figs. 2.44, 2.45).

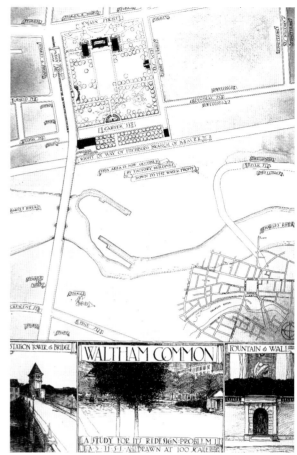

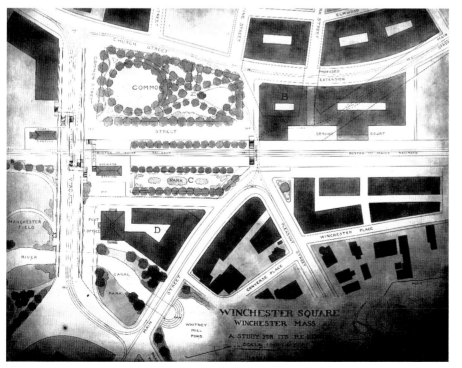

2.44 General plan for the development of Lower Falls Park, Mass., Frederick Noble Evans, February 1911.

2.45 A study for the development of the western portion of the Brighton district as a residential area, Bremer W. Pond, March 1911. LA master's thesis.

2.46 Winchester Square, Winchester, Mass., a study for its redesign, H. L. Flint, 1914.

2.47 (above) Waltham Common, a study for its redesign, B. Y. Morrison, 1915. LA 3.

46

2.48 Theodora Kimball Hubbard, Librarian.
From *American Planner*.

Bureau of Industrial Housing and Transportation used a copy with her own annotations. Kimball was a brilliant bibliographer and editor who made major contributions to the field in her own right, for which she was named Honorary Librarian of the American City Planning Institute (Fig. 2.48). She was also the sister of S. Fiske Kimball, a graduate of Harvard College, AB 1909, and School of Architecture, M.Arch 1912, who became one of America's leading historians of architecture. Theodora Kimball married Henry Hubbard, her Harvard colleague, in 1924. The Harvard family was relatively small and tight.

The Search for a
Modern Professor of Design

In the midst of growth one major deficiency hindered Harvard's movement to the top ranks of design education: it lacked a star designer. Warren had long known that he would need a full-time teacher of national significance if the school were to hold its own against others. Désiré Despradelle had gone to MIT in 1893, following Eugène Letang; the University of Pennsylvania boasted Paul Cret; and Columbia, Jean Hébrard. In the first recorded student protest, in 1904, architecture students had petitioned Warren to find a distinguished teacher for advanced design, but the slot remained unfilled for seven years.[73]

Warren's task was made particularly difficult because he wanted an American, not a Frenchman, to teach at Harvard.

Throughout his efforts to recruit a professor of design, he reiterated his distaste for the influence of the École des Beaux-Arts: "As you know I do not want a Frenchman for our work in design here. The undiluted French influence seems to me to have done great harm to the development of Architecture in this country. . . . But in maintaining an independent position we are clearly going against the current."[74]

One man above all others appeared to be the best candidate in America: John Galen Howard, a successful San Francisco–based practitioner. He had worked for H. H. Richardson, taught at the University of California at Berkeley, and designed the Saxon Theater in Boston in 1903. Warren recommended Howard to President Lowell as "a Boston boy" who was born in Chelmsford and educated at the Boston Latin School and at MIT. Howard, however, resisted the lure of a high salary of $5,000 and a full professorship because he was overwhelmed with business commitments.

On the heels of Howard's refusal, Désiré Despradelle of MIT, assisted by Henry Frost, agreed to teach advanced design in 1910 for a year. In 1911 Cass Gilbert, architect of the Woolworth Building in New York, came to lecture on professional practice; in the same year, John Sanford Humphreys of the New York firm of Carrère & Hastings came to assist with the teaching of design. Humphreys had studied at MIT and at the École des Beaux-Arts but had received no degree. He had entered Carrère & Hastings in 1899, becoming a junior partner in 1907.

His work on large and monumental buildings had supplemented his training in France, and he had just finished working on the design and construction of the New York Public Library. He entered Harvard as an assistant professor and, though not appointed full professor until 1927, provided a steadying presence for thirty years. He was very popular with the students, who cleverly punned his name by calling him "Strawberry Man" (*homme fraise*, a near homonym for "Humphreys" in French) because of his ruddy cheeks.[75] But none of these was the stellar figure needed to lead the school in design.

In 1911, Warren found a professor for the design slot. He was not, however, an American. Eugène-Joseph-Armand Duquesne, though French, was not dogmatically Beaux-Arts in approach, and he was an active practitioner. Winner of the prestigious Prix de Rome in 1897, Duquesne had opened his own atelier in Paris in 1905, which attracted a large number of American students that included graduates of the Harvard architecture program. Duquesne declined Harvard's initial offers but capitulated when President Lowell wrote him: "Your presence here would be not only a distinction and a great pleasure for us and inspiration for our students, but it would provide you with a unique opportunity, whose importance for leaving an indelible influence on our young American architects is difficult to exaggerate."[76]

Duquesne's arrival at the School of Architecture received the official sanction of the French government, which saw

2.49 Harvard architecture students in studio, c. 1909. From Jules Huret's *L'Amerique Moderne* (Paris, 1911).

2.50 Harvard architecture students in a life drawing class, c. 1909. From Jules Huret's *L'Amerique Moderne* (Paris, 1911).

him, ironically, as transporting the architecture of the École des Beaux-Arts to the United States. It also made France take a closer look at Harvard: the French publication *L'Amerique Moderne* noted, in 1911, the comprehensive education students at Harvard were receiving (Figs. 2.49, 2.50).[77] The U.S. ambassador to France underscored the importance of the event when he sent President Lowell a French governmental decree stating that Duquesne was an official representative of the École who had come "to propagate this French art in one of the greatest intellectual centers in America."[78]

Hiring Duquesne was a coup for Harvard and just what it needed to compete with other schools of architecture and further its own efforts to create a modern design agenda. When he arrived in Cambridge in the spring of 1911, the school held a reception with participants costumed as the personifications of various styles of architecture. The highlight of the event was a tableau "representing the union of ancient and modern architecture." The *Harvard Alumni Bulletin* reported that the pageant, staged at the Harvard Union, portrayed a visit of King Edward VI and his court to the University of Cambridge, where an entertainment entitled "A Masque of Prophecy" depicted the future of the art of architecture. Guests included members of the faculty and representatives of the Boston Society of Architects and other organizations representing the arts. The party degenerated into an exuberant drunken bash about which President Lowell complained![79]

Duquesne's arrival at Harvard indeed symbolized "the union of ancient and modern architecture." At the time of his arrival, Harvard's architecture school was a synthesis of a Protestantism inherited from H. H. Richardson and a Romanticism that reflected the entrenched attitudes of Bostonians with their penchant for Ruskin and the Gothic. Many considered the school the most anti–Beaux Arts in its ideology, although, as Warren had pointed out in his writings and public lectures, the school took from the École its methods of planning and composition. It was the nineteenth-century taste and artistic judgment of the École that the Harvard school—and many Boston practitioners—repudiated.

Duquesne came to this critical environment not only because the French government charged him with a mission but also because he expected his professional practice to continue in America. For its part, Harvard wanted Duquesne precisely because he both practiced and taught. At Harvard—ever pragmatic—this judicious principle of assigning French teaching methods to practitioner-teachers was a cornerstone of the program. Duquesne was a true believer in this mode of education.

Duquesne lost little time in publicly stating his practical views on the teaching of architecture. Immediately after his arrival, a journalist quoted him as saying: "There is no better teaching in architecture than that which is given by one who is himself applying in actual work the principles laid down in a course of teach-

ing. . . . I believe that from the day the students realize that the theories of the professor receive their complete expression in the work which he executes, from that day they acquire the conviction that the art of architecture is above all the art of constructing well, and consequently that of composing always with construction in view." He also stated his views on teaching in an article in *The Architectural Quarterly of Harvard University.*[80]

Duquesne began teaching advanced design in the fall of 1911, and by the following spring he was ready to resume his practice. In the first collaborative urban design project for the faculty, the mayor of Cambridge asked Harvard to study improvements for Harvard Square. The university assigned the project to the architecture school with Duquesne as chairman of the study, along with Warren, Humphreys, and Henry Hubbard from landscape architecture. The plan and perspective, reproduced in a pamphlet entitled "The Future Development of Harvard Square and Its Neighborhood," expressed a search for formality and axial vistas.[81]

The urban redesign of Harvard Square—and the plans of the School of Architecture—were delayed as an ominous event erupted: World War I. In the summer of 1914 Duquesne, feeling a patriotic sense of responsibility, suddenly departed for France, leaving his wife, children, and students in Cambridge.[82] After drilling troops for six months in France and realizing the potential longevity of the war, he returned to Cambridge in the spring of 1915 to close his affairs and bring his family back to France. His resignation dealt a severe blow to the School of Architecture. Duquesne did not quickly forget the school, despite the war raging around him. In fact, he arranged for the Société des Architectes Diplômés par le Gouvernement to recognize Harvard's School of Architecture with two medals, one for the student with the highest ranking and the other for distinguished work of a student in the summer school.[83] With Duquesne's initial departure, the search resumed for a professor of architectural design. In June 1914, Warren asked John Howard, his first choice five years before, to accept the position, but again Howard refused. However, he recommended another San Francisco architect, Arthur Brown, Jr., who in 1912 had won the competition to design the city hall there.[84] In August 1914, Warren wrote President Eliot that Brown might be willing to replace Duquesne.[85] The pursuit of Arthur Brown represented another series of frustrating delays and indicated how difficult it was to bring to the school an American who was trained in the methods of the École. Brown was offered the same financial terms as Duquesne and opportunities for leave to pursue his practice, but he declined the position at Harvard, as he had declined offers from Cornell University and the University of Pennsylvania. He had lost office staff to military enlistments and did not want to leave his family in San Francisco. Furthermore, his former master at the École, Laloux, had advised him not to teach.[86]

The situation became so desperate that Warren tried to hold open an option for Brown by finding a temporary teacher—even if the substitute was a prisoner of war. Warren hoped that through the intercession of architect Cass Gilbert, the German army would release Ernest Hébrard, winner of the 1904 Grand Prix de Rome, from its military prison in Magdeburg. As an alternative to Brown, two prominent New York architects, Thomas Hastings of Carrère & Hastings, and Chester Holmes Aldrich of Delano & Aldrich, recommended John Humphreys. Brown formally refused the position in a letter to President Lowell in January 1915, Humphreys never measured up, and Hébrard was not released.[87] Harvard was still without its "star."

The Effects of World War I on Harvard's Collaborative Vision

Concurrent with the search for Duquesne's replacement, the Visiting Committee sent its evaluation of the first academic year the schools of architecture and landscape architecture acted as separate entities (1914–15) to the Harvard Board of Overseers. The committee approved of the new arrangement, stating that it allowed the schools to display their "fine endowments," which lifted them beyond being a "mere slice" of the Graduate School of Applied Science, and that the schools were just where they should be—"under one Faculty: both are architecture, and involve the same fundamental laws of design."[88] The Visiting Commit-

tee judged that equality was important to both schools and requested that a practicing landscape architect be appointed for the first time to its own membership.

The committee also reported that enrollment had steadily increased in architecture and landscape architecture through 1915. The School of Architecture had continued to assert its independence from the Beaux-Arts orthodoxy by engaging in joint academic ventures with local Boston schools. These joint ventures took the form of a new experimental program sponsored by Harvard, MIT, and the Boston Architectural Club, the three architecture schools in the Boston area. The program called for a cooperative effort in giving one design problem, which would be collectively critiqued, to the students of all three schools. In the third year of this local "competition," the committee reported that "results have been highly satisfactory."[89] This effort to focus more on local competitions was an overt statement of resistance to the national competition sponsored by the Beaux-Arts Institute of Design in New York. It also allowed Boston architects to control the local scene and prevent interference from New Yorkers, who adhered more dogmatically to the Beaux-Arts style. From the local perspective, national Beaux-Arts competitions were unnecessary—the annual exhibition of student work at the convention of the American Institute of Architects provided sufficient opportunity for national comparison.

Local cooperation was another matter, and the Visiting Committee recom-

2.51 A study for a city plan based on the topography of Chelsea, Mass., anonymous, 1910. LA thesis.

mended that, to conserve teaching resources, lectures given to large classes should be open to all three schools in the Boston area with the costs shared. It also specifically recommended that Warren's history courses and an experimental course on modern art given by C. Howard Walker, a Harvard graduate, architect, historian, and editor of the Boston *Architectural Review*, be open to students of MIT.[90] The Visiting Committee had sponsored Walker's course on a trial basis for Harvard College. Modern art had a unique cast, since no canon of modern art existed at the time. Reminiscent of the broad foundation of Charles Eliot Norton's lectures, the course was intended to provide a knowledge of the fine arts beyond a general introduction to architecture, painting, sculpture, and decorative arts, and thereby benefit the Schools of Architecture and Landscape Architecture. The Visiting Committee on Architecture decided to propose Walker's undergraduate course to the Visiting Committee on Fine Arts. The collaboration between the two was not surprising: "Your Committee further believes that the closest possible relation should be established between the School of Architecture and the Department of Fine Arts. They are indeed not two subjects but one. The ideal school of architecture is a school of Fine Arts."[91]

Despite the upbeat picture at Harvard, the war soon had insidious effects. When the United States finally entered the war, it took a toll by enlisting students. Herbert Langford Warren, an American born on foreign soil, became swept up in the war

effort and patriotic debate. He so exerted himself, according to one of his obituaries, that he died of exhaustion on June 27, 1917, two months after the United States declared war on Germany.

Warren's tenure as the first dean of the Faculty of Architecture had lasted only three years. A contemporary critic, while acknowledging his role as the founder and director of the architecture school, noted that his greatest achievement may have been his "his brilliant teaching of the history of architecture. It is not exaggerating to say that nothing surpassed it in any school in the world."[92] Warren's teaching rested on the conviction that the study of history would lead America out of the miasma of eclecticism and into the modern future.

By 1917, under Warren's guidance, Harvard had created two small schools of design that lacked the experience of older and larger schools such as MIT. From a single program of architecture in 1895 to a second program of landscape architecture in 1900 evolved two independent graduate schools in 1914. Warren filled his role as professor and dean with a collaborative vision. In these early years, the

schools drew their strength from his indefatigable energy and a coterie of teachers who were largely Harvard products.

As noted above, many of the teachers remained at the schools until the 1930s: Humphreys, Killam, and Frost in architecture; Pray, Hubbard, and Pond in landscape architecture and city planning. Hired as young men, they became the "old guard," a cadre of aging gentlemen during the 1930s in a time of cultural, political, and economic change. Students and ideologues rebelled against them as the bastions of entrenched tradition and obstacles to a radical modernism. But these practitioner-teachers were anything but entrenched; after all, they had founded and shaped schools that were open-minded and eclectic, collaborative and practice-oriented. Their curricula used the study of history as its core while attempting to balance Beaux-Arts ideas with a receptivity to other models of design besides classical Greece and Rome. They focused on training professionals at a graduate level, and they searched for American solutions to American problems even as they expanded their scope of inquiry to consider the problems and needs of cities. Though young and vulnerable to the needs of professional independence for each field, the schools idealistically pursued interdisciplinary collaboration as the modern answer to contemporary problems. Despite inherent tensions between the schools, these practitioner-teachers considered architecture and landscape architecture to be interconnected and believed that students of both fields should study together in their early training.

More innovative and significant than any of the specific results produced by students' projects was this ideal that the fields of architecture and landscape architecture could benefit from the mutual support and fertility found in collaboration. The founders of design education at Harvard actively sought collaboration between architecture and the fine arts, landscape architecture and, eventually, city planning. This philosophy of collaboration accompanied the evolution of these programs from undergraduate to graduate levels, producing the first such programs in these fields anywhere. Even at this early phase, the principle of collaboration testified to a nascent professionalism that lifted design studies beyond liberal arts, engineering, and horticulture to their own distinct disciplines. Professional graduate training and the creation of courses in city planning addressed modern needs. In response to the demands of the world around them and the interests of their faculty and students, these innovators launched an important American initiative: the first professional training in city planning. Regard-

less of how rudimentary we may find their proposals, the denizens of Robinson Hall identified the city itself as the locus of the problems of modern life (Fig. 2.51). For this end, the call for city planning had been raised. The modern city would become the focus of social change.

How did the future look in 1917? Where was Harvard's American project, and what kind of modernism did interdisciplinary design represent? The prospects looked mixed: Harvard's School of Architecture had lost its central leader—Warren. It had, however, charted a course towards uniting the disciplines, identified history as the key to the future of architecture, raised money from endowments, and hired and retained some seasoned teachers. Despite the lack of a strong design program, by 1917 Harvard had high aspirations in seeking to use design to define an American identity through architecture, to claim what Warren had called the country's "birthright." Although unsuccessful, Warren's efforts to find a suitable American professor of architecture placed the Harvard schools squarely in the effort to establish a national identity. In Warren's and the schools' view only an American could establish architectural principles that would respond to the conditions of an American land, its citizens, and their needs.

The pre-war era had spawned a genteel, progressive modernism oriented towards questions of American identity and American problems; it was not a radical call to action precipitated by a sense of fundamental sociological and eco-

nomic crisis. Harvard's modernism in the first decades of these design schools echoed the national tenor. That architecture remained connected to traditional styles, instead of rejecting them, made little difference. The spirit of progressivism behind these efforts is what counted. The call was for reform, not revolution.

Warren's successor as dean, George Harold Edgell, described his role in the midst of progressive modernism: "[Warren's] had been the energy, enthusiasm, and driving force which, more than anything, created the School. He was not only a profound scholar of the history of art and a creative designer of ability, but a brilliant linguist and broad-minded humanist as well." Edgell further commented (an ironic appraisal since few remember Warren's founding and pivotal role): "His name, more than any other, will always be associated with the School."[93] To trace how and why his name was eventually forgotten is to trace how the modernist agenda played out at Harvard.

CHAPTER THREE

RUMBLINGS OF CHANGE,
1917–1934

3.1 Group photo. Pen and Brush Club, 1921–22, School of Architecture. Left to right: Front rows: Constantin A. Pertzoff; John E. Carlson; Roy Ruhnka; Gouverneur M. Peek; Donald S. Reed; Edward S. Read; William J. Stone; William S. Boice; Stanley R. McCandless; Warren L. Hindenach; Ralph B. Jenkins; Louis S. Ross; Otto J. Teegen; Harold Kneworthy; Gilvert S. Underwood; Alfred T. Granger; Professor Hosmer A. Johnson; Emil A. Lehti; George Archimbeau, custodian; William S. Kussin; Edwin B. Olsen.
Back rows: Edwin M. Lye; Frederick J. Wilder; Stuart C. Welch; Professor Harold B. Warren; Professor H. Dudley Murphy; Professor John S. Humphreys; Ruth Cook, librarian; Sally Symonds, secretary; Professor C. Howard Walker; unknown; Professor Jean-Jacques Haffner; Professor John Wilson; George C. Dahl; Arthur B. Eckbert; George E. Sylvia, Jr.; Langford Warren; George L. Howe; Philip L. Cheney; Harold Gimeno; William H. Russell.

While America boomed economically in the 1920s, Europe withered under the strain of rampant inflation. Straitened conditions had an enormous impact on the architecture of Europe. Pre-war diversity in architecture disappeared with the need for a more unified and pragmatic vision of rebuilding war-torn lands.

Before World War I widely varied strands of modern architecture had coexisted, sharing only an exuberance to be modern, championing technology in a search for forms that represented the present and not the past. These strands crossed horizontally from Barcelona in the work of Antonio Gaudí, to the far reaches of Hungary in the work of Ödön Lechner, and vertically from the *Stile Libertà* in Italy—its version of French art nouveau—to Scandinavia. In the approximate center, both geographically and ideologically, France, Germany, and Austria-Hungary generated their own modern movements. These diverse efforts to define and represent modernity through architecture were described in most conventional histories as styles: *art nouveau, Jugendstil* (its Germanic equivalent), expressionism, rational organicism, and Nordic classicism. They all shared common roots in the arts and crafts movement in England that, from the mid-nineteenth century, not only provided the best models for reforming design and tying it to social improvement but also linked European and American developments in a common enterprise.

After the devastation of World War I in Europe, this composite fabric of many threads of modernism unraveled: *art nouveau* and *Jugendstil* vanished as operative forces; expressionism disappeared, except in the work of Erich Mendelsohn and a few other German architects; organicism and classicism became anathema in progressive circles. An architecture characterized by thin floating planes and flat roofs—all without ornament—replaced them. A call for "Objectivity" as a basis of design reform had stimulated the founding of the Deutscher Werkbund in 1907 and the Bauhaus in 1919, but by 1922 a "New Objectivity" was required that would be more radical in every sense than its predecessors. A radical modernism in Europe steamed forward into the 1920s to produce some of the great iconic buildings of the twentieth century, including Le Corbusier's Pavillon de l'Esprit Nouveau in Paris (1925) and the Villa Savoye in Poissy (1929–31); Gerrit Rietveld's Schröder House in Utrecht (1923–24); and J. J. P. Oud's Workers' Housing at the Hook of Holland (1926–27).

From the perspective of these radical modernists in Europe, American architecture from the Civil War to the Depression expressed a country diverted from its own pure architectural identity (commercial and industrial buildings) by historical eclecticism and a love affair with the École des Beaux-Arts. There were exceptions to this desolate view of American achievements, of course. But by 1922 the heroes of American modernism were invisible. Frank Lloyd Wright, after spending many of the previous six years in Japan, was returning to confront a period

in which he designed far more than he built. Louis Sullivan was at the end of his career, suffering from poor health. The visible appeal of American architecture lay in its industrial buildings, skyscrapers, and methods of production. Albert Kahn's Rouge River Glass Plant for the Ford Motor Company in Dearborn, Michigan, opened in 1922 for the purpose of producing, in a 750-foot-long shed of iron and glass, a continuous flow of plate glass from four huge furnaces. Nothing like it existed anywhere in Europe. And in 1931, only a year after the completion of the Chrysler Building, which had surpassed the Eiffel Tower as the world's tallest building, the Empire State Building topped all others in height, finesse, and efficiency of construction.

Our grasp of American architecture in the first decades of the twentieth century, leading up to the new skyscrapers, is still incomplete. In one of the few studies that comprehensively examines architectural practice in the United States in this

period, Paul Bentel has shown that, by the first decade of the century, the architectural profession had solidified through the efforts of the American Institute of Architects.[1] With professional journals available as a tool for discourse, architects began to critically evaluate what they had to offer Americans. Within this examination was an effort to define a social purpose for architecture with roots in American progressivism and the White City movement that had debuted with the World's Columbian Exposition. Architects and their patrons began to jettison traditional visual formulae as the White City movement wound down, but architects still wanted to affiliate with American political and social trends. Like civic leaders and progressive politicians, architects wanted to participate in creating a "new era" in American life that benefited from scientific human resources management (typified by such philosophies as Taylorism) and innovation. Technology in the service of a better society—the key

concept of modernist ideology in Europe—motivated American modernism in the first three decades of the century. Similar idealistic ambitions, however, were producing very different results in America and Europe. In America, a modernism was evolving that cared more about incorporating efficiency and technological innovation into a variety of styles than expressing revolutionary construction. In Europe, modernism did just the opposite by attempting to put the expression of technology and function above other considerations, while breaking with precedent and denying the validity of style itself.

Defining Modernism at Harvard During the 1920s

As American architecture grappled with defining its own modernism between World War I and the Depression, Harvard's progress in devising an agenda for modern design entered an interregnum after the

3.2 George Harold Edgell, Dean of the Faculty of Architecture and Landscape Architecture, 1922–35.

3.3 (opposite) The annual shindig of the Pen and Brush Club—and how! Alfred J. Panepinto, 1928. Left to right: George Archimbeau, custodian; C. Theodore Larson (in tree); Professor H. Dudley Murphy; Professor A. Lassell Ripley; Dean George H. Edgell; Professor Charles W. Killam; William R. Schaar and W. Douglas Richmond (under table); Professor John Wilson (with pipe); T. Matsumoto and Norman O'Sullivan (at table); John S. Bolles and E. A. Hill talking with Professor Harold B. Warren (behind table); Irvin McCleary (lying on stomach); Henry R. Wood, John F. Fitchen, and G. F. R. Heap (playing guitars); Alfred Busselle, Jr. (in swimming trunks); Professors Jean-Jacques Haffner, Charles A. Whittemore, John S. Humphreys, and Walter F. Bogner (standing); Herbert T. Anderson and Tito Cascieri (sitting); Coleman M. Fitch (in tree); and Keith B. Hudson (standing).

death of Langford Warren in 1917. Acting Dean Charles Wilson Killam, the rigorous architectural engineer, attempted to implement Warren's principles while emphasizing construction, despite the war and dwindling enrollment. For the next five years, the curricula in architecture and landscape architecture remained relatively unchanged with an important exception: landscape architecture students no longer studied the rudiments of architectural design in the same studios with architecture students. In the continual search for balance, this change had the unforeseen effect of reducing collaboration between the fields, subtly inducing a psychological separation between the students and their philosophies of design.

Lacking a clear, and therefore unified, direction, the Schools of Architecture and Landscape Architecture were hardly in a position to define American modern architecture. Their concern was immediate: should the new dean be an architect or an architectural historian? Langford Warren had been both; George Harold Edgell, his successor, was neither. Appointed the second dean of the Faculty of Architecture in 1922, Edgell was a scholar and an art historian, the first student to receive a Ph.D. from Harvard's Department of Fine Arts and a specialist in the art of the Italian Renaissance (Fig. 3.2). However, his academic credits included *A History of Architecture*, written with S. Fiske Kimball and published in 1918, the first such survey written in the United States.[2] After his appointment as head of the Faculty of Architecture,

Edgell continued to teach the general introductory courses on medieval art and modern art in the Division of Fine Arts, an effort that reinforced the close interconnections between fine arts and architecture at Harvard.[3]

Edgell knew he straddled disparate academic and professional realms. With respect to his own appointment, he commented to his college classmates: "I was appointed Professor of Fine Arts in 1925. This was three years after President Lowell had tried the audacious experiment of making me Dean of the Faculty of Architecture—and the only member who was not a professional architect. Since then I have been assuming the lion's skin of architect, and concealing the bray."[4]

Edgell, a dog lover and hunter, was well liked by his students, respected by his colleagues, and seen as a facile administrator (Fig. 3.3).[5] The changes occurring during his deanship, from the relative security of the 1920s to the turmoil of the 1930s, required the full use of his skills. Edgell confronted the fact that unity and collaboration between the schools of architecture and landscape architecture had begun to dissolve. He oversaw a shift from a focus on history to an emphasis on design. He played a key role in establishing a School of City Planning, which formed a triumvirate with the architecture and landscape architecture schools. And he attempted to confront the changing academic perceptions of modern architecture while reformulating an educational program in response to desperate global economic conditions. Edgell heard the

rumblings of the European avant-garde, but he could not have foreseen the radical changes that would eventually reshape his school—and design education throughout America—in the late 1930s.

Among the most important changes that Edgell oversaw was a shift towards design in the School of Architecture. In some ways this was an obvious move for a school that had lacked consistent studio teaching at an advanced level. In 1922 Edgell addressed this deficiency by appointing not an American but another Frenchman, Jean-Jacques Haffner, the winner of the Grand Prix de Rome in 1919. Haffner, known as "Jake" to his students, became a Nelson Robinson Professor, the principal instructor in advanced design.[6] Teaching until the late 1930s, Haffner encouraged a wider range of experimentation than would be expected of a graduate of the École.

Upon his arrival, Haffner took over the intermediate and advanced design stu-dios, which he co-taught with John Humphreys. Under Haffner, students designed a broad range of building types from suburban cooperative apartment houses to war memorials and vaudeville theaters. Even Humphreys moved away from the classical Beaux-Arts of Carrère & Hastings to allow his students to design art deco steamship terminals. Haffner also revised the existing design theory course, "Composition in Plan and Decorative Composition," shifting the focus from decorative design to discussions about "current problems" regarding the ele-ments of architecture, methods of work-ing, principles of composition, and a new emphasis on the use of the human scale as an approach to problems of proportion, character, and plan.[7]

The French Beaux-Arts system returned to Harvard but with a twist: Haffner empha-sized students' individual progress and pace over regimented programs, an approach similar to the innovative and strongly anti–Beaux-Arts training being offered then at the University of Oregon.[8] At both schools, the effectiveness of the system depended on the quality of teaching rather than the structure of the course itself.

Harvard's emphasis on design in the 1920s occurred at some expense to the teaching of architectural history, and its history's role, relative to modern design training, would continue to fluctuate. In 1922 the course in ancient architecture was reduced to a half year, joining the sta-tus of medieval, Renaissance, and post-Renaissance architecture, which had been shortened by half before the war. The reduction from full- to half-year courses signaled a de-emphasis on the role of architectural history long before the radical modernist critiques of this his-tory in the 1930s. Although history was Edgell's domain, he was unaware of the extent to which reducing the emphasis on history would subvert the continuity of architectural tradition.

Jerusalem — Sepulchre

Rotunda of Anastasis

3.4 Sepulchre in Jerusalem: Rotunda of Antasis, Alfred J. Panepinto, 1928. Drawing from lantern slide, history course, Professor Conant.

3.5 Original design for a chapel in the French Gothic style, Edwin J. Peterson, 1932. Arch. 4c, 10-day history problem, Professor Conant.

Though his courses were shortened, Kenneth Conant, a graduate of the School of Architecture who was on his way to becoming its premier architectural historian, continued to teach history rigorously and thoroughly.[9] In the 1920s the traditional drawing problems no longer included exercises in dictation; instead, Conant's students made sketches from projected lantern slides (Fig. 3.4). Reconstruction problems asked students to execute complete renderings in the manner of historic structures, which they did to often stunning results (Fig. 3.5). These exercises taught both drawing and visual skills, ensuring students' lifelong familiarity with important buildings. As one student recounted: "Sixty years later I can recognize any important building in Europe if I see it in photographs, or through a train window, or if I drive by it in a car."[10]

Changes in the role and teaching of architectural history also reflected larger trends. On one hand, the field itself was evolving beyond connoisseurship towards a more rational and scientific basis. On the other hand, doubts about the essential validity of the field as a basis for contemporary practice were growing. In Europe, the cataclysm of World War I had focused the modernist reaction against history as a model for the present and a guide for the future. By the early 1920s, radical European modernists saw reliance on history as a corruption of the modernist agenda. Though Henry Ford famously said, "History is bunk," Americans generally took a more benign view.

Yet, even so, the belief in the lessons of history as a model for modern life had begun to wane.

Doubts about the validity of history spawned further doubts about the history-entrenched methods of the École des Beaux-Arts, which had long dominated American design education. Indicating a nascent inclination towards radical modernism, one critic described architectural education in 1925 in negative terms: "[The Beaux-Arts method] emphasized theory and 'unreality,' gave little encouragement to creative ability, lacked integration of subjects, overemphasized design, lacked instruction in business, and failed to provide a transition between school and the office."[11] The same critic asserted, however, that the schools stressed professional ethics and had fully developed common standards. Students trained under these conditions absorbed the skills of drawing and rendering and the logic of the Beaux-Arts plan techniques used to produce monumental designs. But the conditions of design were artificial, and the results were two-dimensional, only partially informed by engineering theory. In sum, the architecture student "had become an habitual plagiarist rather than a creative artist," an observation supported by students producing baroque temple fronts spliced into arcuated colonnades of the Florentine Renaissance (Fig. 3.6).[12]

In 1927 William G. Perry, a Boston architect who had taught briefly at Harvard, pointed out that the French method, applied to American conditions, provided

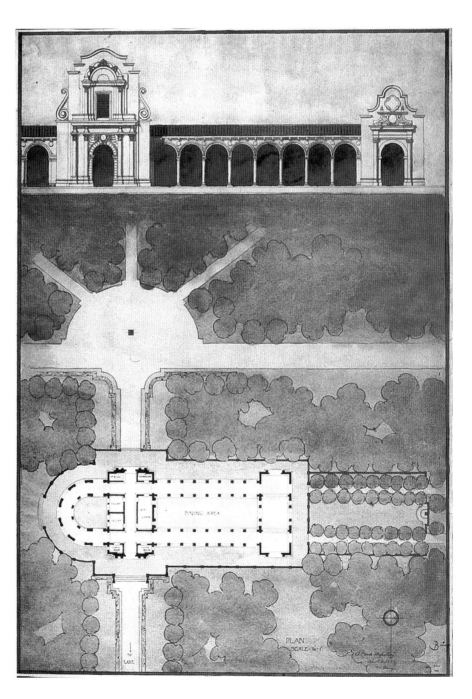

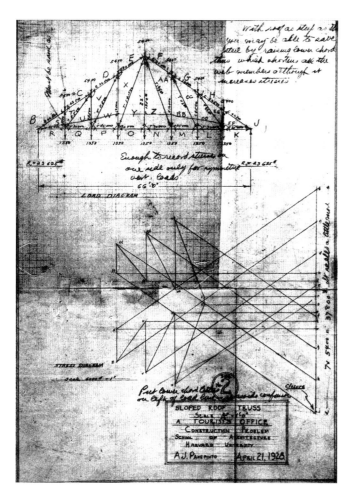

3.7 Sloped roof truss, a tourist's office, Alfred J. Panepinto, 1928. Construction problem, Professor Charles W. Killam.

an effective education but had limitations. The masters of the École, such as Jean Louis Pascal (Duquesne's mentor), Julien Guadet, and Victor Laloux (Haffner's mentor), might train their students with methods that were "more beneficial than any other influence whatsoever," promoting the alleged "superior" logic of the "French Mind" for an American people,[13] but the *methods* of the École did not confront social conflicts, changing attitudes toward business, or global economic crises—all factors beyond the scope of visual solutions alone. With a proper training an architect should have expertise in theoretical, practical, and aesthetic matters, but this public role was not yet effectively taught in architectural education: "unlike the education of law and medicine, it has not convinced the public."[14] *Procession*, *allée*, bilateral symmetry, and axiality no

longer sufficed as the sole means of building organization.

At Harvard, however, the student work became more informed by engineering rigor than the critic assumed, even if the rigor did not show itself stylistically in a new and self-conscious vocabulary. The *Official Register* of the School of Architecture declared that architects still needed "artistic imagination enriched by the knowledge of the great art of the past," but during the early 1920s this injunction was amended to link it to the present, "with knowledge of the needs of today and of the materials and methods now available for expressing those needs."[15] The official addition of this goal to the written program for architectural education at Harvard implied that new technology demanded an appropriate new expression. Langford

Warren had earlier considered the relationship of new design to "modern" building techniques, but it seemed as if no new language of modernism had appeared to 1920s Harvard.

While the forms remained largely traditional, students could take advantage of technological innovation. As seen in the student notebooks of the period, architectural theses incorporated thorough engineering studies and construction calculations. For example, Alfred Panepinto's design for a tourist office, executed in Killam's class, presented 38 pages of drawings and a loose-leaf notebook of 124 pages containing construction calculations (Fig. 3.7). Panepinto had graduated with a BS in civil engineering from Villanova College (now University) and believed that Killam taught the latest construction techniques of the period and that his work was comparable to that of Carl Humphrey, an MIT engineer who taught at Villanova.

Killam carefully checked and corrected every computation amidst a sea of red pencil checks, copious notes, and suggestions. According to Panepinto, Killam "welcomed the new styles especially where unusual construction called for applying basic principles of engineering."[16] Killam's thorough approach to building construction complemented Henry Frost's teaching of drafting skills and knowledge of timber construction. In 1926 the technology sequence was expanded when Frost conducted a problem requiring construction drawings for a wooden frame house. The problem was considered so important by the faculty that design studios were sus-

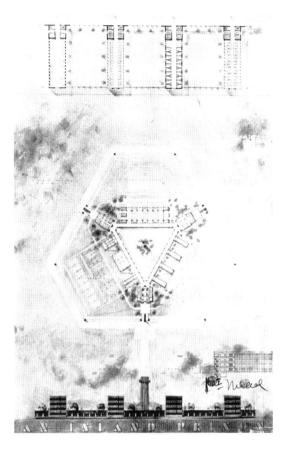

3.8 An island prison, Frederic von Grossmann, 1932. Class "A," V project. 1st medal. National competition organized by the Beaux-Arts Institute of Design, New York.

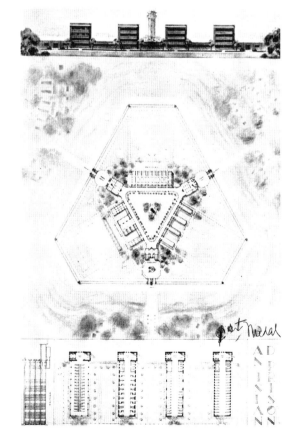

3.9 An island prison, Mario Ciampi, 1932. Class "A," V project. 1st medal. National competition organized by the Beaux-Arts Institute of Design, New York.

pended while students prepared plans, elevations, framing plans, and details. The search for a thorough understanding of construction and engineering was a crucial aspect of the program.

From the radical modernist perspective, however, a search for new forms linked modern architecture not only to new materials and technology but also to changes in society itself. European modernists, unfamiliar with Beaux-Arts training in America and its deviations from the moribund practices in Europe, condemned traditional education in this country. To them America was void of social conscience—an easy assumption considering the proliferation of luxurious buildings for capitalist tycoons and technological marvels such as skyscrapers nicknamed "cathedrals of commerce." In the words of Henry Cobb, who trained under the coming generation of European modernists in the 1940s, "Modernists wanted us to believe the Beaux Arts were anti-social. Students believed it."[17]

But the programs for some of the problems in the 1920s and 1930s—though not focused exclusively on projects for the improvement of social realities—showed more social sensitivity. For example, a sketch problem for "A School of Americanization" in 1930 required students to create a complex that would support immigrants' efforts to "make themselves understood in a country where habits, ways of the people, customs and a general understanding of environment, behavior and life are sometimes very different from their own."[18] The problem

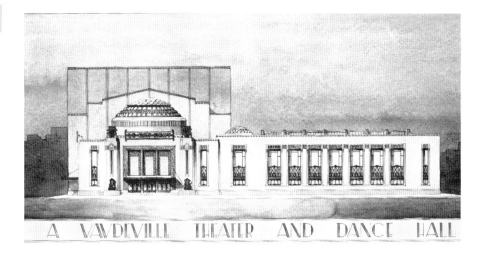

3.10 A vaudeville theater hall, Edward J. Aisner, 1926. Arch. 4c, conjunctive problem, Professor Jean-Jacques Haffner.

3.11 A steamship terminal pier, Alfred J. Panepinto, 1928. Arch. 4b, conjunctive problem, Professor John Humphreys. Elevation.

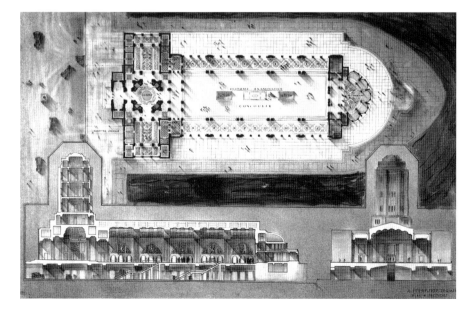

3.12 A steamship terminal pier, Alfred J. Panepinto, 1928. Arch. 4b, conjunctive problem, Professor John Humphreys. Plan and sections.

3.13 Monument to World War I, Walter H. Kilham, Jr., 1928. Arch. 4b, conjunctive problem, Professor Jean-Jacques Haffner. Interior perspective.

3.14 A parish church, Alfred J. Panepinto, 1930. Arch. 4c. Professor Jean-Jacques Haffner.

required an administrative building to provide social services and clerical offices, space for interpreters, a nursery, a kindergarten, health facilities, a cafeteria, and a small post office. A second building was to have thirty classrooms for the study of English and other subjects held in the evenings, complemented by a court with covered galleries for recreation between courses, and an assembly room, seating a thousand people, for lectures and educational movies.

Other studies showed concern for government projects for the struggling, the dispossessed, even the incarcerated. The prison served as the subject for competition designs by F. R. von Grossman and Mario J. Ciampi, who produced conventional plans based on platonic geometry. Remarkably similar, both designs turned the prison blocks into slabs with horizontal bands that resembled the austere, abstract, and planar styles of European modern architecture (Figs. 3.8, 3.9). Ironically, the Beaux-Arts Institute of Design in New York, dedicated to propagating Beaux-Arts methods, organized both competitions in 1932. Though it referred to the categories by the French term *projet*, even the official organization was yielding to economic and social reality.

Perhaps most telling of Harvard students' awareness of current social conditions in the United States, however, was Robert G. Cerny's project for an unemployment camp. Designed in 1932–33 in the midst of the Depression, the camp was clearly intended to address the ram-

3.15 A suburban cooperative apartment house, Alfred J. Panepinto, 1930. Arch. 4c. Professor Jean-Jacques Haffner.

pant unemployment of the time by providing communal housing to those looking for work. At one end of the complex were interview rooms and an employment bureau; at the other were workshops to occupy the men while they waited for gainful employment. The design won second prize from the "conjunctive problem" jury. Collectively, these student design programs that addressed immigration, crime, and unemployment show an obvious concern for larger social issues coexisting with the self-indulgence of the preceding "Golden Twenties."

In 1929, six years after his appointment, Edgell appraised the progress of the School of Architecture and the contributions of his predecessors: "On the whole, it is fair to say that during the regime of Dean Warren special emphasis was laid on Architectural History; during that of Acting Dean Killam, on Architectural Construction; and during that of Dean Edgell, on Architectural Design."[19] Edgell's succinct characterization neatly summarized trends in the school, but where exactly did this place the school's modern agenda? On the eve of global social and economic crisis and after three decades of experience, Harvard still extolled design, in all its professional manifestations, as a fine art, yet an art grounded in physical principles and practical necessities.

Although utilizing an inherited visual vocabulary, the school expressed a sensitivity to the needs of a "modern" society as it perceived them; it began to search for answers to American problems. To the his-

A CHVRCH PORTICO

3.16 A church portico: Corinthian order, Alfred J. Panepinto, 1928. Arch. 4a, Professor Walter Bogner.

3.17 Memorial group, World War I, Edward J. Aisner, 1926. Arch. 4b, conjunctive problem, Professor Jean-Jacques Haffner.

toricism and stylistic plurality that had been the school's legacy were added the latest styles of European and American modern architecture. The students of the 1920s used an array of styles—art deco and the beginnings of *art moderne*—to synthesize a new expression. The results, which at times were spectacular, ranged from designs for a vaudeville theater and dance hall to a dramatic steamship terminal, war memorials, and apartment buildings (Figs. 3.10–3.15). At the same time that students showed expertise in the current styles of modern architecture, they still studied and replicated the classical orders—but with a skill that far surpassed the efforts from twenty years earlier (Figs. 3.16, 3.17).

The Evolution of Education in City Planning

Harvard's evolving modernist agenda was most evident in the city planning program. If the architecture program, despite its innovations and its emphasis on modern conditions and technology, still appeared outwardly conservative, the program in city planning was more obviously modern. A later assessment of the program's early years characterized it as querulous and visionary, as opposed to MIT's pragmatism.[20] The young field had benefited from a series of formative events stemming from the 1910s. The first American conference on city planning was held in Washington, D.C. in 1909, the second in Boston in 1910. Locally, Frederick Law Olmsted, Jr., wrote on aspects

of planning and lectured to Harvard students on the financial aspects of city planning; at the same time, James Ford, a pioneer in the field, lectured on housing. At the outset of World War I, Theodora Kimball's updated *Classified Selected List of References on City Planning* demonstrated the global interest in the subject, particularly in England and Germany.[21] Congresses and conferences on city planning occurred annually in North America, and exhibitions were held in Cologne, Leipzig, Ghent, Dresden, London, and Berlin, with American participation, despite the trend towards isolationism in the years before the war.[22] The first American planning quarterly, *The City Plan*, appeared in 1915, with the stated mission "to teach planners to distinguish between temporary schemes for beautification and sound planning for city development."[23]

Another stimulus for city planning was the passing of the first zoning ordinances, which were enacted for New York in 1916. This momentous legislation prompted hundreds of communities during the following years to analyze their buildings; to establish restrictions on building height and coverage of air, land, and light; and to work on the planning of parks, sanitary systems, streets, and slum clearance—all tasks that became the provenance of the just-emerging field of city planning.[24] Governmental recognition of the new field, from the national to the local level, also helped confirm the need for city planning. Moreover, increasing public interest in urban development stimulated the expansion of the field and

gradually increased the demand for expertise in city and regional planning. In 1917 the American City Planning Institute (later the American Institute of Planners) was formed; seventeen of its 52 charter members were associated with Harvard.[25]

At the same time, a new direction in city planning towards political science and away from design began to undermine the City Beautiful movement. Only two years after its founding, *The City Plan*, a quarterly, formalized this new direction by announcing the "shift from the City Beautiful movement to the City Scientific."[26] This shift reflected the tendencies of American practitioners to emphasize a rational rather than an aesthetic organization of systems: water and rail transportation; the location of major and minor streets, rapid transit, industrial centers, parks and recreational facilities; and legal issues involving public control of private real estate, city financing, and city planning legislation. In the relatively newly industrialized, bustling, and sometimes chaotic American city, pragmatic order and the distribution of services preceded aesthetic considerations.

Arthur Coleman Comey, a Harvard instructor, supported the growing role of the field of city planning to address urban demands for physical order and social well-being. A teacher of city and regional planning at Harvard into the 1930s, Comey, a Harvard graduate in landscape architecture, integrated landscape architecture, city planning, and garden suburb housing in his classes.[27] As early as 1913 his design for Billerica Garden Suburbs in

Billerica, Massachusetts, responded to both pragmatic and social needs for the first instance of public housing—the first such housing in the country and one of the first planned suburban communities. A pioneering effort to eliminate speculation in real estate, Comey's ambitious scheme was intended to provide ownership of low-cost housing to working-class people, establish a community center, and provide jobs. The state of Massachusetts was supposed to provide construction capital; workers who purchased homes would pay back the state. The only stipulation was that a dwelling could not be sold for less than its cost. Comey was the project's chief designer; Warren H. Manning, who had been associated with the Olmsted firm and had an active practice, was advisor. The overarching goal was to create a viable social fabric; its visual appearance was secondary—style was almost irrelevant. The concepts of co-partnership and linking the location of industry to worker housing were attempts to create a "potent economic invention," in which collective ownership would reduce the power of the speculator to inflate the cost of land and buildings.[28] A second housing project was planned for Lowell, Massachusetts. However, the Boston and Maine Railroad reneged on its agreement to provide employment in Billerica, and World War I caused the federal government to absorb these innovative housing efforts in an effort to provide federally sponsored housing.

More influential than Comey's housing projects in stimulating public awareness

about planning was the *Regional Plan of New York and Its Environs*, published in 1922 as the first detailed regional plan in the United States.[29] It pointed to zoning as the dominant issue for planning boards, which were, even then, spreading across the cities and towns of America.

At this time in the 1920s, Harvard provided only one course in planning, taught by James Pray and his colleagues in the School of Landscape Architecture.[30] After Edgell's appointment as dean, the school strengthened its roster of instructors in preparation for a major expansion of its city-planning program. Charles Eliot II, namesake of his uncle, joined the faculty in 1923 upon graduating from the School of Landscape Architecture; he was soon to become nationally influential in city planning. He served on the National Capital Park and Planning Commission from 1926 to 1930 and then became director of planning for Washington and its environs from 1931 to 1933. From 1933 to 1943 he held many important directorships of national planning organizations in Washington, D.C.[31] The school also formulated a definition of the landscape architect as a professional who "designs and directs the development of, or advises regarding" work that ranged from private gardens and country estates to government buildings (including penal institutions) to public park systems, to "land-subdivisions and residential and industrial suburbs; villages, towns, and cities, and larger areas involved in regional planning, and even state and national planning."[32]

In 1923, in response to the national demand for planning expertise, the School of Landscape Architecture announced a new master's level program in city planning, the first such degree offered in the United States. The school justified the new program on two grounds: World War I had demonstrated the economic value of large-scale land planning for residential development of industrially-related housing, and for the layout of military camps and cantonments; and there was an unprecedented demand for trained practitioners of landscape architecture "in its civic aspects."[33] Here was the "social conscience" of Harvard that seemed to be somewhat absent in the architecture program.

The new city planning program was implemented by doubling the length of some courses and halving others to provide flexibility for a regular option in landscape architecture and a special option in city planning.[34] With the creation of the two tracks within the School of Landscape Architecture came a new generation of assistants and junior male faculty members, including Arthur Comey, Ralph N. Cram, Bradford Williams, Howard K. Menhinick, Herbert D. Langhorne, and Carol Fulkerson. Visiting lecturers—lawyers, city and regional planners who predated formal training programs in the field, and experts in housing—kept students and faculty in touch with the latest developments in planning and landscape architecture. Lecturers included Alfred Bettman, Frank Backus Williams (who later endowed a professor-

3.18 Plan of Villa Papa Giulio, Rome, Clarence D. Platt, 1925. Landscape Architecture, Charles Eliot Traveling Fellowship.

3.19 A modern pool in the Alcazar Gardens, Seville, Herbert B. Campbell and Thomas D. Price, 1928. Measured drawing.

3.20 Grading plan for the estate of Lord Hourockie, Middlesex Fells, Stuart Constable, 1924. LA 2b, problem 3.

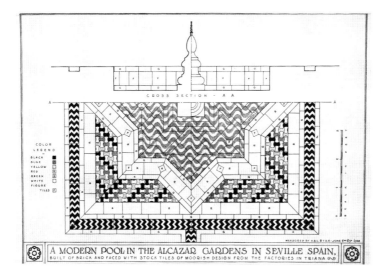

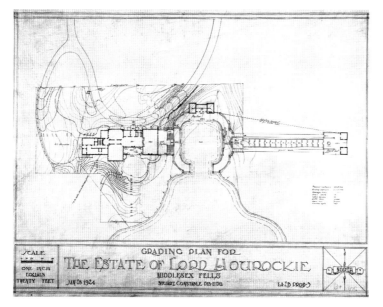

ship), George B. Ford, Harland Bartholomew, Edward Bassett, James Ford, and Robert Whitten. Arthur A. Shurtleff came occasionally from his practice in Boston to speak to the landscape architects, one of whom was his son Sidney Shurtleff.[35]

Another development in its curriculum affected the School of Landscape Architecture during this same period: courses in architecture and the fine arts that had been relegated to the domain of undergraduate prerequisites were reinstated. In the continual vacillation between training students collaboratively and training them separately, landscape architecture and architecture students were—for the moment—rejoined in the common endeavor of design. Students of both the regular landscape option and the planning option were now required to take, in addition to fine arts courses, the introductory course in the history of art and "Materials and Methods of Building Construction" with Charles Killam, the master architectural engineer. These requirements expanded the length of study and recalled Warren's original curriculum that encouraged colleges to supply training in the history of art and architecture for landscape architects and city planners. However, it also meant that the planners would have direct experience in design.

Ambiguity in Landscape Architecture

While city planning courses provided an in-depth means for studying the planning of cities, landscape architecture still

3.21 Kingsley Park Seminary for Young Women, Fresh Pond, Mass., S. Herbert Hare, 1909. LA 2, problem 3, Professor Henry Hubbard.

3.22 A coeducational school of landscape architecture, Fresh Pond, Mass., J. Allen Myers, Jr., 1925. LA 2b, problem 4, Professors Hubbard and Pond.

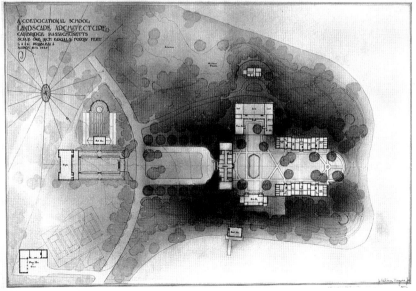

focused on planning estates for the wealthy and only secondarily gave attention to large-scale public projects. On one hand, the landscape architecture training at Harvard was tethered to tradition, and on the other, it responded to modern conditions with innovative studies in the planning of cities and regions. While the new planning courses were integrated into the study of landscape design, landscape architecture still revolved around two familiar styles. The first derived from an Olmstedian adaptation of romantic, picturesque English traditions resulting in designs related like cousins to English ancestors, yet often freer and looser. The second style was derived from continental models of Italian, French, Spanish, and even Dutch designs, which Harvard students in Cambridge and their traveling fellows studied, measured, drew, and redrew (Figs. 3.18–3.20). Students produced variations of the great European models as they mined material for new designs in the creation of an American tradition.

The skills of landscape students improved during the 1920s.[36] A growing number of designs for more populist projects, including comfortable middle-income houses and gardens suitable for suburban sites as well as suburban parks, balanced the continued emphasis on a wealthy clientele. Basic design was studied in problems that were repeated annually. Henry Hubbard chose a site (often Fresh Pond in Cambridge), issued topographic surveys from a standing collection, and had his students fill in site and

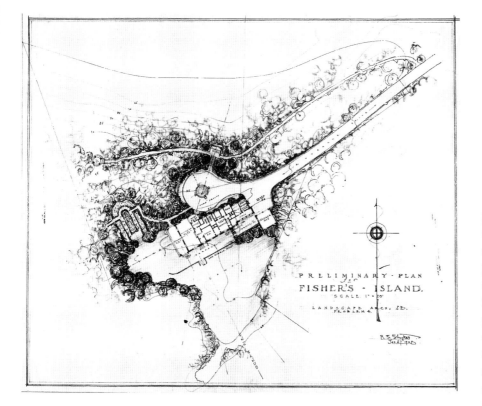

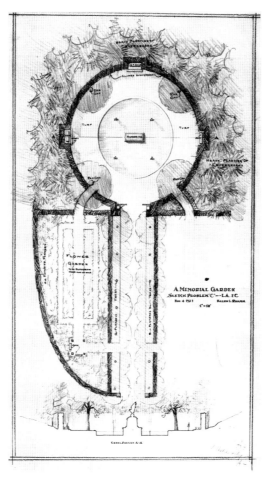

3.23 Preliminary plan for Fisher's Island, Donald W. Stryker, 1928. LA 2d, problem 4.

3.24 A memorial garden, Ralph L. Reaser, 1928. LA 2c, sketch problem "C."

planting plans. The students not only designed various gardens for the site but also provided the Latin names of all the plants, their exact locations, and their costs. They also prepared letters presenting their designs to clients. The design problems called for formal flower gardens, vegetable gardens, and rose, herb, and water gardens. The same site often served for several different assignments, ranging from a seminary for women to a proposed coeducational school of landscape architecture (Figs. 3.21, 3.22). The projected ideal of these landscape school projects reflected a reaction to the persistent male chauvinism of the university, and the ever-simmering desire of landscape architecture to separate itself from architecture—even though collaboration was the credo of both schools.

By the late 1920s Harvard-trained landscape architecture students were producing complex and detailed architectural components in their designs (Fig. 3.23). An entry from the School of Landscape Architecture for a grouping of four houses won first prize in a special category in a competition sponsored by the Garden Club of America in 1924. The designs showed a pioneering use of models built to convey a sense of plant forms and control of architectural details, which resulted in a tactile harmony between architecture and garden. The prize announcement profusely noted the architectural details: "The houses are plain, light stucco, varying in shade; mottled roofs to simulate tiles in four separate tones—green, brown, and blue blending harmoniously. Kitchens and

3.25 Entrance to a funerary isle, Alfred J. Panepinto, 1929. Arch 4b, conjunctive problem, Professor John Humphreys.

garages toward the street, giving the gardens and lawns privacy. Large maple trees on the corners and smaller maples and poplars on the central boundary line. The four adjoining gardens were varied. Vases made of carved red rubber and a clothes reel made of a little Japanese umbrella were features that attracted attention [sic]."[37]

Other successful competition entries from Harvard landscape students addressed monumental designs, such as war memorials; landscape architecture students designed both the planting plans and the memorial structure itself (Fig. 3.24). Benjamin S. Pray, son of the chairman of the department, won first prize in the seventh annual competition for the Topiarian Trophy Club with a campanile that was lauded for "the bold conception of carrying the feeling of the tower to the base of the cliff." The program required a monument for a New England city of 200,000 inhabitants that "shall be a dignified architectural or sculptural subject and that it shall be related, as far as possible, both to the city and to the park." Second prize went to Harvard schoolmate Robert S. Stryker for his design of a marble shaft supporting a perpetual flame, supposedly lit on Armistice Day.[38] Perhaps the most impressive memorial design by a Harvard architecture student was the result of a "conjunctive" problem—the then-contemporary term for *collaborative*—given to architecture and landscape architecture students by Jean-Jacques Haffner. The result shows an impressive consideration of site, scale,

and the spirit of mourning appropriate for the proposed entrance to a funerary isle commemorating the lives sacrificed in war (Fig. 3.25).

Establishment of the School of City Planning

Although Harvard's teaching of landscape architecture addressed the challenges of modernity ambiguously by accepting the traditions of historical examples, ambiguity was nowhere in sight when the decision was made in 1929 to upgrade the program in city planning to its own school in order to train cadres of professional planners equipped to wrestle with modern urban needs. The first such graduate school in the country, its founding was the culmination of twenty years of interest in the field. Major financial gifts to Harvard made possible the establishment of the School of City Planning, which expanded on the existing option in city planning offered in landscape architecture. Behind the financial catalysts that made possible this historic step was a series of protracted negotiations, initiated by James Pray and Dean Edgell, that explained the initial intentions of the school and revealed the factors operating at its creation.

The possibility of creating a graduate school devoted to the study of city planning began in 1928 when the directors of the Regional Plan of New York and Its Environs met at Columbia University to discuss the purpose and nature of a new institute, or school, of city planning. Touching on subjects ranging from the status of building in the United States over the next twenty-five years to the question of whether or not the proposed school's director should have teaching responsibilities, discussions pointed to the ultimate goal of initiating a fund-raising drive for such a school at Columbia.[39] Bearing in mind the existing unprecedented growth in city building, the committee proposed that ample financing should be provided for developing a city planning profession, and that a written set of statements should guide the conception of a school or institute of research and instruction. In drawing up this guide, the New York committee faced many crucial questions: Should a school of planning be associated with a university? If so, should it be part of an existing department, such as architecture, or organized as an independent unit able to interact freely with various departments? Should degrees be awarded immediately, or would it be better to devote a few years to assembling materials and methods for instruction, and students with advanced standing could participate in preparing the program? The committee even considered salaries and expenses for books, but it avoided the central problem of specifically defining the field of city planning.

When Edgell heard about the conference at Columbia, he realized its organizers had ignored Harvard's extensive experience in studying and teaching city planning over a twelve-year period. Regardless of Columbia's prior claim as the locus of the new school, he proposed that the committee consider building upon Harvard's curriculum and the superb planning library that it had developed. Sensing a major opportunity for Harvard, Edgell called in family connections by asking his uncle, Fredrick A. Delano, who happened to be chairman of the Regional Plan in New York and Its Environs, to inform the committee of Harvard's efforts in city and regional planning. Edgell pointed out that "Here, and here only, there are teachers of a dozen or more years experience who have studied the problem, taught the subject, and viewed it in its broadest possible way." He acknowledged that although Harvard was very conservative, it nevertheless wanted to take this progressive action. He also pointed out that the committee had apparently overlooked the pioneering work of Hubbard and Pray in landscape architecture, which had established a master's degree in landscape architecture in city planning. Hubbard, in particular, had made important contributions, not the least through his attention to Harvard's library, so that it had become "the best library in city planning in the world." Edgell amplified the position of Harvard vis-à-vis city planning, which was "not merely an adjunct to an architectural development. That is the last conception that anyone here has. It is an adjunct to civilization, and not any of the arts and crafts. We conceive of it as a sort of three-legged stool, with architecture, landscape architecture, and engineering representing the legs. But of course, it is really far more than that. In our teaching here, we collaborate not only with engineering, but of course with social ethics and with the legal side."[40]

Edgell's efforts and the work of the conference bore fruitful results. Hubbard applied to the Laura Spellman Rockefeller Memorial Foundation for an endowment of one million dollars to provide an income of $50,000 annually for a complete program of teaching and research in city planning.[41] He proposed that this teaching and research be conducted, ideally, by three groups of people: experienced Harvard faculty and outside practitioners, as well as younger program fellows. Other American universities submitted plans for city planning programs at the request of the committee; Hubbard's plan was chosen.[42] The Rockefeller Foundation responded enthusiastically and approved $240,000 for distribution over the next seven years.[43] The foundation wanted the program to be self-supporting by the end of the grant period, so it further agreed to supplement its gift by $5,000 annually if Harvard raised its own funds. Another benefactor was James Freeman Curtis, a graduate of Harvard College and its law school, who donated $150,000 in 1929 to establish a chair in regional planning in memory of his friend Charles Dyer Norton, the first director of the Regional Plan of New York and Its Environs, a prominent civic leader, and a sponsor of regional plans in Chicago as well as New York.[44]

In February 1929 one of the longtime proponents for city planning at Harvard, James Pray, died; Henry Hubbard, the rising star, assumed the chairmanship of the new school.[45] In the fall of 1929 a press release announced the founding of the School of City Planning at Harvard and the offering of a new degree, Master of City Planning.[46] Harvard now had three separate schools, each with its own council and chairman, but all under the general jurisdiction of the Faculty of Architecture. The curriculum of the new planning program differed from the predecessor landscape option in city planning by reducing courses in planting design and adding courses in city planning design, drafting, and topographical surveying. By emphasizing drafting and drawing skills, principles of construction, and the theory of city planning from both the social and the designer's perspectives, the city planning curriculum fostered a justifiable and worthwhile connection to physical design.[47] The planning students drew, took studios, defended their projects in juries, and worked collaboratively with their peers in architecture and landscape architecture. During the first two years of a four-year program, students took design, construction principles, planning principles, drawing, drafting, horticulture, topographic surveying, and fine arts. The subjects of the third-year studio were plans for airports, civic centers, parks, transportation systems, and zoning. In the second semester of the third year, the subject was an ideal town. In the fourth year, students produced a thesis. The curriculum in landscape architecture changed, in turn, to reflect the new program offered by the School of City Planning: the planning option in landscape architecture was obviously dropped, the traditional introductory course in city planning was renamed, and the elementary course on the theory of landscape design included special references to city planning.

The School of City Planning struggled to balance data analysis and formal representation, the polar positions inherited from the City Scientific and the City Beautiful movements. The resulting city plans produced in the young school remain unknown, since little of the student work has been preserved, and much of it was commingled with courses in landscape architecture. Only fifteen people were graduated in a six-year span. A lone example of a study model for aspects of a city plan is found in a report, "Evansville Railroad Problem."[48] The model points to the coordination of rail traffic as the key to future growth and prominence in manufacturing for Indiana. The railroads transported mostly freight, but population studies indicated the need for a new passenger terminal, and the report described existing conditions and documented them with aerial photographs. A typical thesis topic was the study, "Cabrillo—Port of Los Angeles," submitted in 1930 by Shigemaru Shimoyama, for which Comey, Hubbard, and Pond were jurors. The focus of the subject was prescient; a port, when finally built, became an important feature in the prosperity (and traffic congestion) of Los Angeles.[49]

Despite the lack of student work, faculty members of the School of City Planning left impressive writing and research as they tried to define the field itself and,

72

3.26 Henry V. Hubbard's pronouncements for the future in John F. Cogswell's "What spectacular changes would you see if you returned to Boston 1,000 years from today? And would you like it?" *Boston Sunday Post*, 8 February 1931.

inadvertently, the tension between analysis and design. Hubbard set the tone in 1929 by publishing a position paper on education in the field of city planning, justifying the field as a "profession by synthesis" and defining planning as "the official record of the will of the community as to how it means to use the physical areas which it controls." He spelled out a fundamental position espoused by the School of City Planning that "one of the essential requirements is the appearance of the result. The planner must be an artist. His profession is a fine art."[50] By calling city planning a fine art, Hubbard was respecting the traditional categorization of architecture and landscape architecture as fine arts, yet he also knew that rational and scientific inquiry had to support this "art." The following year, in an effort to draw the public's attention to the benefits of planning for the future, Hubbard pondered, in the *Boston Sunday Post*, the possibility of spectacular changes, such as immense skyscrapers, huge apartment complexes, aerial monorail systems, expected a thousand years hence (Fig. 3.26). Models of the city of the future included the futuristic American tower of William Van Alen's 1930 Chrysler Building—a possible "pygmy" compared to the skyscraper of the future—and the latest German and Austrian examples of modern architecture, with Georg and Hans Rottmeyer's immense dry-dock elevators, a scheme for Alexander Platz, Berlin, representing "a new type of building planned for German cities [where] all blocks within a certain

radius are to be part of a central construction scheme," and socialist Vienna's Karl Marx Court, "Europe's largest apartment block [providing] quarters for 5,000 people . . . schools, laundries, medical clinics, a library, post office, and several stores."[51]

Other faculty of the School of City Planning, including charter member Arthur Comey, published the "Harvard City Planning Studies," a series of research monographs that included discussions of the location and administration of airports, the uses of zoning to maintain land values, the revision of zoning laws, and the impact of parkways and boulevards on land values and social values. This series was the most influential result of the first years of the school, for it demonstrated the range and scope of its subjects, that the school was on the cutting edge of developments in planning and had great ambitions to bring new ideas to light.[52] With low enrollment, however, a research institute, rather than a thriving school, had been created. Despite wanting to balance analysis with design, the school soon leaned towards supporting the agenda of the City Scientific philosophy—the utilitarian pursuit of social goals to the exclusion of the physical appearance of cities. Norman Newton, the landscape architect who inherited the mantle of Hubbard at Harvard, succinctly described the results of this initial phase of the School of City Planning: "On the whole, they [the students] tended to be verbally rather than visually oriented and accordingly concentrated

their attention on statistical analysis, formulation of broad programs of action, legislation, administration, and political science in general rather than on design."[53] This orientation tended to polarize policy and design, thus dividing socioeconomic and programmatic issues from physical design solutions, preventing an integrated planning process. This fundamental conflict recurred periodically over the next five decades in the history of city planning at Harvard without permanent resolution—and, possibly, beyond resolution.

Creating a "Laboratory" for Design

In 1929 Edgell and his colleagues evaluated their three schools and the mature student body of college graduates. Their concluding view: "The results are beginning to show; the Faculty believes that in another generation they will show brilliantly."[54] Not only were the programs of architecture and landscape architecture running smoothly, but a school in city planning had been created; and Harvard was also advising the professions and other schools. The growth of the schools and consolidation of the curricula led to their serving as a model for other schools throughout the country. This role began in the late 1910s and was well established by the 1920s—long before Harvard's fame as a model of modernist education after World War II. In addition, the university's summer school (the oldest such program in America) had been offering

What Spectacular Changes Would You See if You Returned to Boston 1000 Years From Today? And Would You Like It?

Prof. Hubbard of Harvard Describes Amazing Problems of Congestion Future Cities Will Face---Imagine What Our Modern Traffic Would Do to Nero's Nerves for a Glimmer of How You Would Feel in 10 Decades From Now

Huge drydock elevator, capable of lifting largest ocean liners to a height of 200 feet, projected by two noted German architects, Georg Albert and Hans Rottmayer.

BY JOHN F. COGGSWELL

THIS is a story about the folks who will come after us; quite a long way after us—the men, women and children of the year A.D. 2500, more than 500 years ahead—the sort of lives they'll lead and the cities they will live in.

Part of it has been plotted out in curved lines by erudite investigators with thick-rimmed spectacles.

Biologists, sociologists, geneticists, archeologists and a whole mess of other 'ologists have told a portion of the story. They got together in Cleveland, a week or so ago, and probed deeply into the subject. Their conclusions are mighty interesting.

Also there's a landscape architect mixed up in the tale. He's a home-town product for us of Greater Boston. His name is Henry Vincent Hubbard. Besides being connected with a leading firm of landscape architects, he is Norton professor of regional planning at Harvard. His job in life is planning cities—cities that instead of outliving their usefulness in virtually a few years, will be laid out with sufficient intelligence so that they will serve efficiently many future generations.

The World Does Grow

Of course, none of us will be around to see how Professor Hubbard's works fit in with the needs of our descendants. However, what he is doing and planning is of great immediate importance to all of us. The pace of present day development is so rushingly swift that right now we're faced with the task of planning and building more efficient cities. There'll be no letup in development, that's certain. Development is an accumulative proposition. Consider inventions. By their curved lines, investigators show that inventions and scientific discoveries are swiftly accumulative. In short, the more inventions we make today, the more there will be tomorrow; the more technical discoveries the engineers of the present generation make, the more there will be possible for the scientific men of the next generation. One invention leads to another, one discovery makes another possible.

So the prospect seems to be that what we of the present day consider swift development will be considered mighty slow by our descendants. We have seen the coming into usefulness of the telephone, the phonograph, the automobile, the airplane, the radio, the X-ray, radium, and a host of other inventions and discoveries, most of which have meant an acceleration of the tempo of life.

Truly, if generations that come after us are going to have to keep pace to an even faster acceleration, there'll be need of supermen and women and of super-cities to give them shelter. What will the man of the year 2500 be like? What will be the appearance of his cities?

Dr. East of Harvard University takes up the subject from the standpoint of the geneticist.

"Much good will come," said Dr. East, "when we learn how to supplement nature in a sensible way, a way that will bring about a happier, fuller life.

An International Race

"The year 2500 A.D. will mean only 20 generations. The population of the world then will be about 35,000,000,000, about double the size it is now; but it will have reached 30,000,000,000 by 2100 A.D., after which the rate of increase will slow down considerably and finally reach a level state."

That last is an interesting statement. Remember the dire word picture painted by our old friend Malthus, who studied out the famous Malthusian theory, which tries to prove that the increase in population will be so progressively swift that eventually there'll not be food enough to feed us and we'll starve to death. Present day investigators say that Malthus was right to a certain extent, but that present indications prove that the world's population increase will gradually slow down and eventually reach a level condition.

According to Dr. East, the population of the earth will then be a pretty mixed condition. As the population increases the white and yellow races will spread more and more over the less-populated regions of the earth. This will result in a struggle for survival between the original inhabitants of Africa and the newcomers and the outcome will be an absorption of the original races.

"The old are" continued Dr. East, "will have passed by then and the total supply will be tremendously low. The demand for power will far outrun the supply; so will the demand for one water, tides, much moisture, he will have to use water, tides, the wind, light and the heat of the earth.

"We will probably continue to be far ahead in invention. As the next generation are more progressive they become more assured of the language will develop through necessity. A universal world system will develop through necessity. Parasitical diseases

Women Slow in Adaptation

Professor William F. Ogburn of the University of Chicago tells us that in 2500 A.D. men will enter their life's work at a somewhat later age than at present. Due to technological progress, eventually, life will have become much more complicated. Each new invention, in a way, means a new problem of adaptation we mentioned.

Women, he points out, have not yet adapted themselves to the tin can, although one of their chief concerns in past days was simple cooking.

"She which shows it that there'll be a tendency in this rich milking machine and farm tasks to be natural instead of the feminine; women are turning more and more to the place out labor to all of us. Professor Ogburn believes that it may become necessary to keep men and women in school and

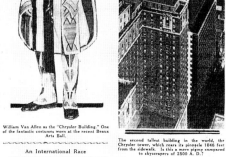

William Van Allen as the "Chrysler Building." One of the fantastic costumes worn at the recent Beaux Arts Ball.

The second tallest building in the world, the Chrysler tower, which rears its pinnacle 1046 feet from the sidewalk. Is this a mere pigmy compared to skyscrapers of 2500 A.D.?

college until the age of 40; they'll not be ready to fit into the life of the period without that much preparation.

"Technical improvements," says Professor Ogburn, "will mean a greater efficiency for the food grower, so that fewer and fewer growers of food will feed more and more consumers. If the population of the United States approaches soon the stationary point, then we may expect to see the sub-marginal lands turned back into forests, inhabited by wild beasts.

"Technological progress means increase in the facility of transforming the products of the soil, of the sea and the minerals into objects that fulfil men's wishes. New discoveries in power and new discoveries in raw materials that can be transformed will bring wealth and abolish poverty.

No More Poverty

"So, then, with a restricted population, a rapidly-growing technology and with, perhaps, a slightly-growing base of materials to be transformed, we should expect to find untrue the often quoted Biblical prediction, 'the poor ye have with you always.'"

There you have something of a composite picture of the American citizen of the year 2500. He'll be a healthy specimen that, to very few diseases. Racial lines will have disappeared to a great extent, although one will be a mixture of all the races, with perhaps the white race predominating.

His dependence upon machinery, tools and all sorts of products of gadgets will be far greater than even that of the present use; the constantly increasing number of inventions will give him a two or a threefold benefit. Machines to do through the working hours much shorter, and there'll be plenty of time for recreation. There will be work for every one, and no such need as poverty stricken.

Here is one picture of 2500 A.D. Will a level of comfort be attained many improvements in our conditions of living and for home. We Bostonians have some trouble with the thermometer the housing accommodations to help a few present-day developments with sufficient accuracy to paint a

No Limit to Skyscrapers

word picture of metropolitan conditions 500 years hence is "talking through his hat." However, there are certain observable trends that give the Harvard man some indications of what the metropolis may be like.

"As a premise," Professor Hubbard told this Sunday Post reporter, "I believe that it is safe to assume that there always will be cities. From the beginning of civilization, men have gathered themselves into communities on account of the benefits that accrue from close association. These communities have become increasingly large, and each year finds a greater proportion of the population living within the limits of cities.

"Surely that condition indicates that the cities have proved their worth. If they were not good, people wouldn't live in them. But, when a person takes up residence in a city, he must give up many things. He must give up some portion of his personal liberty; he can't go partridge hunting through the back yards of the community, nor can he build himself a log cabin in the centre of the main street. Were he to reside in a wilderness, he could shoot or build where he chose.

"He must give up providing for himself several items that make for health and happiness—light, air and the space for outdoor exercise, for example. In short, the modern city is something of a blessing and something of a handicap. It offers many advantages, but takes away a lot to which our rights should be perpetual. If the city of the future is to be successful, it must give back, in the way of substitutes, and in as full measure as possible, the things it has taken away.

"It must be built in such manner that there will be plenty of room for the citizen to get outdoor exercise and fresh air, and he must be provided with ample transportation to get to these places of recreation. In addition, the citizen and his family must be provided with decent living quarters, with conditions that make for health and happiness

"From present indications, large business structures will probably continue popular. No one can say with accuracy what the limit in size will be; discovery of new materials and new designs of construction may remove present limitations, and the sky, in truth, become the limit. The modern skyscraper has been forced upon us. Let us see how this works. A man has a tremendously valuable lot of land in, say, the downtown section of New York. Interest on his investment and the city taxes make that lot a terribly expensive article to own. The owner simply must make it revenue-producing in a big way to stop the drain on his resources. His only recourse is to erect a tremendous skyscraper on the lot. Certainly, if downtown real estate prices continue to soar, the business block of the future will be increasingly large.

Elevated Streets

"However, there is one school of city planners, who have another idea. They say that if the value of a lot is so great and taxes on it so high, that that value can be supported only by a building not fit to live or work in or one that is so large that it will congest the approaching streets, thus shifting the burden from the owner's shoulders to those of the city at large, then restrictions should be placed on the lot that will lower its value sufficiently so that such a great building need not be built.

"Who can say that the contention of this school will not prove itself right? In that case, the tendency will be toward buildings much smaller than those that are being built today.

"One thing seems certain from this distance. The city of the future will have to have much wider thoroughfares. Indeed there may have to be a system composed of several different streets of perhaps three or four levels, so as conditions prevent the widening of streets. Then will have to be great roofs, streets leading out of the city—super-highways under the city level which will be necessary unless some of our roads, streets be necessary unless some of our roads, streets

"You are right there too as the difficulties of

(Continued on Page 10, This Section.)

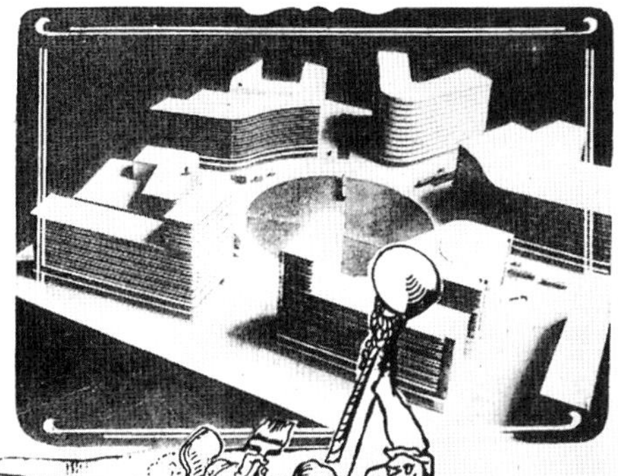

The new type of building being planned for German cities. All the blocks within a certain radius are to be part of a central construction scheme. Photo shows the way Alexander Place, Berlin, will look.

Europe's largest apartment block, which is in Vienna, and is known as Karl Marx Court. It provides quarters for 5000 people, contains schools, laundries, medical clinics, a library, postoffice, hospital and several stores. It gives one a glimpse of the future.

Above—The chap who doesn't care how high they go. One of James Daugherty's illustrations in Carl Sandburg's "Early Moon." (Harcourt, Brace & Co.)

acclaimed training for teachers from other schools in architecture (since 1914) and landscape architecture (since 1917)—a factor that helped spread word of Harvard's design programs.

By answering the frequent queries of other schools, Harvard leaders articulated the university's core principles and goals, particularly the benefits of cultural courses, graduate training, and collaboration among the fields of design. As early as 1917, Acting Dean Killam advised the secretary of the Bureau of Appointments at Oberlin College of Harvard's position on the necessity of courses in history and the fine arts: "Our School is based on the belief that as many as possible of the architects of the country should have a broad cultural training before they begin their technical studies."[55] In another effort to share experience in design education, in 1925 Edgell considered a student exchange program with Joseph Hudnut, a Harvard College graduate who was then director of the McIntire School of Fine Arts at the University of Virginia. Edgell proposed an exchange that would involve a six-year course—four years at Virginia and two years at Harvard—leading to double degrees with a bachelor's in science and a master's in architecture.[56] When Edgell advised Dartmouth College on the establishment of its department of architecture in 1926, he had a chance to explain further the relationship of "culture courses" to the rest of the curriculum and to recommend that Dartmouth institute a course similar to Harvard's. Edgell advocated an emphasis on history to provide a

cultural and political context for architecture; on drawing; on the development, especially for Americans, of "colour-sense"; and on city planning courses, which should follow basic skills, since planning was "a practice for the master rather than the pupil."[57]

In response to another inquiry, Edgell explained Harvard's approach to entrance requirements: since only a master's degree was given, a bachelor's degree was essential. If a student had the bachelor's degree without any previous architectural training, "but with all of the cultural work out of the way, we concentrate on the technical training pure and he gets his degree in about four years."[58] Edgell also received an inquiry from the Agricultural and Mechanical College of Texas (now Texas A & M) concerning a question that Harvard had already faced: taking landscape architecture out of a horticulture department and placing it in an architecture department. In his reply Edgell encouraged collaboration between architecture and landscape architecture, and although his two schools were under the control of one faculty, he felt they should be combined: "Indeed, if we make a mistake, I think it is in having separate schools of architecture and landscape architecture, and not getting enough architectural design into our study of landscape design."[59]

In this domain of interdisciplinary collaboration, Harvard was now not only a model but also a player in a larger American effort towards cooperation. By 1929, experiments in new curricula for a design

education amalgamated with the applied and fine arts were being carried out at many American universities. Arthur Morgan seeded the idea of a cooperative system at Antioch College in Yellow Springs, Ohio, about the same time as University of Cincinnati Dean Herman Schneider established a department of architecture in the College of Engineering and Commerce. This program quickly expanded into the School of Applied Arts, which consisted of a department of architecture, "art-in-industry," interior decoration, landscape architecture, and ceramics. During 1930–31, Schneider, now university president, proposed a "cooperative system" of education in which an amalgamation of basic laws of design would be taught instead of the traditional elements of architecture. In an effort to combine practical and aesthetic education, outside experience in an office practice was required to supplement "cultural courses."[60] Edgell had a copy of the course announcements in architecture and applied fine arts, and he visited Cincinnati in 1930.[61]

The state of Ohio also sponsored another effort in the spirit of cooperation between academic, artistic, and professional interests by founding the Cleveland School of Architecture of Western Reserve University (now Case Western Reserve). The Cleveland Chapter of the AIA funded the first professional courses of this school, and charter provisions required that three representatives of the chapter sit on the Board of Trustees. Consequently, the school's involvement with the profession was mandated by charter, making Cleveland the first school to be governed by the profession.[62]

In the midst of these evolving efforts at collaborative approaches to design, Harvard's design enrollment was growing, and the faculty grew accordingly. Around 1920 there had been 37 students in the School of Architecture and 11 in the School of Landscape Architecture. In 1931, enrollment had grown to 75 in architecture and 50 in landscape architecture, with further increases anticipated from the addition of the School of City Planning. New faculty supported the expanding student body, doubling the total of full-time instructors to eight.[63]

In 1930 Richard K. Webel joined the School of Landscape Architecture as an instructor in design, landscape construction, and municipal planting design (in the city planning program). German-born Webel (1899–2000) had first discovered his propensity for landscape architecture after taking an aptitude test. He read Hubbard's book on the topic, wrote him for advice, and was told to get a first-class education; Webel then received professional training at Harvard. In 1926 Webel won the Sheldon Fellowship, and after going en loge for a month, won the prestigious Grand Prix de Rome in landscape architecture for the first time in the school's history. Having taken the prize from the perennial winners from Cornell, he spent from 1926 to 1929 abroad. Upon his return, he was offered a job in New York with Ferrucio Vitale to work on a general plan for the Chicago World's

Fair. He was an assistant professor of landscape architecture from 1930 to 1938 and commuted from Long Island where he and Umberto Innocenti opened a practice in 1931. At Harvard he taught courses in municipal planting design, advanced landscape design, and elementary landscape construction. Course changes, reflecting the planning program, occurred at the time of Webel's appointment; the requirement of a half-year course in planning was reinstated—instead of the whole sequence. Webel also developed an extremely successful practice as one of the few remaining designers of grand country estates.[64]

New faculty also arrived to staff the School of City Planning in 1930–31. The first of these, Thomas Adams, brought important practical experience to the school, ranging from his position as manager of Letchworth, the first garden city in England, to one as director of plans and surveys for the Regional Plan of New York. Adams (1872–1940) initially came to Harvard as a visiting lecturer and had a temporary office in Hunt Hall while working with Henry Hubbard; in 1930 he became an associate professor of city planning. He had recently informed the readers of the *London Times* that Harvard's School of Landscape Architecture was providing "the desirable link . . . between architecture and landscape engineering" and that the quality of "equipment for student and research" at Harvard had outstripped efforts in England. Adams's opinion was reinforced by his knowledge of its graduates, whom he had

employed and who had "the right training and outlook to do town-planning work, including the planning of parks and parkways"—a necessary training for advancement of land and road development in Great Britain.[65] While in Cambridge, he also lectured on civic design at MIT. When financial problems hit the School of City Planning in 1936, Adams returned to England and resumed his flourishing career there.

Arthur Comey, now assistant professor of city planning, had achieved international recognition in connection with his regional planning theory proposed in 1923, which he subsequently titled "Reply to the British Challenge." A response to the Garden City concepts of Ebenezer Howard, Comey's work showed an expansion of the scale of planning to include large geographical areas, an approach particularly appropriate to America's vast spaces. In addition, Howard K. Menhinick, who had graduated from Harvard in 1928 with an MLA in city planning, began teaching principles and techniques of city planning the following year and taught until 1935. He visited cities throughout the United States, compiling material for Hubbard's *Cities Today and Tomorrow*, and was coauthor (with Hubbard) of the section "Airports in the Plan" in *Airports: Their Location, Administration, and Legal Bases* (1930), one of the more widely used publications sponsored by the School of City Planning in its publication series.[66] All these faculty members shared an interest in regional planning.

3.27 Main drafting room for architecture students, second floor of Robinson Hall, c. 1928. Figure 2.25 shows an earlier view of the same room, with the same casts of the classical orders on pedestals above the drafting tables.

The schools' teaching materials had also expanded: the architecture library and the landscape and city planning library had 34,000 books, 20,000 photographs, and 12,500 lantern slides.[67] In addition, the galleries, lecture hall, and library of the new Fogg Art Museum became available when it opened (in June 1927; the old Fogg Museum in Hunt Hall became an annex to Robinson Hall). In 1930 courses in modeling were held in Hunt Hall's basement; the first floor contained offices of the dean and his secretary, the Hall of Casts, and studios for landscape architecture; and the entire second floor was devoted to studios for architecture and its library (Fig. 3.27). Even these expanded quarters turned out to be inadequate for the schools.

In 1931 Edgell asked John Humphreys, with students Richard M. Bennett and George L. Larson, to study the problem of fitting an addition to Robinson Hall on a triangular plot between the hall and the wall of Harvard Yard (Figs. 3.28, 3.29). The proposed wing was to be linked to Robinson Hall by an angled transitional space consisting of an oval hall, stairwells, and service rooms in the remaining space, or *poché*, of the joint. This connecting space would provide a western entrance to Robinson Hall and allow expansion of the two libraries. The extension, together with the installation of new floor-to-ceiling book stacks, would allow the collections of architecture, landscape architecture, and city planning to increase to over 50,000 volumes. The addition would house only the School of Architec-

ture; the rest of Robinson Hall, except for the Hall of Casts which remained communal, would be appropriated by the landscape architecture and city planning schools. The new spaces would provide drafting rooms for 120 students and were configured to respond to traditional teaching requirements. Lastly, a basement was planned to house a large hall for lectures and exhibitions as well as a recreation room for students, a permanent exhibition space for building materials and models, and a room for instruction in motion-and-talking pictures—"a possibility in the not distant future."[68]

The proposal was for a radically modernist building and generated intense local controversy. While the interior responded to traditional needs in its arrangement of space, the exterior deliberately made a polemical modern statement (Fig. 3.30). Edgell bluntly claimed that it would be impossible for the addition to harmonize with the existing building except in material and color. He pointed out that the elevation facing Harvard Yard was "in strict harmony with the present pseudo-classic brick and stone architecture of Robinson Hall," while "on the Broadway side, allegiance to the type of exterior architecture that has come to be associated especially with the new structures of the University has been frankly abandoned. . . . It would be more sensible to experiment with a boldly original and practical design suggested by the modern architecture of France, of Germany, of Scandinavia."[69] The irregularity of the site and economical and practical

3.28 Proposed addition to Robinson Hall. John Humphreys with Richard M. Bennett and George L. Larson, 1930–31.

3.29 Plan, proposed addition to Robinson Hall. John Humphreys with Richard M. Bennett and George L. Larson, 1930–31.

3.30 Elevation, proposed addition to Robinson Hall. John Humphreys with Richard M. Bennett and George L. Larson, 1930–31.

considerations produced an eccentric plan and elevation that would not "look" Georgian. However, he claimed that the addition did indeed provide a "demure" face to Harvard Yard in deference to its historic context.

Anticipating opposition, Edgell asked his potential critics why the School of Architecture should not take the opportunity "to prove by the opposite elevation that it is not only aware of the heritage of the past, but alive to the problems and the possible developments of the future?"[70] He further defended the radical proposal by noting that the university had already abandoned the Georgian style for a more practical solution to the laboratory, as seen in the new biology laboratory on Divinity Avenue, surprisingly designed by the university's architects, Coolidge, Shepley, Bulfinch & Abbot. The tall vertical glass windows in the laboratory allowed maximum light to enter while providing adequate wall surface. Edgell maintained that designers also required maximum light on their drawing boards so that, while panels of glass were desirable, an expanse of wall was not—thus justifying the proposed use of a glass curtain wall.

The new "laboratory" of design had three serious drawbacks: awkward proportions, a disharmony between its plan configuration and its façade treatment, and its size—it infringed on Sever Hall, its nearest neighbor in Harvard Yard. Yet it was a brave attempt to grapple with a modern architecture that few students and practitioners had experienced first-hand. Thus in 1931 did Edgell, in effect,

announce publicly the school's embrace of European modernism and attempt to integrate it into the neo-Georgian context at Harvard.

The outcry was swift and loud. Ralph Adams Cram, the prominent Boston architect and nationally leading proponent of the collegiate Gothic style, objected that designing "'pseudo-classic,' then without any modulation whatsoever, [having] another style which has no historical precedent, is violently antagonistic and represents a fad in design which I confidently believe to be as ephemeral as the 'Eastlake' or the Romanesque of 40 years ago." The vehemence of this attack revealed the profound antipathy for modern architecture that dwelt in the heart of the American traditionalist. The proposed building "was not architecture . . . [and it] would do more toward implanting in architecture students false ideas of architecture as a profession and an art than any other course that could be followed at the present time." Cram proposed to solve the needs for new space by erecting a separate building on Broadway (on the western edge of Harvard Yard) that would connect to Robinson Hall by a low vestibule or enclosed arcade: "If you are persuaded that suggestions of the architecture of the past are no longer of value in architectural education, then let the detached building be as 'modernist' as you please. You would then have a structure of sufficient unity even though to many of us it might seem of abnormal ugliness."[71]

Edgell replied to this barrage after first diplomatically disclaiming that Harvard

officially had anything to do with his scheme. He answered Cram's objections with practical explanations that he too would prefer to erect a separate building, as Robinson Hall was outmoded, but that financial constraints prevented it. The proposed addition, therefore, made economic sense, and its location took into account the combination of functions in both buildings, with special attention given to the relationship of the new drafting room to the libraries. With respect to Cram's objection to two different façades, the art historian pragmatically replied, "I know of no law, aesthetic or otherwise, that requires the same treatment for the front and the back of a building." In practical terms, the larger fenestration would have provided northern light ideal for studio work. In a lucid demonstration of his grasp of the basic arguments of a modern style, Edgell added: "I see no objection, aesthetic or logical, which should condemn the use, in a certain part of a building, of a treatment which reveals the function of that part. Nor does it seem to me that this implies a persuasion that 'the suggestions of the architecture of the past are no longer of value in building,' but merely that certain problems of architecture in the twentieth century are different from those of the eighteenth or earlier, and that their solutions will be different."[72]

The provocative proposal, however, was doomed to remain a sketch. Within two years the Schools of Architecture, Landscape Architecture, and City Planning staggered, like much of the world around them, in the face of the Depression. A depletion of funds for planning reduced the number of students in two of the schools—landscape architecture alone dropped from 58 students in 1931–32 to 18 in 1932–33—making the expansion unnecessary and impractical.[73]

The End of "the Purple"

The economic crises precipitated by the stock market crash of October 1929 occurred at the height of development in the Schools of Architecture and Landscape Architecture, just as their efforts towards experimentation and innovation were taking off. The scope of the national disaster demanded rethinking all that America stood for and the ways that it had handled itself—its economic and social policies, its values and identity. Reform at all levels was not only desirable as a means of charting the future but also necessary for economic and social survival. Somehow, the usual ways of conducting life and business had plunged Americans into the morass they now confronted. A break with tradition appeared more necessary than ever. Reliance on history as a guide to the future seemed pointless. All these conditions brought calls for reform that no longer allowed a conservative position—only a radical move would suffice. The Schools of Architecture, Landscape Architecture, and City Planning at Harvard participated in the reform efforts as they moved from a conservative to a radical modernism without knowing it.

Even as the nation's giddy optimism was heading towards disastrous specula-

tion, the profession of architecture had started to register tremors of instability. Just six months before the 1929 crash, Dean Edgell learned the results of a survey conducted by the American Collegiate Schools of Architecture (ACSA) that indicated serious shortcomings in the education of design professionals, particularly in their training in business practices. On one hand, those surveyed preferred that an architect receive a liberal education, "giving him an understanding particularly of the humanities, enabling him to interpret the spirit of the times, to meet his clients on every plane of culture, and to express himself reasonably well orally or in writing." On the other hand, approximately three-quarters of the respondents suggested that schools include more professional instruction, confirmed the benefit of practical experience as a prerequisite for an architectural degree, and dismissed the current curriculum requirements as inadequate.[74]

The general direction of the Harvard architecture program in the late 1920s coincided with the desired direction expressed in the survey: it embodied a no-nonsense approach to building, to dealing with clients, and to design education. The training provided by the Harvard design schools had also succeeded in placing students in the profession: over 70 percent of the schools' 147 graduates in architecture were practicing by 1925; 22 percent were heads of firms, almost 14 percent were teaching, with some practicing and teaching, and 15 percent were in other fields.[75] Though innovative new pro-

grams had been introduced, the curricula generally adhered to traditional teaching attitudes and methods. Freehand and life drawing, taught by artists, remained integral to the curriculum. Local independence from national and New York competitions continued while conjunctive competitions with MIT and the Boston Architectural Club remained a means of collective evaluation of the quality of work. Promotion in courses was still attained by achieving suitable standards of work and not by mere completion of the courses in the curriculum.[76] Haffner continued to teach advanced design, altering his theory course to reflect current thinking about professional practice.[77] Edgell developed his course material based on past lectures, including a series he presented at the Sorbonne in 1928–29 that showed his increasing focus on the history of American architecture.[78] His lectures—a pioneering exploration of the architecture of the United States, which was just beginning to receive academic attention—indicated at least some awareness that historicism had its limits: "After the romanticism of the [18]70s, 80s and 90s the early twentieth century saw an enthusiastic colonial revival in all parts of the country. That this revival was an excellent thing for American Architecture few will deny. This Revivalism, however, has become too archeological in its approach."[79]

Edgell still advised other colleges about pre-professional preparation for design studies.[80] Among the students he helped was Harvard undergraduate

Garden Gate
CHASTLETON HOUSE
Orfordshire, England

3.31 Garden gate, Castleton House, Oxfordshire, England, Charles C. Pinkney, 1935. Landscape Architecture, Charles Eliot Traveling Fellowship.

3.32 Professor Walter Chambers (right) with landscape architecture student, 1932.

Henry-Russell Hitchcock, a fine-arts student who studied at the School of Architecture during his senior year at Harvard College (1923–24). Edgell wrote R. Clipston Sturgis in Boston to introduce the young man who was planning to enter the School of Architecture and currently "doing a brilliant piece of work."[81]

The School of Landscape Architecture tried to carry on its traditional approaches to design, but at the price of losing touch with economic and social reality. A student traveling on a Charles Eliot Fellowship had no qualms about relying totally on the past as a guide to the future when preparing measured drawings of historical precedents (Fig. 3.31). A temporary expansion of the curriculum and the faculty continued to promote the profession as provider of luxury environments to the leisure class. Responses to the changed economic conditions and an integration of the practicality of engineering occurred gradually and subtly through the introduction of courses that dealt with these realities. In a bow to the call for increased scientific rigor, Walter Chambers was appointed to teach landscape engineering (Fig. 3.32). Chambers had received a BLA from Ohio State University in 1929 and an MLA from Harvard in 1932, and he taught at Harvard for twenty-six years, during which time he became chairman of the Department of Landscape Architecture.[82]

Joining Chambers was Bremer Whidden Pond, one of the new instructors who had filled the gap after Pray's death in 1929 by taking over his courses and assuming the chairmanship of the landscape architecture program.[83] Pond was a member of a profession with two kinds of clientele: a comfortable elite who maintained country estates and a hard-working public with an ever-growing awareness of community identity and needs. The country estate era had allowed the developing profession to provide high standards of design at a manageable scale that countered English picturesque traditions with studies of Italian gardens.[84] Many landscape architects, though, focused on commissions for a rich elite, giving substance to the public's perception of landscape architecture as a service solely for the wealthy.

Though Pond came from a long line of "gentleman scholars," he immediately began to respond to the public's negative perception of landscape architecture.[85] In 1930 he addressed the issue in the *Christian Science Monitor*, acknowledging that the profession was perceived as "a luxury . . . appreciated largely by persons of education enjoying a certain amount of leisure. This is true of private estate work, certainly; public work, on the other hand, is frequently controlled by the local politicians." By describing the extensive training necessary for successful landscape architects and the special skills of its practitioners, Pond hoped to justify the profession to the public and perhaps even attract a few potential students. His approach was reasonable, though not radically modern. According to Pond, landscape architecture made it possible to "see . . . the opportunities in

the barren" and bring them to fruition. For Pond, design meant both "the pleasant grouping of objects on the ground" and "a knowledge of the different types of design and of their relation to various kinds of ground surfaces." He maintained that the field appealed to its practitioners because the geographical range of the work was broad and required travel. To acquire the background and knowledge about soils, geography, geology, climates, sociology, the economics of land values, and how to deal with clients required a long training period: at least ten years were necessary, which included a general four-year college education, three years of graduate school, and three years in the office of a well-trained landscape architect. This extended training was based, according to Pond, on the premise that landscape architecture is "the fine art of arranging land [and] the objects upon it for maximum human use and enjoyment." He explained that the field differs from engineering because the results must be not only logical but also attractive, and that while a knowledge of horticulture is necessary, design is the "all-important requisite." Pond also asserted the validity of a stylistic pluralism in which historical models remained relevant to contemporary problems: "Designs developed in the time of Imperial Rome for the great sports areas are applicable to modern problems for similar areas. Public and private buildings today range through every known architectural period and style. The landscape architect must be

familiar with all of these in order to make his plans conform to the buildings."[86]

The profession, however, had to confront Pond's assertions. Did there exist in 1930, in the midst of a global depression, areas and conditions similar to those of Imperial Rome or Renaissance Italy? And in the midst of every known style in use, did one style have more validity over another? Furthermore, what and whom did these styles represent?

The Faculty of Architecture soon began to scrutinize its purpose and accelerate its efforts at reform. Subtle changes appeared in the *Official Register of Architecture* of 1930–31. On one hand, the old requirements were present: "Still more does [the architect] need artistic imagination enriched by knowledge of the great art of the past, combined with knowledge of the needs of today and the materials and methods now available for expressing those needs. . . . "[87] The basic purpose of the school continued to be that of providing technical training for a professional career, with the roles of teacher, historian, and theorist as ancillary. Architecture was still considered to be a fine art based on a knowledge of construction and practical requirements of buildings, and the history of architecture was still viewed as essential, for the "growth and meaning of architectural forms . . . may enable [students] ultimately to use precedent, not blindly, but intelligently and with freedom."[88] On the other hand, facility with the constraints of then-modern business realities were needed in addition to artistic imagination. Harvard now maintained that its program had "developed into a graduate school because of the very general feeling of the profession that an architect should have, if possible, a liberal education as a background for professional studies. The architect needs business ability and integrity on account of the large sums of money entrusted to his care. He needs ingenuity and scientific knowledge to plan buildings conveniently and to construct them safely and economically. . . . "[89] This pragmatism was clearly present at Harvard by 1930.

Further fueling the reform efforts was the fact that by the early 1930s the schools of design were well aware of the developments of modern architecture in Europe. Periodicals, guest lecturers (as long as funds were available), and special exhibitions supplemented the study of modern European architecture. By 1930 representative photographic reproductions were available of German, French, and Dutch modern architectural styles that would dominate design in America after World War II. One style of modern architecture was characterized by an unemotional, planar vocabulary in which mass and void were used to create strong contrasts of light and dark. This was the idiom of *neue Sachlichkeit*—the "New Objectivity" that updated the efforts that had begun in Europe in the first decade of the 1900s to moderate artistic concerns with rational ones—which would evolve into the International Style. Still, no single, clear definition of modernism existed in America. Kenneth K. Stowell, editor of *Architectural Forum*, claimed in 1931 that the International Style had no specific aesthetic determinants but found its forms in methods of production and the usefulness of the objects it made.[90] Stowell spoke with the authority of experience: a graduate of Harvard School of Architecture in 1921, he had worked for a number of architects in New York and taught at the Georgia School (later, Institute) of Technology.

Other magazines that transmitted European modernism to America included *L'Architecture d'aujourd'hui*, which began publication in 1930 and included the work of Le Corbusier; students kept this magazine near their drawing boards.[91] They learned of concrete—the most representative building material of modern design—from Dr. Francis S. Onderdonk, author of a basic study on the subject, in his lecture, "The Influence of Concrete on Modern Architecture."[92]

Exhibitions too played a role in disseminating European developments, though Harvard students just missed an opportunity, in 1925, to view an exhibition of developments in Germany—whether it was officially the work of the Bauhaus remains unclear. The *Blaue Reiter* group, comprised of Paul Klee, Vasily Kandinsky, Lyonel Feininger, and Alexey von Jawlensky, had their first exhibit in America at the Daniel Gallery in New York City.[93] President Lowell sent Edgell an announcement of an exhibition of student work of "the German Architectural School" with the telling comment, "I suppose that such an exhibit might be useful in instructing students what to avoid."[94] Edgell agreed, in part, but was more open-minded: "I think you are right that the German architectural exhibits could tell us a lot about what to avoid. On the other hand, it is always interesting to see what other people are doing, and I think it might be interesting to have the exhibition here."[95] No evidence, however, indicates that the exhibition came to Harvard. Although the Bauhaus had exhibited its student work in the 1920s, the material hardly circulated, even in Germany. Lowell was more likely referring either to an officially sponsored exhibition whose content would have been more conservative, but still foreign to Americans, or to an exhibition that included examples of Bauhaus work.

While work of Bauhaus artists had appeared in America occasionally in exhibitions during the 1920s, in December of 1930 the first exhibition exclusively of Bauhaus work was held in Cambridge under the auspices of the Harvard Society of Contemporary Art, curated by Harvard student Lincoln Kirstein, who had learned about the Bauhaus through Philip Johnson and Alfred Barr.[96] The society's first year of exhibitions in 1929 had included Buckminster Fuller's Dymaxion House, paintings by Paul Klee, and expressionist paintings by Max Beckman, Oskar Kokoschka, Max Pechstein, and Karl Schmidt-Rottluff (13,500 people saw the exhibits).[97] In the 1930 exhibition the work of Lyonel Feininger, Johannes Itten, Wassily Kandinsky, Klee, Gerhard Marks, Oskar Schlemmer, and small metal works and photographs by Philip Johnson of the architecture of Walter Gropius and Mies van der Rohe were among the objects displayed. The Bauhaus exhibition at Harvard subsequently traveled in 1931 to New York and Chicago.[98]

The seminal "Modern Architecture: International Style Exhibition" that was sponsored by the Harvard School of Architecture and the Fogg Museum and held at the Museum of Modern Art (MoMA) in New York in 1932 introduced the International Style to America. Edgell, Edward W. Forbes, director of the Fogg, and Paul J. Sachs, associate director and trustee of MoMA, were personal subscribers.[99]

The MoMA exhibition not only presented a selection of work from European and American architects and planners but also provided the cultural imprimatur of MoMA on modern architecture and planning. Henry-Russell Hitchcock and Philip Johnson's book, *The International Style: Architecture Since 1922*, published in conjunction with the exhibition, codified the principles represented by the works and became a kind of Bible at Harvard and across the United States.[100] In particular, Walter Gropius's celebrity status, first promoted by his recognition by Paul Sachs of the Fogg Museum, was solidified by the exhibition catalogue. Although the exhibition was justly famous as a milestone in the history of modern architecture, Hitchcock acknowledged (in retrospect) that the International Style he and Johnson introduced had expanded by the mid-1930s beyond the definitions they had provided. The International Style arrived as a style that was already dead in Europe—its own best practitioners, such

as Le Corbusier, were already in the midst of humanizing its austerity and expanding its scope, focusing on the domain of the city, with the support of the Congrés Internationaux d'Architecture Moderne (CIAM) group, founded in 1928. Though CIAM's "Functional City" philosophy would later greatly influence Harvard's programs, in the late 1920s and early 1930s CIAM was virtually unknown in America.[101]

For actual modern buildings, students now could turn to the work of American architects, ranging from the prolific Chicago firm of Holabird & Roche to Frank Lloyd Wright.[102] Edgell particularly admired Wright's work and showed images of it—the Imperial Hotel in Tokyo and Prairie-style houses—in his lectures as early as 1926. Edgell's opinion of Wright was so high that he recommended Wright for an honorary degree at the university's tercentenary celebration. He bravely wrote the director of the event: "If you want to honour an architect, I have a rather Bolshevik suggestion. Far and away the most famous American architect in thoughtful circles in Europe is Frank Lloyd Wright. Much that he has done I disapprove but his philosophy is progressive and intensely interesting."[103] The reply to the suggestion was distinctly negative; the degrees were intended for "recognition of *scholarship* as such."[104] Edgell recanted and suggested for honorary degrees Bernard Berenson and S. Fiske Kimball, both Harvard men. Edgell considered Kimball "the best historian of architecture in the United States."[105]

Despite the vicissitudes of Frank Lloyd Wright's career in the late 1920s and early 1930s, Wright's ideas were known at Harvard, as can be seen in a student's adaptation of his stylistic devices in a design for a swimming pool bath house (Fig. 3.33). The sculptural figures on pedestals could have been borrowed from Wright's Midway Gardens in Chicago. However, further evidence of the influence of some of the most exciting developments in American modern architecture—including Wright's contributions, the New Architecture of the Midwest, or Chicago's skyscrapers—does not appear in the work of students at Harvard.

Adding to their knowledge from magazines, lectures, site visits, and exhibitions, Harvard students had the rare opportunity of studying modern architecture in their history courses. Edgell led students on tours that included such buildings as New York's Ziegfeld Theater, which was particularly noted for its acoustical problems, unremedied by the expenditure of huge sums of money; Radio City Music Hall; traditionally designed buildings, such as the J. Pierpont Morgan Library; and modern architecture-as-engineering in the George Washington Bridge.[106] In Edgell's estimation, modern architecture had discarded the practice of copying past achievements, while still allowing a multiplicity of styles whose designs had boldness of line and harmony of mass and surface, often executed with a sensitivity to context. He defined an all-encompassing eclecticism in 1928 in his book, *The American Architecture of To-day*: "At the

84

3.33 An open-air swimming pool and bath house, Charles Carroll Colby, 1930–31. Arch. 4c.

outset, therefore, let us agree that by modern we mean contemporary. Modern American architecture includes all the architecture of America which has recently been built, or is being built today. It includes the conservative and the radical, the archaeological and the original."[107]

Presumably students could choose among these contemporary modes of production, refine the product, and make "modern" architecture as the result. Edgell's reasoning provided for a wide latitude in time and scope—but it lacked criteria for judgment of any sort. A house as historicist as Richard Morris Hunt's Joseph R. Busk Mansion of 1889–92 in Newport, Rhode Island, was the work of "literally a modern architect" because its mass and surface conformed to the rugged and rocky landscape of its site and its bold new lines elevated it above mere copyism. Bertram Grosvenor Goodhue's Los Angeles Public Library of 1925 and H. Van Buren Magonigle's design for a Liberty Memorial in Kansas City, Missouri, both illustrated in Edgell's selection of University Prints, provided needed models for students (Figs. 3.34, 3.35).[108] Kenneth Conant greatly admired Goodhue's work, and Edgell called the Memorial design "one of the most important and most discussed"—and even though the building was harshly compared to a chimney, Edgell maintained that it was "a refreshing attempt to get away from the trite and conventional in monumental design."[109] It might have continued to be discussed except that it was constructed

without its intended base, producing an unfortunately awkward appearance.

Conant made his own selection of modern buildings in *Modern Architecture: University Prints, Series GM*, published in 1930. A bound collection of black-and-white plates created as study guides for students, this was the first American compilation devoted exclusively to the study of modern architecture. Its "modern" chronology began in the late eighteenth century and concluded with the "functional" style that was contemporary in the early 1930s. Conant, like Edgell, broadly equated modern architecture with all contemporary architecture—a facile position that made critical assessment difficult. Conant grouped every modern building under the general category of "functional style." In his collection, published the year after the well-publicized World Exhibition in Barcelona of 1929, Conant included an eclectic variety of buildings, some that still represent modernism today as well as others that never made it into the canon that began to develop in the early 1940s.

On one hand, Conant's selection could be seen as uncritically eclectic, including buildings with little aesthetic, cultural, or technological merit. On the other hand, it included works of architects who would soon find themselves outside the canon of modernism. While to Europeans functionalism meant buildings defined by use, efficiency, and an abstraction of aesthetic expression that included little ornament and flat roofs, Conant's definition was more like Edgell's: from

3.34 Los Angeles Public Library. Bertram Grosvenor Goodhue, 1925. From University Prints GM Series.

3.35 Liberty Memorial, Kansas City, Missouri. H. Van Buren Magonigle. Winning entry, design competition, 1921; building dedicated, 1926.

3.36 Schocken Building, Stuttgart. Erich Mendel-sohn, 1927. From University Prints GM Series.

3.37 Bruchfeldstrasse Housing Group, Niederrad, Frankfurt, May, Boehm, and Rudloff, 1926–7. From University Prints GM Series.

their American perspectives functionalism was a style that could barely be distinguished from contemporary design in general. For example, Erich Mendelsohn's Einstein Tower in Potsdam (1921) continues to be a touchstone of modernism, but his Schocken Building (1927) and May, Boehm, and Rudloff's Bruchfeldstrasse Housing Group in Niederrad, Frankfurt (1926–27), both classified as "functional style," are no longer recognized exemplars (Figs. 3.36, 3.37). Conant's ecumenism had the benefit of encompassing Scandinavian architecture, including Lars Sonck's Lutheran church (1910) and Eliel Saarinen's railway station (1918), both in Helsinki, Finland, and Ragnar Östberg's city hall in Stockholm (1912–23), described as a "Baltic Style adaptation."[110] According to one of his students, Conant seemed to choose buildings of clean, simple forms in a search for modern monumentality; later Conant called the Scandinavians "half-moderns," a reflection of their abstract forms and retention of vernacular traditions.[111]

If German and Dutch models provided Conant with one current of modern architecture, France provided another through the work of Auguste Perret and Le Corbusier, whose design for the League of Nations Building was the final plate in his primer, described as "a manifesto against conventional and official architecture and all its works by a brilliant practitioner of, and propagandist for, the Functional style."[112] For Conant, the functional style also included examples of art deco, such as Robert Mallet-Stevens's casino in St.

3.38 Department store entrance, Silas Snider, 1935–36. Arch. 4a.

87

Jean de Luz (1928) and Pierre Patout's Bely Shop in Paris (1929), which was recognized as ideologically and stylistically similar to the work of Le Corbusier.

Edgell's published books on American architecture and Conant's University Prints picture books were integral to the teaching of modern architecture in the history sequence at Harvard. Beginning in 1929 they began to include more lectures on recent architecture in the standard course, which covered the history of medieval, Renaissance, and modern architecture. Assisted in 1931 by the young G. Holmes Perkins, a recent graduate of the School of Architecture, Conant took over the general survey course in 1934. Modern architecture was important enough to merit its own course, which Conant taught from 1936 to 1954.

In addition to the study of modern architecture, Conant introduced Meso-American architecture. These courses were unique and characteristic of the expanse and curiosity of Conant's intellect.[113] No other school at the time offered the study of either modern or Native American architecture. Entitled "Architecture in the Americas," the latter began with Mayan architecture and included the Pueblo architecture of the Rio Grande Valley, subjects Conant knew first-hand from the archeological excavations in which he participated in 1926. Conant even allowed graduate students from Robinson Hall to substitute for a final exam a scale model of any building discussed in the second term. Holmes Perkins recalled in retro-

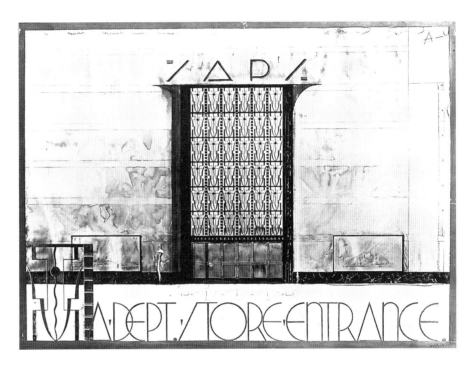

spect that he and others had taken the course for granted.[114]

Despite remnants of Beaux-Arts methods, Harvard's architecture students used a variety of styles to express what they considered to be an evolving modern American architecture. While they revered the historic styles, their work showed a vibrant creativity and skill. Some students used the styles for surface treatments, as seen, for instance, in S. Snider's sumptuous deco treatment for a department store entry (Fig. 3.38). Others used the taut planar surfaces and cubic massing of European modernist designs in combination with deco detail, as demonstrated in P. M. Heffernan's elegant "Airport Station" and Eustis Dearborn's design

for an eight-room house (Figs. 3.39, 3.40). Cubic massing with restrained deco detailing characterizes the thesis project of Alfred Panepinto, "An Architect's Building" (Figs. 3.41–3.44). On one hand, the formal vocabulary shown in this project is spare, like that of European modernism's "New Architecture," as some Americans called it at the time. On the other hand, the design is full of color and texture that typifies the more relaxed American perception of modernism in architecture. The program of this idealized architecture office also gives a glimpse of the needs of a modern designer in 1931. Included are rooms for writing building specifications and contracts, a real estate department, bookkeepers' offices, materials display,

88

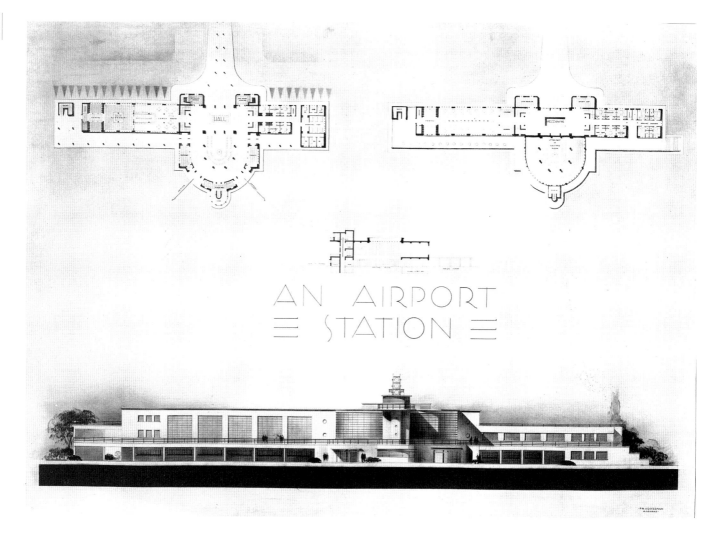

AN AIRPORT
STATION

3.39 "Airport Station," Paul M. Heffernan, 1934. Arch. 4c, regular design problem.

3.40 An eight-room house, Eustis Dearborn, 1932–1933. Arch. 4a.

3.41 (opposite, top left) "An Architect's Building," Alfred J. Panepinto, June 1931. Arch. master's thesis, Professors Haffner and Killam. Plan, ground floor.

3.42 (opposite, middle left) Panepinto, "Architect's Building." Plan, second floor.

3.43 (opposite, bottom) Panepinto, "Architect's Building." Perspective.

3.44 (opposite, top right) Panepinto, "Architect's Building." Elevations and section. Even in Panepinto's modern, streamlined design for an architect's office, there is still room for homage to the masters of architecture: just below the classically inspired frieze he includes panels with the revered names Michelangelo, Bramante, Raphael, and Palladio.

AN EIGHT-ROOM
HOUSE

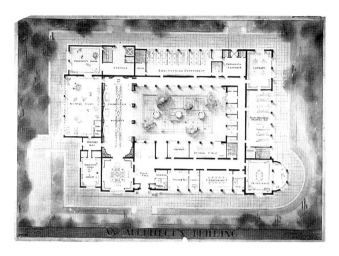

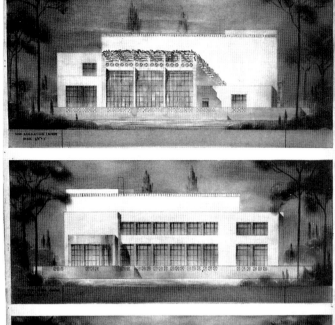

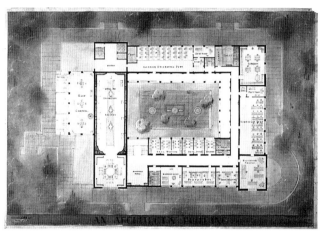

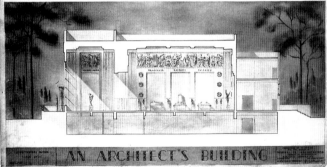

AN ARCHITECT'S BUILDING

AN ARCHITECT'S BUILDING

89

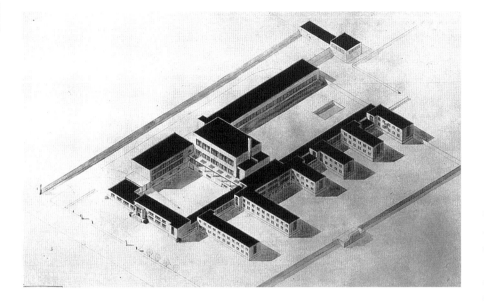

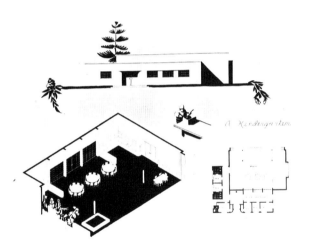

3.45 A prison of medium security, Henry A. Bettman, 1934–35. Thesis.

3.46 A kindergarten, William B. Tabler, 1935–1936. Arch. 4a.

3.47 Episcopal church, Max Abramovitz, 1934-35. Arch. 4c.

3.48 (opposite) A "Little Theatre," Richard M. Bennett, 1931. Architecture, master's thesis. Bennett's designs for the Wheaton College campus would later be chosen over those submitted by Gropius and Breuer in 1937.

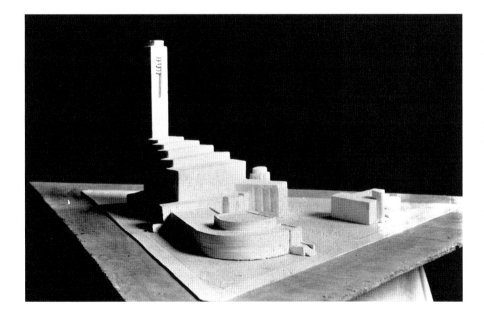

departments of engineering, landscape architecture, interior decorating, a delineators' studio, an architectural drafting room, a sculptor's studio, a library, and an exhibition gallery. These necessities for the production of modern architecture were to be located around an open courtyard with fountains.

The stark effects of the New Objectivity seemed particularly well-suited for the prison designed by Henry Bettman (Fig. 3.45). But the idiom could also apply to a kindergarten, reinforcing the idea that a style applying to any architectural problem could be called an International Style (Fig. 3.46). In a variant of Dutch modernism, the traces of Willem Dudok's towers at Hilversum can be seen in Max Abramovitz's model for an Episcopal church (Fig. 3.47).

Both French art deco and the work of Le Corbusier resonated in the work of students at Harvard: art deco, because it had American counterparts transmitted largely through the Paris Exposition des Arts Décoratifs in 1925; and the designs and theory of Le Corbusier, because they had no counterparts in America and were, therefore, fresh and new and applied to the design process—unlike Wright's precepts of organic architecture, which were not easy to translate into design. Le Corbusier's five elements of a new architecture, developed over time and published in 1926, called for *pilotis* (wide columns) to elevate building mass off the ground; a free plan that resulted in liberating walls from their load-bearing function; a free façade analogous to the liberated plan;

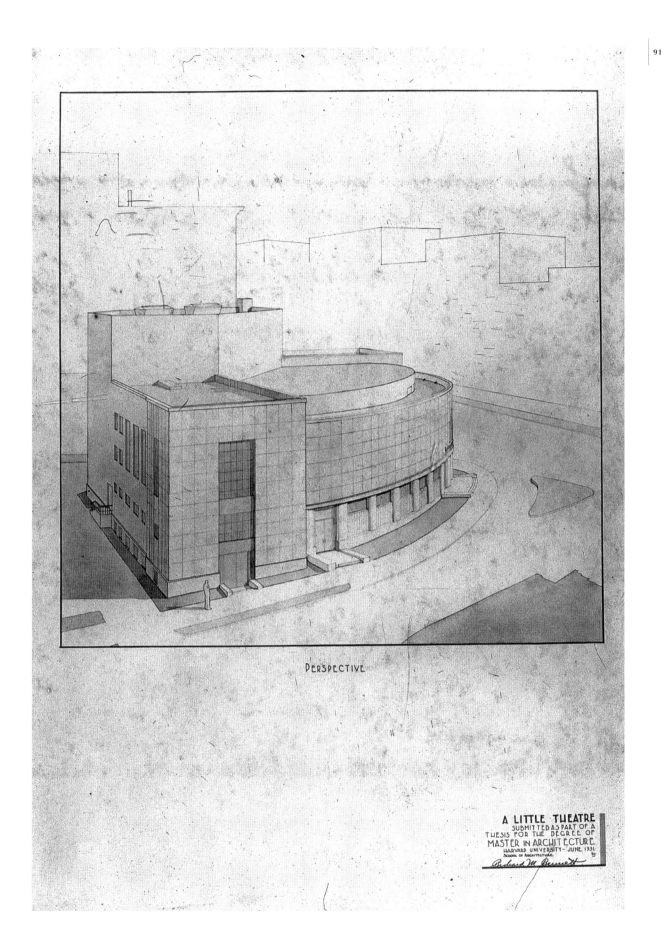

PERSPECTIVE

A LITTLE THEATRE
SUBMITTED AS PART OF A
THESIS FOR THE DEGREE OF
MASTER IN ARCHITECTURE
HARVARD UNIVERSITY ~ JUNE, 1931
SCHOOL OF ARCHITECTURE.
Richard M. Bennett   by

3.49 A monastery in the Rocky Mountains, Richard M. Bennett, 1930–31. Arch. 4c.

long, horizontal sliding windows; and a roof garden. These elements quickly found their way into the work of students, as can be seen in Richard Bennett's thesis for a "Little Theatre" (Fig. 3.48), a more elegant scheme than his addition to Robinson Hall. Here, the engaged columns at the entry level are intended to serve as the floating *pilotis* that free the function of the wall from structural obligations of supporting floors or ceiling above. The regularized scoring of one surface material contrasts in tension with flat, bare textures of other surfaces. The mass of the building curves in response to the street, and, as in the work of Le Corbusier, purpose and form coincide. Bennett's skills extended to other architectural options, as seen in his complex, contextual design for a monastery snuggled deep into the Rocky Mountains (Fig. 3.49).

The careful study of Le Corbusier can also be seen in Samuel Paul's "Test Sketch," which has the rooftop gardens of Corbusian theory as well as a clear and simple construction appropriate for cast concrete (Fig. 3.50). This appreciation for Le Corbusier reached a pinnacle of homage in the studio apartment building by Marc Peter, Jr. (Fig. 3.51). Clearly, the dominant forces in the Harvard design studios, employed in the hope of producing a new monumentality, were Le Corbusier, *art moderne*, streamlined architecture, Dutch architecture, and the recurring classicizing vocabulary of the late Beaux-Arts.

While MoMA's 1932 exhibition became a benchmark for reform in American arch-

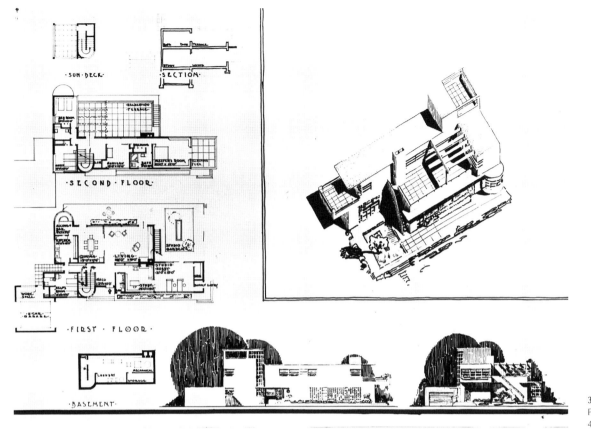

3.50 A house, Samuel Paul, 1935–1936. Arch. 4b, 4c, test sketch.

STUDIO APARTMENT BUILDING

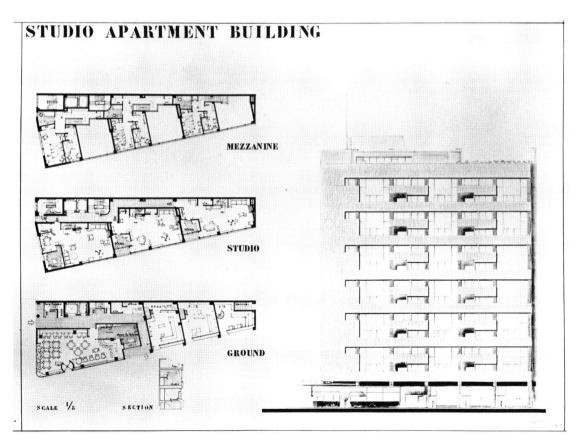

MEZZANINE

STUDIO

GROUND

SCALE ⅛   SECTION

3.51 Studio apartment building, Marc Peter, Jr., 1935–36. Arch. 4c.

3.52 A wine cellar and tap room, Hugh A Stubbins, 1934. Arch. 4c and winner of the Boston Society Prize.

itecture, the election of Franklin D. Roosevelt in 1933 signified the beginnings of reform for the whole nation that would gradually bring the country out of the Depression. Though landscape architecture had lost students, the architecture school was flourishing: it maintained its strong enrollments, took its best students on the usual trip to New York, held many exhibitions displaying the work of practitioners and traveling fellows, and sent its designs on public display. For a second time these designs won an unsolicited Gold Medal from the Société des Architects Diplômé par le Gouvernement Français of the Beaux-Arts Institute of Design, the organization that promoted standardized teaching of French procedures in America.[115] Locally, Harvard students, such as Hugh Stubbins (who later taught at Harvard and practiced in Cambridge), were winning prizes, too. His design for a wine cellar and tap room included sumptuously rendered marble veneer, a treatment that contrasted with the abstract, planar, monochromatic architecture that later dominated his work—a pattern common to many architecture students at Harvard (Fig. 3.52).

In 1933 enrollment in architecture plummeted; the full impact of the Depression now jolted the Schools of Architecture, Landscape Architecture, and City Planning. As Edgell reported, 95 percent of architects in America were out of work, although 65 percent of Harvard's graduates in architecture had jobs.[116] Many of the graduates in landscape architecture began working in the emergency projects

of the New Deal, as part of the Civilian Conservation Corps, particularly in the state and national parks and on other landscape projects. Almost any student with undergraduate training in landscape architecture could skip further professional training and get work; students who had completed all requirements except the thesis withdrew in substantial numbers to take advantage of work opportunities. Ironically, the availability of jobs did not encourage students to enroll—the future may have seemed too uncertain. After substantial drops in the prior year, in 1932–33 the student body in landscape architecture decreased even further, and faculty members had received no salary increases in several years. Lack of enrollment also prompted discontinuation of landscape architecture courses offered in the summer session. On the brighter side, a number of undergraduates in Harvard College enrolled in the landscape architecture program; seven men graduated. The topics of their theses summed up the dichotomy of purpose within the profession: five were designs for country estates, yacht, beach, and country clubs; two were projects for state parks.[117]

While America began to seek reforms that would reverse economic disaster, the Schools of Architecture and Landscape Architecture launched their own series of reforms. These included focusing the curricula on business issues, adding a new course on "The Principles of City Planning" as a degree requirement for graduation in architecture and new courses on

professional practice, and reinstating the collaborative problems between architecture and landscape architecture that had languished and became irregular. New classes on the financial management of architectural practice were to be taught by an expert from the Graduate School of Business. Edgell justified the course: "It is particularly necessary at a time like this—when the profession of architecture is very slack, when the erection of new commercial buildings has almost ceased, and when monumental building has been curtailed—to link, as far as possible, the courses in *Design* with the practical courses in *Engineering*, and the *Business Aspect of Architecture*."[118]

Another response to the profession's demands for rigor were new courses in the "Functions of Buildings," given by Walter F. Bogner, a graduate of the School of Architecture (who would have a long career at Harvard, retiring in 1966);[119] "Architects' Drafting Methods," by Killam and Bogner; and the courses on contracts, specifications, and mechanical plants that were combined into a new course on "Professional Practice." In addition, special problems in advanced design programs were now written from the point of view of the structural engineer as well as the designer. The problems were critiqued both by professors of design and by experts in structural engineering, heating, plumbing, and ventilation for the purpose of determining the practicality of students' designs, and students built complete models of the projects—probably for the first time—to

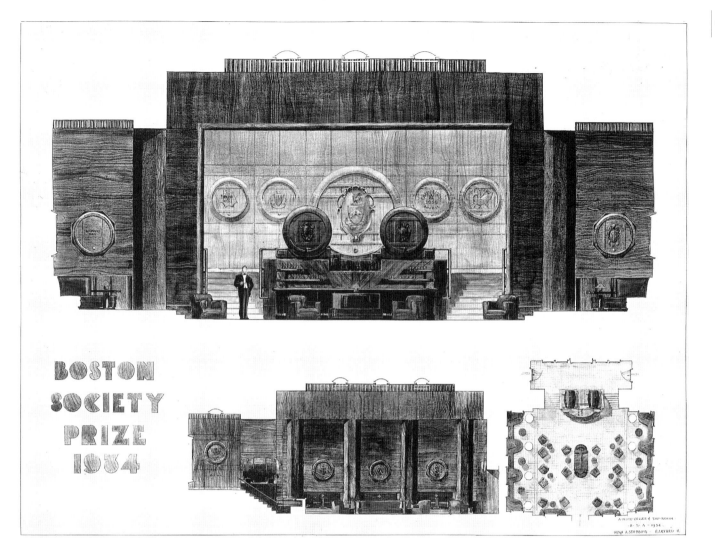

BOSTON
SOCIETY
PRIZE
1934

understand precisely "what their designs would look like from all sides."[120] An impressive array of lecturers, including Alfred Bettman, Charles Eliot II, James Ford (the housing expert), John Nolen, and Lawrence Veiller, added substance to the students' knowledge of the conditions of practice.[121] A knowledge of city and regional planning was essential. As Pond explained, "City Planning looms so large in the modern field of architecture that it was felt that some general review of the subject should be made by any man entering the architectural profession."[122] The role of history was again reconsidered, and the curriculum was altered to decrease emphasis on ancient architecture and increase emphasis on medieval

and Renaissance contributions. Whole courses in the history of architecture were split into half courses to allow for more flexibility in the topics covered.

While the School of Architecture implemented reform through examining business, function, and the content of what passed as modern, the School of Landscape Architecture participated in the post-crash reform efforts by adding more practical courses to its curriculum and reintroducing courses in architecture and history. The school also embraced the reinstatement of a regular collaborative design problem. Despite the curtailment of the program's size, it hoped to plan for the future by acquiring scholarships as well as by educating the public on the

benefits of land planning, especially in the area of public recreation.[123] Two new groups of clients became identifiable: the upper middle class who needed designs for suburban sites and rural residences, and the federal and state governments whose agencies increasingly needed landscape architects to create parks, state forests, and even public utilities. The shift to meet the needs of these clients was fundamental to the profession and, in turn, to the education of landscape architects. This change in demand reconnected with the Olmstedian tradition of socially conscious design, which called for public parks to relieve urban crowding. Within the next decade, students in landscape architecture would learn to serve a clientele of a thousand rather than the single client. Already by 1934, the trend towards public service had become apparent—an equal number of recent graduates chose government employment as chose private practice.[124]

Like the School of Architecture, the School of Landscape Architecture sought to strengthen its instruction on professional practice and offered, for the first time, a course in office practice.[125] Taught by Henry Hubbard as "Professional Practice, Construction, and Specifications," the course represented the new pragmatism and joined the other new offerings in 1934, such as "Materials of Construction," "Theory of Design in Special Relationship to Landscape Architecture," and "City and Regional Planning." An additional course in elementary architectural design was also added. Even the structure of the curriculum was soon made clearer by publishing—again, for the first time in the school's history—a breakdown of course requirements by academic year, instead of the usual sequential list that was unrelated to the actual progress of students through the program.[126]

During the gestation of reforms in the Schools of Architecture and Landscape Architecture, the School of City Planning experienced the irony of an increasing security in its identity and purpose while its source of funds gradually evaporated. In 1933 Henry Hubbard reported to President Lowell that he foresaw increasing "governmental guidance and regulation of the activities of individuals, communities, and states and larger regions," thus

ensuring a need for city, regional, or even national planning.[127] Staffing New Deal programs had created a demand, in excess of supply, for men who could create a physical plan, starting with present physical conditions and organizing land allotments for desirable uses. In addressing this demand, the School of City Planning had found its purpose. It approached this responsibility by requiring candidates in architecture to pass the introductory course in city planning, and by announcing a new course on national and state planning that addressed a larger scale—regional planning—the first such course given in an American university.[128]

Despite the recognition of the public need for planning and the professional activities of the faculty and library, however, the School of City Planning was training very few professionals. Hubbard opened the introductory course in city planning to Harvard undergraduates, so that it "might reasonably form a part of the preparation of an educated man to take his place in modern society," but although it trained students from other professional schools, it had only five students in its program in 1932–33 and no candidates for the degree; nine were enrolled in 1933–34.[129]

In December 1934 the Visiting Committee on city planning assessed the condition of the school and claimed it was the most well-balanced program in city planning in the world.[130] In the six years since its founding, twenty-five candidates had enrolled for its special degree, five from Brazil, China, Denmark, Ger-

many, and Japan; ten candidates had enrolled in 1930–31. One hundred and six students had taken one or more courses. According to the committee's report, the numbers appeared small because the profession was new and students were unaware of its possibilities, despite the fact that most recent graduates were employed.

Clearly, the initial efforts of the school had not included recruiting large numbers of students, focusing instead on maintaining a small student body and a faculty involved in investigative research. The committee applauded these efforts and praised, in particular, the publication series produced by the school. The committee also summarized the issues confronting the field of planning: the convergence of populations in towns and cities, the consequent unguided growth that derived from the uncontrolled play of individual enterprise, the assumption of planning by the real estate subdivider, and the "monotonous, uninspired and expensive consequences of his limited outlook."[131] The committee defined the planner as an organizer who would guide the work of collaborating specialists, weighing and balancing social, industrial, administrative, architectural, engineering, and landscaping concerns. To accomplish this end, the city planner needed two complete educations, one focusing on the "breadth and intensity of social awareness," the other on technique and the principles of design. In defining the educational requirements of a planner, the committee outlined an ideal goal:

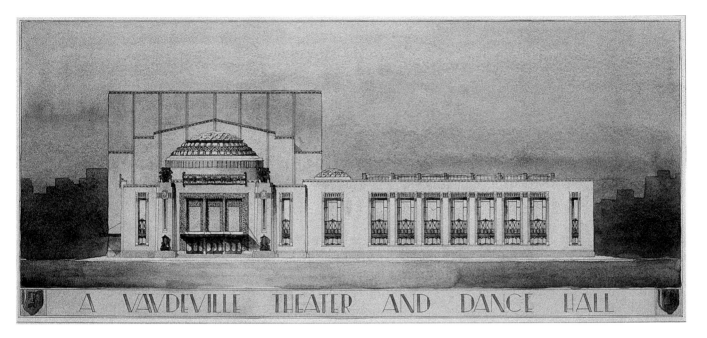

A VAVDEVILLE THEATER AND DANCE HALL

A STEAMSHIP TERMINAL

3.10 A vaudeville theater hall, Edward J. Aisner, 1926. Arch. 4c, conjunctive problem, Professor Jean-Jacques Haffner.

3.11 A steamship terminal pier, Alfred J. Panepinto, 1928. Arch. 4b, conjunctive problem, Professor John Humphreys. Elevation.

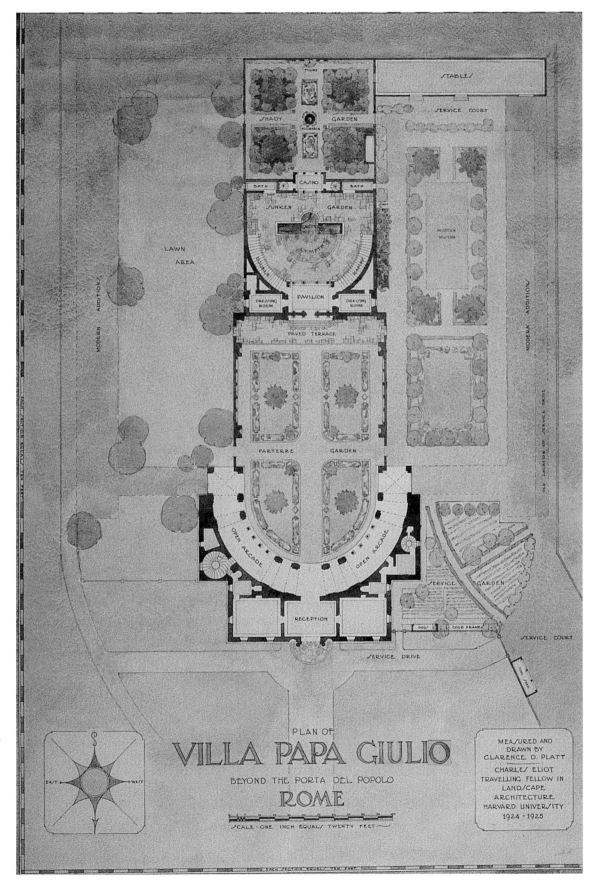

PLAN OF
VILLA PAPA GIULIO
BEYOND THE PORTA DEL POPOLO
ROME

SCALE · ONE · INCH · EQUALS · TWENTY · FEET

MEASURED AND
DRAWN BY
CLARENCE D. PLATT

CHARLES ELIOT
TRAVELLING FELLOW IN
LANDSCAPE
ARCHITECTURE
HARVARD UNIVERSITY
1924 - 1925

3.13 Monument to World War I, Walter H. Kilham, Jr., 1928. Arch. 4b, conjunctive problem, Professor Jean-Jacques Haffner. Interior perspective.

3.18 Plan of Villa Papa Giulio, Rome, Clarence D. Platt, 1925. Landscape Architecture, Charles Eliot Traveling Fellowship.

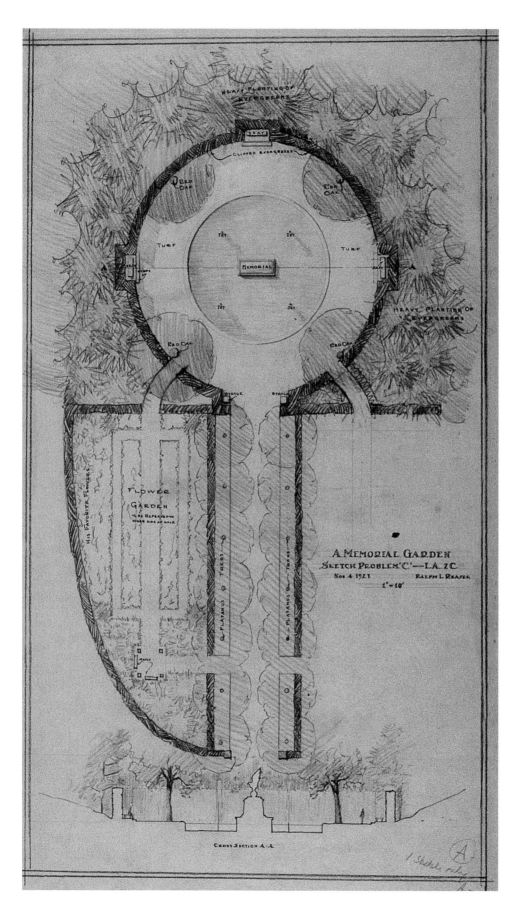

3.24 A memorial garden, Ralph L. Reaser, 1928. LA 2c, sketch problem "C."

3.25 Entrance
to a funerary
isle, Alfred J.
Panepinto,
1929. Arch 4b,
conjunctive
problem,
Professor John
Humphreys.

Built about 1605 when the house, which is now standing, was erected by Walter Jones; now owned by Miss Whitmore Jones.
Scale — One inch equals one foot.

Garden Gate
CHASLETON HOUSE
Oxfordshire, England

Measured and Drawn as an Envoi for the Charles Eliot Travelling Fellowship 1934-1935
School of Landscape Architecture Harvard University

3.31 Garden gate, Castleton House, Oxfordshire, England, Charles C. Pinkney, 1935. Landscape Architecture, Charles Eliot Traveling Fellowship.

5.12 a,b Project for a lodge. Robert A. Little, 1939.

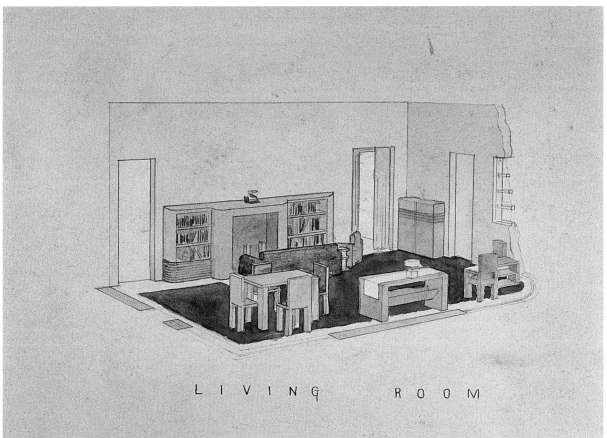

LIVING ROOM

the planner must first formulate the complex social conception of the plan and then give form to the plan or map. Technique, including the principles of design, should be learned as architects and engineers learned it, as a professional enterprise available in a school. An understanding of social and political sciences that deals in human and cultural issues, however, could only be obtained from a "collective assemblage of departments." Consequently, city planning students should already have a "cultural course" equivalent to a bachelor's degree prior to technical studies. Conversely, city planning courses should be made available to non-majors. At that point, the school's introductory half-course on the principles of city and regional planning could be taken for credit only by students in the Schools of Architecture, Landscape Architecture, or Engineering. The committee wisely surmised the implications of this policy: either the course was too poorly taught and deficient in content to deserve outside credit, or the Faculty of Arts and Sciences was unable to recognize that "the physical structure of our modern communities binds up their social and economic structures and is deserving of the attention of sociologists, economists, and students of governments." Overall, the committee found that the young, small school was well on track, and it requested time and patience as the school attempted to raise funds to support its further development. Despite the committee's highly favorable evaluation and Hubbard's efforts to raise funds, the

School of City Planning faced closure in June 1936 due to budgetary shortfalls.[132]

The Visiting Committee for the Schools of Architecture and Landscape Architecture took stock of conditions and called for dramatic change: despite the persistent rhetoric of collaboration, too much autonomy had developed among the three schools. Though the schools were grouped together in the university curriculum, shared buildings in Harvard Yard, and had common instructors, courses, and dean, a chasm had gradually grown between them. This was a major criticism in light of the fact that Edgell was approaching retirement and a new dean and chairman of the architecture school would inherit the problem of how to better maintain the collaborative ideal. The committee somberly pronounced: "This lack of co-ordination between these three schools is not a good thing."[133]

The Visiting Committee noted that the *professions* of architecture, landscape architecture, and planning were increasingly working together and expanding mutual understanding and cooperation. Since friendly cooperation was essential to modern practice, the committee asked, why should it not be equally necessary among the schools? To the committee, this was the most vital need in design education at Harvard. Despite the years of effort spent focusing on collaboration, it called for new connections between the schools that echoed the sentiments of their founders at the turn of the century: "We suggest more mutual undertakings, each school in its own sphere. The schools must

be brought more closely together. The Dean to be selected is the man to do it."[134]

Otto J. Teegen (Harvard AB 1922, M.Arch. 1924), member of the Visiting Committee and practitioner in the New York firm of the art deco architect Ely Jacques Kahn, believed that the issue of cooperation between the schools was so important that he appended a lengthy letter to the report in which a new program for the combined schools was presented. Teegen pointed out the city planning profession's broad criticism that architecture schools had not kept up with the rapid changes that had occurred in the real world within the last three to five years, and that blaming "the terrible state of architectural training" for the profession's problems was not constructive.[135] So far only a few schools had made radical attempts at change, principal among them the School of Architecture at Columbia University. Its program, directed by Joseph Hudnut, was a standard of comparison for Harvard's efforts. Teegen directly compared the two programs on points that covered most of the basic issues of design education, including, among others: cultivating imagination versus copying; increased awareness of social factors; practical considerations of construction and materials; increased awareness of economic effects on communities; research; study of the history of architecture from a philosophical and cultural rather than a chronological point of view; knowledge of manufacturing and construction, illustrated by models and reinforced by site visits; and coordination of teaching landscape with architecture. Finally, he included the issue of creating a broad training "to make [the students] men of the world" through a flexible curriculum without grades, in which creativity and instinct are encouraged, the branches of design exist in true relationship to one another, and students have contact with leaders of the professions of architecture, art, drama, and music. Teegen implied that Harvard had done the best it could, given that it could not have foreseen the political and economic changes that had affected the profession. From Teegen's point of view, at Harvard the desire for change was present but the means had not been formulated. For attempting to deal with these issues, Columbia had already received much attention, including publication of its report in *Architectural Forum* in February 1935. Harvard's reforms of 1932–33, however, were known only to a few people outside the staff, and its efforts were as yet unrecognized.[136]

Although Harvard had already independently enacted some of the principles reported by Columbia, it still needed to address other specific points. To increase cooperation between the Schools of Landscape Architecture and Architecture at Harvard, Teegen suggested that the schools seek "young blood with energetic ideas" to replace the professors who had sadly "grown old in service." His outspoken position reflected a view that the schools were experiencing "growing pains" and that, despite criticism, "Harvard need not feel that it should throw its

curriculum overboard and start from scratch again for it has too much that is good on which to build."[137]

Teegen's observations confirmed that the Schools of Architecture, Landscape Architecture, and City Planning had drifted far apart. By the end of the 1920s architecture students were not even aware that Harvard had a School of City Planning.[138] The widening gaps between architecture and landscape architecture students were such that they experienced no fraternal or professional connection with their peers. A former architecture student recalled: "To us on the second floor, the Landscape division might as well have been an annex to the Law School. We didn't have any combined problems in the curriculum and no collaboration with them of any kind. . . . Our annual picnic was only for the School of Architecture. The attitude towards the Landscape Architects was friendly but the general feeling was as though they were a foreign group attached to the university."[139]

The validity of a "conjunctive" problem between the Schools of Architecture and Landscape Architecture was recognized anew at an administrative level in 1931. The faculty now claimed that this approach had never been attempted at Harvard. Ironically, they failed to realize that the conjunctive problem between architecture and landscape architecture was also a return to the founding principle, enunciated in 1900, that architecture and landscape architecture were two aspects of the process of design. In fact, this method was not a sudden or unique

innovation—it had been successfully used at the American Academy in Rome, the design bastion of expatriate conservatism. Practiced intermittently in the past at Harvard, the conjunctive problem was reinstated in 1931 as a crucial element in the reform movement. A team consisting of a landscape architect and an architect explored design problems with the intention of creating them "on a more comprehensive and better scale."[140] In addition to participating in the reinstated joint studio, the School of Landscape Architecture supported the interdisciplinary approach by adding a course requirement in the history of fine arts and by separating its introductory course into two parts, one in design theory and the other in principles of landscape architecture.

The Visiting Committee reported the benefits of the collaborative approach: "This means much more, much better, and much more thorough architectural design for the men in Landscape Architecture, and also has the great advantage of breaking up more the distinction between Schools."[141] However, the products of the collaborative problems reflected the tensions of architects and landscape architects attempting to reconcile their divergent interests in clients and sites (Fig. 3.53).

In his report of 1934 to the university, Dean Edgell defined the purpose of the reforms as a response to pragmatic demands of the modern world of the mid-1930s: "These changes were of course designed to try to meet modern problems and better equip young men to

3.53 An island estate. Philip P. Pasqualino (architecture) and A. Hopkins (landscape architecture), 1931–32. Arch. collaborative problem.

3.54 Restaurants on promontory. Left to right: Carl A. Strauss, Francis B. Hayne, and R. D. deRham, 1934. Arch. 4a.

3.55 (opposite top left) A hotel, P. W. Jones, 1934. Arch. 4c, special problem.

3.56 (opposite top right) A hotel, Richard H. Cutting, 1933–1934. Arch. 4c, special problem.

3.57 (opposite bottom) A hotel, student designs for a special problem in Arch. 4c, 1934. The models, made of both clay and wood, were placed for this group photograph in a bed of sand on the floor of the Hall of Casts in Robinson Hall.

obtain jobs and adjust themselves to the changing conditions in architecture when they graduate from the School."[142] The reforms in response to contemporary economic and social conditions were precursors to the amalgamation of the schools in 1936 and provided the basis for renewal of collaboration between the fields. In many guises, the "modern conditions" leading to the International Style had already arrived. Modernism in America, however, was developing in an ironic fashion: both progressives (such as Edgell) and radical modernists conceived of modern architecture not as a style but as the correct approach to solving problems at hand. Despite the fact that radical modernists hated styles, their modern architecture became increasingly identified in the mind of the public as exactly that: a *style*. Progressives, too, were exploring modern architecture, but only as one style among contemporary idioms of design.

Poised between radical and progressive attitudes, between European and American visions, no single perception of modern American architecture yet dominated. Mirroring the world around them, Harvard students in 1934 were confronted with different expressions of

modern architecture that had not coalesced into a single style. One group of models showing a restaurant on a promontory included an example of the International Style (left), one with features of Mediterranean Renaissance revival (center), and a third example defined by the curved forms and stripped classical details of late *art moderne* (Fig. 3.54).

Symptomatic of the multiple "modernisms" that coexisted was the assembly of the schools' own "City of Modernism"—an exhibition in December 1933 that met with public attention and favorable comment, and was even mentioned in Sunday newspapers.[143] While there were several building types, including concrete ribbed halls with glass ceilings, apartment buildings and hotels dominated. Utilizing clearly rectilinear urban lots, the students had assembled buildings to create urban spaces with two open blocks at their center (Figs. 3.55–3.57). Gone were the straight axes of Beaux-Arts methods. Now an underlying urban grid provided a pattern of placement. Installed on the floor of the "Great Space" in Robinson Hall, home of the former Hall of Casts, sand was used to create ground forms,

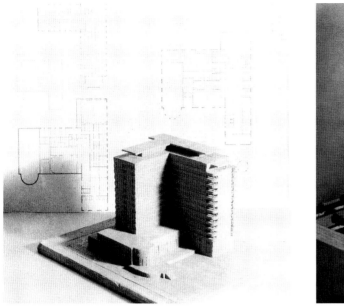

and the plans of these buildings, rendered in wash on boards, were propped against the fragments and capitals of classical architecture. Upon these relics of the past, these icons of tradition, Harvard intended to build the modern world of the future.

Sand was an appropriate base with its shifting, formless topography—the fully developed modern landscape did not yet exist. The American field of landscape architecture existed outside and independent of European developments, in which modern conditions shaped the designer's approach, allowing adaptations to the contemporary demands of business and government but not to aesthetic values. In the mid-1930s the only experiments at Harvard in modern landscape architecture were those of Jean-Jacques Haffner, whose work received little recognition. Jostling among various stylistic approaches and ideological positions, modern architecture itself lacked a cohesive identity.

Further articulation of a response to the demands of modern design at Harvard rested on the ability of the fields to collaborate. To move forward, teachers would have to respect and cooperate with their colleague-cousins and encourage tolerant, mutual understanding. Students would need to come into closer contact with the conditions and problems of the architectural profession as it was practiced in the "real" world. Students would need to realize that beauty results from a full consideration of function, construction, and materials rather than from

design alone. In Teegen's view, Harvard was on the right track: "The potentialities are all there, the stage is set, the actors are ready. Now bring on the new director."[144] Like the reforms themselves, however, the discovery of the "new director" of this drama needed a powerful catalyst within the university. That catalyst was Harvard's new president, James Bryant Conant.

While the School of City Planning awaited financial rescue, the reforms contemplated by the Schools of Architecture and Landscape Architecture and suggested by the Visiting Committee were dependent upon the appointment of a new president at Harvard. In September 1933 James Bryant Conant assumed his duties as Harvard's twenty-third president.[145] Conant (only distantly related to architectural historian Kenneth John Conant) was a chemist who became a major figure for change at Harvard and nationally known as an educational reformer in both private and public sectors. He received a Harvard Ph.D. in chemistry in 1916 and, after serving in World War I, returned to Harvard to teach, attaining the rank of full professor in 1929. During his presidency from 1933 to 1952, Conant authored numerous significant changes: among others, he emphasized research and graduate education as being of comparable importance to undergraduate training, instituted the eight-year maximum on non-tenured appointments, created ad hoc committees to screen tenure appointments, created university professorships, reorganized the engineering school into the Division of

Applied Sciences and Engineering Sciences, and reinvigorated the Graduate School of Education. As Harvard's new president, Conant immediately involved himself in the Schools of Architecture, Landscape Architecture, and City Planning and played a pivotal role in their reformulation.

The national context in which Conant enacted his major reforms at Harvard, and in which graduate design education would be altered, was one of broad-based reforms in education, the return of liberal politics, and antipathy for traditional teaching methods in history, art, and archeology. Though at first this larger context may appear unconnected to reforms in the design schools, it ultimately had significant impact. One immediate factor impinging on the local scene was the need to resolve problems in the elective system of Harvard College that existed under President Eliot and had remained unresolved under President Lowell. In 1910 Lowell had abolished his predecessor's innovation of free electives, which had allowed complete, if random, choices of courses, and replaced it with a system based on the concepts of "concentration" and "distribution" (taking courses outside the major to balance the liberal arts education). But since that time, there had been no agreement on what courses or groups of courses an undergraduate should take to supplement his area of concentration. Survey courses that involved linear expositions were seen as too superficial to satisfy this need; furthermore, in the 1930s "general education,"

which was associated with the survey courses, was not in favor at Harvard. Conant addressed this issue of general knowledge versus specialization broadly and specifically noted the challenge in his tercentenary oration of 1936. In his speech, Conant cited "a wave of anti-intellectualism which was passing around the world," a weariness that resulted from the accumulation of knowledge, and "intellectual anarchy in our schools and colleges [that] has been more or less rife for the better part of a hundred years." The mission of the liberal arts curriculum was to provide order; the classical tradition of education was replaced by its "modern equivalent." [146]

Conant based his search for the "modern equivalent" on the premise that people must understand the nature of their culture in order to perpetuate democratic ideals. He saw this search for culture as providing (1) fertile ground for the discussion of collaboration among a wide array of fields, (2) the stimuli for new integrative teaching methods, and (3) the exchange of information and ideology among many disciplines. The vehicle for this search was a new concept of liberal arts training that included core courses in the humanities, social sciences, and natural sciences. In defining a new purpose for education, Conant defined a new audience for the educated to serve: "The primary concern of American education today is not the development of the appreciation of the 'good life' in young gentlemen born to the purple. It is the infusion of the liberal and humane tradition into our entire educa-

tional system. Our purpose is to cultivate in the largest possible number of our future citizens an appreciation of both the responsibilities and the benefits which come to them because they are Americans and are free." [147]

A new goal was set to synchronize public schools with universities in the promotion of a pluralistic, "open" society. Precursors in place, the stage was set for the emergence of a modernism that offered opportunities for change and that was backed by the rigor of moral conviction and liberal ideals. Over the ten years in which a "liberal and humane tradition" was developed as the basis for a free society, not only for Harvard but for America, design education at Harvard was transformed. Conant sanctioned and promoted the creation of the new Graduate School of Design, appointed its dean, and approved its curriculum and famous European teachers. In short, he set the intellectual tone and supported the ideals of radical reform.

MODERNIST VISIONS,
1934–1936

The national call for an open society resonated with a core goal of modernism to express a liberal, democratic agenda. At Harvard, and throughout the design professions, the early 1930s was a time of much soul-searching about the future place and potential for American designers and design education. The reform movement in the School of Architecture that had been evolving for a decade still needed a catalyzing figure to push forward its agenda of modernism and to give physical form to this new open American society. Pending the discovery of a new leader for Harvard's design schools, the concerns about the future centered on two interrelated fronts: assessment of the current educational programs and the search for a new dean.

Students and faculty of the School of Architecture were asked to write formal critiques of the program. In their 1934–35 report to President Conant, the students stated that they wanted to give credit where credit was due, while also identifying the elements of an antiquated system. They reiterated the fundamental call for collaboration between the fields of design, doubting its feasibility, given the lethargy that permeated the school as a whole. Their report ascribed the lethargy to insufficient give-and-take between instructors and students and unclear didactic purposes. Students wanted to expand discussion to events taking place in the architectural world at large and to increase contact with the profession. They pointed out that medical students met with prominent physicians in their labora-

tories, those in the business school were placed in a variety of jobs, and the law school maintained a legal aid society and law review. Why couldn't the School of Architecture expose its students to more actual practice? They also criticized aspects of the Beaux-Arts educational methods and its competitive system—critiques that squarely supported the noncompetitive approach to design courses such as the program offered by the University of Oregon. While raising these criticisms, the students also acknowledged how thankful they were for the recent additional courses that dealt with professional practice and the functions of buildings, such as mechanical systems.

The students also submitted a remarkably perceptive critique of the school's curriculum at this transitional moment, analyzing the courses in design, technology, drawing, and history. Though design needed to dominate the curriculum, they felt they were studying too many decorative details for façades and neglecting the overall organization of plans. But focusing on the plan seemed to unearth a quandary. Beginning students were forced to "consider the question 'shall I be modern?' If they design in the classic style, they can have little feeling for it; whereas if they attempt modernity, they are merely substituting one style for another, and it becomes modernistic paper architecture in the worst. Modernity is not a style: it is an approach . . . foreseeing a modern problem demands a modern plan; and modern elevation follows as a matter of course and the question does not present

113

4.1 Garden plan. Jean-Jacques Haffner, from *Compositions des Jardins* (1931).

itself."[1] Students thus expressed the fundamental dilemma that had confronted all designers of the period, professional and student: defining modernism as an approach rather than a style.

With respect to technology, the students said they believed that the engineering courses on steel-reinforced concrete construction and the use of the materials were not only good but the best in the school. Comments about freehand drawing reflected the clear perception that the old guard offered too many courses and overemphasized design sketches at the expense of life drawing. Students advocated free and loose sketching that showed an impression or part of a process for a client instead of the formality and frozen quality of rendering from still lifes, plaster casts, and photographs. Modeling classes also appeared irrelevant in their current form, as modern architectural embellishment no longer required variations of the acanthus leaf, classical consoles, or modillions; instead, such

courses should turn to explorations of abstract design. The grandest tradition in the school, the history courses, also came in for reasoned criticism: they were more for the intellectual than the artist and put too much emphasis on memorizing facts about buildings. History courses were indeed taught from an "intellectual" perspective because the scholarship of the period had begun to address actual methods of construction, even in Gothic cathedrals (Roman work had already undergone a fair amount of analysis by archeologists). Despite the fact that no student would construct buildings in a Roman or Byzantine manner, the romance of knowing the construction system was what counted. Nevertheless, the usefulness of history courses—which provided the cultural and historical context of design—was being questioned.

The students also hit upon one of the key planks of the program that eventually took hold: moving prerequisites for professional study to undergraduate education.

4.2 Professor Henry Frost with Dick Merrick, landscape architecture student, c. 1938.

The students recommended that the history of architecture, for instance, be studied prior to the graduate program to alleviate some of the heavy burden of first-year studies. Regarding other course requirements, the report emphasized that a student should have the broadest possible background in order to deal with the architect's role as coordinator, creator, and competitor with promoters, contractors, and hard-headed speculators. Not only should the school emphasize mathematics, physics, shades and shadows, history (if studied as an undergraduate), and freehand drawing, but it also should recommend courses that "rationally broaden the prospective architect's mind toward relating to existing problems. Courses in the fields of economics, business administration, government, and the social sciences may be tentatively mentioned." The students acknowledged that the requirement of such courses raised a question concerning the type of professional the School of Architecture desired to produce: did it intend to create a "big man" who could handle complex problems in an independent practice, or a variety of talented individuals who had "a flair approaching genius in design, in construction, or in some limited sphere"?[2] Once the goal was clarified, an undergraduate could plan his pre-architectural studies with the purpose of attaining a broad cultural background and still follow courses later that related to the type of professional pursuits he intended to follow.

Finally, the students expressed optimism that the three fields of architecture, landscape architecture, and planning could share a unified vision, believing that present and future economic conditions called for greater cooperation among the professions. The separation in training arose, they believed, from the physical separation of their workplaces and their lack of social contact. Some architecture students took a condescending attitude towards the role of the landscape architect: one went so far as to suggest that architects learn the rudiments of landscape design so that they could practice it themselves and reduce landscape architects to the category of master gardeners. The authors of the report, however, felt that this prejudice should be attacked at its root, in school. Various methods were suggested for establishing a closer relationship between the Schools of Architecture and Landscape Architecture, including again the resumption of the original tradition of the collaborative problem. However, the students recommended a combined course as perhaps the easiest and most effective means of bridging the fields. The sole cross-disciplinary course at the time, in city planning, was considered beneficial, though not inspiring.

Faculty also discussed the future of the schools. In spring 1935, the veteran teacher Henry Frost responded to President Conant's ideas for a new formulation for the schools and potential changes in the curriculum of the School of Architecture (Fig. 4.2). Frost supported Conant's consideration of an amalgamated school,

since a single faculty could both administer the three curricula and provide greater opportunity for collaboration. Frost was so enthusiastic that he prepared a preliminary, detailed chart showing how such a course of action could be achieved.[3] The extent and detail of Frost's observations show how thoroughly and seriously the faculty considered the transformation of the schools. He asserted that the three professions had a definite place in modern life and that, of the three, city regional planning might assume leadership over architecture and landscape architecture. Promising students, he felt, should be encouraged to choose city planning since the future of landscape architecture was uncertain; it might merge with architecture. This opinion reflected both the effects of the New Deal on the professions and the belief that in the last twenty years, landscape curricula had become increasingly more architectural. He saw the three professions as so interdependent that a practitioner of one could not be considered well trained unless he understood the other two. Ideally, that interdisciplinary understanding should be acquired at school.

Having stated the broad conditions, Frost, like his students, recommended a collaborative approach to design education that would provide a broad-based, professional training, foster the flexibility needed to respond to changing economic conditions, and help dispel the antagonism that existed among the professions. The specific changes involved support courses: history should be team-

taught with emphasis on (1) analysis and criticism, (2) the study of plans, massing, and detail in terms of their materials, and (3) how buildings related to the social and economic conditions of their times. Graphics should be presented with more lectures and fewer exercises, a reduction that allowed more time for architecture students to study landscape architecture and city planning; freehand drawing should be retained as a means of studying form and color and training hand and eye. The design studios, Frost felt, would require little alteration in a new curriculum.[4]

Frost, however, anticipated difficulty in implementing the principle of collaboration. Construction, for instance, required such different knowledge among the three fields that it should be taught separately. While collaboration should begin in early courses, construction should be taught later in the process. And in the twenty years of his teaching career, Frost confessed, he had never found great success in teaching plant materials and plant design to architects. Neither had he found plants and planting anything but the particular domain of landscape architecture. He felt that their integration needed further study. Another subject that required further study before being incorporated into a new program was that of professional practice, which was still quite new as a topic of academic pursuit.[5]

With respect to undergraduate preparation for graduate training, Frost concurred with his students by recommending that Harvard College could create a new concentration in planning and design, bringing Harvard to the forefront of architectural education. Frost summarized his views: "There is an opportunity for us to build the greatest school in the country. Our decisions and changes must be progressive. . . . Catch phrases and revolutionary measures will be dangerous and are, I believe, entirely unnecessary. . . . The plan is broader and more comprehensive than any offered at present by other schools (so far as I know). It has the advantage of suggesting a graduate rather than an undergraduate point of view."[6]

President Conant also listened to recommendations from the Beaux-Arts–trained Jean-Jacques Haffner, who advocated progressive change. He wrote to President Conant in May 1935 that the changes then under consideration had been, in part, a response to recommendations made by the Faculty of Architecture in 1932. According to Haffner, changes to the curriculum then were adopted only in part because the dean and the faculty council of the school hesitated in the face of uncertain economic conditions in the country and the impending retirement of Lowell, the former president of the university. Haffner pointed out that during the following three years, the changes outlined had become completely necessary and that it was urgent to adopt them for the creation of a new curriculum.[7]

Haffner basically reiterated Frost's position, giving the justification, advantages, and means of creating a dramatically new and modern training. Successful courses that attracted the present

student body should be kept; new courses and material should be added to fill in the gaps in architectural education and enlarge the field of professional opportunity; unnecessary courses should be eliminated; courses of a general preparatory nature should shift to undergraduate training; new and present courses should be woven together so that the interrelationship of the subjects of architecture would be more clearly understood by students; and, finally, courses in architecture, landscape architecture, and city planning should be integrated through cooperation with the existing schools in these fields. He also proposed establishing an undergraduate program in design in Harvard College.

President Conant finally heard from the last senior faculty member when Charles Killam wrote to him. Even the crusty autodidact engineer grasped the essential issues in establishing an educational program for modern design. He reported that, in the best judgment of the members of the profession, "schools should emphasize design rather than business but that the design should be taught in the most practical way. They would give the student a background (not a smattering) of economics and sociology, but there is no widespread belief that the school should spend very much time on teaching real estate methods or details of office practice. As to the dean, his experience, character, personality and breadth of view are more important than his own predilections as to design based upon precedent or design gone modernistic."[8]

Killam argued for an architect as dean of a school that contained architecture, landscape architecture, and planning because all three fields are based on training in planning and design, although in varying degrees. An architect, he thought, could rise above internecine jealousies and coordinate the activities of all other fields and, crucially, could act as advisor on education to the profession at a national level. Killam believed that this advantage had been lost during Edgell's deanship because Edgell was not a professional architect: "We need leaders who will be noted and respected in their own profession because these are professional schools, not undergraduate departments of the university."[9] Sidestepping this dilemma, Killam joined Frost and Haffner in asserting that the statement of principles was far more important than the man chosen as the dean—but that did not prevent him from making two recommendations: William T. Aldrich, a Harvard College alumnus, Boston practitioner, and teacher at the Rhode Island School of Design and the Museum School in Boston; and Ellis F. Lawrence, the dean of the School of Architecture at the University of Oregon.

The Search for a New Dean

After faculty and students articulated their critiques of the past and hopes for the future, Harvard began its search for a new dean for the Faculty of Architecture. By January 1935 rumors of the search began to circulate, but it was not until March that Dean Edgell formally announced his retirement and the need for a successor. President Conant took a direct and serious interest in the recruitment, which showed not only the seriousness of the endeavor but also the role this new dean would play in propagating Conant's own modern educational agenda for the entire university: expand the focus of the university beyond Boston and New England to a more national—and international—level. The changes contemplated in the design schools were part of this agenda and of such importance that he consulted, among others, Frederic Delano, a long-term advisor to the Regional Plan of New York and head of the National Planning Board established by his uncle, President Roosevelt, in 1933. Delano had a major impact in the nascent planning field, but his ideas of large-scale planning were not incorporated into the reformed planning program and had little impact on the new curriculum.[10] Edgell suggested to President Conant that a new dean—not an acting dean—be found, and that this appointment should solidify the collaborative efforts of the three schools.[11]

For an overview of appropriate candidates for the deanship, and for the latest observations on architectural education, President Conant turned to his brother-in-law, Harold Bush-Brown, a graduate of Harvard's School of Architecture and then chairman of the Department of Architecture at the Georgia Institute of Technology. Bush-Brown mentioned a recent report, *A Study of Architectural Schools*, by F. Hunt

Bosworth of Cornell and Roy Childs Jones of the University of Minnesota, which divided the professional training of an architect into six main topics: architectural design, construction or architectural engineering, history of architecture, graphics, freehand drawing, and professional practice.[12]

Bush-Brown concluded his tutorial by sending a draft report on architectural education which he had compiled for the Association of Collegiate Schools of Architecture (ACSA). He also explained the basic elements that compose the professional training of an architect, and how Americans had adapted the educational system of the École des Beaux-Arts, with its *esquisses* and national competitions, summing up: "While it is not perfect, I believe it serves a good purpose, and with some reservations, does its job surprisingly well."[13] Bush-Brown acknowledged that Harvard differed from other American universities in its application of Beaux-Arts principles by only occasionally participating in the national contests, emphasizing instead local competitions through shared juries with MIT and the Boston Architectural Club. The School of Architecture at the University of Oregon had gone even further, he noted, and was one of the few schools to abolish the competitive method in favor of encouraging students to find their own means of expression. Oregon's dean, Ellis Lawrence, the former president of the ACSA, became a serious contender for the Harvard deanship. Among his supporters, beside Killam, was Grant LaFarge, a lecturer for the

Committee on Education of the AIA, who wrote: "Nowhere do I know so happy an atmosphere, so successful a fusion and integration of architecture and its allied arts as in Oregon." LaFarge and his colleagues had previously recommended Lawrence for deanships at Columbia University and Washington University in St. Louis.[14]

In his specific recommendations for Harvard, Bush-Brown confirmed that the School of Architecture had already begun to follow a more modern direction: "That there is a progressive spirit in the school is shown by the fact that certain reforms and methods, new emphasis on certain phases of the work to meet modern conditions, and an attempt at better correlation of work has been made in the schools recently. Also announcement has been made that the school is committed to the new or modern architecture, which is a bold step. . . ."[15]

Bush-Brown also recommended a man who would continue to come to the attention of President Conant: Joseph Fairman Hudnut, who had attended Harvard College and worked with the School of Architecture in the 1920s in the creation of a joint program with the University of Virginia. Like Herbert Langford Warren, Hudnut practiced as an architect and taught the history of architecture. He was now dean at Columbia. Bush-Brown suggested that "if you want to go into architectural education further, I think the man who has the soundest ideas on the subject and has expressed himself most clearly on the matter as far as the modern problem

118

of present day needs are concerned, is Dean Hudnut of Columbia. His last year's report, and this year's report and his address to alumni, all of which have been issued in pamphlet form, are well worth reading."[16]

A slew of recommendations from various sources followed, discussing both the deanship itself and new directions for the school in general. Collectively they reflected a spectrum of views about the phenomenon of modern education. Edgell suggested a host of architects as consultants but specifically recommended Kenneth Stowell of *Architectural Forum*.[17] Fiske Kimball suggested an appointment from within the university: Henry Hubbard, who represented a major force in planning and the Olmsted tradition in landscape architecture. Hubbard's Harvard colleague and former student, Howard Menhinick, circulated a petition that fifteen faculty members signed— Hubbard was clearly the inside candidate.[18] Even Hudnut was asked to make recommendations, and he suggested Ellis Lawrence and Roy Childs Jones.[19] But Hudnut himself emerged as the leading candidate. Edgell felt that any candidates from Princeton and Yale would not leave their present positions. He informed President Conant, "If you are out for seduction, however, I should start with Hudnut anyway. . . . [He is] the best man to steal."[20] President Conant met with Hudnut in New York in March. After their meeting, Hudnut wrote, saying that he wished he could have been of greater help at their conference. With his note he

included a copy of a magazine article that contained his comments on the architecture of Yale University and a copy of his recent report to the president of Columbia University.[21]

Conant clearly had not made up his mind. Because Hudnut was currently a dean at Columbia University and because Conant wished to avoid the appearance of unscrupulousness, his name did not appear on the official list of candidates under consideration.[22] After winnowing, Conant solicited confidential opinions on Ellis Lawrence, the dean at Oregon; Roy Child Jones, the dean at Minnesota; W. Pope Barney, at the University of Pennsylvania (whose reputation was conservative and old-fashioned); Dennis Moore, an archeologist; and, finally, Otto Teegen, the perceptive Harvard alumnus on the Visiting Committee.

Based on the input from Harvard faculty and students, architects in Boston and New York, and at least one dean of another school of architecture, Conant defined his position in a letter to Bush-Brown:

It would seem that what we should aim for here is to try to amalgamate further the schools of architecture, landscape architecture and city planning. In fact amalgamating them as far as possible, only leaving the reservation that there is a recognition that they are three separate vocations. It seems to me that the training should be so flexible that it would be much easier than at present for a graduate of whichever vocation he chose to jump into another, if economic condi-

tions made it desirable. I also feel that we should emphasize our graduate work, that as far as architecture is concerned the move should be definitely to the left, if I may use that phrase. We should move away from archaeology and towards engineering and a greater contact with economics and politics.[23]

Here was the fundamental summation of the reformulation of the schools of design at Harvard—to provide professionally trained students with the ability to work in one or another of the professions as they responded to their own desires and changing economic conditions. Tied to this intention was a fundamental belief in the necessity of a political orientation that associated the university and its president with the progressive ideals of the liberal left. The modern world required the input of pioneering fields and new developments in engineering, economics, politics, and the national programs of the New Deal, while the lessons of the past appeared to recede in terms of what they offered.

Oregon's Ellis Lawrence emerged as the leading contender in President Conant's view, but Edgell brought up, once again, the name of Joseph Hudnut. Having heard several speeches on education at a dinner given by the Boston Society of Architects, Edgell reported to President Conant that though Haffner and Barney spoke well, "the last and longest speech was Hudnut's and it made all the others sound like milksops. I know that you are an honest man and a gentleman, and if you stick to your opinion that it would not be cricket to try and steal Hudnut from Columbia, I shall respect your decision. Nevertheless, putting it in the baldest terms, if the Harvard School is not the greatest school in the country, it ought to be. If it is looking for a dean it ought to get the best man in the country. That man is Hudnut, I am now convinced. I doubt very much if we could steal him, but if you become sufficiently unscrupulous shake me off the lead and at least I can try."[24]

With such an extraordinarily strong recommendation from Edgell, President Conant began to put his own scruples aside and wrote Bush-Brown for a confidential opinion on Hudnut. Bush-Brown replied favorably: "He is a good architect, a good teacher, and has an excellent mind, and is thoroughly alive to the modern problems. I do not believe that you could do better. . . . [Hudnut] is not very impressive on first acquaintance but of all those I know in the educational field I believe I would place him first for the job in question."[25] As the academic year closed, President Conant, loaded with recommendations from both inside and outside the profession concerning candidates for the deanship and proposals for a new curriculum, suddenly offered the position to Hudnut, apparently over the phone. Conant then wrote to Hudnut on June 7, 1935, to confirm Hudnut's acceptance as dean of the Faculty of Architecture and tenured professor of architecture. He would start officially on July 1, 1935, at a salary of $12,000. He concluded his invitation: "Let me say

again how delighted I am that we have the good fortune to secure your services, and how sure I am that under your guidance the School of Architecture will develop something of great value and of unique character."[26]

Hudnut planned to meet with Dean Edgell while in Boston for several days in June to attend the twenty-fifth reunion of his Harvard class.[27] He had been dean at Columbia for only one year, and his departure left Columbia reeling; temporarily dividing the deanship among a committee of three, it lost its momentum as an innovator of an experimental modernist program and reverted to its former Beaux-Arts habits.[28]

Joseph Hudnut's Modernist Perspective

Hudnut's appointment at Harvard signaled the beginning of a transformation that would overturn many of the school's traditions and fundamentally alter architectural education in America. Born in Grand Rapids, Michigan, in 1884, he attended Harvard as an undergraduate (1906–9) but left, before graduating, to spend two years in a Chicago architectural office.[29] He received a B.Arch. from the University of Michigan in 1912, assumed a professorship at the University of Alabama until 1916, and then took a master's of science from Columbia in 1917. In World War I he saw overseas service with the American Expeditionary Force, and began his architectural prac-

4.3 Dean Joseph Fairman Hudnut, c. 1938. Hudnut, after becoming dean in 1935, led the Harvard schools as they amalgamated into the Graduate School of Design and was responsible for bringing Walter Gropius to the GSD in 1937.

tice in New York in 1919, where from his small office he built churches, country homes, and commercial buildings in historical styles. His published buildings were executed in a thin, abstracted, classicizing style.

Hudnut's conversion to modernism began in 1917 when he met Werner Hegemann, the German city planner, for whom he worked on and off until 1921.[30] Hegemann had become well known in American planning circles after organizing a major city-planning exhibition in Boston in 1915. From Hegemann, Hudnut appears to have absorbed key modernist concepts: city planning as the basis of architecture; the incorporation of social and human realities into architecture and planning; and the need to integrate scientific with aesthetic expression. Hudnut also apparently came into contact with the ideas of John Dewey, the philosopher, psychologist, and educator, whose views of progressive education and pragmatism further shaped him. From Dewey, Hudnut absorbed the idea that education was the backbone of a democratic society and should provide not merely training but experience. A complete education moved beyond the walls of academia to the social unity of the community.

When Hudnut accepted a position at the University of Virginia in 1923, to direct its architecture school, he set about creating the joint program among Virginia, Harvard, and Alabama Polytechnic Institute, mentioned in chapter 3. Over the next three years he disengaged from his practice and focused on teaching architectural history and design, searching for a means of reconciling architecture's past with the present needs for practicality and social relevance. When Hudnut returned to New York to teach the history of architecture as a professor at Columbia University in 1926, he could draw on the concepts of Hegemann and Dewey, whose ideas were much discussed at Columbia, as well as his own experience as an educator. Part of his awareness of modern developments in art and architecture came from reading Lewis Mumford's *Sticks and Stones*, published in 1924.[31] Added to this was the buzz of modernism in the arts that could be sensed in New York as in few other places in America. Life in New York must have only reinforced the seeds of reformist fervor that were planted in the young, classically trained, Midwestern architect who would "desert the stylistic school for the organic."[32]

Hudnut began to articulate his own perceptions of modern art in 1929 when his article was published in *Modern Sculpture*. By 1931 he began to attack the traditional system of design education, revealing the fundamental principles of his design ideology. Amid the beginning reform movement at Harvard, Hudnut spoke with greater clarity and vehemence about the two basic responsibilities of architecture schools: to teach the science of construction, particularly in its abstract principles and general processes, and to teach the economic facts and intellectual forces that affect students' lives and work. At the same time, Hudnut revealed a humanistic attitude that balanced his call for technocratic and social enlightenment when he proposed a third responsibility: "the encouragement of those qualities of the mind—or the soul—of which the creation of beauty is the tangible expression."[33]

From the modernist perspective, the classical language of architecture, when unthinkingly replicated, impeded this rational architecture of beauty. Classicism had begun to fail because of its own irrelevancy during the eclecticism of the previous decades. It was further subverted during the 1920s by the doctrines of functionalism, attributed (with a religious fervor) to Le Corbusier. However, even at this early date in 1931, Hudnut recognized a danger in the overzealous application of functionalism, which already had precedents in the pragmatic Chicago School, and in a romanticized version of traditional city planning. Hudnut not only called the old City Beautiful movement, updated with theories of function, "defunct," but also questioned functionalism, a core dogma of modernism. In the public's mind, functionalism meant that architectural beauty could be created by logical processes, and that it is experienced, in Hudnut's paraphrase of Vitruvian principles, when "we perceive the fitness of an instrument for its use." By this reasoning, design education need not concern itself with beauty. And yet, according to Hudnut, beauty in design required intense discrimination and concentration, combined with an ephemeral quality, if architecture were to transcend function and assume a timeless presence.[34]

In 1933, Hudnut began to make his mark on American architectural education. When William A. Boring resigned after fourteen years as director and then dean of the School of Architecture at Columbia University, its president, Nicholas Murray Butler, faced a similar situation to Conant's at Harvard. Butler appointed a committee which issued a report in late spring 1934 that called for the Columbia School of Architecture to respond to the social and economic realities of the moment. Joseph Hudnut, who had become acting dean the previous year, gave similar recommendations to President Butler.[35]

After assuming the Columbia deanship in 1934, the forty-eight-year-old Hudnut launched a radically experimental program that foreshadowed his actions at Harvard.[36] The key points in Hudnut's program were creating a flexible curriculum independent of the usual academic hours, classes, and lectures; emphasizing realistic demands of practice; eliminating competitive design programs; freeing the students to pursue individual interests; and integrating the various courses of the program. In a report of June 30, 1934, Hudnut outlined the new thrust of the school: architecture of the future would not be based on the goals of creating beauty and comfort but "with an exigent desire to improve the environment of the human race."[37] Hudnut implied that a pursuit of this direction should maintain a scientific attitude, similar to that of the chemist and the engineer, and that sentiment and feeling, which were unreliable, would be suppressed.

By 1935, Columbia was creating a model, that if followed by other schools, would have launched a revolution in design education. It added city planning to its curriculum as the best means of achieving the social goals of the new architecture and of inculcating a scientific and rational approach to design. Community planner and housing expert Henry Wright, Werner Hegemann, and Carol Aronovici, a nationally recognized housing expert, provided additional courses on urbanism and housing.

Hudnut's proposed changes at Columbia reflect the attitudes he brought to Harvard. At Columbia, he espoused the problem method over competition and allowed students to enter only one competition per year. He proposed two types of design problems, one executed by the individual student, and the other done as sketches of short duration, executed in groups competing within the school.

At the core of these changes was a surprising notion: the new modern agenda was actually a return to earlier American tendencies in architectural educations. Those methods, espoused fifty years earlier by William Ware, and then by Langford Warren, had been overshadowed by French influence; now was the chance to redress the situation by returning to American roots.[38] Indeed, Hudnut acknowledged that his approach was "in many ways . . . merely a return to methods which obtained before the French influence became predominant in this country."[39] Hudnut carried his call for change

to his colleagues in the profession. He stunned a New York meeting of the American Institute of Architects in 1935 by declaring, "Students of Architecture should not design buildings which they cannot build. Our architecture has lost its vitality, its power to command the imagination and to interpret our civilization."[40] So known for this ardor did he become that his obituary would describe his position as "an obsession for realism which indelibly marked the character of American architecture," a realism that demanded that "an architect must understand the art of management in its relation to capital and labor; he must have knowledge of the law."[41]

According to Hudnut and his modernist contemporaries in the mid-1930s, emphasis belonged on the business and social aspects of the profession, and design efforts should be directed towards the creation of great social institutions, such as public utilities and large-scale housing schemes, rather than palaces and cathedrals. The call for economic and social rehabilitation that generated New Deal policies based on a new social conscience required support from architects as well. Hudnut responded.

Implementation of Harvard's Modernist Agenda

Even before his arrival at Harvard, Hudnut's ambitions to strengthen and further coordinate the fields of design had created a sensation. He found a receptive home at Harvard, where he immediately began to enact major changes, guided by three objectives. One was the desire for Harvard to create a synthetic approach to education, a move towards "total design" based on preexisting American traditions that unified the design arts. On one hand, from the late nineteenth century Harvard had wanted to connect the fine arts and decorative arts to cultivating a sensibility for design; on the other hand, American architects and artisans drew on the total-design ethos of the arts and crafts movement to invigorate their work; American landscape architects and planners continually had called on the Olmsted tradition. Hudnut's second aim was to link professional training in design with practical and rigorous pursuits that appeared scientific in their methods. His third aim was to transfer all courses that provided cultural background to undergraduate education. This transfer would make way for graduate-level courses that focused on engineering and construction.

He began to take steps to actualize his objectives and, at the same time, to get acquainted with his new faculty, colleagues, and students. They gave him the chummy nickname "Vi" (from a popular manufacturer, Hudnut's, whose best-selling fragrance was named "Violet").[42] Among other practical—and popular—issues needing attention, Hudnut sought equitable salaries for the younger instructors like G. Holmes Perkins, a Harvard architecture graduate who had returned to teach design at Frost's request, and who was also teaching design and history at the Cambridge School of Domestic Architecture and Landscape Architecture. Hudnut also approved an increase for Walter Bogner, who had returned to teach in 1931.[43] They soon played important roles in the school.

The first faculty meeting under Dean Hudnut, on October 16, 1935, lasted only fifteen minutes with nothing extraordinary reported except that a large number of undergraduates were taking courses in the program.[44] Two weeks later, Hudnut prepared the first in a series of memoranda to President Conant proposing changes in the curriculum of the School of Architecture. Hudnut outlined a degree of structure that would alter the existing program not only within the School of Architecture but within the university at large. The former master's program would be overhauled to become the new professional B.Arch. program. Significantly, this bachelor's in architecture was, in fact, a professional degree and a graduate degree as well—admission to the GSD's bachelor's program required the student to possess a bachelor of arts degree. Once students had earned the B.Arch. from the GSD, they could continue for an additional semester to obtain a master's degree by enrolling in the school's new advanced studio, known as the master's class. The master's degree in architecture became solely a postprofessional pursuit, open only to students who already had a professional degree in architecture, the B.Arch. or its equivalent. Students from other universities who held a B.Arch. would be admitted with advanced standing to the GSD's new postprofessional master's program. Its degree requirements consisted of a series of courses in design, engineering science, history of art and architecture, construction, city planning, and a thesis. This new program of instruction obviously would require an intense restructuring of the design programs. A central premise in that restructuring was the GSD's transfer of the teaching of history and drawing to its undergraduate students to the Fine Arts Department. Furthermore, the longstanding traditional courses in archeological reconstruction, life drawing, and modeling in clay completely disappeared from the course offerings. In order to create a body of Harvard undergraduates qualified for entrance to the GSD's professional degrees, Hudnut proposed a new program in Harvard College called Architectural Sciences. Granting an AB degree, it was a cornerstone of the GSD's vision of the properly educated architect.[45] The Council of the School of Architecture approved the new undergraduate area of concentration in Harvard College at the end of November 1935.[46]

Meanwhile, a problem arose within the existing School of City Planning. The school's financial difficulties were brought to the attention of Henry James, a Harvard alumnus who was a representative of the Rockefeller Foundation (the School's benefactor), a member of the Board of Overseers, the son of William James, and a New York lawyer.[47] In conversations with James, Hudnut made clear that the city planning school was too narrow in its perception of itself "as a highly specialized field."[48] James suggested that a wider view might come from bringing in an eminent scholar in the field of economics. James then wrote to President Conant with his own report of a meeting with Hudnut and Henry Hubbard. According to James, while the School of City Planning had not realized anyone's ideals, he believed it was still the best school of its kind anywhere. Recognizing that Hubbard had both strengths and weaknesses, he suggested the following solution: "If you are thinking of merging architecture and landscape architecture, why not merge city planning also into a division or department or school presided over by Hudnut, and establish the understanding that Hudnut is to be the real dean of all three phases of the one department or school. That would enable Hudnut to supplement Hubbard where he is weak but would give Hubbard scope enough for teaching and researching his own particular line." James saw that Hudnut genuinely recognized the fact that city planning, housing, and related issues were primarily economic and social problems that were impossible to resolve without the techniques and tools of the architect and planner. Architects, however, gave lip service to this recognition and generally waited for others to provide the "requirements for an edifice that they are then delighted to design."[49]

Finally, James revealed some bad news, not revealed earlier to Hudnut: the Rockefellers were reluctant to go ahead with funding the program in city planning because "it appears that the university isn't doing anything in particular for City Planning beyond allowing the Rockefellers to pay for it."[50] If the university took the lead in reorganizing and reshaping the program, James felt it would impress the Rockefellers, although he did not know if that alone would persuade them to make further grants. President Conant therefore bought time for a resolution of the problem with the city planning school while Hubbard and Hudnut more clearly defined their plans, and a new program for a graduate school of public administration unfolded. Hudnut asked for a short delay in approving the undergraduate program so that he could push ahead with the reorganization of the graduate programs.[51]

The resolutions for the master's and bachelor's programs in architecture, though, quickly went to President Conant in December 1935. Hudnut's recommendation, which still needed approval by the Harvard Board of Overseers, included an outline of administrative responsibilities and proposed the creation of "two or more departments," each with its own faculty council.[52] Pencil notes at the bottom of the original draft of the proposal outlined the advantages of the new school: too much independence had handicapped the school, whereas departmental cooperation and the new structure—with its resulting savings and simplification—would allow two degrees.[53]

In mid-January 1936, all previous memoranda were summarized in a statement that Hudnut presented to the Corporation and outlined, for the first time, the formation of a Graduate School of Design, under the immediate control of the Faculty of Architecture (which then would be renamed the Faculty of Design). Comments appeared in red pencil in the margins, and Joseph Hudnut's initials concluded the memorandum. Ironically, a comment in the margin by the former instructor of architectural history had significant repercussions for architectural education—and, ultimately, professional practice itself: "Architect[ural] Research in History not in the School of D[esign]." This final memorandum officially stated the position of the new configuration: "Such knowledge and experience (of the proposed school) will include of course a knowledge of the history of art, but it is recognized that the enlargement of this knowledge through the science of archaeology and historical research, as well as its arrangement and interpretation, forms a special field of scholarly activities only indirectly related to the practice of the arts. These activities properly belong to another division of the University and will not be included in the School of Design."[54]

This document defined the philosophical underpinnings for Harvard's teaching of architecture, landscape architecture, and city and regional planning for the next fifty years. By this action, Harvard institutionalized a policy of relegating any course of study not directly related to professional practice—particularly the culture courses of the traditional programs—to the undergraduate domain. History courses went to the Fogg Museum along with Professor Kenneth Conant. This move reflected Hudnut's personal resistance to the methods and aims of archeology and a preference for architecture to be seen as a viable response to social and communal needs.

Four guiding principles for the new GSD were identified in this memorandum. First, *design* would have primacy: "The word 'design' is to be understood as including all those processes by which the visual arts are created: processes by which materials are assembled in such a way as to afford aesthetic satisfactions. Design therefore includes architecture, landscape architecture, and regional planning. The fundamental knowledge and experience necessary for the successful process of all of these visual arts may logically be included in the curricula of the School of Design."[55]

The second principle required that students of the new GSD complete preparatory work in college before entering graduate study. Consequently, graduate students were expected to have a clear vision of the world and the intellectual capacity that derives from the disciplined experience of college training. Preparation for the study of design included a basic knowledge of history and the theory of arts, experience in drawing and painting, and an introduction to the process of design, as well as courses in economics and sociology. These were required, "since it is highly probable that the practice of the visual arts will be in the future closely identified with industry and since these arts will be more immediately serv-

iceable to the population as a whole than to individuals, it is also important that the college course for students who are to enter the School of Design should include scientific studies such as economics and sociology."[56] This view reflected the struggles of the Depression that pressed people to believe that economics and sociology were "sciences," as if science itself offered a replacement for outmoded tools of teaching and a means for social rejuvenation.

The third principle called for a spirit of collaboration, given that the basic processes of design are common to all three professional fields and their related arts. Thus students sharing training and association during their first years in the allied fields of architecture, landscape architecture, and city planning could start to grasp the similarities of their work. Ideally, this beneficial association in the first years of training would be reinforced in the later years by continuing collaboration.

The fourth principle asserted that the future might require a professional expertise and experience beyond anything currently contemplated. The proposal for the Graduate School of Design was the first step for what, in time, could expand into a small university school that could include other arts. It could also provide preparation for other professions in a series of ateliers where students could explore fundamental knowledge and get experience in all fields of design as well as exposure to the specific processes and materials of the distinctive arts. In effect, the new school

defined itself in terms of providing flexibility for the future, the changing role of art, and the demands of the design professions.

The Harvard Corporation approved Hudnut's proposal on February 3, 1936, and forwarded it to the Overseers (the other main governing body) for a formal vote. The corporation, however, did make one amendment and omitted the sentence "the Schools of Architecture, Landscape Architecture and City Planning are to be together under the immediate charge of the Faculty of Architecture."[57] The amendment reflected a continuing discussion of whether or not to include the city planning school under the Faculty of Architecture. Rather than make the decision at that time, the door was left open for city planning to be either included or excluded in the formulation of the new school. With the approval of the Overseers (an assumed formality for the new Graduate School of Design), and with the proposition for a new design concentration in Harvard College on its way to the Faculty of Arts and Sciences, Hudnut refocused on budget concerns, faculty appointments, and dealing with the lingering issues about the School of City Planning and the physical site for the new GSD.

The manifestation of this grand agenda for modern design education involved an irrevocable reference to the past: Robinson Hall itself. It was still filled with the artifacts of the old order—paintings, casts of classical fragments, original marbles, drawings, paintings, and objects in glass cases—and Hudnut was anxious to

remodel the building to reflect the school's new direction. He also felt that the building was not well suited for teaching purposes, and he proposed a series of alterations to make it more effective and to accomplish a considerable amount of deferred maintenance.[58] He requested $20,832 for alterations and improvements to Robinson Hall. The largest expenditure, $5,722, would go for the Hall of Casts. The Harvard Corporation provided a special fund for the reorganization and remodeling in February 1936.

Giving priority to such an expensive remodeling project in the midst of the Depression in itself expressed the university's support for the change. The large drafting rooms received new lighting and desks. The libraries were reorganized, and new files and lights were added. The large drafting room in the southeast corner of the building, formerly used for advanced design and thesis projects, was subdivided into offices for instructors. The basement, which had been used for the activities of the Pen and Brush Club, became a laboratory for the plant materials course, a studio for life drawing, and a new room for juries. The major change was the removal of all the plaster casts and most of the architectural fragments from the Great Hall. The visual legacy of the school's past was swiftly expunged and, with some exceptions, ultimately lost. These artifacts—the sculptural fragments of which the school had been so proud— now represented an antiquated approach to design. Modern exhibition cases were installed on the bare walls, and the formerly richly decorated Hall of Casts now resembled the spare, monochromatic, planar architecture of European modernism and became known casually as the Great Space (Fig. 4.4).

4.4 Hall of Casts, Robinson Hall, c. 1935. The modernized Hall as it was remodeled after the arrival of Dean Hudnut, containing instead of classical and medieval sculptural casts and fragments, sterile museum cases. The impulse to remove the cast collection predated Hudnut's arrival, however.

It is easy to imagine Hudnut's modernist fervor prompting him to jettison the artifacts of the Hall of Casts as a symbolic rejection of classical architecture and a moribund past. The irrelevance of the classical fragments had been apparent to Edgell before Hudnut arrived. In the late spring of 1935, in response to questions for an official guide to University buildings, Edgell admitted that he did not know the identity of the stone reproductions on the façade of Robinson Hall, that he had no idea of the location of the original urns from which the school's travertine copies had been made, and that "the long list of casts in the Hall of Casts is superfluous. Nobody cares much about casts anymore."[59] He suggested keeping only the stone originals, full-scale objects (such as the reproduction of the Arch of Trajan), the balcony, and copies of Ionic columns from the Mausoleum at Halicarnassus.[60] All the minor casts were slated to be removed by the end of that academic year to make way for an exhibition of building materials. The fabric of the modern world was officially replacing the long-dominant language of classicism. Edgell knew the tide had turned, and with his approval, the dean designate would be free of antiquated baggage. The removal of the casts at Harvard mirrored the changes at other institutions, for example, the Metropolitan Museum of Art in New York, whose renowned collection was being put in storage and whose own Hall of Casts was to be reconstructed as the Hall of Armor.[61] The changes to Robinson Hall and the removal of paintings and

objets d'art became a delicate issue for donors who had made gifts to the school. When a friend of the Department of Landscape Architecture offered paintings to the school, she was informed that "the Hall of Casts is a thing of the past, bare walls or walls with glassed cases being the vogue at the moment."[62] The offer of a portrait of Charles G. Fall proved especially embarrassing because classes in landscape architecture had annually visited Fall's estate in Cohasset, Massachusetts.

In addition to launching a remodeling in his first academic year at Harvard, Hudnut also made changes in his faculty. In March 1936 he reappointed or eliminated a number of faculty positions to suit the newly constituted Graduate School of Design.[63] Appointments in architecture were largely routine; the one exception was architectural engineer Jean Georges Peters, a Harvard alumnus and office manager for William T. Aldrich, a Boston architect. Peters' appointment was partly in anticipation of the retirement of Charles Killam and partly to signify the new approach to scientific rigor. Hudnut, with the agreement of Bremer Pond, believed that the landscape staff could be reduced without seriously impairing instruction. Hudnut recommended that assistant professor Morley J. Williams and Herbert D. Langhorne, an instructor, not be reappointed. Hudnut mentioned that, due to the demand for the services of landscape architects in the various governmental agencies, both Williams and Langhorne would be able to obtain good appointments quickly.[64] Hudnut recom-

mended the reappointment of Steven F. Hamblin as assistant professor of horticulture, and Hamblin, together with Bremer Pond, Walter L. Chambers, and Richard Webel (who now taught design as a part-time assistant professor) formed the remaining core of the Department of Landscape Architecture.

In keeping with the principle of eliminating extraneous courses from the curriculum, Hudnut recommended that instruction in freehand drawing be offered through the fine arts division of Harvard College. Reflecting his rejection of one of the fundamental graphic techniques in the system of Beaux-Arts education, Hudnut believed that watercolor drawing was not an essential part of an architecture curriculum. Aiden Laselle Ripley, an artist who offered the fine-arts approach that Hudnut had relegated to undergraduate training, was not reappointed. H. Dudley Murphy's services as an instructor in freehand drawing were retained, particularly since Ripley's freehand courses would be offered in the division of fine arts, not the GSD. Hudnut's proposals for shifting drawing and eliminating watercolor met with concern. Murphy wrote university architect and Visiting Committee member Charles A. Coolidge, who informed President Conant of Murphy's worries that architectural students would no longer have a decent instruction in watercolor and freehand drawing. Murphy pointed out that freehand drawing and watercoloring were important for the architect, "as increasing the sales appeal of his work."[65] Coolidge concurred.

Hudnut's recommendations for faculty reappointments and dismissals during this transition, though not uncontroversial, could hardly be called a housecleaning. Largely at the expense of the Department of Landscape Architecture, Hudnut trimmed his staff to bring it in line with budgetary necessities and to weed out those teachers who appeared to offer irrelevant or unsatisfactory instruction. However, in the spring of 1936 a series of events opened the possibility for a radically new appointment for the Graduate School of Design. Jean-Jacques Haffner decided to resign, effective the following spring, leaving open a position for a new professor of design. Though on the surface his departure might appear to be part of a systematic clearing of the "old guard" in the faculty, Haffner pointedly declared this was not the case. Haffner's wife and daughters had been visiting in France, and he had asked for a half-year sabbatical to be granted a year early so he could join them. Hudnut told Haffner that this was not possible. Haffner's family insisted on staying in France, which was in the midst of increasingly threatening political circumstances, and he wanted to be with them. He expressed deep personal regret at leaving the school and had no resentment towards Hudnut: "Leaving this school eighteen months after the appointment of a new dean, may appear, I realize, as a step which might be taxed with ingratitude. No one else more than I has been so fortunate as to see, at last, the new sound basis on which our school is being placed, thanks to the activity and

understanding of Dean Hudnut: no one else more regrets the step which I feel compelled to take. Family circumstances are the only ones to guide me: they are imperative enough in my mind to warrant this decision."[66] Based on Haffner's approval of Hudnut's changes and Haffner's own suggestions for alterations of the curriculum, there is no indication that he was under pressure to leave because of his Beaux-Arts background.[67] Hudnut appraised his efforts as having "developed the work in design to a level not excelled by that of any other school in this country."[68]

Ironically, Haffner may have been one of the few design instructors capable of teaching the new idioms of modern architecture—at least, in stylistic terms. His designs for modern gardens, published in his little-known *Compositions des Jardins*, was the sole work of its kind and introduced modern, cubistic principles of composition to landscape architects (see Fig. 4.1).[69] It contained designs for modern gardens surrounding modern houses that were flat-roofed, planar compositions that crossed the work of Le Corbusier with austere models of German and Dutch housing and recalled the work of Gabriel Guevrekian. In the late 1920s and early 1930s his students explored the vocabulary of art deco, *art moderne*, and the work of German and Dutch modern architects, as well as that of Le Corbusier. Haffner strongly supported the reform movement at Harvard from its origins in 1932 and backed the formation of an integrated Graduate School of Design. Nevertheless,

it is reasonable to conclude that Haffner's reasons for departure were only partly personal, and that he graciously wanted to give Hudnut a free hand in choosing a new leader in design for the school. His students and colleagues honored him with a festive dinner, replete with a charming program that featured his work and included his photograph (Fig. 4.5). Upon his return to France, Haffner became architect to the Louvre in Paris and director in 1938 of the Fontainebleau School of Fine Arts.[70] Haffner's departure marked the end of an era.

With his programs approved and faculty sorted out, except for Haffner's replacement, Hudnut turned to the problems with the planning program. In the spring of 1936 he sent a memorandum to President Conant stating that the new program in regional planning would conduct work at a regional scale that involved research and instruction, and that this should be communicated to the Rockefeller Foundation. Hudnut proposed that the degree in regional planning should be offered not by the GSD but by the new School of Public Administration, which had just been established that year.[71] In effect, Hudnut was opposing the incorporation of the planning department as an equal partner in the new Graduate School of Design. Though collaboration was central to the new GSD, its collaborators were anything but equal in status. The nomenclature is confusing: by 1934–35, the planning program was called the School of City and Regional Planning to reflect its expanded scope, but the school

DINNER

IN HONOUR OF

JEAN JACQUES HAFFNER

CHEVALIER DE LA LEGION D'HONNEUR
ARCHITECTE DU GOUVERNEMENT
GRAND PRIX DE ROME

NELSON ROBINSON JR.
PROFESSOR OF ARCHITECTURE
IN HARVARD UNIVERSITY

12/18/36.

(?)

MR, POND

4.5 Invitation to bon-voyage party
for Professor Jean-Jacques Haffner,
addressed to Professor Bremer
Pond, 1937.

was closed in 1936–37, and reopened in 1937, renamed the Department of Regional Planning since it now offered a variety of degrees in both city and regional planning. Hudnut's objections came from his own conceptions of regional planning. To him, the work of regional planners involved little more than finding ways to physically manifest less tangible plans derived from economic, political, and social concepts—and that to put design first was to put the cart before the horse.

Hudnut gave primacy to the formulation of policy and the coordination of economic and social ideas as the basic generators for plans of cities and regions. However, Hudnut's position on planning as an equal partner in the collaborative endeavor is not totally clear. Proposing the transfer of regional planning to a policy school may reflect his perception of a regional emphasis on governmental policy, while city planning and its adjunct, the history of cities, dealt more with design. The former, therefore, would fit better at Littauer Center's School of Public Administration, while the latter would be better off in the GSD. This lack of clarity suggests that creating the collaborative design model was a process with built-in contradictions—which, nevertheless, did not prevent a pursuit of the overall goal of collaborative education.

In any case, such an interdisciplinary profession necessitated an integrated educational process. Hudnut felt that such an endeavor perhaps could be best undertaken by a university agency that was independent of the departments of social science, on the one hand, and a department of regional planning, on the other, but had aspects common to both. In Hudnut's view, the new School of Public Administration fit this bill; therefore, it should offer the degree in regional planning, not the School of Design. The curriculum of a new Department of Regional Planning could have two parts, consisting of laboratory work and lecture courses. A third part could be added, consisting of conferences, lectures, and readings designed to help students integrate the ideas from the several departments. The problem method of instruction would be used, and promotion would depend upon the successful solution of problems as well as upon the successful completion of the parallel courses of study. The fundamental issue for the field of city and regional planning came down to the ability of its practitioners to master all of the necessary legal, social, economic, and political inputs and come up with a physical result.

The later history of the Graduate School of Design involved the effort to reverse this interdisciplinary approach and establish the primacy of design over socioeconomic and policy issues. Each successor to Hudnut's deanship took a fundamental position, consciously or not, for or against his point of view. From Hudnut's perspective, design was the end product of the process of city and regional planning, not its beginning.

At the conclusion of the 1935–36 academic year the new dean reported on the past year's transition to the president, emphasizing important changes that furthered the cause of collaborative education. Of particular note was the Overseers' official sanction (on February 24, 1936) of the amalgamation of the three schools into one for the purposes of simplifying administration and encouraging collaboration. The principle of collaboration was to be enforced in the first year of training, when all students took the same instruction.[72]

Equally significant was the creation of a new undergraduate program in architectural sciences that accomplished the shift of all culture courses, like history, from the graduate level to the undergraduate, and the potential creation of a highly qualified group of undergraduates for admission to the new GSD.[73] The instruction in this new undergraduate program was provided by three instructors from the School of Design and three from the Division of Fine Arts. The creation of the new undergraduate field also allowed the graduate program to concentrate on courses that were uniquely professional, and made possible—but only for the new Department of Architecture—the granting of the two professional degrees, a bachelor's degree and a master's degree, both in architecture. Although later the degrees for landscape and planning students were also supplemented, granting of the dual degrees in architecture reflected a glaring bias toward one department. The triumvirate would not comprise equal partners; architecture had the highest priority, planning had the lowest.

While Hudnut reported on these structural changes, he was in the awkward position of having to announce that his faculty had voted to discontinue the operation of one of the departments for one year—the School of City Planning had run out of money. The funds that remained were to be used to complete research publications: the *Harvard City Planning Studies*. However, the department planned to reopen in the academic year 1937–38 with reorganized courses focused on the regional aspects of planning. These developments must have been difficult for Henry Hubbard, who not only had been passed over as dean but now also saw his school reduced to a department that had arrived still-born. In addition, Theodora Kimball Hubbard, his wife and colleague, and a pioneer bibliographer in planning and landscape architecture, had died in November 1935.[74] Under her and Katherine McNamara, the landscape architecture librarian known as "Miss Mac," the collection had increased, owning three times as many books and documents (14,010) as the library of architecture (5,875).[75] McNamara had just updated Theodora Hubbard's bibliography in planning and published it as the tenth volume of the *Harvard Planning Studies*.[76] All these efforts must now have appeared for naught.

Paradoxically, while announcing the cessation of courses in planning, Hudnut had to acknowledge that the graduates of the planning program were extremely successful in finding jobs in the midst of the Depression. In particular, Harvard planners were in demand, according to their employers, because they appreciated the relationships of government and economics to physical planning.

All was not harmonious with landscape architecture either: it also entered the GSD on a lower footing than architecture, tangibly expressed in the reduced space allocated to the department in Hudnut's remodeling of Robinson Hall. Then, with the passive consent of the department's chairman, Bremer Pond, Hudnut reduced its budget and staff in order to expand the curriculum in architecture. According to Hudnut, at least, these budget reductions did not significantly lower the standards of teaching.[77]

Hudnut's assessment of the prospects for students in landscape architecture was similar to those in planning: the departments were temporarily weakened, but demand for graduates was high. Although the Depression had reduced the enrollment of students in landscape architecture, there was optimism for the future. The profession had shifted from the pre-Depression work of designing large private estates, parks, and recreational areas to public works that included federal programs such as the National Park Service, the National Resources Board, the Tennessee Valley Authority, the Forestry Service, and the Resettlement Bureau, as well as state, county, and city park authorities. The programs of the New Deal rescued the landscape architect; each recent Harvard graduate had at least two jobs in the profession open to him.

With the details of Hudnut's annual report in hand, President Conant presented his own annual report to the university's Board of Overseers. In the aftermath of Harvard's tercentenary, which had been celebrated the previous September, Conant reiterated the university's roles and goals as broadly reformational in nature. In Conant's words, the academic symposia of the recent celebration of Harvard's three-hundredth birthday "served to symbolize the common tradition which the universities have preserved nearly a thousand years." Study of the history of knowledge could foster the spirit of "essential unity" and point to "the fundamental unity of feeling which binds together the professors in a twentieth century university. . . . An appreciation of this unity is essential if institutions of higher learning are to flourish in periods of uncertainty and social change."[78] Unity was critical as the political disintegration of Europe loomed.

Conant believed that this sense of unity could be reinforced by the study of history in the broadest sense. Here is the principle that had motivated the study of architecture at the microcosmic level operating at Harvard in the larger sphere of American society. It was given form via the creation of a new field—the history of science and learning (usually referred to as simply the history of science)—and it reflected the belief "that in the study of our national culture we may find the principle that is needed to unify our liberal arts tradition and to mold it to suit this modern age."[79] In this context, President Conant announced

the formation of the Graduate School of Design—an integration of the Schools of Architecture, Landscape Architecture, and City Planning—and a demonstration of the essential shift away from isolationism: "The closer union of these three schools . . . is one more indication of a widespread feeling that the separatist spirit of the past quarter of a century has proceeded too far and that a period of coordination and amalgamation must be the next step in university development."[80]

In the following academic year, 1936–37, the Graduate School of Design officially began operation and declared in its *Official Register* its new standard, emphasizing both the high level of prerequisite training required for admission and the school's commitment to professional training that resembled the conditions of an office. Furthermore, despite the school's traditional emphasis on the history of architecture during the previous forty years, from 1936 on, emphasis was clearly on *design*: "Only one subject, *Design*, is taught but this term is understood to include structural design, professional practice, and the social requirements of architecture."[81]

The Arrival of Walter Gropius

The GSD needed a new head for the design programs to further combat the separatist spirit and promote the amalgamation of the arts and sciences in the modernist cause. Just as the early architecture school sought out major practitioners for professorships to establish itself in design, the new school now turned to find a famous leader. But there was a significant difference between past searches for a design professor and the search in 1936: the emphasis earlier had been on finding an American for an American school— even if Harvard ultimately appointed two Frenchmen—and now *only* Europeans were considered. There were no American candidates because no American architectural work was viewed as worthy as that of the Europeans. Furthermore, there was a perception that modern European architects had a more theoretical inclination and a greater commitment to teaching than their American peers.[82]

By the summer of 1936 three candidates were under consideration to replace Haffner and lead the school into the era of modernism.[83] Walter Gropius and Mies van der Rohe were German architects and educators; J. J. P. Oud, a Dutch architect, was one of the first to articulate the "New Objectivity" that defined architecture as created by technology and social determinants.[84] They constituted three of the four major architects at the "Modern Architects" exhibition at the Museum of Modern Art in 1932, which had announced the International Style to America; Le Corbusier was the fourth: though he had visited the United States for two months in 1935, sponsored by the Museum of Modern Art, and lectured at numerous architecture schools, he did not figure in the competition at Harvard.[85] Perhaps his inability to speak English was a factor, or more sig-

nificantly, his lack of experience in running a school, as Gropius and Mies had.

During the summer of 1936, Hudnut and Holmes Perkins traveled to Europe, visiting Mies in Berlin, Gropius in London, and Oud in Holland. Hudnut met with Gropius in August 1936 and returned to the United States the second week of September.[86] Perkins then accompanied Gropius to La Sarraz, Switzerland, where they vacationed with other members of the European modernist circle, including László Moholy-Nagy. The forty-seven-year-old Gropius was returning to a place associated with the ambitions of the modern movement in Europe; the Château of La Sarraz, the 1928 site of the first meeting of CIAM (Congrés Internationaux d'Architecture Moderne), the leading organization for disseminating modernist ideas. The château was also the location of September planning meetings held to organize the fifth CIAM congress, which Perkins apparently attended.[87] Having gained recognition in his early architectural practice with Adolf Meyer through the Fagus Factory in Alfeld, Germany (1911–13) and the Werkbund Exhibition building in Cologne (1913–14), Gropius had begun to concentrate on developing an ideology that responded to the social need for, and benefits of, mass housing. His goals for addressing social issues through visual means found an optimal vehicle in 1919 when he became director of the old Kunstgewerbeschule in Weimar and transformed the arts and crafts school into the Staatliches Bauhaus Weimar. The manifesto of the Bauhaus announced that

"the ultimate aim of all visual arts is the complete building," and that the amalgamation of "architecture and sculpture and painting in one unity . . . [would] one day rise toward heaven from the hands of a million workers like the crystal symbol of a new faith."[88] Though its teachers and curriculum became famous, the Bauhaus was fraught with conflict and met with disapproval from the conservative local bourgeoisie.

In 1925 the city of Dessau invited Gropius and the Bauhaus to move there and erect a new building for its use. However, despite progress in developing their total-design curriculum, criticism from local craft unions, art academies, and the far right of the National Socialists resulted in Gropius's resignation from the Bauhaus—though the prospect of large-scale architectural commissions also entered into his decision. Despite the severe rebuff of his countrymen, his resignation allowed him, in 1928, to fulfill a longstanding intention of visiting the United States (Fig. 4.6). Once there, he became fascinated with utilitarian buildings; he demanded that local architects in Detroit and Chicago show him concrete grain elevators, and he could not understand why Americans did not admire them more than they did.[89] After returning to Berlin, he practiced, published his writings, lectured widely in Europe, and continued his research, particularly on housing. Unsure of the political situation in Germany in 1934, Gropius and his wife, Ise, moved to England. His arrival went generally

4.6 Bon-voyage gathering for the Gropiuses at the Sommerfeld Villa prior to their departure for a trip to America in 1928; showing (left to right): Minister Braun, Renee Sommerfeld, Walter Gropius, Frau Martin Wagner, Adolf Sommerfeld, Ise Gropius, and Martin Wagner (later Gropius's associate at the GSD).

unheralded; he entered the small circle of modernists, which included Isokon and the Modern Architecture Research Group, and began a small practice with Edwin Maxell Fry.[90]

After the summer travels, Hudnut discussed the results of his interviews with President Conant and forwarded to him biographical sketches of Mies and Gropius. Oud was soon dropped from consideration; he suffered from depression and his psychological condition may have been a factor in his elimination.[91] Hudnut's presentations of Mies and Gropius appeared to show little favoritism; however, Gropius's publications were noted, and Hudnut commented that in view of Mies's taciturn nature, Gropius might be a somewhat easier fellow overall. The two men were friends and colleagues: Gropius had invited Mies to head the Bauhaus in 1931, which he did for two turbulent years until it closed in June 1933, a victim of Gestapo harassment and lack of funds.[92]

As deliberations continued, Mies made a major blunder. Misunderstanding the intentional vagueness of Harvard's approach, he thought he had been offered the job in early September 1936. Hudnut informed him to the contrary; a formal request could be made only to the president of the university to offer a chair for a professor of design, and there was opposition to the appointment of a modernist architect.[93] Hudnut explained that to reduce the opposition, President Conant had suggested that there be two nominees. Mies replied on September 15 that he would accept the appointment, but would not be a candidate.[94] Hudnut testily answered that he had not intended that Mies consider himself an official candidate, but that he was only trying to ascertain if Mies would accept if he were nominated. Hudnut also informed Mies of further difficulties with licensing that would limit the work of a foreign architect—an obstacle that did not appear relevant in Hudnut's negotiations with Gropius.

Gropius now emerged as the main candidate. Nevertheless, he anticipated some difficulties, and on September 1, 1936, he began to move behind the scenes to solicit the support of a powerful ally, Pierre Jay, chairman of the Fiduciary Trust Company of New York.[95] This wealthy banker had helped Gropius in 1931 by trying to arrange for him to meet Dean William Boring, Hudnut's predecessor at Columbia.[96] Gropius asked Jay to encourage President Conant to support his nomination for an appointment because Gropius expected "resistance from the part of some rather old-fashioned colleagues who would principally contradict an appointment of a modern architect."[97] President Conant, however, had no objections to Gropius's appointment to Harvard, and Hudnut wrote Gropius that Conant would submit the nomination to the Harvard Corporation and Board of Overseers, "probably on December 1 [1936]."[98]

On November 16, 1936, Hudnut informed Mies that President Conant and members of the governing boards deemed it was "impracticable" to invite Mies to Harvard.[99] On the same day Hudnut also wrote to Alfred Barr, Jr., director of the Museum of Modern Art in New York, saying that Gropius was the "practicable" person because he had run a school and had an educational background. Although there is no precise indication of the reasons for the choice, Mies's misunderstanding of the search process, or his arrogance in refusing to be considered a candidate on a list of two, may have knocked him out of the running. Having lost at Harvard, Mies accepted a position to direct the architecture department at the Armour (later Illinois) Institute of Technology (IIT) in 1937 and the following year began his own translation of Bauhaus ideas, which differed from the Beaux-Arts model as well as from the collaborative model that Hudnut and Gropius would develop.[100]

President Conant began to canvas the opinions of the faculty in the Graduate School of Design about the possible appointment of Gropius; he elicited an overwhelming approval from the faculty, with two exceptions. Charles Killam cast the lone outright objection to Gropius; the engineering aesthetic of the new architecture represented by Gropius did not appeal to him.[101] The other exception was Henry Hubbard, who expressed a qualified approval. As chairman of the disintegrating program in planning, he feared that Gropius's appointment might threaten his department. He wrote President Conant a rambling, equivocal letter explaining that although he agreed with the fundamental principles of what Gropius called the "new architecture," to which any Beaux-Arts architect would subscribe, he had reservations about the models of German city planning.[102]

Hudnut told Gropius in England that there had been only one faculty vote against his nomination and no negative votes from the governing boards, concluding, "I am more than ever certain you are urgently needed in America."[103] Shortly thereafter, Hudnut wrote to Gropius to express his hopes for "the beginning of a new era in American architecture" and to articulate three objectives that he had in mind: "to obtain [Gropius's] collaboration in the study of the educational problem in American architecture as a whole, in the hope that we may devise a new and more rational program in our educational process"; to create a master's class of advanced students, "the best American students in Architecture," to be selected and taught by Gropius; and to reestablish an architectural practice for Gropius.[104] The "best American students" became the nucleus of the master's class for students pursuing the master's degree in architecture; Gropius would hand-pick the students of this elite group.

The general approval of the faculty prompted an official offer to Gropius, and in December 1936 he wired his acceptance and confirmed his thanks for the offer of a chair as professor of architecture.[105] After official confirmation, Gropius was appointed commencing April 1, 1937, though he assumed no named chair (Fig. 4.7).

What no one at Harvard realized was that Gropius's reputation as educator, author, architect, and founder of the Bauhaus had carried him through one of the most difficult periods of his career for the past several years.[106] The Bauhaus had closed in 1933; Gropius's situation in England in the mid-1930s was precarious. Though he had friends and supporters, the "new architecture" met with resistance there. Out of five projects designed by Gropius and his partner Maxwell Fry, including three apartment buildings and a residence hall for Christ College in Cambridge, only a community school and activities center at Impington (1936) was built, and it was heavily altered to fit its budget. Though Gropius never acknowledged as much, Harvard's offer virtually, if not literally, rescued his career and ultimately gave him a fame in America that he might never have known had he stayed in England.

Before his arrival, Gropius needed to make delicate arrangements to transfer his possessions from Germany to the United States. His relationship with the Nazi government was ambiguous; he had not gone to England as a refugee or renounced his citizenship, but he was now outside the regime—though his drawings and papers remained in Germany. President Conant telegrammed German officials to announce Gropius's appointment, which may have encouraged them to view Gropius's emigration to the United States and Harvard as signaling the supplanting of French influences by German ones, despite the censure of the Bauhaus. In any

case, Gropius was allowed to arrange for his papers and drawings to be transferred from Germany to America, where they were safely stored in Harvard's Busch-Reisinger Museum. Gropius and his wife set sail for America on March 12, 1937, aboard the cruise ship *Europa*, arriving five days later in New York, where a telegram from Hudnut greeted them: "Welcome to America where Happiness and Success await you."[107]

Meanwhile, at Harvard and beyond, approval of the appointment came from a variety of sources, including Alfred Barr, who had met Gropius ten years earlier.[108] Social and political figures even took note; Leverett Saltonstall, the renowned Boston lawyer and politician who would become governor of Massachusetts in 1939, inquired if Hudnut was hosting a welcome dinner for Gropius.[109] True to his word, Hudnut arranged for many dinners and other events designed to introduce Gropius and promote his reputation. Even before Gropius arrived, Hudnut, in a report to the university president, praised his major contributions to the field of architecture, such as his development of multiple dwellings, his widely accepted theories of design, and the Bauhaus—"the most important contribution to education technique of our profession . . . in recent years."[110]

The local and national press thoroughly covered Gropius's imminent arrival in America nine years after his first visit in 1928. At the announcement of his appointment, the *Boston Evening Transcript* wrote that Gropius was bringing modernism to Harvard; upon his

arrival, the *New York Times* sought his views on the American scene.[111] Publicity was central to Gropius's efforts to introduce modernism to America, and he responded to the media naturally and enthusiastically.

After Gropius arrived in New York, Hudnut arranged a round of introductions and presented Gropius to people of social, political, and financial importance. In the itinerary for New York, Hudnut even included a confidential memorandum that contained brief biographies of important dinner guests, a detail that reflected Hudnut's familiarity with prominent New Yorkers and members of the architectural press—all of whom considered Hudnut one of their own.[112] A similar round of introductions awaited Gropius when he arrived in Boston.

Once installed at Harvard, Hudnut arranged for Gropius to have his own secretary and an office in Hunt Hall. As for teaching assignments, Gropius would teach a studio course in the spring of 1937, with the assistance of Holmes Perkins, whom, Hudnut noted, "is very popular with the students and is genuinely in sympathy with your work. He is also widely known in Boston, here his family is a very old one, and I think that he would be of great help to you in many ways not directly associated with work at the School."[113]

In addition to providing the contact with Perkins, Hudnut also advised Gropius on appropriate ways to obtain architectural influence and commissions. At one point, Hudnut advised

4.7 Walter and Ise Gropius in 1937.

Gropius not to enter a competition: "I think you will have no chance with that jury. The competition will be seen by Ralph Adams Cram" (a leading proponent of traditional architecture and the Gothic style, in particular).[114] On another occasion, while suggesting that Gropius try to influence the design of the Littauer Center, the new building for the School of Public Administration at Harvard that was headed for the conservative firm of Shepley, Rutan & Coolidge, Hudnut reiterated to Gropius: "I believe you will be able—perhaps gradually, but surely—to effect a great reform there [at Harvard]."[115]

Hudnut later asked for Gropius's support in pushing forward the modernist agenda in a project of more national significance: the proposed Jefferson Memorial in Washington. Hudnut, a member of the committee responsible for selecting the architect, explained to Gropius: "I don't see any other way of making sure that modernism will have a fair chance of winning. [Richard J.] Neutra is the only man I can think of (except Wright) who is competent to judge modern architecture and who has enough strength of character to balance the really strong man who will have to be put on to represent the conservatives—unless you serve [on the committee]. . . . This is the first time modernism has had the slightest chance to build an important building in Washington."[116] Hudnut's aspirations in this instance did not succeed, but it was only one battle in a war that he and Gropius would ultimately win.

Gropius's Campaign for Modernism

Before Gropius had any commissions of his own, he began to clarify his intentions in public lectures and in the forum of the architectural press. The public often reacted enthusiastically, but the private responses were, at times, negative and acerbic. Shortly after arriving, Gropius lectured to the Boston Architectural Club on the "The Development of the New Architecture" and included slides of his own work.[117] The club members, comprising a group of local architects, many of whom were Harvard alumni, were repelled by Gropius's work, seeing not architecture but engineering; their disenfranchisement from Harvard began immediately.[118]

The following month Gropius launched a publishing campaign to explain his educational philosophy. One statement of his philosophy of design education—a brilliant ideological justification for, and explanation of, the program of the Bauhaus—appeared in the *American Architect and Architecture*. Gropius began by explaining how late-nineteenth-century progressives saw "the machine as the modern vehicle of form." The struggle to integrate the machine of industrialization into daily existence had caused the dissolution of the arts as a unified expression of social life and the community. The worship of art for its own sake, an obsession with business, and nostalgia for the past and its historical forms had replaced this unity. According to Gropius, a principal cause of these conditions was the rise of the academies, which had undermined the last Golden Age, the Middle Ages, when craftsmen and arts were united and bound by a common training in the workshop. Royal patronage had lifted practical restraints from the craftsman, swelled his ego to that of a genius, and consequently caused the death of "true national art."[119] Without a sense of community, badly designed goods became the impersonal result of manufacturing, and the subdivision of labor and consequent loss of creative control had enfeebled life itself.

For Gropius, the solution to this detrimental situation lay in collaboration: "a collective form of labor [that] can lead humanity to a greater total efficiency."[120] Here was the intersection of his long-standing educational philosophy and the goals of the educational program at Harvard. Regardless of the fact that America never had academies; regardless of the traditions, practical considerations, and local conditions that generated the motivation for a Graduate School of Design; when Gropius heard of the program of collaboration between the fields of design, an entirely intellectual, preformed construct must surely have resonated in him. After all, in founding the Bauhaus he had already created a successful, if controversial, model.

The Bauhaus, Gropius explained, was based on the belief that the machine would liberate people from the oppression of labor and thereby open the space for creative impulses, and that its educational programs of theoretical and manual

training would lead to creative industrial production. Necessary for this production was learning "a special language of shape" and a scientific theory of "objectively valid optical facts." This common visual language and theory of knowledge was paramount to the creation of a harmonious collective design. The academy should have provided this theory of the visual arts, but since it had not, it had fallen to the Bauhaus to determine the grammar of proportion, optical illusions, and colors. The practice and investigation of these "natural laws" would further the emergence of a "true tradition" more than imitation would.[121]

Gropius described the training program at the Bauhaus with its emphasis on optical qualities, spatial sense, and manual skills, and the crucial "preliminary training" in design and handicrafts.[122] He then proposed its principles as a universal system of education for America from the earliest training of the child to advanced technical education. Gropius considered U.S. education to be flawed: children were exposed to basic art materials in kindergarten, and some might take an art course in high school, but no real art education was conducted across the school years. Consequently, when students reached college, they had little artistic knowledge, not to mention development. He saw rectifying this situation as the responsibility of the entire community: "It is an urgent problem as to how the generation should be taught and influenced for this common task from the beginning and how the State could intervene."[123]

The German architect called for no less than a "homogeneous fundamental" training in all the schools in America—an exhortation that revealed both the fervor of his convictions and their inherent limitations. Although logically argued, his promotion of a national system of education displayed a misunderstanding of the autonomous and democratic forces that formulate the varieties of the American system. In the first place, his idealistic belief in the universality of visual laws that would unite people in creative efforts ignored the cultural relativity of aesthetic sensibilities and the absence of scientific proof that such universal laws even existed. Secondly, Gropius fundamentally misunderstood the American system of government. He was accustomed to the central authority of the German state and assumed that, in America as in Germany, there was a national mandate determining the content of educational systems. He did not realize that there were national standards of education only in the broadest sense, and that local and state conditions, supported by democratic process, exerted tremendous influence—for better or worse—over the content of curricula. This misunderstanding led Gropius to form a grandiose belief in the general applicability of *his* system of education—a belief that also reflected his ignorance of the unique conditions at Harvard.

Gropius's second statement, published in *Architectural Record,* concerned the future of architecture at Harvard. It was clear, articulate, concise, noble, irre-futable in principle, and even tinged with humility. Gropius began by praising the extraordinary systems of construction, the enormous scale, bold planning, and amazing technical perfection in America. In light of these developments, and since Gropius only knew America directly from a previous visit in 1928, he would be a student as well as a teacher. He vowed not to introduce a style—a "Gropius architecture"—but rather approaches applicable to particular problems: "I want a young architect to be able to find his way whatever the circumstances; I want him independently to create true, genuine forms out of the technical, economical and social conditions in which he finds himself instead of imposing a learned formula onto surroundings which may call for an entirely different solution."[124]

Gropius then clarified some misunderstandings concerning his work. Instead of being merely "the peak of rationalization and mechanization," his work also emphasized a "new spatial vision" over structural economy and the perfection of function, and sought beauty—"perfect proportions and colors in a well-balanced harmony." Architecture for Gropius was expansive, not reductive, "a projection of life itself and that implies an intimate knowledge of biological, social, technical and artistic problems." This design method required a patient search for intellectually derived forms, in contrast to the process of traditional architects who relied on a miscellany of styles. Despite the fact that the field of education was limited in the degree to which it could foster inculcation of the strong character necessary to achieve this unity, the goal was to produce men of vision and to save them from becoming "absorbed too early into the narrow channels of specialization."[125]

Here was the power of the modern polemic in its most articulate form, reasoned and reasonable, too well intended and too general to raise suspicion, so artfully expressed that one could easily agree that the "learned formula" of the irrelevant past stood in the way of creativity. Having traveled partway around the world to Cambridge, Gropius at last found a colleague in arms. Together, Joseph Hudnut and Walter Gropius were ready to wage a war for modern architecture.

THE CRUSADE FOR MODERNISM,
1936–1944

5.1 Joseph Hudnut and Walter Gropius, May 1942.

Walter Gropius and Joseph Hudnut forged a modern, unified approach to design at Harvard that resembled a war, replete with battles, victories, and defeats. Hudnut began to dismantle parts of the educational establishment and to implement a new training for future practitioners of the "new architecture." Gropius settled into an American scene where he explored the possibilities of inculcating the rational principles of his ideology. For the moment, a jointly held belief in the power of collaboration propelled both as partners in the creation of a radically modern design education (Fig. 5.1). Nevertheless, it took ten years for the new collaborative programs in both the university and the Graduate School of Design to reach their optimal levels. Three phases divided this development: the first between 1936 and 1939, during which Hudnut and Gropius made their first plans for the GSD; the second during war emergency conditions from 1940 to 1944 during which their initial program was set aside; and the third from 1945 to 1952, the apogee of collaborative education at Harvard.

The Crusade for Modernism

In its first academic year, 1936–37, the GSD underwent changes, both before and after Gropius's arrival. There was a new kind of master's degree in architecture; and a new master studio, intended to simulate the conditions of a professional office, was begun under Haffner for one semester in the fall of 1936, then taken over by Gropius during mid-spring of 1937. Gropius personally selected the students, the first group of which came from nineteen different architectural schools—a sign of the widespread notice, via the press, of Gropius's arrival.[1] In 1937–38, Gropius's first full year, enrollment in the famed master's class soared by more than 100 percent and it soon became a training ground for numerous future practitioners.

Gropius's first class indicated the direction his design program would follow. He and Holmes Perkins gave students the problem of designing public housing to surround Fresh Pond in Cambridge. Circumscribed by strict requirements that each dwelling unit should have sun for at least two hours every day and that each should have a view, the optimal solution became long rows of tall buildings, all with the same orientation. These buildings resembled the *Zeilenbau* that Gropius and other German architects had proposed as solutions for mass housing. The basic elements of the problem—consciousness of the large-scale needs for economical mass housing and rational design requirements of light and view—set the tone for subsequent problems.

The study of housing types embodied the modernist goal of harnessing architecture to a social agenda. In both the bachelor's and the master's program the new emphasis on housing as a means of improving social conditions paralleled the reality-based efforts to incorporate con-

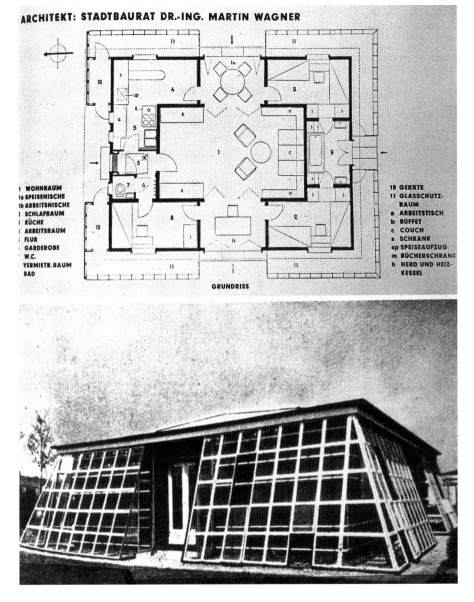

ARCHITEKT: STADTBAURAT DR.-ING. MARTIN WAGNER

1 WOHNRAUM
1a SPEISENISCHE
1b ARBEITSNISCHE
I SCHLAFRAUM
I KÜCHE
I ARBEITSRAUM
I FLUR
I GARDEROBE
W.C.
VERMIETB. RAUM
BAD

10 GERÄTE
11 GLASSCHUTZ-
RAUM
a ARBEITSTISCH
b BÜFFET
c COUCH
s SCHRANK
sp SPEISEAUFZUG
m BÜCHERSCHRANK
h HERD UND HEIZ-
KESSEL

GRUNDRISS

5.2 Ecological, economical house, Martin Wagner, 1932. From his book *Das wachsende Haus* (The Evolving House).

struction, engineering, and professional practice into design studios. Students could now experience professional architectural practice during at least six months of their academic training. The return to courses such as statics, algebra, and graphics, offered in the university's Department of Engineering, ironically reversed the intentions of the original founders of the School of Architecture, for whom architecture was a cultural phenomenon that included mathematics but went beyond them.

Another significant indication of the socially directed agenda of the new modernist education was the appearance of "Site and Shelter," the first course that dealt with design implications of broad issues. Offered to both graduate and undergraduate students, it became an immediate requirement for all bachelor's degree candidates in architecture, landscape architecture, and planning. Taught by Martin Wagner, a recent émigré from Germany, the purpose of the course was "to give a general understanding of man's many activities in planning, building, the design of outdoor areas, and their mutual relationships."[2] An ardent socialist in Germany, Wagner had been the chief city planner of Berlin, directing its vast escalation in public housing.[3] His research focused on ascertaining maximum density levels for cities and rational urban organization; and he had also published designs for economical *and* ecological houses in 1932 (Fig. 5.2). For models of total control of land and economy, Wagner looked to Soviet planning. However, his career in

5.3 MW house, plan view. Martin Wagner, 1939. From "A Fresh Approach to Housing," *Architectural Forum* 74 (February 1941).

5.4 Project, Martin Wagner, 1940. "A Fresh Approach to Housing," *Architectural Forum* 74 (February 1941).

Germany ended under political pressure from the Nazis: in 1933, he was expelled from the Deutscher Werkbund at the same time that Gropius was removed from its Board of Directors. Wagner came to Harvard in 1938, after spending three years in Turkey. He was one of several associates and friends whom Gropius and his wife assisted in their flight from Nazi Germany as refugees.

In America, Wagner continued to search for rational forms of mass housing, using technology to produce primary forms. In 1939 he designed a prefabricated dwelling, the MW House; in 1940, another scheme followed whose units, resembling aluminum igloos, could be clustered (Figs. 5.3, 5.4).[4] Wagner was motivated to search for dwellings whose forms were not bound by tradition and whose construction would lend itself to mass production. Underlying such projects was the assumption that new forms would support the new way of life in an egalitarian society.

Wagner's course included the study of typical designs for shelter from the elemental forces of wind, water, heat, cold, fire, smoke, and noise. The course also explored how earthquakes, traffic, and air raids affect buildings.[5] Using prefabrication and the planning principles of the Garden City movement, Wagner intended to show how societal and economic problems influenced the shape and construction of houses, towns, and regions. These topics represented a search for first principles reached through analytical inquiry. The process of design, not style, was

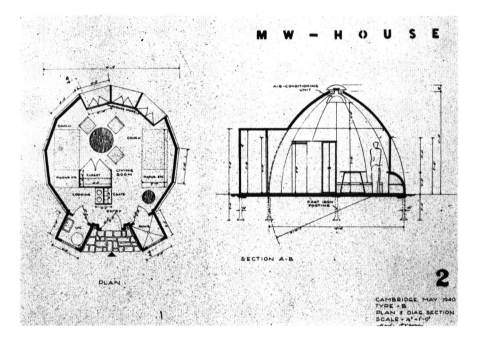

paramount—a position that reflected the fundamental modern ethos embedded in attempts to respond to a new social and economic environment and that subverted all traditions that put style before other considerations.

Implementation of the new graduate-level architecture curriculum involved a complicated three-year-long process of restructuring the course work. The previous master's degree program was converted to the professional bachelor's degree in architecture in 1936–37. The changes that followed showed a continued emphasis on shifting the study of drawing and history out of the GSD to make way for the new modernist curriculum. New courses like "Site and Shelter" continued to supplant traditional ones; "Contemporary Architecture," taught by Hudnut, replaced Haffner's more traditional course on the theory of composition and the former course on professional practice. An attempt to include construction and professional practice courses in a design sequence failed; there was too much material to be taught in a studio. As a consequence, the design and engineering courses were restructured during 1939 and 1940. While intermediate and advanced design still included aspects of building construction and professional practice, separate courses were reinstated in construction and architectural engineering, and new courses were created to teach construction problem resolution and to provide practical experience in construction, including a minimum of three months' experience in the field.

The study of history and drawing was deemphasized to make way for new requirements. The prerequisite of three history courses—ancient, medieval, and Renaissance architecture—became two courses on the history of architecture and one in site planning; thus, six courses were reduced to three. Drawing courses were even more reduced to allow expansion of practical, "realistic" study of engineering and construction; the longstanding courses in archeological reconstruction, life drawing, and modeling in clay were eliminated. Fine arts courses in drawing and theory of design, theory and practice of design, and descriptive geometry were replaced by one course in architectural sciences, "Descriptive Geometry and Its Applications." The prerequisites in the Department of Fine Arts were reduced and replaced by courses in the new undergraduate Department of Architectural Sciences, taught by Hudnut and his faculty.

Hudnut's new Department of Architectural Sciences was the undergraduate companion program to the GSD. Accomplishing the creation of the new reality-oriented graduate programs depended on undergraduates obtaining a broad liberal arts education to provide a cultural foundation for advanced training in modern design.[6] This policy made it possible to transfer the "culture courses" from the graduate to the undergraduate level of the liberal arts program, thereby providing the time and space for the reality-oriented courses on professional training at the graduate level. Hudnut developed the

department over two years and placed it within Harvard College where it would be a combined effort of the faculties of fine arts and design: its curriculum included courses in the history of art and architecture, fine arts, drawing, basic design, and an introduction to architecture. Interestingly, it took some finesse to obtain approval for this new program. Harvard had already rejected a proposal to establish a Department of Geology on the grounds that it was too pre-professional for the liberal arts curriculum—but it *had* approved a Department of *Geological Sciences.* Hudnut grasped the nuance needed and created the term *architectural sciences* for his program.[7]

When the program in architectural sciences was officially announced in 1938–39, its stated purposes were to organize a scholarly survey of general knowledge underlying the professions of design and to establish the "habits of thought and vision" essential to success in the professions. As part of the regular Harvard undergraduate programs, it combined courses in the student's major with courses not immediately related to the central field of interest. Pointedly, the announcement noted that the program contained only one course in professional studies, an introductory studio class in architectural design. Seven courses were initially offered as architectural sciences: two on the history of architecture and planning, a course on landscape architecture, two studio courses on the theory and practice of design, a course on descriptive geometry, and one professional studio in architectural design (which counted as a double course).[8]

To facilitate implementation of the new undergraduate program, the GSD had already established a special design studio on the second floor of Hunt Hall. "Productive work"—using their hands to draw and to make objects—supplemented theory, an idea John Dewey would have loved. Despite the emphasis on production and manual work, Hudnut stressed that "[it] is not intended that the study of history and the critical analysis of works of art should be neglected, but rather that these studies should be united with a practical experience with tools, techniques, and the processes of assembling and shaping materials."[9] Hudnut provided the intellectual and financial resources to make the Department of Architectural Sciences—or *Arc Sci*, as it was later nicknamed—a reality. Much of the funding and several of the faculty for it came from the Graduate School of Design. As a testimony to his conviction about the importance of the program, Hudnut assumed the chairmanship and responsibility, with Kenneth Conant, of teaching undergraduates the history of architecture and planning. The program became very popular in Harvard College: once created, the new department grew from 9 students in 1941 to 116 immediately after the war, and it averaged between 75 and 85 students until a new program superseded it in 1968.[10]

As seen from his interest in this undergraduate program and his writing during the 1930s, Hudnut had started to define the role of history, in the context of modernism, as it should be pursued in America. His position had two basic premises: historical models should not be replicated in the contemporary world, and the principles of history should form part of a student's liberal arts education and be studied *prior* to professional training. History was, in this model, still an important part of designers' education—just not a part of their professional training. Hudnut's conviction about the role of history was demonstrated by his teaching the subject himself. Initially, while Kenneth Conant was on sabbatical in 1935–36, he taught post-Renaissance architecture, which one student recalled as "broad-based and ruminative."[11] He then taught a course on contemporary architecture (1937–47). For him there was no conflict in being both a modernist and an historian.

Another key factor in modernist education at Harvard was the establishment of workshops that offered the practical experience of working with building materials and studying manufacturing processes associated with buildings and landscape construction. These workshops, offered in the Graduate School of Design, were intended to supplement the studio courses offered in Harvard College, thereby linking graduate and undergraduate programs. The workshops also would bring the teaching of design closer to reality, as desired by Hudnut, by exposing students to the materials and methods of production and by providing them with the hand skills that Gropius had considered fundamental to basic training at the Bauhaus. Experimenting with wood, stone, and glass would replace the traditional arts of drawing, modeling, and painting. The approach had drawbacks, however, as few buildings were then being made of stone, and wood frame construction was concealed in a finished building. The pedagogical intent was to encourage the potential usage of such materials in design rather than their literal incorporation.

Hudnut reported to President Conant at the close of GSD's second year that the most urgent priority was implementing the workshops. He also pointed out that practical training had met with great success during the preceding year: the standard of work in design and building construction had, in his opinion, never been higher, and students and faculty were "working together with unfailing optimism."[12] The design programs focused on buildings that could actually be built in practice instead of fantasy projects. Studio work expanded to include field trips, the direct study of building operations, and factory processes (although these were unspecified). And the "new and more realistic methods" were producing a "new character" of design, seen not only in the vitality of regular student work but even in the work of the summer school students under Walter Bogner (Figs. 5.5, 5.6).[13]

In his annual report of 1937–38 President Conant, reiterating Hudnut's positive reports, praised Gropius's success: "Under his guidance and with the assistance of able collaborators, the School of Design has become the leading center in

5.5 Walter F. Bogner instructing summer school, 1935.

5.6 GSD summer school project, 1938.

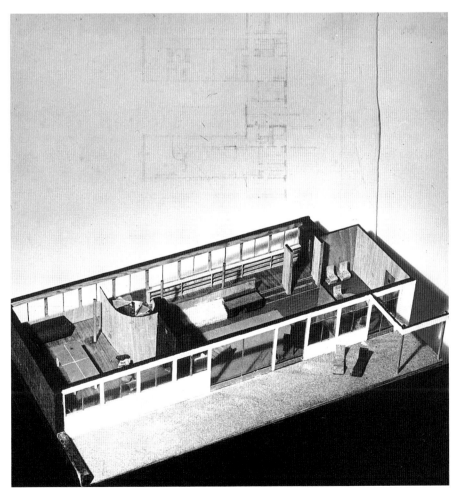

this country, if not in the world, for the development of what is commonly referred to as modern architecture."[14] According to Conant, this success was due to the unified curriculum of the Graduate School of Design, which led to the master's degree of architecture, and to the increased practical character of courses in the techniques of integrating building construction and design. The curriculum reflected the latest technology and was effective because the graduate students were being "hand-tooled."[15]

President Conant also pointed out the innovation of creating the Department of Architectural Sciences that not only could prepare students in Harvard College for entry into the School of Design but also could provide an educational scope appropriate to a liberal arts college. Conant paid the GSD the high compliment of comparing its development to programs in biochemical sciences, or engineering sciences, which had long provided a preliminary education for Harvard undergraduates who eventually became scientists or professional engineers through graduate study. Underlying this view was the premise that the quality of the student and the length of education helped ensure career success as much as a practical approach to a field of study.

But while Hudnut and President Conant proclaimed an immediate success for the reality-oriented graduate architecture programs and the new undergraduate architectural sciences program, a difficult impediment still blocked the creation of a unified school from three design disciplines: in the first year of the amalgamated school, 1936–37, the city planning program offered no courses and accepted no new students. Hudnut had to report that the department chairman had to sanction independent work for two students because he had no expertise in their fields of interest. The only alternative for the students was to transfer to another school—a situation of acute embarrassment for Hubbard.

The hiatus lasted one year. In September 1937 the planning program reopened as the Department of Regional Planning, a new name that emphasized its approach to issues that extended beyond the peripheries of cities and towns. Accompanying the name change was a revised curriculum requiring courses in economic principles, municipal government, statistics, and theory for all students who had not studied these subjects in college. The growing involvement of the federal government in regional planning and the expansion of the field of planning to a scale much larger than the city necessitated familiarity with these subjects. The study of horticulture and planting design, which had been required for city planning, was eliminated, but planning students still were involved with design issues even as their domain of study expanded. They also studied principles of construction, as taught in the Department of Landscape Architecture, and their design studios benefited from support courses in drawing and engineering courses that dealt with infrastructure.

With this new beginning in 1937, the program appeared to have recovered from the lack of funding that halted its operations.[16] Research projects by Arthur Comey, Hubbard's recently graduated student, Max S. Wehrly, and Howard K. Menhinick, among others, progressed fitfully.[17] Enrollment remained low: eight students were enrolled in its first new year of operation, and seven the next year, while landscape architecture had 24 students and architecture had 25.[18] Nevertheless, the Department of Regional Planning had worked with the other departments on collaborative problems, and Hubbard dutifully avowed that his department looked "forward eagerly" to more extensive collaboration in the following year.[19]

The Department of Landscape Architecture underwent none of the conceptual or structural upheavals of the planning and architecture programs; however, it too existed on borrowed time. Despite low enrollment and a budget reduced to support programs in architecture, enthusiasm about the profession of landscape architecture remained high: all recent graduates in landscape architecture had jobs related to the field, and commissions for park designs were abundant. Indeed, two graduates reported the extraordinary annual income of $30,000.[20] According to Hudnut, landscape architecture adopted the approach of bringing students into direct contact with aspects of professional practice, as exemplified by the field trip to the North Shore where designs and topography were studied. However, the claim for the novelty of this practice meant little, given that site visits had been introduced in 1900. New courses in freehand drawing remedied the deficiency in the subject that Pond had predicted a few years earlier. Consistent with the new policy in the architecture program, students who had no previous experience in drawing and art had to take fine arts courses in Harvard College. Compared to the overhaul that architecture programs underwent, the Department of Landscape Architecture appeared to exist in a state of superficial tranquillity—which would soon dissolve, as students reacted against the status quo.

In the midst of this atmosphere of change, the old guard departed. Charles Killam ended his twenty-eight-year career in 1937; H. Dudley Murphy, a traditional artist who had studied at the Académie Julian in Paris as a pupil of Jean Paul Laurens and of Benjamin Constant, whose landscapes and watercolors had received medals, and who had taught freehand drawing since 1902, was obliged to resign without emeritus status—Hudnut ignored his protests.[21] John Humphreys remained to represent the original foundations of the design programs, and he was to retire, as emeritus professor, during 1944–45; only his student, Walter Bogner, remained from the old school, and he had crossed into the modernist camp.[22]

Although the GSD was operating at a deficit, Hudnut added faculty members whose work supported Gropius. The new wave of arrivals included Paul Willard Norton, who was appointed instructor of building construction but resigned after

Gropius, and the cooperation between them had within it all the benefits and antagonisms that accrue to most partnerships. From the start of Gropius's career, with the 1911 design of the Fagus Shoe Last Factory in Alfeld, Germany, with Adolf Meyer, Gropius had relied on collaborators.[27]

Exhibitions, Student Projects, and Collaborative Endeavors

Students in the late 1930s benefited from exposure to two worlds: the vestiges of the Beaux-Arts traditions—transformed into art deco and the streamlined designs of *art moderne*—and the austerity and rigor of the modernist architecture coming from Europe. Exhibitions and lectures at the GSD exemplify these dual intellectual forces. In 1936–37, for example, the diverse exhibition schedule included a display of photographs and models from the offices of the Olmsted Brothers; Arthur A. Shurcliff, who had taught at Harvard at the turn of the century and still lectured during the year; his son Sidney N. Shurcliff; Vitale & Geiffert, designers of beautiful Italianate gardens; and Gilmore D. Clarke, dean of landscape architecture at Cornell. Other exhibitions displayed the work of H. H. Richardson (organized by Henry-Russell Hitchcock); European posters; drawings for government housing developments at the new town of Greenbelt, Maryland; photographs of new architecture in Mexico; and color prints illustrating the work of living American artists. During the same academic year, visiting

only two years; Samuel F. Hershey, instructor of freehand drawing; and Robert G. Scott, instructor of drawing. Bogner and Comey were promoted from assistant to associate professors. Finally, the teaching of modern construction was pursued with the appointment of Jean Georges Peter, a graduate of the Harvard engineering school, as an assistant professor.[23]

Most importantly, Hudnut hired Marcel Breuer, the Hungarian architect and former Bauhaus student and instructor. Breuer's successful career in Germany was interrupted when, like Gropius, he fled Germany for London in 1934. Despite a precarious appointment and salary, Breuer arrived at the GSD in early 1938 as research associate in design.[24] Although Breuer's architecture was relatively unknown in America, Hudnut described him as "widely known as a writer on architecture and also as an industrial designer," referring to Breuer's designs for chairs made from tubular steel. At the end of the spring semester in 1938, Breuer organized an exhibition of his own work using photographs and models

that aroused wide interest during Harvard's commencement.[25]

The nearly immediate American publication of Breuer's work in *Architectural Record* showed an approach to modernism that distinguished him from the emulators of the most austere, objective, and planar styles. His project for a small ski hotel in the Austrian Alps was intended "to prove that modern forms are not dependent on steel, glass, concrete, or cantilevered balconies, and that modern architecture is based on a mentality, an approach to planning, and not on a certain technique."[26] In his project, all load-bearing walls and partitions were stone, and the window walls were made of wood so light that they needed no steel or concrete lintels over the strip windows (Fig. 5.7).

In late summer of 1938 Hudnut secured funding to recommend Breuer's more permanent appointment as associate professor. Breuer had demonstrated his abilities as a teacher and researcher, had received the unanimous endorsement of the faculty, and was popular with the students. He had also entered into a professional partnership with

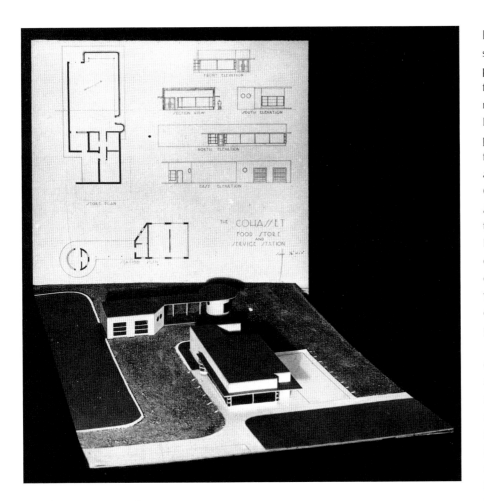

5.8 Cohasset gas station, student project designed under Walter F. Bogner, 1938.

lecturers emphasized more clearly the school's growing connection to the European modern movement: Josef Albers, from Black Mountain College and a former instructor of basic design at the Bauhaus; and Walter Curt Behrendt, a planner and architectural critic ousted from Germany in 1933, who had received a position at Dartmouth College.[28] Gropius hoped that Hudnut would offer Albers a teaching position at Harvard and thereby reinforce his own efforts to bring Bauhaus methodologies to a new basic design course.[29] Hudnut, however, declined to make this appointment, which would have only served to further emphasize the Bauhaus-based approaches of Gropius's reign.

In the following years, exhibits of modern architecture became more prominent at Harvard, as seen in the show "British Architecture Today" and an exhibition of architecture from the U.S.S.R., sent to the school by the American Russian Institute (both 1937–38). The heterogeneous schedule continued, though, showcasing the relationship between modern architecture and modern housing in an exhibit circulated by the U. S. Housing Authority and in an exhibition of drawings and maps of the Tennessee Valley Authority (both 1938–39). Among visiting lecturers, *émigré* European modernists appeared with more frequency: Richard J. Neutra, the Viennese-born architect who had worked with Frank Lloyd Wright and practiced in Los Angeles; German-born Albers; and Gunnar Asplund from the Stockholm Institute of Technology. Finnish

architect Alvar Aalto also lectured in November 1938, in conjunction with an exhibit of his furniture and decorative arts designs.[30] Despite the school's increasing modernist voice, the lectures given by Robert LaMontagne Saint-Hubert during 1937–38 kept alive, temporarily, the presence of the École des Beaux-Arts.

Students' work reflected this eclectic intellectual atmosphere. For example, a project that combined a food store and gas station for Cohasset, Massachusetts, was, at once, a forerunner of the convenience stores of the future and a demonstration of the transitional character of modern architecture in general (Fig. 5.8). The design displayed a new building type that leaned towards functionalism yet had the curving forms and porthole windows of American modern architecture. Emphasis on the pragmatics of construction—a cornerstone of modernist doctrine—can be seen in the framing model of a small studio residence by another student in his 1939 project (Fig. 5.9). The structural complexity was no advance on the rigorous methods taught by the old guard engineer Walter Killam, but the use of models as a tool of design became increasingly important.

A group of projects by student Robert A. Little demonstrates, in microcosm, the journey from the realm of an eclectic American modernism to a radical European modernism. His designs for a hydroelectric station (highlighting a locomotive, the icon of modern speed and efficiency), for a railroad station, and for a modest lodge still reflect an architecture of mass, of volumes whose solidity is

reinforced by the curving of corners (Figs. 5.10–5.12). These aggregated cubes are relieved only by the piercing band of horizontal windows. In his project for a School of Design, Little reveals his familiarity (like that of many of his peers) with European modernism (Figs. 5.13–5.15). The surfaces of his design school are fields of windows, screens for light, that illuminate the interior of the building, just as in the most advanced modern factories in Germany, or in the Bauhaus at Dessau itself. Rendered in light gray and blue, highlighted with touches of white gouache, this project, like all his early designs, is vibrant with polychromed buildings of solid mass.

Little's thesis, a house for his father, shows how the new European modernist

aesthetic continued to replace American art deco and streamlined *art moderne* (Figs. 5.16, 5.17). Submitted in January 1939, it immediately conveys the rationality of the new architecture in the regular grid of the floor plan. The solar angles indicated on the plans testify to the scheme's rational adaptation to climate. Here, in embryonic form, was an architecture that denied mass in a search for an architecture of space. As seen in their rendered interiors, these spaces have only a few details in color, utilizing instead the spare details of a machine aesthetic, as in the railings made of industrial metal. These details are part of an architecture of surfaces without moldings, of floors without patterns or carpet; a rectilinear architecture, the linearity of which is inter-

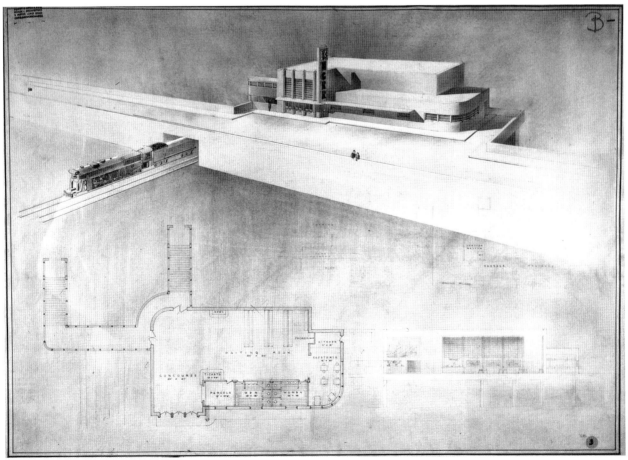

5.10 (opposite top) Project for a power station. Robert A. Little, 1938.

5.11 (opposite bottom) Project for a railway station. Robert A. Little, 1938.

5.12 a,b Project for a lodge. Robert A. Little, 1939.

rupted only by a curving partial wall opposite the entry. Emblematic of this modernist aesthetic is the replacement of double-hung windows—the "guillotine" of traditional architecture, in the words of Frank Lloyd Wright—with a casement window that cranked outward.

Only one feature of the modernist checklist of design elements is missing from Little's thesis: the interpenetration of spaces in the vertical dimension. In Little's project economic factors allowed no double-height spaces. He attempted to lighten the mass of his buildings, to "dematerialize" them, but instead his walls appear merely as voids defined by outlines. Clearly, the transition from the architecture of mass and volume to the expanding space of the modernist aesthetic was difficult for the student (as it was for many practitioners) to master.

Beyond the design of individual buildings, the test of the philosophy of unified design at the GSD can be found in the revival and revision of collaborative problems between 1936 and 1939. Much to its credit, the Department of Landscape Architecture attempted to embrace the collaborative spirit by proposing a joint problem with the Departments of Architecture and Regional Planning. The subject was a housing group with an adjoining recreational park, executed by six teams of five advanced students: three architects, a landscape architect, and a regional planner. The results, according to Pond, showed that the three departments were indeed capable of collaborating; Holmes Perkins, however, thought

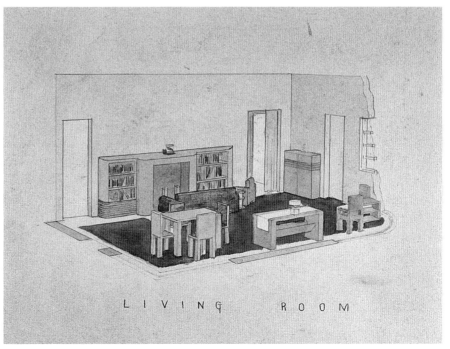

LIVING ROOM

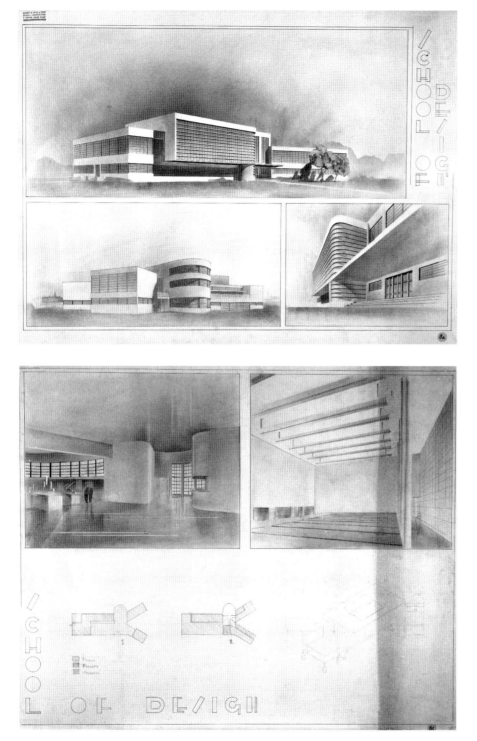

5.13 Project for a School of Design. Robert A. Little, 1939.

5.14 Project for a School of Design. Robert A. Little, 1939.

that these first-phase efforts lacked seriousness.[31]

The regional planning students, though few in number and in an underfinanced department, showed their particular approach by participating in a problem to study the control of roadside development in New Hampshire. Their job was to provide an analysis of conditions in the state, beginning with an assessment of land, water resources, population, economy, and government—all of which pointed to New Hampshire's favorable role in recreation. The students recognized that the stimulus for development—the automobile and its potential for personal high-speed travel—was also a threat to conservation. Acknowledging that new links between time and space defined the modern world, one student observed that "the auto has brought and makes possible still further changes in established time-space concepts. When the automobile gets a suitable living space, the human being will have a new living space. In this new living space New Hampshire may well be as much in the nature of a backyard to metropolitan Boston as it is now a summer refuge of seclusion."[32] The writer was prescient: New Hampshire became a backyard for many New England urbanites.

In their final report the planning students called for a program of education to inform both visitors and residents (particularly untrained members of local planning boards) about licensing regulations to control health conditions, trailer accommodations and the visual appear-

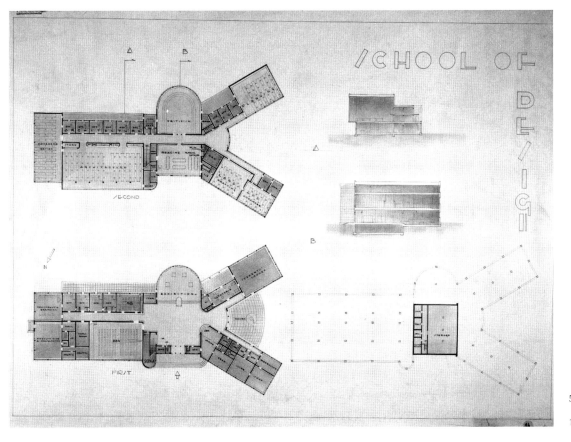

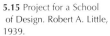

5.15 Project for a School of Design. Robert A. Little, 1939.

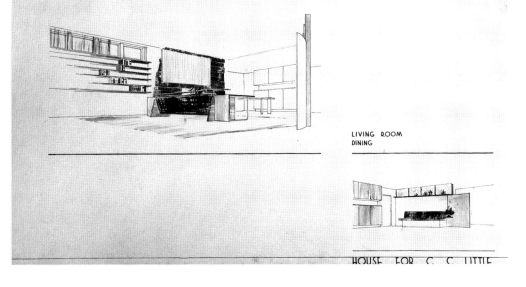

LIVING ROOM
DINING

5.16 House for C. C. Little, Robert A. Little, 1939. Arch. master's thesis project.

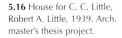

5.17 House for C. C. Little, Robert A. Little, 1939. Arch. master's thesis project.

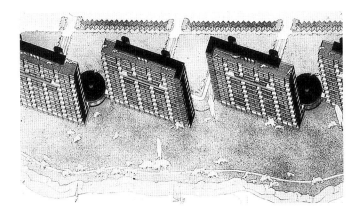

5.18 *Zeilenbau,* proposals for mass housing. Walter Gropius, 1931.

5.19 South Boston housing project and residential park. Collaborative problem, 1939. Model created by student group 2.

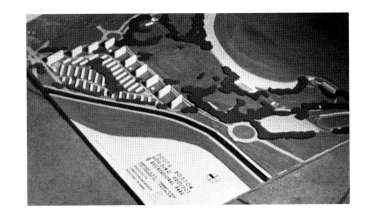

5.20 South Boston housing project and residential park. Collaborative problem, 1939. Model created by student group 4: Robert Ashland Sundt, Ulrich Weil, Architecture; Elkan W. Groll, Dean Newton Glick, Landscape Architecture; Millard Humstone, Regional Planning.

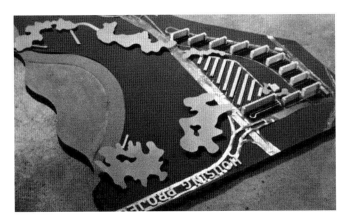

5.21 South Boston housing project and residential park. Collaborative problem, 1939. Model created by student group 3: John F. Kausal, William B. Tabler, Robert B. Murphy, Architecture; Wiley T. Jones, Landscape Architecture; Angel E. Nakpil, Regional Planning.

5.22 (opposite top) Apartment house block, South Boston housing project and residential park, perspective. Group 3 architects: William B. Tabler, Robert B. Murphy, and Paul F. Schelp, 1939.

5.23 (opposite bottom) Apartment house block, South Boston housing project and residential park, plan and elevations. Group 3 architects: William B. Tabler, Robert B. Murphy, and Paul F. Schelp, 1939.

ance of the juncture between the road and the landscape, highway zoning, easement purchases, "title" purchases along roads, and new rights of way. These recommendations, while unsophisticated and lacking in complex statistical or graphic analyses, made sense and could be easily understood and translated into the solution to the collaborative design problem.

One collaborative project that did net striking results was for a housing project and recreational park in South Boston. The site soon became a revisited location for studio projects, just as Fresh Pond in Cambridge had been a favorite subject of the old schools. Several teams, consisting of landscape architects, architects, and planners, provided alternatives with slight variations. One team elaborated the sports facilities of the complex and provided a mix of high- and low-rise housing units. Another team elaborated the access to the development by providing a complex cloverleaf intersection at the feeder road to the site. Another iconic form, or stylistic marker, of the period appeared in the treatment of landscape features as amoeboid organic shapes to represent trees. All the projects used slab buildings reminiscent of the German *Zeilenbau* (Figs. 5.18–5.21). This building type can be seen in the design by the architecture students—William B. Tabler, Robert B. Murphy, and Paul F. Schelp—who even signed their elevation drawing as if they were a professional firm. Ten stories high and flat-roofed, their buildings provided minimum accommodations for occupants

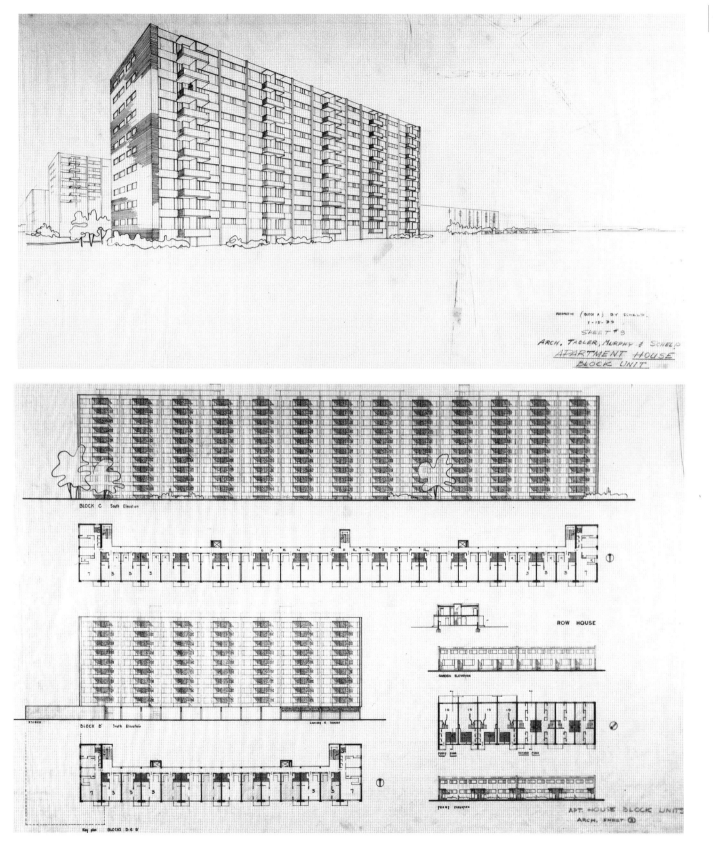

PERSPECTIVE (BLOCK A) BY SCHELIP.
1-15-39
SHEET #9
ARCH. TABLER, MURPHY & SCHELIP
APARTMENT HOUSE
BLOCK UNIT

BLOCK C   South Elevation

OPEN CORRIDOR

BLOCK B'   South Elevation

Key plan   BLOCKS B & B'

ROW HOUSE

GARDEN ELEVATION

FIRST FLOOR   SECOND FLOOR

FRONT ELEVATION

APT. HOUSE BLOCK UNITS
ARCH. SHEET 8

and small balconies of little use. However, having the corridors single-loaded, with apartments only on one side of the hallways, reduced the overall density of the buildings (Figs. 5.22, 5.23). These schemes foreshadowed the mass housing of the future; indeed, the flat-roofed apartment slab became an icon for mass housing in the post-war era.

Hudnut's March for Modernism

The fledgling collaborative problems were but one sign of deep structural changes occurring not only in the amalgamation of architecture, landscape architecture, and city planning schools but in Harvard itself. Within the institution, the changes were more complicated and subtle than a mere conflict between an "old school" and an avant-garde. One kind of teacher was on the way out and along with this departure went a whole tone and atmosphere. The conservative gentleman scholar who often had deep Harvard or New England roots was being replaced by the teacher as an ideologue: a fervent disciple, often from the "outside" (meaning New York or Europe), who dispensed with tradition and orthodoxy in the pursuit of a vision based on social commitment and the implementation of a curriculum based on actual practice.

Paralleling the replacement of American aristocratic scholars by European radicals was the rejection of everything associated with the traditions of the École des Beaux-Arts. Although criticism of the methods of the École had been a distin-

guishing feature of the Harvard program from the turn of the century, outright rejection of the École spread throughout the American architectural profession during the 1920s, reaching a crescendo by 1936. The *realpolitik* of the modernist curriculum required the defamation of the preceding generation, which consisted largely of the claim that the Beaux-Arts had nothing to offer the modern design professions. The polemic against it asserted that students educated under its system were deficient in engineering studies, knowledge of building techniques, and facility in construction. In other words, the Beaux-Arts system produced only paper architects whose designs could not be built.

At Harvard this claim could be justified partly in view of the few buildings attributed to the traditional instructors, who, though they began as practitioners, devoted so much time to teaching and to intellectual pursuits that they ultimately built very little. But labeling the students of the "old school" as paper architects is unjustified. The theses of architectural students in the late 1920s and mid-1930s contained more detailed engineering calculations than those of the late 1930s or 1940s, and their knowledge of construction matched or surpassed that of later students. The older generation had used models to study structure, and their abilities to render light, texture, and color provided tools that better communicated at least the visual appearance of reality. Modernist polemics ignored teaching that had given the previous generation skills in

engineering and construction, and they also denigrated them as exclusively elitist and insensitive to the driving social agenda of modernism. In simplified terms, the GSD of 1937 saw that the old school reveled in architecture as art over technology; in the new school, architecture served a social purpose, even if that social purpose was often a generalized and vague goal rather than a specific program. The reduction of the past to such simplicities made way for a political zeal and polemical intensity that put an ideal social order—with its vision of a transformed, rational, fair, and humane life—above all other considerations. For Gropius and his colleagues, composition was immaterial compared to the harnessing of technology and functional analysis in the pursuit of a social agenda. Within this framework Breuer became associated with technology and fabrication, Gropius with teamwork and social consciousness.

Concurrent with the introduction of their modernist agenda at the GSD, Hudnut and Gropius pushed the war for modernism beyond the walls of Harvard Yard.[33] Hudnut assaulted tradition and conservatism in a series of eloquent, polemical statements justifying modern architecture. His target in 1937 was the last major public American monument designed in the Beaux-Arts tradition (by John Russell Pope), the Jefferson Memorial in Washington, D.C., which Hudnut called "an egg on a pantry shelf in a geometric Sahara" (Fig. 5.24). Originally given as a speech, Hudnut titled his diatribe "Twilight of the Gods" and called for

5.24 Jefferson Memorial model, Washington, D.C. John Russell Pope. From J. Hudnut, "Twilight of the Gods," *Magazine of Art* (August 1937).

the end of Beaux-Arts–derived architecture in America. He claimed that the current understanding of neoclassical architecture failed to provide an "abstract and universal expression in art."[34] For Hudnut, the conservative tendencies of the proposed monument associated with Jefferson's character were inconsistent with the great American figure. In Hudnut's view, the form of the Pantheon did not fit the man. "In spite of [Jefferson's] sympathy for the classic," Hudnut exhorted, "shall we commemorate his simplicity and reticence by the most grandiloquent and splendiferous of monumental forms, his devotion to American culture, his democratic sympathies by an Imperial utterance?"[35]

Hudnut continued his outcry over the Jefferson Memorial (and a neoclassical Washington) in the architectural press and, later, in the *New Republic*, where he declared that monuments and buildings in the neoclassical style, such as Grant's Tomb, resulted from a national insecurity in architecture's ability to express appropriate dignity.[36] He mocked the view that honor, particularly in the nation's capital, is derived from the columns in a building and is proportional to their number and weight. Hudnut poured invective on the Jefferson Memorial: when completed, he said, it "will embody so grotesque a presentation of Jefferson's character as to make him—if such a thing is possible—forever ridiculous."[37]

Hudnut's opinion about the corruption of history was not limited to John Russell Pope's classicism; he also challenged Le Corbusier's *Plan Voisin*—a polemical scheme for a modern city on the site of Paris—not because of its cost in land or money, but because by wiping out the medieval center of Paris, the scheme eradicated a historical legacy. Supplanting such cultural fallacies was the architecture of modernism, which offered, beyond mere function, an opportunity for representations of "dignity and power": "Modern architecture is essentially an effort to return to this unity of process, to arrive at expressive forms, not as elements added on to structures in the name of taste, but as necessary consequences of a need for order and grace in our way of life. Not because they are functional but because, being functional, their harmonies bring us an assurance of unity in the total phenomena of human life, our new vocabulary of constructed form, conditioned directly upon our way of life and developed from a contemporary technology, will regain the dignity and power we discover in the great traditions of our art."[38]

5.25 Smithsonian Gallery of Art, Washington, D.C., competition jury 1939. Left to right: Joseph Hudnut, John A. Holabird, Henry Shepley, Frederic A. Delano, George Howe, Walter Gropius, and Thomas Mabry.

According to Hudnut, modern architecture would be misunderstood, resisted, and unpopular in conservative circles, which he denigrated as "Bronxville." Despite such resistance, however, Hudnut asserted, in the diction of epiphany, that modern architecture would "illumine in new orderings of space and objective form that responsible and compassionate impulse which guides these heroic enterprises. Here will be mirrored for the first time the collective soul of a new and splendid age. Beauty, a spirit inaccessible to thought and skill, will enter unbidden into the heart of structure thus conceived and fashioned."[39]

Hudnut continued his crusade from Cambridge, even as he set his eyes on Washington, D.C., and the competition for a new Smithsonian Museum in 1939, which he saw as an opportunity to build a modernist project in the nation's capital.[40] As a professional advisor to the competition, he promoted Eliel and Eero Saarinen's design for a museum of modern art in an important place on the Washington Mall.[41] According to architectural histo-

rian Walter Creese, in this competition Hudnut tried "to win all of America over to modern architecture in one fell swoop in 1939, after he completed the deed at Harvard in 1937. He was an extraordinarily effective adversary in such contests because he spoke and thought in simple, clear, and bold terms; and academics and government figures were hardly used to that. It threw them off balance. Moreover, those were depression times, and real leaders could propose outrageous new things and still find acceptance."[42]

Hudnut also invited Gropius to a meeting of the jury, and the competition soon became a focus for their students, faculty colleagues, and graduates of the School of Architecture. Holmes Perkins and the recently graduated Robert Little submitted a bold and austere project utilizing an asymmetrical plan; Hugh Stubbins and Marc Peter, Jr., both recent Harvard graduates, entered a project that was laid out symmetrically on a regular grid of columns; and Edward Durrell Stone, who had studied at Harvard for a year before transferring to MIT, emphasized the role

of large figurative sculpture in his submission (Figs. 5.25–5.27). Collectively, these designs represented a rupture with all classical traditions that had dominated architecture in the nation's capital. However, Gilmore D. Clarke, a powerhouse in landscape architecture who was dean at Cornell and the chairman of the president's Fine Arts Commission (at times responsible for commissions for federal art and architecture), thwarted Hudnut's plans. Clarke objected to a modernist project interfering with the sanctity of the green of the Mall, and he succeeded in suppressing Hudnut's efforts.

Hudnut's campaign for modern architecture brought attention from unusual quarters. For example, in the spring of 1938 discussions ensued between him and A. Conger Goodyear, president of the Board of Trustees of the Museum of Modern Art in New York. Goodyear and the board were apparently considering trying to establish a "progressive school of fine arts" under the auspices of MoMA, and they approached Hudnut to be its director. Though Hudnut declined the offer, the MoMA board's consideration indicates his standing in American modernist circles.[43]

Reinforcements in the campaign for modernism arrived in the form of Sigfried Giedion of Zurich, the secretary-general of CIAM, the working arm of the modern movement in Europe.[44] With the assent of President Conant and the recommendation of Gropius, Hudnut, though not very familiar with Giedion's work, arranged for him to deliver Harvard's prestigious Charles Eliot Norton Lectures in 1938–39

5.26 Smithsonian Gallery of Art, Washington, D.C., competition drawings. G. Holmes Perkins and Robert A. Little, 1939.

5.27 Smithsonian Gallery of Art, Washington, D.C., competition drawings. Hugh Stubbins and Marc Peter, Jr., 1939.

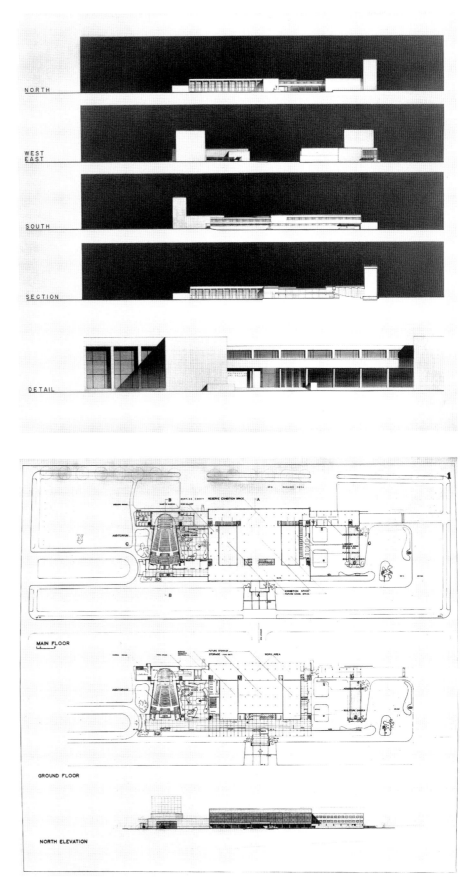

(a year before Igor Stravinsky held the same position).[45] His appointment signified the university's official embrace of the ideology of the modern movement. Giedion gave twelve lectures during the academic year, which provided the basis for *Space, Time and Architecture*, the most significant book to appear on the modern movement and the principal text for courses on modern architecture through the late 1960s.[46] Giedion's thesis was more complex than that introduced by Henry-Russell Hitchcock, Philip Johnson, and Alfred Barr, Jr., at the 1932 Museum of Modern Art exhibition, which had emphasized formal considerations at the expense of the social and intellectual issues that still concerned and motivated Giedion and his CIAM colleagues. Giedion's thesis was that the "New Tradition," inaugurated through the engineering advances of the late nineteenth-century modernist pioneers, needed further elaboration in the ongoing effort to reconcile the individual with production and the new concepts that linked space and time.

Giedion's position was in direct contrast with that of Kenneth Conant, who was the principal architectural historian of the GSD—and an immediate target for Gropius. Conant provided the explanation for the reduction of history courses: "Three full courses in history was really overbalanced, considering what had happened to architecture. The emphasis had shifted entirely from retrospective to the new architecture. History courses necessarily would show that, and my courses were showing it. My thesis was that you have to know the basic construction in order to understand any side of architecture, and there had been a radical change in construction. It really was different, and that implied a new style. *Stilus*, of course, is the Greek word for column. You named your architecture according to the column. And now we had the extruded 'H'column."[47] This observation reflected both Conant's archeological side and his view that modernism was rooted in technological innovation.

On the surface, materials (steel, glass, and concrete) and methods of construction (including fireproofing) had transformed the architecture of many European and American modernists since the mid-nineteenth century. The ethos of modern design held that new materials and means of production demanded new forms—and these new forms should benefit society. Beyond this ethos was the symbolic role of traditional form—a role, however problematic, that was ignored. Conant could acknowledge that, despite the use of steel framing and the expansion of space it allowed, despite the fluidity and mass of concrete and the illumination of buildings by immense sheets of plate glass, modernism demanded a rejection of the symbolic content of tradition in order to establish its own stylistic identity.

Conant recalled the time when, despite his progressive philosophy, Gropius initially opposed his courses and discouraged students from taking them: "Gropius thought that our history, which I was giving, would be like the history that he had

in the German schools. It was not so at all. The School [of Design] was paying about two-thirds of my salary, and during the first years I would get only three or four students from the School. . . . I was really very much up-to-date. People said that I was a very, very good teacher of architectural history. At the end I had a third of all the registrations in the Fine Arts Department . . . and my classes had run [from] 125 to 150 [students]." According to Conant, Gropius eventually "realized that I was dealing with a very different course on architectural history [and] his opposition disappeared."[48] Clearly Conant was receptive to, and equipped to teach, modern architecture; he had control over his material and had enthusiasm even for the controversial Frank Lloyd Wright, whom he knew personally. Walter Creese, who studied under Conant, recalled his lectures as fast and spare and given with enormous enthusiasm: "He had an encyclopedic mind and could take up and order quantities of information and imagery. He was hugely energetic—and he had been to see almost everything. His analyses tended to be artistic, esthetic, and in snapshot-like terms, showing many pictures with quick summaries. He was not much interested in theories and philosophies. To be aware and eclectic is a kind of American attitude—that was carried on by Conant's pupils as disciples."[49] Such an eclecticism, however, was open to the criticism that the scope was too large and insufficiently critical.

Despite his familiarity with modern architecture, Conant lacked the polemi-

cal taste and fervor necessary to limit himself to one cause. Another former student, Landis Gores, recalled Conant's office in the basement of Robinson Hall and how his desk was piled with sketches, abstracts, artifacts, and large-scale renderings in China ink—much of which was dedicated to his efforts to reconstruct the Cluny monastery. At this time, in the early 1940s, Conant's fall course was on Renaissance, baroque, and neoclassical architecture and the spring course on American architecture from colonial to federal styles, with a summary of modernism that ranged from Chicago's tall buildings to the triumph of the International Style as somewhat disappointing in substance. Gores, who had studied the history of architecture with Baldwin Smith at Princeton, perceived Conant's teaching in the first semester as "hardly more than a slide-show run-through of Bannister Fletcher: venerable buildings galore, but woefully short either on analysis or on synthesis."[50] According to Gores, the discussion of Henri Labrouste and the Meunier Chocolate factory—canonically identified as proto-modernist—could have come directly from Sigfried Giedion's *Space, Time and Architecture*, which all the students had read on their own.

Countering this view, however, was the perception that Conant provided complete data about the buildings to supplement the sequence of flashing images, and a kind of synthesis that placed buildings under titles of schools or groups.[51] After his course, many students felt they had seen everything worth seeing, and that Conant was looking at the full scope of history, not at a small, detailed segment. The broad receptivity that allowed Conant to embrace modern architecture also created his weakness in presenting it. A perusal through his *Modern Architecture* in the University Prints Series GM—the first American pictorial collection of modern architecture—shows a catholic taste whose standards of selection are difficult to discern.[52]

Despite the limits of Conant's approach to history, the first years of the GSD were marked by an excitement that spread quickly through the student body, spurred by Hudnut's outside agitation, Gropius's charisma, and Giedion's fervor. In the midst of these dramatic changes in outlook and personnel, the veteran Bremer Pond tried to put the best face on his department, describing in his report of 1938–39 the usual contributions of the library in collecting books and publishing aerial photographs of work by former students who now worked with the New York Parks Department. In the heyday of Robert Moses in New York, these photographs, exhibited in late February 1939, showed the vital significance of parks, parkways, and recreational areas to the economic and social configurations of congested cities and the range and complexity of park design. Pond saw these photographs as "an impressive document of the landscape architect's answer to the trend of modern times for the greatest good of the greatest number."[53] In addition to the

usual tour of estates, the annual landscape students' tour promoted an awareness of social and economic conditions, including inspections of recent parks, housing developments, boulevards, parkway arteries, and the New York World's Fair, then under construction.

A traditionalist, Pond tried to accommodate modernism, as can be seen in his *Outline History of Landscape Architecture*, written in 1936. Despite its cursory text and the uneven quality of the illustrations, it gives a taste of the typical attitudes towards both the teaching of landscape architecture and appropriate models for its students and the profession. Pond described what he saw as modernist conditions: a decline of distinct national styles, changes in hiring conditions, and changes in transportation that affected large-scale design of the land. The stylistic problem pitted classicism against functionalism, a battle in the context of a rising interest in contemporary art and a desire for "novelties." One response to modern requirements was the heightened interest in community and recreational planning and the introduction of new materials. Another response was found in large-scale designs that related to topography, climate, "land-scape effects," use, and traffic.[54] Pond's discussion clearly shows that when landscape architecture began to deal with modernist issues, it began to resemble planning as a discipline.

Ironically, Pond's illustrations showed how thoroughly issues for landscape architecture now fell within the province

of the profession of planning. His bow to modernism was to show an unidentified illustration from Harvard colleague Jean-Jacques Haffner's series of cubistic gardens in *Compositions des Jardins*.[55] The only other mention of modern garden design included the unidentified (and possibly redrawn) dynamic design by Gabriel Guevrekian of a garden for the Vicomte de Noailles, the patron of modern architecture and gardens, friend of Adolf Loos, and friend and commissioner of Robert Mallet-Stevens, who designed the villa for Guevrekian's garden. Pond was so accustomed to Beaux-Arts principles of organization that he positioned the illustration perpendicular to the page, giving the impression that the design was axially oriented and thus traditional—though, in fact, it was neither.

Two basic approaches were unavailable to students of landscape architecture: the pastoral visions of the Olmsted tradition and the axial planning of the Beaux-Arts. Some students, however, began to question if there were not something else that landscape architecture could offer. Faced with the predictability of Pond's banal views, they reacted: was that all there was to the modern landscape—one token garden and one fantasy? How could landscape architecture relate to the exciting developments in modern art? What was the relationship of their design efforts to society? And what was the appropriate aesthetic for the pressing needs of the day? Pond's token acknowledgment of modernism was an empty gesture to some of his students who wanted to relate land-

5.28 Garrett Eckbo, landscape architecture student, 1938.

5.29 Garden plan, Garrett Eckbo, 1938.

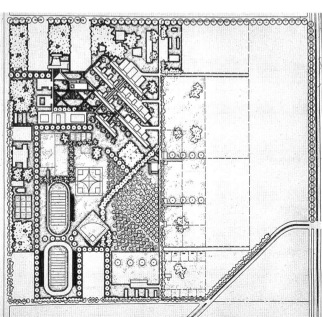

scape architecture to the latest developments in modern architecture and arts.

The conservative bent of the landscape architecture program became painfully obvious to three students—Garrett Eckbo, Dan Kiley, and James Rose—who arrived in the late 1930s (Fig. 5.28). They challenged their professors to demonstrate the social role of landscape architecture and to explore its commitment to modernism.[56] Eckbo came to Harvard in 1936 after studying at Berkeley and quickly found Harvard's atmosphere fusty and outdated. He later recalled that "while architecture in Robinson Hall fiercely debated the relative merits of, and proper responses to, the new European masters, the landscape faculty was telling us carefully that, since trees were not made in factories, we need not worry about a modern landscape architecture. . . . Rose, Kiley, and I were unconvinced, and continued to explore in our individual ways the works and theories of modern art and architecture and their possible implications for landscape architecture."[57]

Pond, perceived as formal and rigidly old-fashioned, became a focus of revolt as his students took their objections to the forum of the design journals. The rebellious trio explored the modern possibilities, currently neglected at Harvard, through a series of publications that both attacked the profession's present state and proposed new directions for it. James Rose, the angriest member of the group, wrote in 1939 that a drastic change of approach was necessary for landscape architects.[58] It was "fear" that kept schools

and their "conventional instructors" from moving beyond their Beaux-Arts educational system.[59] Science and a new attention to economic expediencies were destined to save the field, ensuring its relevancy in a new era of social and fiscal responsibility.[60]

One of Eckbo's articles in the *Magazine of Art* explored the relationship of landscape architecture to modern painting and allied arts.[61] His response to the necessities of modernism could be seen in his own garden designs and in his Harvard thesis: the design of "Contempoville," a 1938 project for a World's Fair in Los Angeles in 1945 (Figs. 5.29–5.32). His "World of [the] Day After Tomorrow" included a range of flat-roof modernist buildings as integral to his project. Eckbo's continuing criticism of Harvard's program eventually provoked Richard Webel, the traditional landscape designer, to expel him—which did not interfere with the progress of his prolific and groundbreaking career.

Dan Kiley coauthored two articles with Eckbo and Rose that appeared in *Architectural Record* in 1939. Beginning with a historical outline of man's manipulation of the landscape, then moving on to the demands of the modern urban areas, the three called for clearly outlined systems of parks, play lots, greenbelts, and recreation areas to be incorporated into the plans of all modern cities. They wrote, "Contemporary landscape design is finding its standards in relation to the new needs of urban society."[62] They also insisted on the importance of the land-

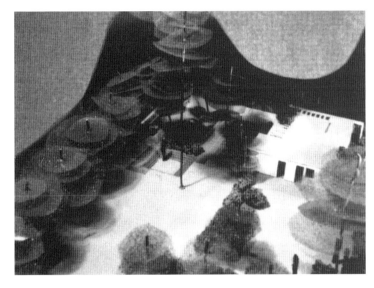

5.30, 5.31, 5.32
Garret Eckbo,
Los Angeles
World's Fair, LA
master's thesis,
Contempoville,
1938.

scape architect's participation in the expansion of America into its undeveloped hinterlands. Only with the trained hand of professionals could the beauty of the landscape be preserved as it was developed.

The students' position conflicted not only with Bremer Pond's but also with that of their teacher Richard Webel, a brilliant and experienced designer with an Italianate inclination. His practice centered on Long Island, New York, in the heart of its elegant estates—though after the stock market crash of 1929, this type of work was relatively rare. Webel reacted to the call for a modern approach to landscape design by simplifying design elements and focusing on individual plant specimens for a clearer effect.

Landscape students took sides either for or against the new policies of Dean Hudnut, creating so much tension that, by mutual consent, Webel eventually stopped teaching design and returned to practice full-time. Webel's replacement was Norman T. Newton, whom he had known when they both worked at the firm of Vitale & Geiffert in New York City. Newton provided an incomparable combination of practical experience, design skills, and knowledge of the history of his profession and field. A student of Gilmore Clark at Cornell University and a fellow of the American Academy in Rome, he had wide experience in the National Park Service and had opened a practice in New York City. He arrived at Harvard as an assistant professor in 1939 and became a major figure in the Graduate School of

Design over the next forty years.[63] Newton represented a thoroughly American tradition that, while open to modern developments, still looked back to its Olmstedian roots and the great precedents of historic gardens.

Newton's arrival coincided with the appearance of Canadian Christopher Tunnard. Appointed a lecturer in 1939, he brought a fresh approach to the teaching of landscape architecture.[64] He had worked in England as a designer and site planner and had won a special award for landscape design in the Paris Exposition of 1937. He was chairman of the town planning committee of the Modern Architectural Research Society (MARS) in London from 1938 to 1939, signifying his membership in the fledgling modern movement in Great Britain.[65] Tunnard's views on the significance of the international debates on modernism were revealed in his 1938 book, *Gardens in the Modern Landscape*.[66] It was the first book on the modern garden, and its second edition, revised with American material, included a note by Hudnut. At Harvard Tunnard demonstrated his position as a proponent of modernism, a prolific historian, and a critic of the city. He shared an extensive knowledge of Great Britain and America, had a broad, humanistic view of design, and had the courage of his convictions.[67]

With students critiquing their professors in the press, a wider community also began to form its opinions and perceptions about the arrival of "modern" architecture at Harvard. Lawrence Dame, a travel

writer, viewed the pioneering efforts to propagate modern art in Boston as evidence of an intellectual and economic resurgence in the somnolent land of the Yankee. Dame noted that the "Harvard Architecture School" and "a little group of teachers headed by Walter Gropius" were already exerting a great influence on contemporary American architecture; that their efforts had surpassed the Beaux-Arts system, which had not taken into account the influence of industry on architecture; and that, consequently, "a new attitude, a new order in architecture was coming forward."[68] The Machine Age called for simpler, streamlined functional forms, Dame said, and President Conant had recognized the shift and taken the needed action by hiring Hudnut and Gropius. According to Dame, Gropius was notable for his bold experiments in the adaptation and teaching of industrial architecture as applied to modern housing, which "was the keynote of the new trend at Harvard."[69]

Dame realized, however, that Harvard had no plans to become a copy of the Bauhaus at Dessau; much of the American system was to be retained, with German methods applied only to American building problems introduced by Hudnut. Though New England industry was in bad shape, students were encouraged to recognize the importance of the "industrial regime" in which they lived and to see the relationship of architecture to social and economic factors.[70] Beauty was still the objective, but only because it was seen as inherent in the forms that emerge out of present-day life.

According to Dame, a rapid increase in enrollment with students from all over the United States coming to study modern architecture and planning in "the proverbial land of colonial and Cape Cod houses," further confirmed the renaissance at Harvard.[71] However, Dame made no reference to developments in landscape architecture or regional planning as contributing factors in the resurgence of cultural life in New England, and no mention of detractors of these modernist developments.

Dame's assessment was highly favorable, but there was still the risk of public dismay and protest in response to the tumultuous changes. When a former student in landscape architecture sent his enthusiastic comments to Hudnut, the student received a cautious reply: "We are pleased by your comments on our recent changes. These changes do not comprise anything very radical but are merely in line with the general movement towards more realistic methods in which all of the important schools of architecture are sharing."[72] Hudnut's caution was on target. The battle to shift out of the entrenched status quo and into the new and unknown was far from over, and even his own role was changing. Despite the recognition and importance of his pioneering role, the local crusade for modernism increasingly became identified with Walter Gropius within the Graduate School of Design. The public response to Gropius's arrival in America had been publicly more positive than negative. One admirer in Chicago wrote

to express his hope that Gropius would change architectural taste. "We suffer terribly from 'Collegiate Gothic' and the young think it beautiful," the man lamented.[73]

But even in the midst of acceptance, Gropius saw difficulties close to home. As he wrote to Pierre Jay, the financier, "I think there has been quite a little opposition against introducing modern architecture to Harvard."[74] And the opposition was coming directly from friction within the faculty of the GSD. Gropius, going over the authority of Henry Hubbard, attempted to arrange the appointment of an associate (probably Martin Wagner) in the planning department. Hudnut had to implore Gropius, at some length, to cooperate with Hubbard, who was Gropius's equal as chairman of the Department of Regional Planning. Despite the progress made toward a collaborative model of design education, there were also disgruntled sentiments in the Department of Landscape Architecture, where both students and teachers expressed a token resistance to Hudnut and Gropius. Hudnut informed Gropius about some awkward questions concerning his office: "It was low-down (to say the least) for our landscape friends to complain about your office in Hunt Hall—but I am inclined to believe that the intention was not so much to hurt you as to embarrass me. Not long ago my accounts were gone over very thoroughly with the same objective in mind."[75]

The practical difficulties associated with the arrival of modernism, however, created

a common opposition that brought Gropius and Hudnut together. Their efforts to bring modern architecture to America began with a shared vision. Writing to Hudnut at the conclusion of their first year of working together, Gropius confessed: "I must tell you that I admire very sincerely your grand manner of fighting your way through with suppleness and tact to a very determined aim. I know what courage is necessary to overcome the general stupidity and laziness of hearts and brains in order to change the ordinary beaten track. So I feel very happy about the good luck of having become your companion in this fight for preparing a better architecture in this country."[76] Little did either man know that Gropius was soon to overpower his "sincere friend" and that, in the future, they would work at serious cross-purposes, ending up as enemies on an intellectual, if not a personal, level.

Gropius also encountered opposition from sources outside Harvard. When he and Herbert Bayer, his former colleague in Germany, organized an exhibition on the Bauhaus at the Museum of Modern Art, their unrealistically high appraisal of its achievements created a furor that was reported by the New York Times.[77] Gropius ran afoul of the museum's director, Alfred Barr—who earlier had approved of Gropius's appointment at Harvard—when Gropius attempted to excise material in a history of the Bauhaus. Barr acidly reprimanded Gropius for attempting to impede an objective assessment of the Bauhaus: "This book [on the Bauhaus] is not complete even within its field . . . calling

eventually for a more definitive and dispassionate study. I must ask you to replace these omissions in the interest of the Museum's scholarly integrity."[78] Barr had already chastised Gropius for promoting ideas as new that had been in practice in America for twenty-five years—even at Harvard—adding that Gropius's misunderstanding of American culture made him appear foolish.[79] In still another rebuff, Frank Lloyd Wright, who attacked the Bauhaus as a destructive foreign import, initially refused to meet with Gropius when he wanted to visit him in 1937; they later met in 1940 when Wright came to lecture in Boston and at Harvard.[80]

Gropius's crusade to promote his vision of modernism was demonstrated in his own architectural work, which also elicited mixed reactions. His aspirations to revive his architectural career with public buildings did not occur immediately upon his arrival in America in 1937. His scheme for Wheaton College, with Marcel Breuer, only won second prize in the college's design competition; Richard M. Bennett, a recent Harvard graduate, and his partner, Caleb Hornbostel, were awarded first prize. Giedion wrote that though Gropius's design "faced a wall of prejudice," it was also "premature"—however, according to Katherine Cook, the Harvard librarian, members of the GSD traveled to Wheaton to protest the decision.[81] Other large schemes were not built: Black Mountain College, with Marcel Breuer, at Lake Eden, North Carolina, 1939; and a recreational center, with

Konrad Wachsmann, for Key West, Florida, 1942.

The houses of four Harvard professors—Gropius, Bogner, Breuer, and Perkins—in Lincoln, Massachusetts, near historic Concord, well displayed the new influence. Breuer, however, was mistakenly singled out by Dame as being known for his progressive and practical ideas on city planning.[82] Although each house distinctly expressed the owners' preferences and needs, they were all visually related and, with their flat roofs and open expanses of glass, unmistakably modern.

Gropius and Breuer and younger colleagues built their own homes in Lincoln, Massachusetts, in an area called Half Moon Hill; these were the houses Dame wrote about (Fig. 5.33). Gropius sited his house for its views and began construction in April 1938; a modernist icon, it soon became an architectural landmark (and, eventually, a property of the Society for the Preservation of New England Antiquities).[83] Gropius and Breuer received commissions to design other single-family homes in Massachusetts: the Ford House, in Lincoln (1938); the Hagerty House, in Cohasset (1938); the Chamberlain residence in Sudbury (1939); and the residence of Dr. Abele in Framingham (1941). They also designed a luxurious residence for Cecilia and Robert Frank in Pittsburgh (1939) and executed the Pennsylvania State Pavilion at the New York World's Fair of 1939.[84]

The examples of Gropius's built work were not lost on his pupils; one student, Paul Schelp, later explained that one of

his interior designs was "somewhat inspired by Gropius's own house." In witty annotations on one of his student drawings from 1938, Schelp points out all the important components of his appropriately modern design for a domestic interior: an Aalto chair, a Breuer chair, and, of course, abstract art on the wall (Fig. 5.34). Schelp's work was but one proof that Gropius's domestic style—flat roofs, simple open spaces, monochromatic walls, and expanses of glass—quickly gained a well-known, though not necessarily respected, currency among students. Schelp even used Gropius's design of the Bauhaus in Dessau as a model for a high school in Concord,

5.35 Project for a school, Concord, Mass. Paul F. Schelp, problem 1, 1938. Pencil notations added 1986.

Massachusetts: much to Schelp's surprise, Breuer criticized the design as "too commercial" (Fig. 5.35).[85]

Gropius's first large-scale building contract in the United States came in 1940 when he was hired to build housing for defense industry workers in New Kensington, Pennsylvania.[86] Here was his first opportunity to demonstrate, in America, his skills in creating rational housing systems, a passion that spanned his career. "Aluminum City Terrace," consisting of 250 one- and two-story units of wood construction, was built to house workers of the nearby factory of the Aluminum Company of America (Alcoa) (Fig. 5.36). The units had from one to three bedrooms and were grouped in rows of six to eight units. Semi-detached two-family dwellings were also distributed throughout the site.

The housing at New Kensington, however, initially failed to garner public acceptance and created a reaction similar to that elicited by Gropius's Torten Housing near Dessau in 1926.[87] Local realtors opposed it, the local press attacked it, and residents rejected it on both aesthetic and functional grounds. Their complaints appeared in TASK, the international journal whose purpose was to prove the validity of the modern movement by solving material problems that went beyond aesthetic revolutions. A sampling vividly conveys the gist of public sentiment: "Why, you can't tell the front from the back . . . no cellar, no place to hang your clothes when it rains . . . those funny wood fronts—that's the kind of house

poor farmers live in."[88] After its completion only thirty-four tenants were willing to occupy the housing. With the lifting of the requirement that only defense workers were eligible to rent the units, the "Aluminum Edition" of the *C.I.O.* (*Congress of Industrial Organizations*) *News* staged a publicity campaign for the project. Gradually acceptance increased, and by the spring of 1944, 188 units were occupied, 121 of them by families of Alcoa workers. Bad drainage—an economy move that eliminated site grading—and poor soundproofing plagued residents.

Defense-sponsored housing projects by other architects were more successful. Richard Neutra's Channel Heights was commended for its completeness, for the usefulness of its community facilities (which New Kensington lacked), and for its promise as a housing type for the future.[89] Certainly the reception of Gropius's first major project in the United States must have been disappointing, if not embarrassing, and may well have caused him to start considering what would be more acceptable in America.

The partnership between Gropius and Breuer itself posed difficulties and provided another opportunity for latent opposition to surface. Mirroring the resistance and apprehensions of some graduates of Harvard's former Schools of Architecture and Landscape Architecture, a landscape alumnus accused Gropius and Breuer of running their business from Hunt Hall.[90] The secretary of the Harvard Corporation wrote Gropius and asked for

an explanation.[91] Gropius replied with surprise at the objection, explained his work with Breuer, and even sent a sample of letterhead stationery to show that he and Breuer were not conducting business on university property.[92] Despite subsequent apologies from the alumnus, the tension dragged on in a long series of letters of explanations and counter-explanations. At best, the inquiry could be seen as an innocent misunderstanding. Nevertheless, it aroused the suspicion of Gropius, who was still getting accustomed to a foreign environment, and it fueled his resentment towards his colleagues in landscape architecture. This kind of personal affront played a role in undermining the effectiveness of collaboration among the departments and further polarized the architecture and landscape architecture departments.

A more fundamental obstacle emerged in Hudnut's plans to unify the school: despite the overarching goal of achieving a truly collaborative education, the Departments of Landscape Architecture and Regional Planning feared losing their autonomy in the process. According to Holmes Perkins, the two departments were "one hundred and ten percent independent" by this time. Hubbard, the man who had lost the deanship to Hudnut, and who was a very powerful figure in the field of planning, began to oppose any collaborative problems that risked sacrificing the autonomy of his fields.[93] He stood squarely in the way of Hudnut and became an impediment to the collaborative program.

Richard Webel, in recalling the struggle that preceded his own departure, saw the difficulties as arising from Hudnut's wily political maneuvering to obtain for the Department of Architecture the endowment intended for the Department of Landscape Architecture.[94] Perkins also saw the struggle as a fight for the independence of the landscape architecture department. Students took sides in favor of, or in opposition to, the dean. The views of some of the students who witnessed the transition from the traditional to the modernist era show what is was like to experience this upheaval. While the proponents of the modernist agenda were clear about their purpose, their students were not always so certain. Students knew that they were against the old ways of tradition but were unsure of what they were for in its place. Landis Gores, who graduated in 1942, and who gained international recognition for working and living in his own house in New Canaan, Connecticut,[95] recalled how, in the changes instituted by Hudnut, "advocates of an architectural cosmogony conventional to the outside world were gently sidelined or submerged until retirement could clear the atmosphere while others deemed able to, and indeed often were delighted to, conform to new patterns of thinking were gradually indoctrinated and incorporated into a coherent body of instruction."[96] Gores also noted that in the first year of the GSD, Hudnut assumed a principal role in teaching architectural history (as had Langford Warren), which he intended to provide "operative rather

5.36 Aluminum City Terrace, New Kensington, Pennsylvania. Walter Gropius, 1940.

168

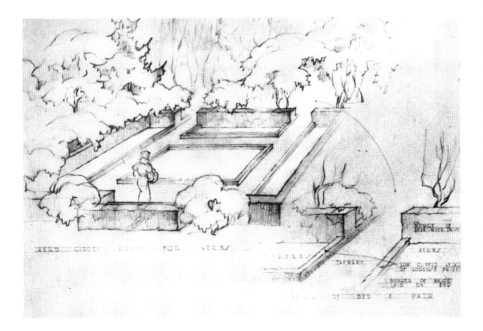

5.37 Garden plan, section of a thesis model of exterior illumination, John O. Simonds, 1939.

5.38 Herb garden, Dickinger Estate. First professional work by John O. Simonds, carried out while he was a student.

than archaeological implications." Gores described the appointment of Gropius in Hudnut's second year as "epochal," and Marcel Breuer's arrival in the next year as filled with "electricity."[97]

John O. Simonds, who received a master's degree in landscape architecture in 1939, saw the arrival of the European modernists as a religious event: "They came as evangelists, preaching a strong new gospel. To the jaded Beaux-Arts student architects, wearied of the hymns in praise of Vignola, beginning to question the very morality of the plaster applied, and stuffed to their uppers with pagan Acanthus leaves, the words of these new professors were both cathartic and tonic."[98]

The rebellious students in landscape architecture sought a parallel expression to their colleagues in architecture. According to Simonds, he and his peers in landscape architecture turned for inspiration to painting, sculpture (particularly the "free form" deriving from Jean Arp and Constantine Brancusi), and even music.[99] In his view this search was for new forms rather than principles, and "the immediate result was a weird new variety of plan geometry, a startling collection of novel clichés. We based plan diagrams on the sawtooth and the spiral, on stylized organisms such as the leafstalk, the wheatsheaf, and the overlapping scales of sturgeon. We sought geometric plan forms in quartz crystals. We adapted 'free' plan forms from bacterial cultures magnified to the thousandth power. We sought to borrow and adapt the plan diagrams of

5.39 First contemporary garden east of the Rockies. John O. Simonds, designed in 1939 as a student. Mitchell/Ritchey designed the structure.

ancient Persian courtyards and early Roman forts."[100] Nevertheless, Simonds's student attempts at modern design show how difficult it was to break away from traditional approaches to composition. Sometimes the response was reflexive, producing rigidly bilateral designs, as seen in some of his garden plans (Figs. 5.37, 5.38). Particularly in public spaces, symmetrical plans with axial progressions could facilitate clarity of movement, orderly systems of understanding, as well as a visual focus with vistas. But asymmetrical plans became the preferred means of expression in the ground plans of the new architecture, along with an immediate suspicion of planning techniques associated with major and minor axes. Ultimately, asymmetrical, nonaxial planning became the prototypical style of design. As modernist practices took hold, something as abstract as a plan configuration attained moral overtones, with symmetry ardently associated with control, particularly totalitarian and fascist control, and asymmetry associated with freedom (Fig. 5.39).[101] Simonds described, in retrospect, the sense of rebellion students felt at the imposition of such a limited focus:

It was a revulsion at the flamboyant excesses and questionable tenets of the expiring Beaux-Arts system of architectural and landscape architectural education. It was a rejection of the mentality that could accept the validity of:

—a fire station "in the style of" a Georgian counting house,

—a bank "in the style of" a Roman Temple,

—stage-set Long Island estates copied, detail by detail, from Tudor country seats, or

—geometric public parks reproducing the plan of a Renaissance palace garden.

Such design solutions, in mode at the time, were to us clearly false and utterly repugnant. Searching for a more valid approach we found inspiration in the Gropius-Breuer-Wagnerian gospel of functional form as first (in recent history) espoused by Louis Sullivan. It was an approach that sought in all design solutions the directness of the New England "salt box" house, the silo, the pitchfork, and the plan layout of the farmstead. This we felt to be "honest."

Simonds noted, however, that even with these convictions about participating in an "honest" architecture, his visual orientation and lack of knowledge about social conditions impeded the direction and muddied the social significance of his student work. He also felt, retrospectively, that the products, the structures, of the new and fervently avowed modernist principles lacked the "ring of reality"—a serious condemnation—and gave little

satisfaction. Absent from the honest approach of the "new architecture" were basic planning principles that are timeless in nature, such as those used in Japanese garden design. These timeless principles could only be found in history, in those models that contained no artificial barriers between architecture and landscape architecture, between the city and its fabric, between nature and human.[102]

Another articulate view of the modernist fervor came from Seymour Howard, who had transferred to Harvard after beginning his training in Cambridge, England, where his discovery of Le Corbusier's writings and the work of Wells Coates and the Tecton Group challenged the Palladian style he and his peers had been urged to follow. When Howard came to Harvard to continue his studies in 1937, he found Gropius's rational approach more satisfying than the emotional appeal of Le Corbusier's publications. This rationality rested more upon implicit principles of analysis and design than on long theoretical justifications. Employing a functional method meant that architects first studied human activities before they defined a building program for them. Form followed logically from the program and means of construction, which consisted of systems of basic structure (building "skin" and partitions) and mechanical equipment. At Harvard the plans of students' designs for everything from objects to buildings had to be rationally justified as efficient; façades had to have similar utilitarian justifications in terms of lighting, ventilation, and protection from the elements. Sections and elevations *followed* plan designs as opposed to being conceived jointly with them.

Howard saw examples of the functionalist approach not only in European architects and theorists but also in the work of Americans. Paul Nelson, for example, an American architect working in France and friend of Fernand Léger, Hans Arp, and Joan Miró, designed an exemplary parasolar envelope for a Suez clinic, whose detailed hospital plans and ovoid operating rooms were models of functionalist architecture. His "Suspended House" project, derived from the work of Buckminster Fuller and exhibited widely in Europe and United States in 1937–38, represented a solution for housing the masses. Students admired and emulated the plans of Le Corbusier for the Centrosoyus (headquarters of the Soviet central cooperatives in Moscow) and the Salvation Army, but Le Corbusier's social theories, according to Howard, seemed overly utopian at Harvard. More appealing to students was the work of Lewis Mumford, heir of British sociologist Patrick Geddes and ultimately the Russian revolutionist Petr Kropotkin, whose message was that architecture and city planning should serve *people* instead of artistic formalism.

For Howard and his peers, the subjects of design in 1938–39 exuded social significance: a hospital, a high school that stayed open at night and on weekends for adults, and low-cost housing in poor suburban areas—they each served the collective and communal well-being. Justification for focusing on individual private dwellings, which were viewed as reinforcing an old elitist order, came from seeing these design experiments in creating new life-styles through new technologies, such as sliding windows, radiant heat, and passive solar heating—à la Neutra's earlier Lovell Health House (1927–29). As they pursued these problems, the students became "proselytes of functionalist doctrine": "We thought of ourselves as pioneers in the search for paradigmatic solutions to the environmental problems of modern life, universally applicable with today's technology."[103]

The drive and commitment of those converted to the modern cause kept all adherents motivated, at times more intensely than their teachers. Paradoxically, Gropius and Breuer both built their houses in Lincoln using light wood framing and granite fieldstone—conventional materials that offered no technological innovation at all, but which were economical, available, and added color and texture. The stark black-and-white photographs of the new architecture portrayed modern houses as "white, prismatic luminous . . . symbols of a new era" to the students. In short, the new architecture had a stunning effect. In Howard's words, "With this atmosphere of fervor, rejection of the past was easy: With-

out any specific knowledge about it, we were of course against any vestiges of the teaching of the École des Beaux-Arts. . . . We were against everything academic, symmetrical compositions, elaborately rendered plans and elevations. Our projects were shown in precisely drawn plans, sections, elevations. Massing and three dimensional spaces were visualized by axonometrics and models. Lyrical descriptions were laughed at, only the logically reasoned counted."[104]

Only a compelling vision could so thoroughly eradicate all traces of the traditions that were present just four years earlier. Only the power of a crusade could eliminate the reformist efforts of the preceding schools; their programs had logic too, but it was channeled into formulae; their purposes also included public needs as well as elite preferences; their forms also could withstand mechanical analysis. And yet the predecessors saw themselves as foremost in the pursuit of art, whereas the modernists pursued social welfare. The former group would not allow a resurgence of socialist fervor after decades of tradition, while the latter group ignored the progressive, reformist motivations of the 1880s and 1890s in America that accomplished much with landscapes and suburbs.[105]

Consequently, in the new architecture a flat roof became a powerful symbol that blinded students to the reality that flat roofs cost more than shingled or pitched roofs. When the opulence of the house designed by Gropius and Breuer for Cecilia and Robert Frank appeared to students to compromise the social commitment of architecture, the students held the design up as a refutation of social ideals and a betrayal of the cause for mass housing.[106]

The mounting intensity of the crusade, with its budding critique from within its own ranks, encountered an abrupt obstruction as the onset of war in Europe stalled the modernist agenda. The short period between the founding of the GSD and the war provided a rare moment of foment and hope. As Seymour Howard recalled, "So it was in the GSD just before the war. Utopian and reformist dreams vanished under the bombs."[107]

Weathering the War Years

As developments escalated in the war in Europe, so many students with college degrees enlisted in the armed services that there was insufficient enrollment of students in the GSD. Emergency measures required reducing the admission requirements and lowering the number of courses required for the degrees in the design programs. During the war, the GSD offered (for the first time) a bachelor's degree in landscape architecture, requiring a college degree or advanced standing for students who had taken professional courses or had pursued a special curriculum option in the architectural sciences department of Harvard College.

During this period of low enrollment, the master of landscape architecture degree was also overhauled to parallel the master of architecture degree: the master's

program in landscape architecture was now conducted in conditions resembling those of a landscape architect's office, with greater freedom from details and wider opportunity for creative design. Only two courses were required: a special advanced design studio and a course in professional practice, contracts, and specifications—both of which were taught by teams of faculty in the Department of Landscape Architecture. Admission requirements to the bachelor's program in architecture were also reduced for new students: the requirement that all candidates must hold a bachelor's degree was waived temporarily; instead candidates were now required to have completed only eight courses towards the bachelor's.[108] Expansion of the war effort in 1942 required portions of the university to mobilize for war-related research: dormitories housed large numbers of men in the military services, severely limiting housing available for graduate students.[109] The war depleted the student body and left the school, and designers in general, in a lull. Columbia's School of Architecture had a similar fate: during the war its student body consisted of women, male students with 4-F deferments, and foreign students; an accelerated program was offered and a supplementary evening degree program was instituted.[110]

Efforts to implement the new modernist agenda at the GSD diminished. Though the years between 1940 and 1944 saw the incorporation of new types of collaborative problems at Harvard, such as schemes for satellite communities, overall

few of the planned adjustments in the design programs took hold. This interval did, however, allow time to contemplate society's needs in the future, and it had the positive effect of forcing one major change in the program: for the first time, Harvard began to accept women students to its design programs.

Buoyed by the addition of women, the GSD managed to continue operating throughout the war emergency. The summer school increased in significance because it compensated for the reduced program and provided an extra opportunity for teaching and for the temporary addition of a faculty conversant with Gropius's attitudes. In the summer of 1941 Josef Albers returned to Harvard from Black Mountain College to teach a course on the theory and practice of design.[111] He taught the principles of basic design that Gropius believed to be the crucial underpinnings of design education: drawing and painting of simple geometric forms (no architectural rendering), emphasizing the use of simple tools and materials. He stressed the inherent qualities of materials, structures, surfaces, plasticity, color, and their "characteristic forms," as well as the effects of color and light on the perception of form. As an investigation of abstraction, Albers's course differed dramatically from the previous offerings of the summer school, wherein the same basic design course required a series of short-term realistic architectural designs on paper, using sketches and models.

Regular design studios in the academic year 1940–41 continued to offer a variety of programs that confronted contemporary problems, from commercial building, to a terminal for Pan American Airways, and a small photographic shop (Figs. 5.40–5.42). As responses to basic modern needs for commerce, travel, and communication, the projects demonstrated not so much that function generated their forms as that their flat roofs, curtain wall glazing, and simple open interiors made them recognizable as modern buildings.

In April 1943 the GSD announced a special wartime curriculum. In addition to reductions in the time required to complete degrees and the university-wide implementation of a three-semester academic year, the program allowed testing of the most collaborative program offered since the turn of the century.[112] Also significant was the format of the courses: integrated sequences whose purpose was "to form a single educational experience." The first year became virtually identical for students in landscape architecture and architecture: they took the same courses in architectural design, building construction, theory and practice of design, descriptive geometry and projective drawing, the history of civic design, statics, and mathematics, with design, building construction, and statics forming three parts of one sequence; an intensive four-week course in topography preceded the construction course.[113] Similar sequences made up the second year when, for landscape students, landscape design, landscape construction, and the study of plant materials were joined; and when, for architecture students, all the courses (except the history of architecture) were sequenced to form an interrelated whole. The renewed effort to integrate the curriculum resulted in one course on both architectural and landscape design, shared between the two programs, with landscape architects taking one term of architectural design. The only variations came in electives: landscape architects studied geology or biology, while architects studied the history of modern architecture or the history of American architecture. Although students were now studying some of the same design courses, they had lost, once again, the links between their fields that the study of history could have provided.

The troika that constituted the GSD still did not have three equal partners—nowhere near. The planning program suffered during the war years as its faculty vanished. As noted previously, by 1940–41 Arthur Comey, housing pioneer and a founding member of the School of City Planning, had departed, his dreams of both mass housing and regional planning unfulfilled. Even more significant was the resignation of Henry Hubbard in 1940. In an unpleasant turn of events, the pressure on the Department of Regional Planning increased to the point of causing Hubbard to withdraw from teaching several months prior to his designated retirement. A former faculty member alleged that Hudnut had ultimately forced Hubbard's resignation.[114] His departure was a statement of protest regarding the inequality among the departments and expressed his intense personal disappointment in the university's inability to support fully the teaching of regional planning. It was a defeat for a man who was distinguished in the professions of both landscape architecture and planning, a dedicated Harvard man who had received its first professional degree in landscape architecture and was a founder in the field of professional planning in America and the driving force in planning at Harvard.[115] Hubbard summarized, in retrospect, the tribulations that befell the planning program at Harvard from 1929 until 1940:

> The teaching of regional planning at Harvard did not soon become, as I had hoped, an integral part of a School of Design recognizing the mutual contribution of the world's developing thoughts whether labeled Architecture, Landscape Architecture, Engineering, City Planning, Fine Arts, Government or whatever else. The first result under the School of Design was, rather, less support of instruction in landscape architecture and regional planning, and a concentration of official enthusiasm on architectural design of a certain kind. . . . I hope and believe that Harvard will yet promote regional planning in America, not as the adopted child of any other profession, but as an essential common effort calling upon all those who can think creatively.[116]

With Hubbard's departure, Gropius was free to exert greater influence throughout the school.[117]

The planning program at Harvard did not recover quickly. Along with the key departures of Comey and Hubbard and

5.40 A commercial building for Boylston, Berkeley, and Newbury Streets, Boston, Mass. Hugh McK. Jones, Arch. 2b, 1940.

5.41 Pan American Airways, Wake Island, Hugh McK. Jones, 1941. Arch. 2c, first problem under Professor Bogner.

5.42 Photographic shop for 1316 Massachusetts Avenue, Cambridge, Hugh McK. Jones, 1942. Arch. 2c, second problem, Professor Bogner.

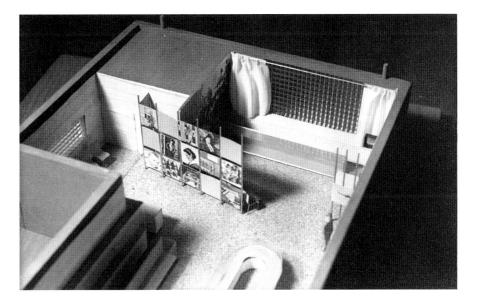

the onset of wartime measures, enrollment in planning plummeted as many students enlisted in the armed forces. Only Wagner's course on housing continued. During the war a bachelor's degree in city planning replaced the master's degree.

Having faltered in the mid-1930s for financial reasons, the program now virtually ceased to train professional planners as master synthesizers, capable of dealing with a broad range of issues at the regional level. Its instability was reflected in the succession of four chairmen over the next ten years. John Merriman Gaus succeeded Hubbard as the Charles Dyer Norton Professor of Regional Planning. He began his chairmanship by preparing, at Hudnut's request, an outline for instruction in planning at the university. Gaus traced the history of planning in America to show how it had evolved from city planning that focused on physical design, to regional planning, which, though still centered on physical design needs, included research into conceptual issues, like the economic and social structure of cities and their surrounding metropolitan areas, land classification, use of natural resources, ecological protection of watersheds, wildlife, and the retention of land for recreation. Within planning agencies and the government-sponsored programs of the New Deal, the shift to regional interests required working with governmental units that were regional in their jurisdiction. As a result, professional planners became less focused on problems of physical design. Given the interdisciplinary components of the regional planning field, training in it required input from several departments, each with a particular emphasis. Gaus believed that the education of a planner at Harvard required two different kinds of training: one covering physical design aspects, offered through the Graduate School of Design, and another that provided "training for general staff work . . . sometimes called management training" provided by the Graduate School of Public Administration.[118]

In 1943 there were only two students and three teachers in the planning department—"a lovely ratio," according to one of those students, Martin Meyerson. His fellow student was William Wurster; the faculty comprised John Gaus, Christopher Tunnard, and Martin Wagner. According to Meyerson, Tunnard's importance stemmed from his understanding of the National Resource Planning Board (headed by Harvard-trained Charles Eliot II) and the different planning approaches of Britain, Canada, and the United States. His modernism was obvious: he was associated with the avant-garde MARS group in England. Gaus, said Meyerson, preferred to affiliate the planning department with a school of government: Martin Wagner was "imaginative and precise," an excellent teacher somehow outside the world of action he had known in Germany and, to a lesser extent, in Turkey.[119]

Wurster, who designed the biggest housing project of the war at Vallejo in San Francisco Bay, was twice the age of fellow student Meyerson. In 1940 he had married Catherine Bauer, the housing expert who would soon teach in the planning depart-

ment of the GSD.[120] He came from California where he had practiced architecture, to accompany his wife and to take some time off to study regional planning in 1943. Meyerson characterized this cabal as all having a readiness "to combine the social sense and the physical sense."[121] Wurster took the initiative in bringing people together to discuss planning issues. As Walter Creese recalled, Wurster "used to hold soirées, with coffee and doughnuts as attractions, in the basement of Robinson Hall, trying to get people enthused over architecture. Down there he endeavored to persuade Harvard professors to exchange weighty views with MIT professors, which at that time would have been a dubious enterprise even in much more conducive surroundings."[122] This informal approach characterized the times and reflected the yearning for new leaders and a belief that good minds, regardless of persuasion, could get together and share ideas. When he left Harvard in 1944, Wurster became dean of the School of Architecture and Planning at MIT, a post he held until 1950.[123]

Gaus also departed. His analysis of the profession was insightful, his requirements for a planner's education were comprehensive, and he drew attention to the fundamental split between training in physical design and management of policy. In the mid-1940s he returned to Harvard to lecture in the Graduate School of Public Administration, the associated program in planning whose purpose he so well understood.[124] Meanwhile, planning at the GSD drifted.

The war affected the landscape architecture department far less dramatically than it had planning, as Hudnut attempted to "keep peace" among fractious divisions.[125] Norman T. Newton and Christopher Tunnard had appeared as competitors for a single position in the department. Hubbard and Pond supported the former, Hudnut and Gropius the latter.[126] President Conant made the Solomonic decision to hire both men, Newton as an assistant professor and Tunnard as a lecturer. The two became close friends, but the war prevented a long partnership at Harvard. After active military duty, Newton resumed his teaching post at the GSD, while Tunnard served with the Royal Canadian Engineers in 1942–43, received a Wheelwright Fellowship for 1943–44, and departed the following year to work as an associate editor of *Architectural Forum*. Ultimately, he became an assistant professor of city planning at Yale, where he spent the rest of his distinguished academic career.[127]

During the war the landscape architecture department also looked more generally at its role in the future. When a colleague at Penn State University questioned Bremer Pond about his views of the future of the field, Pond reiterated Harvard's founding premise that landscape architecture was a fine art that needed to divorce itself from associations with horticulture, but he affirmed his approval and support of collaborative efforts with architecture and engineering. Pond did not mention that his department had already dropped residential problems in order to focus on large-scale public works, starting with Norman T. Newton's first problem in state park design in 1941.[128]

Women and Design Education at Harvard

Despite the progressive and idealistic tenor of the GSD's rhetoric about architectural education, the university as a whole was far from progressive in its attitude towards the admission of women. While the university was undeniably chauvinistic, some faculty from architecture and landscape architecture—notably Henry Frost and Bremer Pond—were active supporters of admitting women to the design program. Katherine Brooks, an early victim of the school's admissions policy, sought out Frost for private instruction with five other women. This group, together with Bremer Pond, founded a school (later called the Cambridge School of Architecture and Landscape Architecture) that became one of the most important training grounds for women in these fields in the first half of the century.[129] The school officially opened in 1916, with Frost as director, a position he retained during the school's several relocations within Cambridge city limits. Frost worked unabatedly, for the rest of his life, for the cause of equality in the professional training of women and men. Charles Wilson Killam also lectured at the Cambridge School after his retirement from Harvard in 1937.

The university, however, inexcusably excluded women students, though it was happy to welcome women staff members, particularly in the traditional role of librarian. Librarians at Harvard were not merely cataloguers and keepers of books but careful bibliographers who made outstanding contributions to the design fields, especially in city planning, and who researched the illustrations for books such as Edgell's American Architecture of To-day. Though largely unheralded as such, in their one-to-one exchange with students, they, too, were teachers. Elizabeth D. Clarke was an assistant in the architecture library from 1902 to 1914, then librarian from 1914 to 1919, a seventeen-year period during which she was also secretary to the School of Architecture. Her successor as librarian was Ruth V. Cook, a graduate of the New School of Design in Boston, who held the position from 1919 to 1956. Cook founded new collections and oversaw a tremendous and rich variety of reference materials, including lantern slides, the blueprint collection, photographs of Renaissance buildings, and material on medieval architecture. A lively and generous person, she read all the books and encouraged numerous student investigations.[130] She kept and classified rare, fugitive materials, which resulted in a unique collection of ephemera. Along with faculty colleague Kenneth Conant, she was one of the founders of the Society of Architectural Historians in 1940.[131]

In a separate library of landscape architecture and city planning, formed on the first floor of Robinson Hall in 1911, Theodora Kimball, its first librarian, accomplished seminal work in defining the context and content of planning literature. Her collaborations with James Sturgis Pray and Henry Hubbard produced classification systems for city planning and landscape architecture that are still of scholarly interest. She worked with Hubbard on an Introduction to the Study of Landscape Architecture, founded the City Planning magazine, was active on Landscape Architecture magazine, and was a member of several city planning organizations. She continued as an advisor when Katherine McNamara became librarian in 1924. The collections they assembled eventually represented the finest library of city planning literature in the world.[132] McNamara continued the traditions of the library, became widely known as the foremost bibliographer of planning in the United States, and developed a sense of depth and range of the subject that far transcended technical reports.

Not only did these women take an active interest in their fields, they directed collections that expanded from 400 books in 1902 to 29,535 books and pamphlets in 1932. Other contributions came from Sally C. Symonds, secretary to the School of Architecture, who had a long and constructive tenure at Harvard.[133] Thus, ironically, while women were deprived of an education at the Schools of Architecture, Landscape Architecture, and City Planning, their intellects and labors greatly supported the professional training of men. Cook, McNamara, and their colleagues at the Fogg Museum helped intellectualize architecture, enriching the

5.43 (opposite top) Walter Gropius at his birthday party, May 1943. Left to right: Elizabeth Ware, John Black, Peter Jenks, Ansui Nimmana-haeminda, Mrs. Halprin, Mrs. Cheang, Gropius, Jorge S. Arango.

subject of design and making it more challenging and thoughtful. Indeed, the initiatives of the librarians at Harvard were paralleled by significant efforts at the University of Illinois, the University of California at Berkeley, and the University of Pennsylvania. The efforts of these librarians form part of the unwritten history of modern design.

MIT had admitted women to their architecture program since 1885; Harvard retained its chauvinism until World War II.[134] In the face of the war, the GSD recognized a need to consolidate both resources and students. In 1940 the GSD's summer school collaborated with Smith College's Graduate School of Architecture and Landscape Architecture, which had been affiliated with the Cambridge School since 1932.[135] This move towards accepting women was not, however, a progressive statement but an expedience to balance the budget. With the continuation of the economic restraints of the war and reductions in enrollment, Harvard next made arrangements to absorb the Cambridge School and open its own doors to women in 1942—with the intention that they be accepted *only* during the emergency. The debate over the acceptance of women into the GSD subtly presaged a coming divergence of political positions: Hudnut wanted women accepted on a permanent basis, while Gropius wanted women admitted only as special students and not as degree candidates.[136]

In describing the transfer of the Cambridge School's programs and students to Harvard in the summer of 1942, Frost explained that the emergency conditions of the war required the elimination of unnecessary duplication in teaching.[137] Women students with college degrees interested in professional design training could now apply to the Graduate School of Design; those without bachelor's degrees were denied entry. Few current students of the Cambridge School chose to pursue their studies at Harvard, and alumnae of the Cambridge School were furious at the closing of their school.[138] Finally, in 1942 Harvard accepted women into the GSD as regular students, fifty-seven years after MIT and sixty-four years after the University of Illinois opened their doors to women.

The insulting words of one member of the Department of Landscape Architecture show the blatant disgust that some GSD faculty members felt at the arrival of women: "In they came scrambling like oysters who walked up the beach with the Walrus and the Carpenter in Alice in Wonderland. We won't carry the simile any further. The aegis under which they entered bore the words, 'for the duration.' They may end up as the oysters did, or, they may be v-e-r-y difficult to dislodge. Anyway, they definitely are here."[139] Within six months enrollment of new female students had dropped from sixty to twenty-three.[140] In the words of their instructors, "while the best girls were not as good as the best men, the poorest were better than the worst men."[141] Despite this grudging acceptance of the adequacy of women's academic performance, the vitu-perative chauvinism lingered, and the Visiting Committee suggested limiting the number of women accepted or allowing them to fill only the places not filled by male students. Nevertheless, from this time on female students were admitted to the school.

A Modernist Vision of the Future

Faculty and students mostly treaded water during the war. Despite the pressures everyone felt under wartime conditions, the school developed a convivial social ambience—which included the celebration of Gropius's birthday, an annual school event (Fig. 5.43). Lecturers and exhibitions captured the pent-up energy surrounding the different manifestations of modern art and architecture around them. The schedule shows, though, that one kind of modernism—Frank Lloyd Wright's organic architecture—was off-limits to students as a model, though Wright did visit the GSD. When he lectured in 1940, he quashed questions of those students who dared challenge him and implied that they were all wasting their time studying at Harvard.[142]

Another project for Hudnut and his faculty was preparation in 1941 for a New York exhibition that would focus on Harvard's training of architects (Figs. 5.44, 5.45). Foreshadowing the further development of the GSD's educational principles, this exhibition would have offered the most cohesive explication of design education—had it actually opened.[143] The

5.44 Jury for the *Hidden Talent Competition* exhibition held at the Museum of Modern Art, New York, 1949. Left to right: Wallace Harrison, Joseph Hudnut (chair of the jury), Ludwig Mies van der Rohe, Eero Saarinen, Wallace Ketchum.

5.45 Jury for the *Hidden Talent Competition* exhibition held at the Museum of Modern Art, New York, 1949. Left to right: Wallace K. Harrison, Eero Saarinen, Ludwig Mies van der Rohe, Joseph Hudnut (chair of the jury).

only parallel was Gropius's version of design education at the Bauhaus, explained at an exhibition at the Museum of Modern Art in 1938.[144] An early version of Hudnut's outline for the stillborn exhibition began by criticizing the last generation's training as based on "book knowledge," the imitation of styles, and a total reliance on the classical orders that resulted in "timidity of imagination caused by lack of spiritual guidance and stimulation towards [students'] own creative efforts."[145]

Hudnut relaxed his diatribe in the revised version, however, and the project took on a more positive tone, elegantly laying out the educational philosophy of the GSD. Design training was shown to begin in college (as illustrated by student work arranged by Josef Albers), where young students were given hands-on experience with materials and tools in determining elementary structure and spatial relations for problems requiring solutions for actual buildings on known sites. The requirements of building programs were shown to be logically determined by applying scientific analysis to economic and social factors. The science of building combined with the art of spatial relations provided the two main disciplines involved in design, with both fueled by imagination, particularly as expressed in construction.[146]

The exhibition laid out the sequence of coursework that would meet these modern demands. In the studio system, students addressed successive problems under the direction of a master, which

required precise drawings essential for execution of the design and models to aid visualization. Teamwork would dominate the studio, specifically requiring the participation of landscape architects. Designs would include not only the building site but also the community and its collective life—a concept requiring each student to complete at least one project in low-cost housing. These studies would lead to the later introduction of city and regional planning. Ultimately, graduates of this training, along with distinguished graduates of other schools, would enroll in Walter Gropius's master studio, "the crown of our system of education."[147] The exhibition was to conclude with the school's credo: "We count as successful only those graduates who, besides technical competence, are able by an imaginative command of form to integrate the thought and feeling of our time into an organic unity with structural pattern. Only in that way can architecture be reinstated as the discoverer and guardian of the spiritual forces or can it recapture its inherent power for human happiness."[148]

Here, then, was the official ideal, to be presented publicly, a vision so clear and complete that illustrations sprang to its author's mind for every proposition. No mere technicians were to be trained at Harvard, but individuals whose spirituality connected them to the fullness of life. The concept of *teamwork* became the key term, replacing collaboration. Unfortunately, the exhibition was unrealized.

Students further defined the agenda of modern design education during the war,

showing their involvement with the social commitment of the new architecture and the philosophical issues of their own education by publishing "Opinion on Architecture," a formal critique of modernism, complemented by recommendations for school policy, dedicated and addressed to Hudnut.[149] The students' purpose was "to change the mild course of modern fashion architecture into a struggle for a revolution in the architectural world." This revolutionary zeal included specific political issues to be addressed by architects and architecture: for instance, how could modern architecture, as an expression of a new society, contribute to the fight against fascism?

The students objected to "mild" modernism and formulated analyses of the pioneers of the modern movement regarding their contributions to articulating the social role of architecture. The generation of the founders—Le Corbusier, Gropius, Erich Mendelsohn, Mies, J. J. P. Oud, and Wright—now was giving way to the next generation—Alvar Aalto, Richard Neutra, Marcel Breuer—each of whom was individually critiqued by the students. The principles of the pioneers had not been assimilated, the students concluded, and they saw "too few good followers" of their own generation.[150]

The students attacked the GSD for remaining too detached from social issues because it allocated only seven weeks to housing, "the main architectural issue of our time." Furthermore, they claimed, despite the ambitions of Hudnut and Gropius, their program was insufficient in its coverage of aesthetics, engineering and

construction principles, and realities of professional practice. Furthermore, it was inadequate in its coverage of landscape architecture, regional planning, and furniture design.[151]

Overarching the criticisms of the school was a fervent statement about the social role of the architect as a propagandist who strove to persuade people of the necessity for modern architecture. Le Corbusier became a role model who, in the competition for the Palace of the League of Nations, "sacrific[ed] his own interest and renounc[ed] the opportunity to win first prize, [thereby doing] more for propaganda of modern architecture than an executed building with compromise could have"—Le Corbusier's project, the most modern of the competition, was disqualified by conservative jurors for a minor infraction of the presentation requirements.[152] Reflecting socialist ideals, the students claimed that solutions in the future lay in "*COLLECTIVE WORK* among architects, engineers, contractors, and the working class" and was the only means to achieve an architecture that was both an "expressive and social activity."[153] The students concluded their broadside by recommending that the school's programs include more exposure to professional practitioners, contractors, local and national organizations, experimental works emphasizing particularly new technology, open juries, visiting lecturers from related fields, increased study of landscape architecture by architects and through collaborative problems, furniture design and household articles, and student discussions, conferences, and publications. Many of these reforms had been sought since the early 1930s—the vehemence of the demand was the new factor.

Despite the critiques students aimed at the school, and the school and faculty's critique addressed to the public, a powerful idealism still pervaded the atmosphere of conflict. A practical fact supported this idealism: after the threat of war diminished the enrollment, the admission of women—long awaited by some of the GSD—made it possible for the school to stay open. Positive and creative forces emerged during these war years, allowing a gradual coalescence of purpose. Also, while many students and faculty enlisted in the military, there was ample time for those left behind to assess where the schools, the professions, and society in general were heading in the future. The combination of the faculty's intentions and students' criticisms created a unique sense of purpose, dedication, and frustration. Rarely had a craving for the ideal role of the designer been so fervently expressed as it was in the early 1940s. The power of this vision, shared by students and faculty alike, was confirmed by how quickly it produced results.

By the middle of 1942, two years after Hubbard's resignation, the Visiting Committee reported a "fine spirit of cooperation which had matured in the past year, and the evident intelligent integration of the different Departments into a unified teaching whole. The frictions and dissatisfactions and personnel difficulties of the past had vanished completely."[154] There

was even a slight budgetary surplus, although the school paid a large price for the undergraduate program, with expenses for the Department of Architectural Sciences running almost half that of the graduate instruction in architecture and almost equaling the budget for instruction in landscape architecture.[155]

The Visiting Committee also pointed out deficiencies and unsettled issues. The Department of Architecture had five instructors in design and only one in engineering. Reinforcing the call for realism, the committee suggested hiring a distinguished engineer with experience in structural engineering and engineering research, even if his employment unbalanced the budget; the skills and expertise of Charles Wilson Killam had to be replaced. Finally, the committee left it to the faculty's discretion to decide if students should perform more practical field work. Operations in regional planning still remained unassessed.

A larger force outside the school supported the general optimism: anticipation of a tremendous building boom promised to stimulate growth in the design fields at the close of the war. Already by the summer of 1942 the budget for war-related building construction in the war program was $11 billion, with larger budgets expected in the next two years.[156] Since no private building was allowed, except for small houses, a tremendous building shortage was developing that would soon stimulate unprecedented growth under a national program of reconstruction. The new social and economic conditions

would call for the planning of cities and regions; the reconstruction of cities was anticipated as well as the design of new cities on a hitherto unknown scale. Landscape architects would be needed for problems of land planning, landscape engineering, and recreational projects at the regional, state, and national levels. The school asserted that research and instruction would not merely continue but would intensify and accelerate after the war.

This prospect of a rosy future for design motivated the addition of the first doctoral degrees in architecture, landscape architecture, and regional planning despite the overall reductions in curriculum that occurred at the same time. In February 1942 Harvard's Faculty of Arts and Sciences sanctioned the degree of a doctor of philosophy primarily for technical research in design and construction and in historical, scientific, and economic problems related to architecture or its allied fields; advanced research for the Ph.D. in the history of architecture—the "history of architectural styles"—remained the domain of the Department of Fine Arts.[157] The reasons for this announcement in the midst of the war are not clear. It may have been a desperate measure to attract students, like those who pushed for enrollment in the summer schools and finally admitted women. It may also have been an attempt to anticipate future needs of the profession. In any case, doctoral training played no significant role in the newly emerging modernist view of the social implications of design; producing modernist-minded practitioners, some of whom would become teachers, was the primary goal.

The daily press confirmed the enthusiasm about the future and the desire for a new vision. Despite the country's involvement in the war and the associated unpopularity of things Japanese or German, Gropius received public acceptance and even favorable publicity. An informative and laudatory 1942 article in the *Boston Herald*, entitled "Profile of a Dreamer Who Makes His Dreams Bloom into Reality," portrayed Gropius as a relentless visionary of the houses of the future. After lucidly explaining the benefits of technical advances in materials and engineering and principles of modern architecture, Gropius stated that the houses of the future would be prefabricated of concrete, glass, and steel, made practical by machine production and transported to sites, where they could be augmented, room by room, as families grew. After the war, armament factories could be converted to manufacturing these prefabricated houses,"and the new era of the artist-technician will be upon us."[158] This version of turning swords into plowshares framed the building type of the future as housing for veterans, which would, in turn, move into mass-developed, pitched-roof houses in the largest expansions of suburbs ever encountered in the United States.

Complementing Gropius's radical pronouncements, the newspaper provided a sympathetic and fascinating biography of his life and work, attributing many innovations in modern architecture to Gropius, along with a stunning portrait.

Despite the fact that Frank Lloyd Wright had already written on the ramifications of a modern expression utilizing glass and concrete three decades earlier, and that Le Corbusier's five principles included roof-top gardens and the abolition of the wall in experiments from the 1910s, the press placed the mantle of modernism on Gropius's shoulders, declaring that "the flat roof is another characteristic of the New Architecture pioneered by Gropius."[159] The wider public, through these kinds of articles, began to identify modern architecture with Gropius.

Machine-made houses were only one prospect in the future; new cities were another. The themes of national and city reconstruction increasingly became the subjects of design as the GSD anticipated America's needs after the war. Preparation for post-war conditions addressed problems in housing and planning as well as the intersection of social institutions and industrial facilities. Landscape architects geared to focus more on collective than individual needs, and regional planners to examine the causes of civic deterioration and formulate remedial programs.

Gropius continued to attempt to put his theories into practice; on the professional front, however, his progress was temporarily blocked. Breuer terminated their partnership in 1941, claiming that he had been publicly insulted by Gropius during a design jury. Privately, Breuer accused Gropius of misusing his authority and deeply offending him.[160] Despite this professional rupture, they eventually resumed their friendship.

After the break with Breuer, Gropius and Wagner collaborated on student projects, focusing largely on designs for mass housing and city planning. Gropius advocated single-family houses on green peripheries and high-rise buildings for urban situations, a precursor of slab buildings that later dominated housing. Their operating premise was that city reconstruction required not so much the rebuilding of central cities as the transferring of populations from urban centers to new satellite cities. Collaboration among the design fields could provide the appropriate expertise for solving such problems on a regional or national level—problems that surely exceeded the scope of any individual's skill. One student project supervised by Gropius and Wagner, "Housing as a Town Planning Problem," embodied their approach. Executed in the winter of 1942, it was published as "A Program for City Reconstruction" in *Architectural Forum* in 1943 (Figs. 5.46, 5.47).[161] To Gropius and Wagner, housing and "town planning" were synonymous. The project proposed that urban rehabilitation could be accomplished by resettling people into rationally organized, self-contained suburban communities called "townships," with populations of 5,000 residents. The program was based on a ten-point manifesto, ranging from the need for large-scale rehabilitation to resettlement of the unemployed. Its points included the need for "square mile" rehabilitation, instead of a piecemeal approach to reconstruction; provision of new legal and financial tools that would operate on a state and national

5.46 "A Program for City Reconstruction." Student project under the supervision of Walter Gropius and Martin Wagner, as published in *Architectural Forum*, 1943.

5.47 "A Program for City Reconstruction." Student project under the supervision of Walter Gropius and Martin Wagner, as published in *Architectural Forum*, 1943.

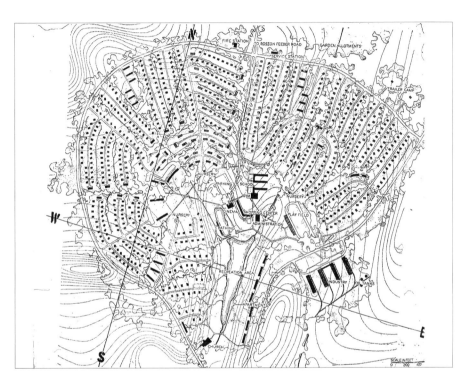

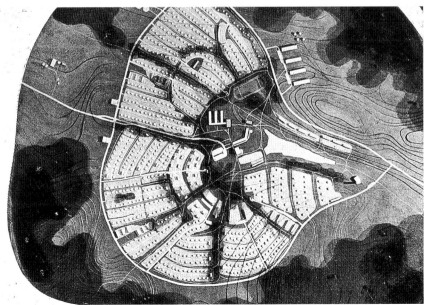

level; integration of industry, commerce, and living places; resettlement of unemployed people into townships; connection of townships by "superhighways"; use of human-scale and time-distance studies to limit the size of townships; surrounding townships with farmbelts; abolition of real estate speculation with its function replaced by communal ownership; autonomous township government; and the combining of townships into "county-ships." Conveying a Marxist orientation typical of the politically motivated modernists, the manifesto provided a guide for students in their attempts to integrate single-family houses into the townships. There were even stipulations for resettling people from the inner cities. Among the questions that went unaddressed was the problem of what would become of the cities abandoned by these new residents.

In addition to schemes for creating housing in the framework of city planning, Gropius and Wagner collaborated on a number of academic research papers and projects of mutual interest: they testified before a select committee of the U.S. Congress in 1941 on the issue of population movement in response to war and war industry[162]; they also prepared "Cities Renaissance" and a report in *The New City Pattern* that was first presented as part of a conference on urbanism in Cambridge, Massachusetts, in 1942.[163]

Despite their joint efforts, a bitter rift had begun to open in their relationship as early as 1940; differing philosophies of innovation in design and social programs in housing were at the core. Wagner, ever

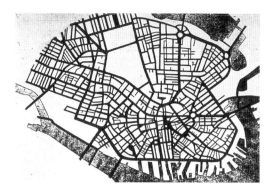

5.48 "Question Mark Boston,"
existing plan of downtown Boston.
Martin Wagner, 1942.

the socialist, questioned Gropius's dedication to radical ideals. This interpersonal demarcation mirrored a fundamental conflict within the entire modern movement as its early diehard protagonists lost their political ardor. Wagner accused Gropius of acquiring a conservatism at the age of fifty-seven that had not been present in their experimental years of the 1920s. In a frank and critical letter to Gropius, Wagner wrote that, in the past, his "beloved Goethe-Gropius of Weimar" had learned from mistakes and blunders—"but the Harvard Gropius seems to have changed his mind in this respect. He believes he can or should stop students [from] making mistakes in pioneering on new building fields on account of getting [here Wagner quotes Gropius] 'too easily to wrong inferences, [and] not overlooking the vast amount of problems concerned.'"[164] The "inferences" referred to students imitating the work of Le Corbusier and Gropius himself. Also, Wagner felt that design problems such as museums, dance pavilions, or farms for gentlemen avoided the pressing social and artistic problems of the time.

In the same letter Wagner further criticized Gropius for no longer being interested in prefabrication. European modernists had long hoped that the use of prefabricated materials would provide economy and speed in the construction of detached and semi-detached dwellings. In response to a comment by Gropius that methods of prefabrication were too difficult to teach to students, Wagner asserted that prefabrication was no more complicated than any other conventional con-

struction method, and it allowed students an opportunity to "learn the real elements of building construction and financing." Wagner informed Gropius that he intended to teach his own students that "prefabrication means simplification in building construction, at least a special kind of simplification which can be carried out much easier than the old-fashioned method of post-fabrication." With respect to the public's rejection of unusual housing forms, Wagner blamed architects, contractors, and politicians "for not having prepared [for] the spontaneous acceptance of new form as is the case in the field of engineering." The acceptance of unconventional housing could occur if prices were low enough and quality high enough. Although Gropius had given student problems in prefabrication, Wagner again challenged him: "You, dear Gropius, had the same idea in 1924, and you fought for this idea, and by now has it become obsolete for you? You do not believe any more in a Henry Ford for housing the masses."[165]

Gropius, however, did make another attempt to implement the ideas of prefabrication in his practice. In 1942 he joined Konrad Wachsmann in promoting the Packaged House System, a system of prefabricated panels developed by Wachsmann and manufactured by the General Panel Corporation. Gropius's enthusiasm for the system, however, may have been aroused only after Wachsmann had developed it considerably, and at least some of the appeal rested in the financial compensation offered to Gropius by the man-

ufacturing company.[166] The advantage of the Packaged House System was that its panels could be assembled both vertically and horizontally. The system "proved its worth," but over a six-year period it failed to garner public acceptance—which Gropius attributed to "psychological reasons," presumably a resistance to change.[167] Giedion attributed the lack of consumer response to a fear that prefabricated housing would lack individuality and noted another hindrance, cited by Gropius, which was that the methods of financing private construction were based entirely on manual labor, not on prefabrication. Part of the reason, however, for the failure of the Packaged House System was that it did not provide an effective means of product distribution, and it lacked sufficient tolerance for field installations.[168] Although Gropius continued to speak about the necessity for the mass production of housing, saying in 1947 that future efforts should concentrate on prefabricated parts rather than whole house units, he was less and less interested in the difficulties of industrial production.[169] In Europe the modernist emphasis was on the container as an enclosure;[170] in America the emphasis shifted to the components within the container—and eventually even the importance of the components faded as the quest for erected buildings at the largest possible scale dominated the field.

While Gropius pursued more pragmatic approaches, adapting himself to the changing demands of America, Wagner retained the aggressive intensity of European mod-

5.49 "Question Mark Boston," a rational reconstruction of downtown Boston, 1942. Student projects under Martin Wagner.

5.50 "Question Mark Boston," a rational reconstruction of downtown Boston, 1942. Student projects under Martin Wagner.

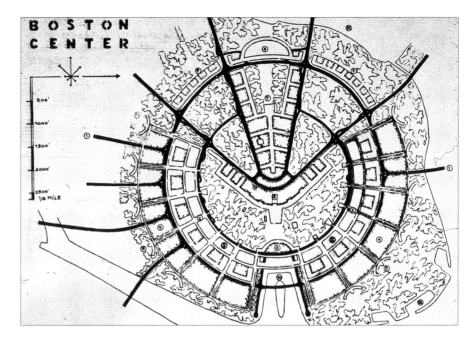

ernism in its heroic phase, proposing utopian and politically radical projects for dwelling units, cities, and regions. From his perspective, the reconstruction of cities posed a major challenge to all design fields, and the housing in cities needed rational reconsideration. Wagner proposed studying new housing types in the summer session of 1942 when he taught courses on "demountable houses" (an introduction to the design of prefabricated housing that included social, economic, and technical problems of this "new branch of construction") and post-war planning and building problems.[171]

Wagner's initial scheme of 1942 for a new city center in Boston culminated with a polemical proposal for the Boston Contest of 1944, "Question Mark Boston," which called for a complete reconstruction of the city's downtown requiring the razing of the entire downtown area (Figs. 5.48–5.50).[172] Shares in the ownership of the new city were to be distributed on the basis of previous property ownership. Activities within the new city would be redistributed in a rational and functional plan: a rationalized transit system with circular road patterns and civic facilities in a curved belt wrapping around the transit circle. Well aware of the polemical nature of his proposal, Wagner subtitled it "A Challenge to the Intelligent Imaginations of the Residents of Metropolitan Boston." Despite its utopian basis, Wagner provided extensive details for its implementation and financing. Wagner's Harvard colleague, Walter Bogner, however, won first prize with a prosaic scheme for urban

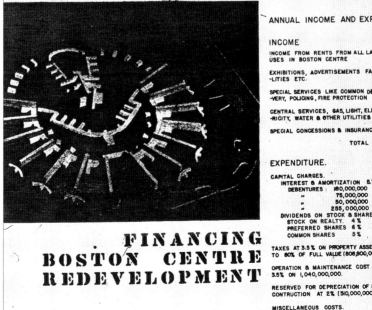

Fig. 23 Boston Center Proposal

5.51 Project for an economic
post-war house, Octavio A.
Mendez, March 1943. "Post-war
Shelter" Architecture 2d, Professor
Gropius.

redevelopment. Ironically, Gropius's 1953
proposal with Pietro Belluschi for a new
Boston Center—ultimately constructed in
a different form than the Prudential Center—was the successor to Wagner's circular utopia.[173]

Contradicting Wagner's criticism of
Gropius's flagging commitment to mass
housing and prefabrication, he gave his
students the problem "The Post-War Shelter for the Average Family."[174] In the brief
for his students, Gropius provided directions for systematic research of a suitable
module, for varying its appearance when
grouped, and for alleviating the rigidity
and scale problems that occur with
grouping the units; here was the clarity of
approach and purpose for which Gropius
deserved his reputation of brilliance. He
also pointed out to his students that "the
true aim of prefabrication, namely to
combine the economic advantages of
machine-made repetition with the human
requirement of justified individual variations, may seem to be contradictory."[175] It
was up to them to create flexibility and
variety of purpose.

Student projects from the master's
classes of 1943 show the results. Octavio
A. Mendez, a student from Panama,
demonstrated Gropius's approach in his
isometric drawing of the project, which
emphasized the service wall as containing utilities and ventilation and functioning as a spine and a divider between utilitarian and living spaces (Fig. 5.51).
Mendez also showed a plan that allowed
for the addition of two bedrooms for the
expanding post-war family.

5.52, 5.53 Project for a post-war shelter,
I. M. Pei, March 1943. "Post-war Shelter,"
Arch. 2d, Professor Gropius. Elevations
and interior perspective.

I. M. Pei, while in the master's program at the GSD, focused more on the development of a constructional system (Figs. 5.52, 5.53). His scheme provided details for wood construction and the all-important module for the prefabrication of units. The use of the module allowed for expansion of the ground floor as well as an addition of a linear, second-floor wing. In addition, Pei explored a series of variations based on the relationship between the main entry of the unit to the point of arrival via an automobile; one variation abutted two garages to form a semi-detached pair of units. Pei's scheme had the aesthetic image that soon became iconic for modern housing: a simple, dynamic façade of vertical and horizontal elements; a sleek interior with exposed framing members; and a butter-fly-shaped roof that inclined from the edges towards the center. This butterfly shape—which later appeared in Breuer's "House in a Garden" at the Museum of Modern Art and Le Corbusier's project for the Errazuriz House in Chile—extended to form a trellis, providing an alternative to a pitched roof while attempting to avoid the problem of water retention on flat roofs.

In another student study for the post-war house, Theodore Prichard designed an elegant library and paid special attention to interior furnishings and details (Figs. 5.54, 5.55). Philip Johnson, who had returned to Harvard to study architecture after establishing himself at the Museum of Modern Art, had the temerity to design not a house for the post-war

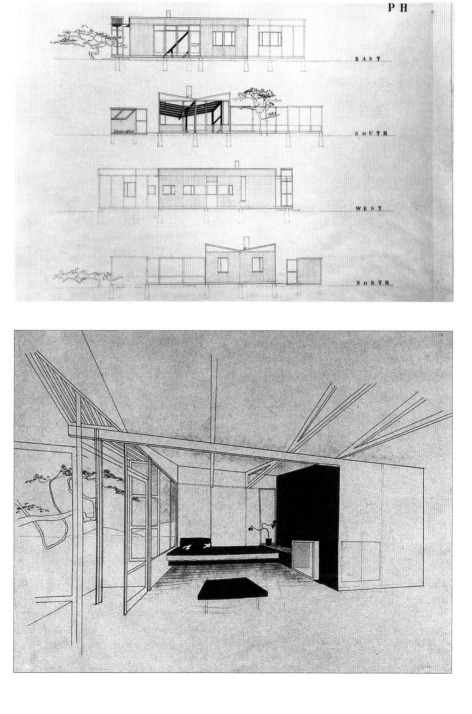

5.54, 5.55 Library, Theodore
Prichard, c. 1944. Master's class,
Professor Walter Gropius.
Elevations and perspective.

5.56, 5.57 (opposite) Student's house,
Cambridge, Mass., Philip C. Johnson,
1943. Master's thesis project.
Perspective and plan.

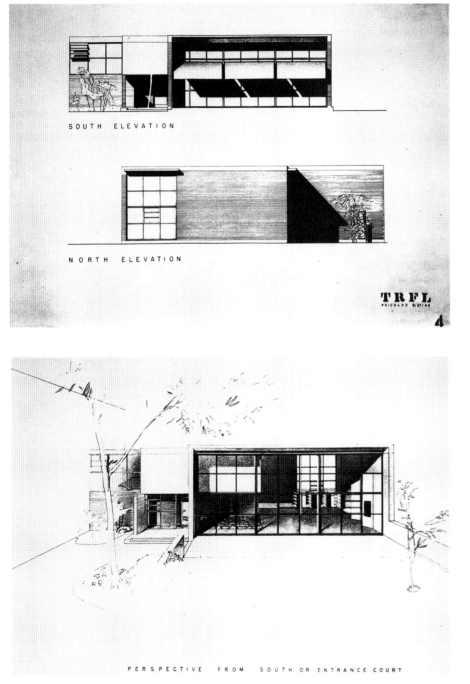

SOUTH ELEVATION

NORTH ELEVATION

TRFL
PRICHARD 5/27/44

4

PERSPECTIVE FROM SOUTH OR ENTRANCE COURT

masses but a house for *himself*, intended for a Cambridge location. A wall wrapped around the front of the lot, forming an enclosed courtyard and completely blocking any view of the house from the street, creating a building that had no relation to the urban "streetscape" of the city (Figs. 5.56, 5.57). The clear plan, variety of materials, and modular use of stone as a surface material showed the influence of Mies van der Rohe, who attained the status of an icon in the 1950s.

The need for collective and single-family housing existed not only in the United States but also in underdeveloped countries. The international students in Gropius's master's class could explore the problem of applying a generic approach, developed in Europe and America, to non-Western cultures. Calling on his own cultural experience, Ansui Nimmanahaeminda submitted a thesis for a summerhouse on Sutep Mountain, Chiengmai, Thailand. It contained a house for five families that was intended to reflect Asia's social customs as well as its economy (Figs. 5.58, 5.59). Gropius asked the student to define the cultural context as well as to provide details of the climate, square-footages, uses of bedrooms and living and dining areas, views, and prevailing winds. The student rose to the challenge by submitting a supplement to his written program. Gropius provided the practical dictates of rational, modern architecture; Nimmanahaeminda provided a stunning vernacular architecture using a pinwheel-shaped plan that admitted the Western pleasures of tennis, bad-

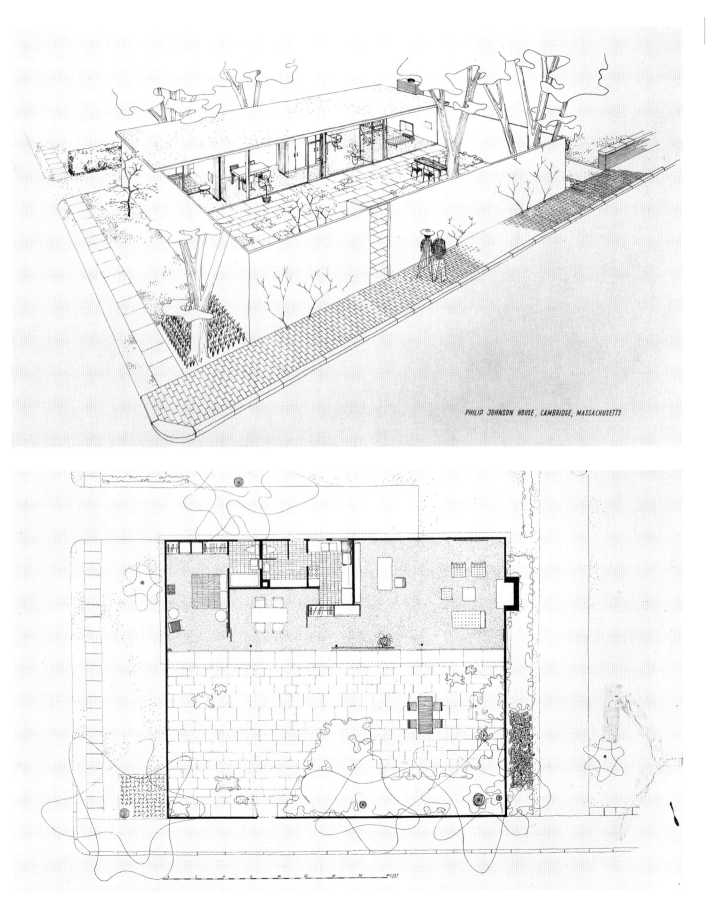

PHILIP JOHNSON HOUSE, CAMBRIDGE, MASSACHUSETTS

5.58, 5.59 Summer house, Sutep Mountain, Chiengmai, Thailand. A. Nimmanahaeminda, October 1943. Master's thesis, Gropius studio. Elevations and perspectives.

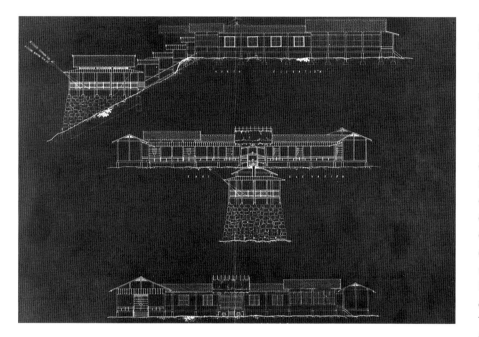

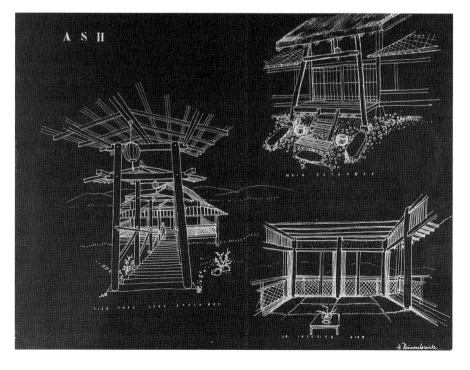

minton, and shuffleboard courts—and a room for ping-pong.

Breuer also gave his students problems in housing. His studio program in the spring of 1944, the "Redevelopment of Boston's South End," synopsized not only the Harvard method but also the basic modernist approach to the development of new communities that would have major repercussions for the next three decades.[176] The program for the redevelopment used "real conditions"—the one constant in the modernist agenda—as described in the recently published reports by the Boston City Planning Board. The site was real, too—a specifically designated area of the South End. The task was to design a residential area for a population of 4,000–8,000 inhabitants in the larger context of the whole development of the Inner South End District, including removal of its industrial section. Except for building code requirements, no design restrictions hindered the solutions conceived. Since the area was slated as residential, all support facilities needed to be included. Breuer stressed that the solutions proposed by students should be economical and realistic, although the actual financial costs for the developments would not be calculated until the conclusion of the project.

The students began their tasks with a site visit in the company of Wagner, followed by discussions of the issues, fact-finding, locating maps, and related tasks. Using the concept of teamwork—the new term for collaboration—Breuer then divided the students into teams, some

5.60, 5.61 Redevelopment of South End, Boston, Jean Bodman, 1944. Arch. 2c, Breuer studio. Plan and model.

189

starting on the design of dwellings and others on site plans. Breuer and the teams discussed the preliminary results; the designers of the site plans subsequently suggested capacities and space requirements for public facilities and the layout of the site models. The other groups began to flesh out the design details and coordinate the plans for dwellings and individual models. Final review of models, rental rate computations, and financial analysis occurred five weeks after the start of the project in April 1944.

Jean Bodman, a Smith College graduate who was to become a founding partner of Gropius's future practice, The Architect's Collaborative, proposed a scheme that identified the support facilities of the residential redevelopment: shopping center, restaurant, school, auditorium, gymnasium, gas station, and tennis courts (Figs. 5.60, 5.61). In addition to this central complex, she provided three housing components. One was a two-story line of rowhouses that had storage and appliance rooms on the lower level with apartments above; parking spaces separated each parallel row. A second housing type was the medium-rise slab, with parking lots in front of each building. The third was a continuous linear building, fourteen stories high, presumably for residents without automobiles; their building fronted the access to the subway that provided the main mass transit link to Boston.

The other general plans used similar approaches of providing neighborhood facilities, high-rise slabs, and medium-rise buildings; only the disposition of

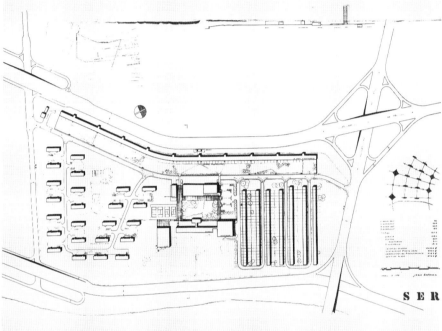

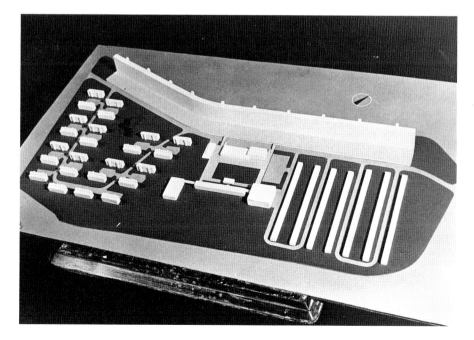

5.62 Redevelopment of South End, Boston, Margaret D. Heath and group, 1944. Arch. 2c, Breuer studio. Plan.

5.63 Redevelopment of South End, Boston, Margaret D. Heath and group, 1944. Arch. 2c, Breuer studio. View of model.

5.64 (opposite top left) Redevelopment of South End, Boston, Ira Rakatansky 1944. Arch. 2c, Breuer studio. Plan.

5.65 (opposite middle) Redevelopment of South End, Boston, Ira Rakatansky, 1944. Breuer studio. View of model.

5.66 (opposite top right) Redevelopment of South End, Boston. Arthur K. H. Cheang, 1944. Gropius studio.

5.67 (opposite bottom left) Redevelopment of South End, Boston, Anne G. Tyng, 1944. Arch. 2c, Breuer studio. Site plan.

5.68 (opposite bottom right) Redevelopment of South End, Boston, Anne G. Tyng, 1944. Arch. 2c, Breuer studio. Typical apartment plan and section.

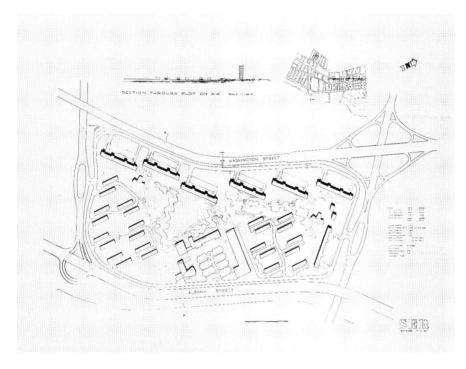

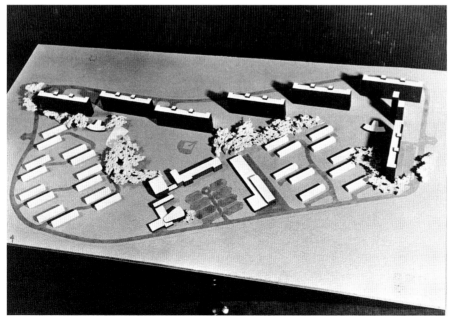

these elements around the site varied. Margaret D. Heath and her group used eight high-rise slab buildings instead of long buildings (Figs. 5.62, 5.63). By pushing the housing slabs to the edge of the site, Ira Rakatansky's scheme had the advantage of creating loosely surrounded open spaces for the residents (Figs. 5.64, 5.65). To confirm the modernist inspiration for the scheme, Rakatansky added a diagram of a partial golden section to remind viewers of Le Corbusier's *modulor* system or proportion. The sole variation on the use of rectilinear schemes was presented by K. H. Cheang when he took on the same problem as his project in Gropius's master studio: he used curved buildings to follow streets and thereby provide more spatial definition to the complex while framing a man-made lake (Fig. 5.66).

Anne G. Tyng, later Louis Kahn's collaborator, proposed for the South Bay Boston site a set of interlocking apartment buildings bounded by four principal streets (Figs. 5.67, 5.68). Simple in their architectural expression, each complex contained the basic elements of the anticipated post-war neighborhood: mixed apartment units and garages, a school, auditorium, and community center, nurseries, and, of course, shopping center. In addition, as in many similar schemes, the existing pattern of blocks—their scale and the scale of any surrounding buildings—was absorbed into the spreading complex, with its low base and disparate towers, all independent of the city grid and oriented towards the sun.

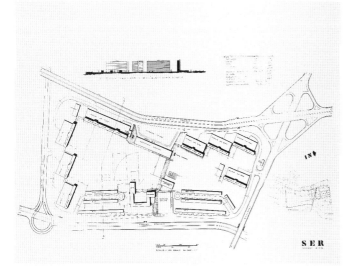

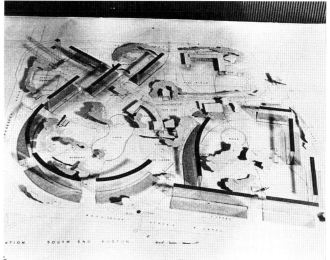

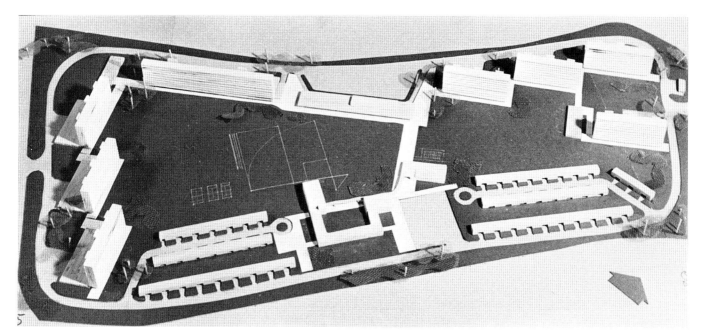

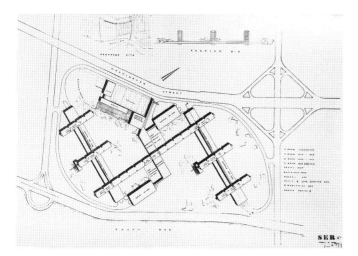

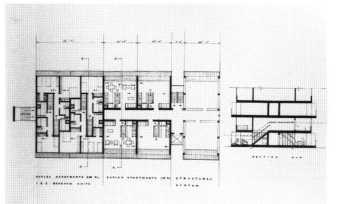

5.69 Redevelopment of South End,
Boston, Lucy W. Hulburd, 1944.
Breuer studio. Apartment building,
elevation, and section.

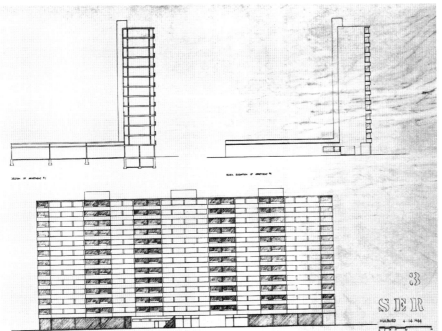

The design of individual buildings within the South Boston Project (and other community redevelopment projects like it) focused on building types that were seen as providing the basic needs of neighborhood life: apartment buildings, shopping centers, community centers, and schools—but no individual dwellings. Apartment building designs were based on a set of basic strategies, and their façades became increasingly abstract and diagrammatic (Fig. 5.69). Basil Yurchenco provided a view of a community center of a typical redevelopment scheme, as seen by residents from the rooftop garden of a high-rise apartment building (Figs 5.70, 5.71). Whimsi-cally, his perspective drawing included a clarion angel that trumpeted, "Come and Live at Troffle Village."

The students' concepts of shopping centers tended to be interchangeable; Lincoln B. Hockaday's proposal for a shopping center in Lincoln, Massachusetts, could have easily fit into the South Boston Complex (Figs 5.72, 5.73). To further ground the project in the social realities of the day, Hockaday used a collage, a preferred modernist presentation technique, to include in his drawing a photographic image of a couple, presumably a wife with her returning GI husband. To complete the aura of practicality and rationality, he circled the details of floor and ceiling construction, pointing out the advantages of each.

Though all the proposals for the redevelopment of South Boston intended to provide new and better accommodations for a typically run-down urban American neighborhood, their deficiencies remained unclear to their authors and their teachers—and to successive generations of architects and planners who used these kinds of prototypes to design mass housing. Untouched were questions about the social impact of living in such densely populated high-rise buildings and the psychological isolation people might feel in response to being physically disconnected from the fabric of the city around them. In essence, the designers of the future did not know who the real residents of "Troffle City" would be or whether these were the community centers the unknown masses wanted and needed.

While Gropius, Breuer, and Wagner attempted to demonstrate their idealistic modernist principles, Hudnut was writing and contemplating what was on the horizon. In this period of introspection during the war, the *Journal of the American Institute of Architects* asked Hudnut to describe the philosophy at Harvard. He replied, quoting Ralph Waldo Emerson's essay "Self-Reliance" (1841), that despite its modernist orientation, the conservative culture of New England supported his school: "Models of American art are in the minds of its citizens, in their climate, soil, needs of the people, and habit and form of government."[177] At this point, Hudnut still believed that the radical

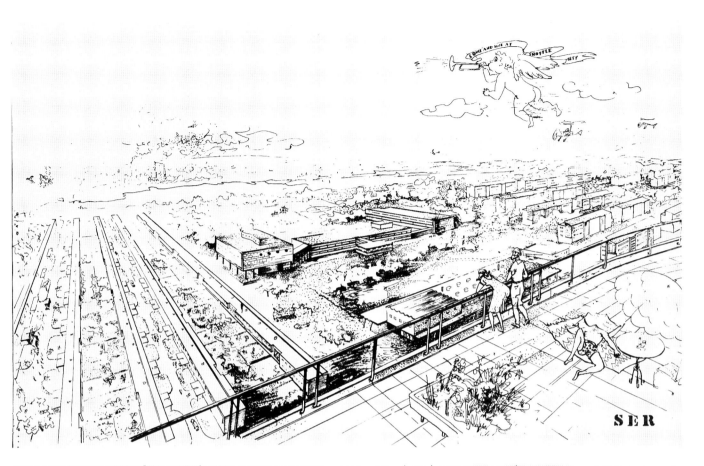

SER

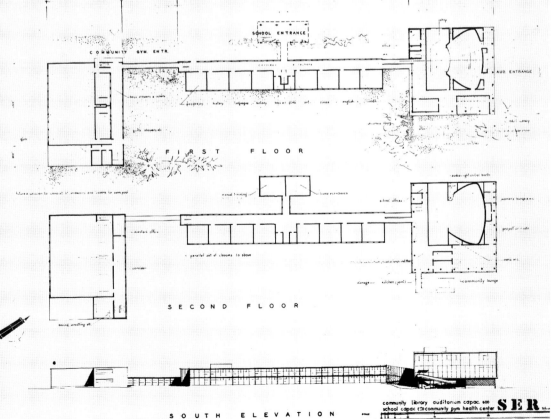

COMMUNITY GYM. ENTR.

SCHOOL ENTRANCE

AUD. ENTRANCE

FIRST FLOOR

SECOND FLOOR

SOUTH ELEVATION

community library auditorium capac. 600
school capac. 650 community gym health center **SER**

5.70 Redevelopment of South End, Boston, Basil Yurchenco, 1944. Breuer studio. "Troffle City," view of community center. Perspective. Sunbathers and sight-seers enjoy the view of their modern community as a cherubic angel proclaims, "Come and Live at Troffle City."

5.71 Redevelopment of South End, Boston, Basil Yurchenco, 1944. Breuer studio. "Troffle City," view of community center. Plan and elevation.

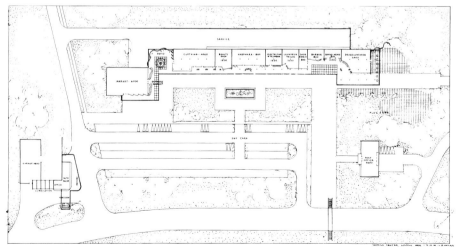

reforms he was shepherding had roots in America's own traditions and identity.

In *Architectural Record* Hudnut explicated a broader perspective in which he claimed that the profession of education had steadily expanded while the profession of architecture had steadily shrunk. Architects had lost ground to engineers, landscape architects (architects' "romantic cousins"), and the new planning professionals ("nebulous as yet but promising of sons"), as well as to interior decorators, contractors, realtors, corporate and institutional entities with "Architectural Departments," and even magazines that furnished house plans with each subscription. The solution, as Hudnut saw it, was to admit the changes and assess their direction. A "renewed comradeship" with all the design professions was required, since they are all "social arts inseparable except in rare instances from the collective life, the smallest unit of which is the family, the largest the population of a town or of a region."[178]

Ideally, this comradeship would result in the reunion of the several professions into one, with both specialists and generalists. The phenomenon of the group practice—present since the beginnings of the Departments of Architecture, Landscape Architecture, and City Planning—allowed the collaborative effort. As Hudnut noted, though, "this idea of a collaborative problem is not new; but we have failed to develop the idea to a sufficient usefulness." Merely working together on a common problem was insufficient to achieve this end; students should have actual experience, as creators, in the allied fields and gain sufficient knowledge and opinions "to the point of belligerency."[179]

Hudnut acknowledged that conflicts between the professions and within architecture itself made collaboration difficult. To make this point, he recounted listening to a city planner selling a city council on the need for a city plan, and the need for city planners, while demeaning architects as "makers of pretty pictures . . . purveyors of a facile romanticism; tailors who can trim up the outside of a house, unconcerned with its interior or environment; or at the best dreamers asleep in a private heaven of 'aesthetic compositions.' Their estimates are unreliable, their ignorance of land forms and land economics a menace to public safety, and their heads are placidly innocent of all those 'social and economic factors' so dear to the planner."[180]

In the face of such divisive attitudes, Hudnut believed that architectural schools should stand together, but that schools alone could not overturn a fixation on conventional images that derived from traditional rendering, perspective, and model-making wherein a building's plan, method of construction, and image were independently conceived. Neither could they indoctrinate students with theories of functionalism or insist that they embrace structural principles without a fundamental change that emphasized the design process as a means of unifying a building's plan with its materials and construction to produce a coherent, expres-

sive character. Process should take precedence over preconceived image. Not only ideology but technology would lead the way. Ironically, the war's urgencies, Hudnut predicted, would accelerate "discoveries and inventions having a scope and adaptability undreamed of in this our antique world."[181] New technology would emerge, as would flexible, light, moldable materials and synthetic fibers beyond present imagination, in addition to the plastics and waterproof plywood that already had been developed. Furthermore, the future promised new organizations of industry, capital, and labor, and new transportation, production, and sources of power.

Relying on precedent or on the analysis of accepted masterpieces could not begin to realize this idealistic and robust vision of the future. According to Hudnut, students would be able to create optimally in these future conditions only if they grasped how forms emerge from the design process—a basic comprehension that would "afford a progressive experience in the integration of structure with plan and expressive form." The courses oriented towards processes would require a method unique to achieving the creation of specific "environments, equipment, conventions." For Hudnut, the result might be a language particular to the objectives, and that process and its products would have to be "enlightened by a liberal philosophy."[182]

Hudnut concluded his visionary statement of dedication and hope for the future on an inspired note: "I should like our stu-

dents to leave our schools of architecture with a wider vision and a broader range of interests than those which I had at the end of my professional studies. I should like them to feel a deeper comradeship for those who, although architects in spirit and in way of working, are yet practitioners of an affiliated art. I should wish them to be armed with a practical and immediate technology, but they should have also minds that are curious and awake to every new discovery and invention; and they should be resolute to use their art, woven into actualities and yet addressed to the spirit, for the reconstruction of our ravaged world. In that direction lies the recovered authority of architecture.[183]

Even as Hudnut spoke so eloquently about the virtues of collaboration, the triad of professions composing the Graduate School of Design still remained unequal: the planning department was rising from its nadir, and landscape architecture was still struggling to integrate itself into the ethos of the GSD. The demands of modernism required a vision of a unified training program for designers and planners that would alter the educational process in America by creating generations of highly successful practitioners as well as teachers and leaders of other schools, and by serving as a model to be considered and even emulated by other schools. Implicit in changing the educational system was the ambition to change not merely America but a world convulsed with war. With the end of the war and an onslaught of returning students, this elegant vision of unity took on a simple and rational clarity.

THE POST-WAR APOGEE,
1945–1951

The post-war period surged with enthusiasm for the reconstruction of a devastated Europe as well as of an America that had finally shaken off the misery of the Great Depression. Cities needed rebuilding; middle-class people needed homes; veterans needed jobs and education—and architecture schools needed to create a new body of modern professionals to satisfy an overwhelming demand for buildings. Modernism now had its greatest opportunity to enter the mainstream of American life.

With the war's end, enrollment for 1945–46 nearly doubled, though the number of women in the school dropped dramatically. Also attending the Graduate School of Design were twenty-five foreign students from sixteen countries; many came for advanced study with Gropius, and they provided the first international nucleus for spreading his principles. Veterans naturally wanted to complete their studies as quickly as possible and get on with their lives, but Hudnut specifically opposed implementing accelerated programs, as other schools were doing, noting that time was needed for proper training and that aptitude for design could not be taught anyway.

Rejecting accusations that a "Gropius style" dominated Harvard, Hudnut cast the developments at the GSD in a progressive, rather than revolutionary, light: "There will be no radical change in our discipline which, as you know, is based upon the problem system developed in the École des Beaux-Arts in Paris with many adaptations to fit this tradition to the American Scene. We do not try to indoctrinate our students in any kind of architecture." The Graduate School of Design, he added, wanted to provide a "wider social serviceability" and consequently steered its students to grapple with problems in city planning, housing, techniques of building construction, and "everything which tends to sustain the happiness of populations."[1]

The New Modernist Curriculum

In the fall of 1945 the GSD responded to post-war conditions and the needs of its incoming students by finally implementing the changes in structure and curriculum that had been gestating since Dean Hudnut's arrival in 1936. The GSD's program for training a modern practitioner of architecture, landscape architecture, or city and regional planning became classically elegant in its simplicity. The new modernist GSD offered a revamped first-year core of courses and electives, a new approach to providing practical, hands-on experience, and a large group of new teachers who had been trained by Gropius.

The core of the program, which provided the basis of all the design disciplines, was formed by four closely integrated courses taught in the first year to all students by an interdepartmental team of instructors. Future architects, landscape architects, and planners once again shared a common training, just as they had under Langford Warren at the turn of the century. During this first year

6.1 GSD students in Hunt Hall examining a model of frame construction, 1946 (*Harvard Alumni Bulletin*, 30 March 1946).

they were exposed to the elements common to the three design fields as well as to the basic techniques of each profession. The purpose was to create a well-rounded professional whose education was founded on fundamentals that involved basic design, considerations of site and shelter, and the principles of construction. These courses specifically reflected the intention of turning social, economic, and physical data into built form. As part of the program's streamlined image, newly simplified course names identified their fundamental character: Design 1, Planning 1, Construction 1, and Architecture 3.

Design 1, a weekly six-hour course, introduced the basic elements of design and expression in abstract formal terms to familiarize students with "fundamental concepts of *space, form, and function* and the primary structural relationships which control them," and to study the effects of color and light on the perception of form and space.[2] The studio exercises of the course also included the teaching of basic design at an abstract level, paralleling principles of basic design at the Bauhaus.

Planning 1 dealt with problems of "site and shelter." The students began with a study of topography and developed "use-ful patterns in space and structure" based on an interpretation of social, economic, and physical data. The course stressed methods common to planners, architects, and landscape architects, and included map reading, the study of ground forms, and topographic analysis complemented by field trips. These experiences and the analysis of the social fabric of the community were combined with a series of increasingly complex design problems related to actual sites and probable requirements. Students also prepared documents and drawings for this course. Reflecting its importance in the core, it met for nine hours per week.

Construction 1, a weekly three-hour course, proceeded from principles to facts to design expression and consisted of lectures, conferences, and class exercises; surveys of land areas, services, and uses; and a consideration of structures and materials. The course also included field trips, whose exercises illustrated problems discussed in lectures, and models were used to study structural systems (Fig. 6.1). Architecture 3, an elective weekly three-hour course, focused on the drawing techniques essential in demonstrating the ideas of these studies and thereby reinforced the other core courses.

In the second year students entered courses specific to their chosen fields. Architecture students took architectural engineering, building technology, professional practice, mechanical equipment—and, of course, design, conducted every semester in a studio. Landscape students studied landscape engineering, freehand drawing, and planting design centered around landscape design studio. Planning students had the most flexible curriculum; in addition to studying planning techniques, their work involved design studio courses that dealt with city and regional planning. They also were offered civic design, economics, engineering, government, history, math, and sociology.

The new curriculum relied heavily on a previous liberal arts education to provide the intellectual groundwork for professional training. The *Official Register* of the GSD recommended that undergraduates seeking admission to the GSD's program should take courses in physics, mathematics, English literature, and philosophy, as well as in the theory and practice of design, especially courses involved in "making and doing." Undergraduates from Harvard and Radcliffe had the architectural sciences program, created by Hudnut in 1936, to provide the groundwork for studies at the graduate level. Indeed, the Department of Architectural Sciences emerged from the stasis of the war emergency with a crisply defined program of liberal arts and preprofessional courses. Among the GSD faculty teaching in this department were Hudnut, teaching history courses in civic design;

Pond, history of landscape architecture; LeBoutillier, introductory design; Frost (the program director), descriptive geometry; and Wagner and Perkins, planning. The combinative power of collaboration among the fields was conveyed by an introductory design problem in architecture and landscape architecture and by courses on architecture design and techniques. The design studio for seniors in Harvard College was taught by Frost, Pond, and Hudnut. A student in the Department of Architectural Sciences at Harvard could replace the final year in the college with the first-year program at the GSD. However, this undergraduate exposure to the visual arts was not adequate even at Harvard—Hudnut reported to the university president in 1947 that training was still lacking.[3]

By 1949 the combination of undergraduate work in architectural sciences with graduate training was seen also as a means of providing the necessary breadth required for the professional education of a landscape architect. Norman Newton proposed an ideal curriculum that Bremer Pond estimated would take an unbelievable nine years of study.[4] Succeeding Frost, Newton was chairman of the Department of Architectural Sciences from 1949 to 1964; he considered a six-and-a-half-year combination as an effective compromise. Like architecture undergraduates at Harvard and Radcliffe College, a landscape architecture student could take the first year of regular graduate study as a senior with first-year graduate students. The student then

entered the School of Design and, after two and a half years of additional study, received the MLA.

Electives during the first year of the graduate program provided the opportunity for students to fulfill requirements not taken at the undergraduate level, such as the history of art and architecture, or mathematics. Students could also take electives outside their programs in order; in effect, electives were intended to keep the student in touch with the intellectual and spiritual growth seeded in their college years.

Another key part of the modernist program was the requirement of working in an office or field setting prior to graduation. During the summers, architecture students undertook an internship, while landscape students studied horticulture and plant materials. In addition, the study of professional practice was combined with the technology of construction and taught by a design studio instructor in order to ensure that the collaborative effort was sustained.

The modernist curriculum took three years of three seminars of study to complete, including study or internships during the summer and a final thesis, which was intended to demonstrate the student's mastery in design and techniques of construction. Despite Hudnut's philosophic objection to accelerated programs, during and briefly after the war a temporary measure allowed students to enter the GSD's graduate programs without having completed a bachelor's degree. These students still received graduate-level status in

order to allow veterans to return to the workplace more quickly. The program began in 1943 and was phased out by the end of the war.[5]

The students who came to Harvard with professional bachelor's degrees from other schools of architecture pursued the master's program under Gropius. This program combined the advanced study of design, construction, and professional practice with conditions similar to those of a professional office. The centerpiece was the design studio, which involved collaboration with city and regional planning and with landscape architecture. The generic design problem required research and gathering of social and economic data; the design itself; detailing of structural elements and installation; computation of financial and operational costs; and issues of professional practice, which included preparing specifications, documents, and legal procedures.

Restructuring the Faculty

The teams charged with collaborative teaching included a mix of continuing faculty and new appointments; many of the instructors were Harvard graduates of various ages: Walter Bogner, who had been a special student in the former School of Architecture in 1922–23, taught advanced design studios; Kenneth Conant offered elective courses in architectural history; Henry Frost taught drawing; Walter L. Chambers assisted in design courses, worked on the new collaborative curriculum, and helped Henry Frost teach engineering drawing; George Holmes Perkins, the new chairman of the Department of City and Regional Planning, taught Planning 1; Jean George Peter, a Swiss-born civil engineer, succeeded Killam as the principal instructor in building construction; and Hugh A. Stubbins, Jr., who had become Gropius's assistant in 1940, taught Construction 1.[6] Bremer Pond, the Charles Eliot Professor and chairman of the Department of Landscape Architecture, taught studio design.[7]

The launching of the new program in 1945 required additional staff. George T. LeBoutillier was appointed a lecturer in architectural sciences, and he hired instructors to teach the design of mechanical equipment and architectural engineering. Edward K. True, a recent graduate of MIT, taught architectural engineering at the GSD for the next thirty-one years.[8] Dean Peabody, Jr., also an MIT graduate, was an expert in the technology of concrete. Several young instructors were recent students of Gropius. Charles H. Burchard, one of Gropius's first students in the master's class, was appointed in 1946.[9] John C. Harkness, a graduate of Harvard College and the GSD in 1941, began as an assistant in Gropius's master's class and became one of his colleagues in Gropius's firm, The Architects Collaborative (TAC), in 1945.[10] He, like several others, chose to build his house near Gropius in Lincoln. Canadian-born Leonard J. Currie, another of Gropius's former students and employee at TAC, was hired as an assistant professor in the Department of Architecture in 1946.[11]

One important experienced teacher, however, did not remain: Marcel Breuer, who was listed in the GSD's *Official Register* as "on leave" in 1946–47 and 1947–48, had left the school by the following year.

In the late 1940s Gropius's former students continued to win positions in the department: I. M. Pei returned in 1946 to teach for two years while working for Hugh Stubbins in Boston, and Chester E. Nagel became an instructor and later a member of TAC.[12] Not only did Nagel assist Gropius in teaching, but in 1947 he also defended Gropius in a controversy concerning the attitude of the AIA towards modernism. Nagel wrote that the institute was "known for its puttering with hashed-up historical forms," and he bashed the Federal Housing Administration as "more inclined to sanction the work of a copyist shyster than that of a genuine creative architect."[13] Nagel had absorbed the fervor directly from the master, as seen in his comment, "I have found in the philosophy of Gropius a mission as broad and compelling as any within the clergy or medicine."[14]

Nagel and Pei were joined by William W. Lyman, Jr., another graduate from the master's class of 1940. Complementing this cadre of instructors was Jean-Paul Carlhian who had received a master's degree in city planning from the GSD in 1947 after training in France. Although a graduate of the École des Beaux-Arts, he taught and practiced using the modernist vocabulary of the New Architecture.[15]

The large influx of new faculty in architecture reflected the growing popula-

tion of the school. When the GSD opened its doors to returning veterans in 1945–46, there were nine times as many students in architecture as landscape architecture. The thirteen students in landscape architecture could easily see that their faculty was not expanding. Bremer Pond provided a legacy that extended virtually to the beginnings of landscape training; Norman T. Newton, trained at Cornell, was his relatively youthful counterpart, along with Walter L. Chambers. But the Department of Landscape Architecture, which had always sought autonomy and whose high status in its profession had often outshone that accrued by the Department of Architecture, shrank.

Planning: Return of the Phoenix

In contrast, the planning department was reborn between 1944 and 1950. Its renaissance began in the midst of the perennial identity crisis that focused on how a planner should be trained. The annual conference for planners in May 1946 provided an opportunity to assess the war's effects and to take stock of the profession. During a series of discussions entitled "What a Planner Has to Know," Hudnut explained that he had asked the chairmen of several departments at Harvard how much training a planner should receive in order to understand the field. One colleague suggested 120 courses of study as essential, with 75 others as desirable. Using his survey results, Hudnut calculated that 33 years would be required for the general education of a planner, and that after the necessary apprenticeship in the field, a planner could begin a professional career at the age of 70. Hudnut then made a series of serious observations, beginning with the recommendation that planners *not* study economics: "If an architect dared to give advice to a planner, I should advise less economics and a larger dose of *politics*: politics being, if I understand it correctly, a kind of economics translated into action." Hudnut emphasized not merely the study of populations, the distribution and use of wealth, or the mechanisms of capital formation, but also the role of government and the people who composed it. The planner, Hudnut suggested, "must be at home amid constitutions, cabinets, legislatures, and laws. He must know how ordinances originate, how they are enacted, how enforced and how evaded. He must know when to bribe and whom to bully and whom to persuade."[16]

In a critique that would resurface in the late 1960s, Hudnut then attacked planning practices that resulted in towns that function but do not transcend utility. He proposed that the art of life, which he viewed as including music, sculpture, letters, theater, dance, and the crafts, must rise above "the shallow level of the market." Furthermore, while the current school of planners was churning out "machines for producing and consuming," they had "no architecture—a term which implies proportion and balance in the buildings, in streets and open places, and form and sequence in their collective whole."[17] After the conference on hous-

ing, Hudnut amplified his views in an article in which he raised the issue of the social objectives of housing in contrast to emphasis on the mechanism of making housing. Here he articulated his view of the city as a work of art, formed by the clash of economics, "ideas, and conscious guidance." In this context Hudnut saw housing projects generated as a response to unemployment, as "agencies for relief," which would resume their function as soon as the war was over.[18]

Martin D. Meyerson, who had graduated from the planning department at Harvard in 1949, and who would return there in a pivotal role in the 1950s, spoke directly following Hudnut.[19] Meyerson pointed out that, in addition to the necessary physical, social, and political knowledge, a planner needed imagination to visualize the future—a quality that made the planner an artist. He also called for the unification of people through "ties of common standards and knowledge," philosophically spelled out in President Conant's recently published *General Education in a Free Society*.[20] Finally, as if to confirm the view Hudnut was formulating thematically in his own lectures and writings, Meyerson reiterated that change in society comes about best by studying man's history, art, literature, science, and technology.

The task of humanizing the planning profession would fall to the next chairman of the department, Holmes Perkins. Trained as an architect during the crucial years of change from the old to the new regimes, Perkins had been groomed by

Gropius and was an eyewitness to the formulation of his and Hudnut's plans. Altogether, he was in an excellent position to bring a synthetic approach to the study of planning. Named chairman of the Department of City and Regional Planning and awarded the Charles Dyer Norton Professorship of Regional Planning in 1945, Perkins attempted to realize his predecessors' plans and to maintain a special role based on his rapport with Gropius. Perkins recalled, in retrospect: "I was invited back because I think they couldn't find anybody else to take over who was a friend of Gropius's. . . . The excuse of bringing me back was that it would really give the architects control of the second department."[21]

Instead of allowing the "second" department to become a tool of the architects, however, Perkins breathed new life into it. Drawing upon his wartime experience in housing programming and legislation in the Federal Housing Agency in Washington, D.C., he immediately augmented his two-man staff (Martin Wagner and himself) with new specialists in geography (Edward L. Ullman) and housing (William L. C. Wheaton).[22] In addition, he pursued a philosophy that the "unserviceability of our cities, occasioned in part by their swift and undirected growth," and in part by technical advances in science, had been exacerbated by the postponement of all projects for civic improvement.[23] Perkins believed that the experiences of the war would reveal a national failure to develop and use natural and human resources at the regional level. An increasing confidence in the "art of plan-ning—that is to say, of the art of creating, by means of applied technologies, a bet-ter environment for communities," along with the growth of planning agencies, however, encouraged his belief that plan-ners could direct change intelligently, and that in the post-war era their skills in plan-ning would be urgently needed. Perkins also believed that rebuilding American cities required correcting—among other things—uncontrolled sprawl. This correc-tion called not only for new approaches to planning but also for a reorientation in the training of architects if they were to make the required contribution to city planning.[24] This new direction would focus on the social and economic forces that mold the growth of cities, an approach that, in theory, was already being pursued at Harvard.

In contrast to John Gaus, who had asked too much of planning education, Perkins and his colleagues realistically acknowledged the limitations of their department: "We do not suggest that a competence in so vast and complex a field as planning can be created by a uni-versity curriculum: we suggest, rather, that the disciplines here made available may help to develop those habits of thought and of action, and that vision of the world, which when augmented by further growth and experience, are the necessary bases for a later competence."[25]

However, Perkins did continue Gaus's practice of involving members from many departments of the university and of opening the seminars and courses of

those departments to students in planning in order to encourage a multifaceted training. According to Perkins, this inter-change would establish a "sense of com-radeship between those students of the social sciences and of design who will be collaborating in the future in the develop-ment of public policy and plans."[26] Con-sequently, Perkins expanded the structure of the planning program by creating an interdisciplinary committee of faculty including, in addition to professors of planning and architecture, professors of government, geography, economics, busi-ness, and sociology. Called the Council of Regional Planning, it was separate from, but partially overlapped, the Faculty of Design. Hudnut, Gropius, and Wagner were on the council, along with five pro-fessors from other departments in the uni-versity; by 1949 the council expanded to twelve members.[27]

By making these changes and relying on an interdisciplinary council, Perkins addressed the nearly insurmountable problem of training planners at the GSD. A key aspect of the program was the belief in the academic "core" principle: that entering graduate students had already received the prerequisites of cultural experience and analytical training in col-lege. Admission was open to a broad spectrum of students, not only to those with experience in physical planning.[28]

The choice of courses was based on each student's past training, experience, and objectives for the future. The program offered a bachelor's degree in city plan-ning, a master's in city and regional plan-

ning, and a Ph.D. in regional planning, each with its own requirements of resi-dency and internship.[29] Six terms of study and an internship in a local, state, or national planning agency were required for the BCP; students who had concentrated in the appropriate program in Harvard Col-lege's Department of Architectural Sci-ences could receive advanced standing. For the master's degree in city and regional planning, prerequisites included the BCP or a master's in a social science or an equivalent, and at least one year of practi-cal experience with a planning agency. Two terms of study were required for the degree. The Ph.D. in city and regional planning required a minimum of two years of additional study (one of which was spent in residency), a reading knowledge of French and German, general examina-tions, a thesis, and a final examination.

The interdisciplinary nature of the pro-gram allowed three people to teach almost all of the courses offered in the Department of City and Regional Plan-ning, with all other courses offered by other departments in the GSD. Perkins taught an introductory studio in the analy-sis and critical study of cities in modern times and emphasized the role of citizens in the planning process. His other intro-ductory course was a review of the previ-ous ten years in the field of planning. Martin Wagner taught the continuation of Perkins's introductory design studio, and a studio involving research and analysis of regional and national planning. The emphasis on programming, design, and implementation was similar to the approach Wagner had followed in Germany. Although conclusions from their data varied, all agreed in the necessity of collaboration—and, in Perkins's words, working collaboratively "was fun."[30] Both Perkins and Wagner taught a course of techniques planning research, which included governmental organization for planning, public control of lands, and principles of city and regional design. Joseph Hudnut, a long-term critic of planning education, taught two half-year courses on the history of civic design. Finally, Catherine Bauer, the national expert on public housing, taught the seminar on housing (with the collaboration of Gropius and Perkins) that Wagner had given previously.[31]

Student Achievements

The vision of an integrated response to modern problems, built around the principle of collaboration, flourished from 1945 to 1950 with an unprecedented impact. Judging from the professional success of its students and its role as a model for other schools, the GSD reached an apogee in this period. The students who attended during this fruitful time ultimately became a *Who's Who* of American and international architecture, landscape architecture, and planning, some of them among the most successful practitioners of the twentieth century. Many became teachers or mixed teaching with practice, so that their Harvard views on design education rippled throughout schools of architecture, land-

scape architecture, and city planning for decades. As teachers, they passed on the ethos of the Harvard training to their students and in the programs they created and implemented.

But even before the long-term success of its graduates, the new program quickly produced positive short-term results. In its report of 1946, the Visiting Committee claimed that the quality of student work was high—although there was some difference of opinion between new guard and old guard. Interestingly, the committee recommended more emphasis on freehand drawing—a great strength of the old schools—and upon "facility in expression": student work may have appeared somewhat dry and austere in its modernist, planar emphasis. The Visiting Committee also noted that the influx of students was overtaxing the facilities but that the high enrollment would eventually subside. Sexist attitudes towards women at the school persisted in the comments of the committee. Finally, the committee noted that Gropius's master's class, intended to resemble office experience, was "as real as possible."[32]

The design problems that focused on the city and suburb served as one reliable source by which to evaluate the results of the school's philosophy. In 1948 Martin Wagner selected the town of Framingham, Massachusetts, just outside Boston, as a "laboratory" for his students. Like the sites used for the studies of city reconstruction conducted during the war, Framingham held potential as a site of post-war development; in just such towns would

the challenges of the suburb be met by dedicated planners. Defining the problem as "Framingham against the World," Wagner gave his planning students the problem of considering the financial structure of the town. The title of the problem was borrowed from a 1946 *Fortune* magazine article, "Oskaloosa Against the World," which raised the question of whether the town had a positive or a negative balance of payments.[33] The typical results are visible in the work of one student, David A. Wallace, whose flow diagram shows the complexity of the city's income statement (Fig. 6.2). Presumably, such realistic analyses would ground all aspects of subsequent designs.

Using this economic groundwork in a collaborative studio, Wagner assigned his students the design of new housing and facilities to alleviate existing shortages and those anticipated from the opening of a new General Motors assembly plant near Framingham. One team produced the essential communal elements in a new settlement called "Felicitas." Consistent with Wagner's pedagogical principles, the project was "work-integrated," which meant that it considered the walking distance between activities. The diagram of the new community showed the relationships of shopping center, community center, power plant and supply building to factories and health centers (Figs. 6.3–6.5). The site plan for housing in "Felicitas" took an amoeboid shape that contained branches of units, both single and in rows, that ended in cul-de-sacs. The branches connected to an

A CITY'S INCOME STATEMENT
19··

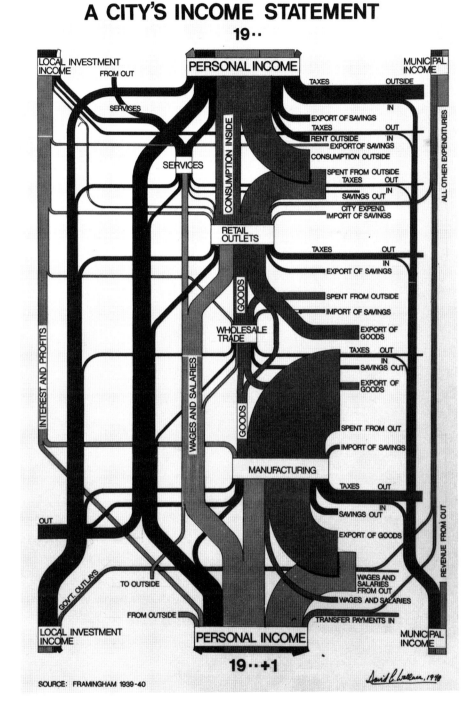

SOURCE: FRAMINGHAM 1939-40

6.2 David A. Wallace, chart for a city's income in a study of "Framingham Against the World," 1948. Collaborative problem for Arch. 2b, LA 2b, CP 2b.

encircling main road, adjusted to the contours of the community site. The wavy amoeboid shape appeared to respond to the topography of the site, although it should also be noted that this configuration recurred in many different modernist designs throughout the 1940s. The layout indicated that proximity of residences to community services was the generative factor in the groupings, not the goal of an asymmetrical or formal arrangement. The buildings themselves (such as the shopping center and community recreation complex) were rectangular in plan, with angled projections. Thin-walled rooms were mixed with sheltered open spaces, and a simple columnar grid provided vertical support. Elevations of the buildings particularly showed an economy of means; every plane was as thin as practicable. No unnecessary detail was present, nor did any element provide transition from horizontal to vertical surfaces. Only the bold, black shadows, slung with diagonals, animated the façades of these buildings. Austere and practical, they recalled the efforts of Gropius and Breuer in their housing at New Kensington.

In another study of the same problem, Zena Prager designed a school that showed similar economy of means (Figs. 6.6–6.8). However, her classrooms were located in appendages off a central core, which tended to isolate the grades from one another and rendered the spaces between the arms empty and spatially disconnected from the building's interior.

Although students began to specialize in their chosen fields after the first year,

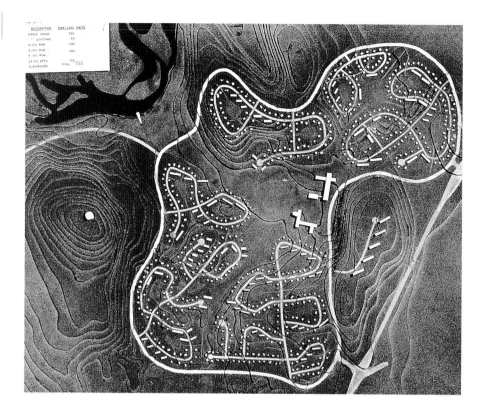

6.3, 6.4, 6.5 "Felicitas," neighborhood plan for Framingham, Mass., by architecture team members William I. Barton, Melvin Brecher, Robert L. Geddes, Peter A. Kitchell, and Paul J. Mitarachi, March 1948. Collaborative problem III, Arch. 2b, LA 2b, CP 2b. Site plan, building plans, and elevations.

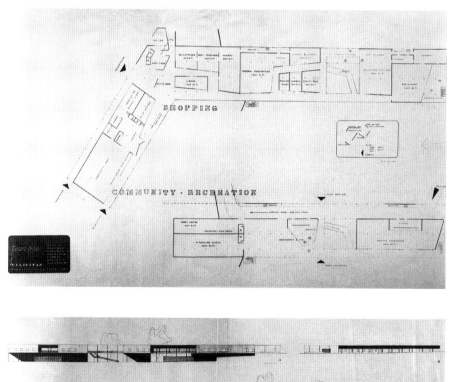

collaborative problems were also assigned in the second year. For example, architecture students designed an entire new community near Natick, Massachusetts—an assignment that lasted six to eight weeks. Students tackled similar exercises into their third year, and even the thesis was intended to demonstrate collaboration as well as relevance to a student's anticipated professional life. The thesis consisted of two long problems for which students wrote their own programs, detailed the problems to be solved, and then developed solutions, with occasional critiques from the faculty. The student's thesis was to be conducted as though he were running his own office and had a group of consultants coming in from time to time.

In landscape architecture a variety of new types of thesis subjects emerged, replacing the previous popularity of the elitist estate plan. Now problems included multiple-unit subdivisions that mixed residential and recreational facilities; a community club and recreational development for employees of a watch manufacturer; a veterans' cooperative; an "air-park community" that included an airport, housing, and recreational facilities on land and water; multiple family housing units for veterans; a summer institute for the arts; a summer resort and recreational area for a labor union; and a decentralized zoo whose units could be located near schools to allow easy access for students. Each problem had a specific site and confirmed the trend, existing from the early 1930s and the end of the country place era, towards public projects

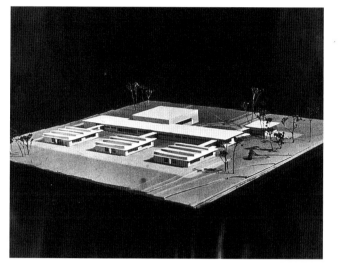

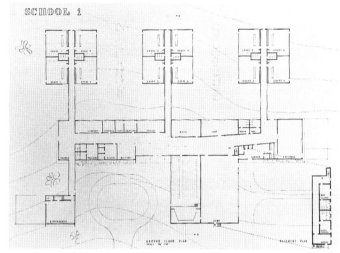

SCHOOL 1

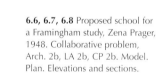

SCHOOL 2

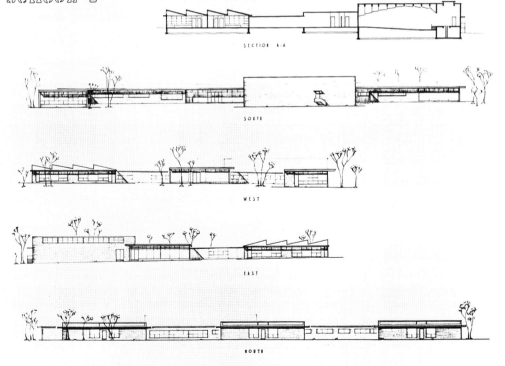

SECTION A-A

SOUTH

WEST

EAST

NORTH

6.6, 6.7, 6.8 Proposed school for a Framingham study, Zena Prager, 1948. Collaborative problem, Arch. 2b, LA 2b, CP 2b. Model. Plan. Elevations and sections.

6.9 Public presentation of collaborative thesis project for the redevelopment of downtown Providence, Rhode Island. Marvin Sevely (left) and R. I. William Conklin (center) presenting model to Walter Gropius (right) and guest jury, including Joseph Hudnut seated left and Charles Burchard seated right. Collaborative thesis by Conklin, Sevely, Robert Geddes, and Ian L. McHarg, 1950. Photo by Raymond Ball.

for large numbers of people, housing, recreation, and the work place. The only neglected client was the wealthy landowner in need of traditional formal gardens.

Norman Newton described the underlying intentions and structure of the collaborative problems in the training of landscape architects at Harvard, giving an extensive project, such as the redesign in 1948–49 of the whole of South Boston, the first exercise, to impress landscape students with the complexity of problems and show "how many factors need to be investigated deeply and thoroughly if the design development, which continues in a series of problems throughout the year, is to be at all valid." To cover the broad issues, students were required to conduct research in libraries, pursue investigations in the field, interview people, and visit offices and private agencies. All these avenues were pursued in order "to put into that First Year a lively sense of reality, to demonstrate what is a profound conviction of the entire School: that the professions we practice are social arts, and that their value depends upon their demonstrated capacity to serve *people*."

This "sense of reality," tied to the vision of design as a social art and composed of the connections between human beings and their environment, was based on the founding premise of modern design education: "the effort . . . is directed toward an understanding of the unity and inseparability of architecture, landscape architecture, and city planning." Not only was the founding premise restated, but the principle of collaboration became more precise

when Newton described that "the process of collaboration is virtually a technique in itself. It is something that is not the prerogative of any one profession, but is pertinent to all of them and needs to be studied as a definite way of working." [34]

Trained in the traditions of American landscape architecture, enriched by the study of Italian gardens and the history of his field, and well grounded in practice, Newton also revealed a sympathetic and characteristic conception of modernism. In the framework of Sigfried Giedion's crystallization of the modern world as a distinct cultural event characterized by Einsteinian spatial and temporal interdependence, Newton perceived the need for a complete revision in general education: to see "events in space-time as *unique* events, we need to see things and people and situations as unique *individuals*." In this context, modern design was not a style but an attitude: "If by 'modern design' we mean anything at all intelligible, we mean a method of attack, an attitude—a careful, analytical, rational approach to problems in terms of today's

knowledge, of today's social facts, and of the psychological needs of today's human beings." [35]

Newton's viewpoint relied on basic modernist assumptions that the light of science would illuminate reality, and that a modern attitude required solving each problem on its own terms, allowing form to emerge from human activity rather than from the old habits of using a style—the *bête noire* of modernists. But the social, economic, and political "facts" kept changing at least every five years, and the problem remained how to equip students to handle such cyclical changes. Ironically, the New Architecture itself was already a style—though none of its adherents could yet face that simple fact.

At Harvard, all the departments under the sway of radical European modernism believed in the interdependence of the design arts, the role of design as a social art, the vision of collaboration as a process and technique, and the conception of modern design as an attitude involving a rational, analytical approach to problem-solving. Reflecting these atti-

6.10 Redevelopment of downtown Providence, Rhode Island. Ian McHarg presented scheme to jury in Hunt Hall. Seated: Walter Gropius (center); Chester Nagel (left); Professor Edward K. True (with pipe); Professor Benjamin Thompson (behind); and Robert Geddes (far right). Photo by Raymond Ball.

through the existing structure of political, economic, and social agencies in the area. Our principal task we felt should be the redevelopment of the central area of the city. Because we believe that planning, architecture, and landscape architecture are interdependent, and no one of them alone can be successful in the creation of the urban environment, we have undertaken as a collaborative thesis the redevelopment of parts of the center of Providence, Rhode Island.[37]

tudes and providing a synopsis of students' efforts in landscape architecture, architecture, and planning to solve modern problems, William Conklin, Robert Geddes, Marvin Sevely, and Ian L. McHarg produced a collaborative thesis in 1950.[36] The team chose Providence, Rhode Island, for their project because its public and private agencies had a strong and sympathetic attitude towards planning, a fully staffed Planning Commission and Redevelopment Agency, as well as the financial and legal ability to carry out urban development. Conklin, Geddes, and Sevely were architecture students, McHarg a graduate student in both landscape architecture and city planning. Their research and planning analyses focused on general conditions of cities similar to Providence; economic conditions in Providence; and analyses of the uses of downtown, including space requirements and financing.

The team wrote its own thesis statement, which clearly reflected both the impact of Hudnut's interest in the history of cities and the GSD's fundamental phi-

losophy on the interdependency of the fields of design:

> Our interest in urban redevelopment stems from our belief that cities are the fruit of civilization. They are at once the product and genesis of culture. Historically, cities have epitomized and characterized the dominant social and economic forces of their times. The center of the city has always held the market, the seat of the temple, the hall of justice, and the academy of learning.
>
> The city centers of integrated civilizations of the past have all had one thing in common: the agora, the forum, the village green all held meaningful and rewarding experiences for the citizen. Today death haunts our city centers. Our new city centers must speak of life and its joys. It is in the belief that it is essential for our cities to recapture this spirit that we have operated.
>
> From the beginning, we agreed that to carry through our beliefs about the nature and function of the cities our work should be directed to the re-development and renewal of an existing urban area. We also agreed that we should work

Here, then, was an affirmation of the value of the city, an identification of it as the locus of the challenge of the future, and an idealistic—even noble—belief in the ability of collaboration among the fields of design to create a practical and humane environment.

The group presented its project to Gropius and his colleagues in June 1950 (Figs. 6.9, 6.10). After the official presentation of their work to the GSD, the *Providence Sunday Journal Magazine* also published the Harvard students' work as "Providence Tomorrow? Face Lifting for Downtown." The scheme intertwined the proposed modernist buildings with the fabric of the city that had evolved over time. While the new buildings resulted from a careful consideration of their function—and their aesthetic qualities—they tended to appear as detached objects in the context of the city. These kinds of self-contained and self-referential buildings that seemed oblivious to the adjoining urban fabric would appear in numerous cities of America—often with less landsome results—as redevelopment of down-

208

6.11 Redevelopment of downtown Providence, Rhode Island. General view of model showing the proposed cylindrical office towers, vertical mechanical parking garages, spiral department store, and shopping courts. Collaborative thesis by William Conklin, Robert Geddes, Ian L. McHarg, and Marvin Sevely, 1950. Photo by James K. Ufford.

6.12 Redevelopment of downtown, Providence, Rhode Island. Detail of model showing, in addition to the three-story shopping courts and parking garages, a new downtown circular church and a new government office building with an atrium. The new circumferential highway proposed around downtown is shown in the distance. Collaborative thesis by William Conklin, Robert Geddes, Ian L. McHarg, and Marvin Sevely, 1950.

town urban centers occurred in the 1950s and 1960s.

The team's proposal for a redeveloped Providence included cylindrical office towers, vertical mechanical parking garages, and shopping courts (Figs. 6.11–6.14). A close look at the model shows, in addition to the three-story shopping courts, a downtown circular church and a government office building with an atrium. In the distance is another feature that would become common in urban renewal projects: a highway ringing the downtown area. The team developed individual buildings in detail, including the proposed federal office building with a triangulated and faceted skin over a cylindrical tower. Its section shows a constructional system influenced by Buckminster Fuller in the use of stainless steel trusses and polarized glass; the building would provide services on ground level and a pedestrian access at the second level.

Ian McHarg's contribution to the development of central public open space is of particular interest because it shows the approach of a landscape architect in a collaborative context as well as some of his own intellectual roots. His section of the project began with a historical preamble discussing the general appropriateness of the current styles of landscape architecture, pointing out that Bremer Pond had said that Renaissance garden design served the ostentatious tastes of a social aristocracy; such a tradition, McHarg stated, would not suit Providence. Nor would English concepts of

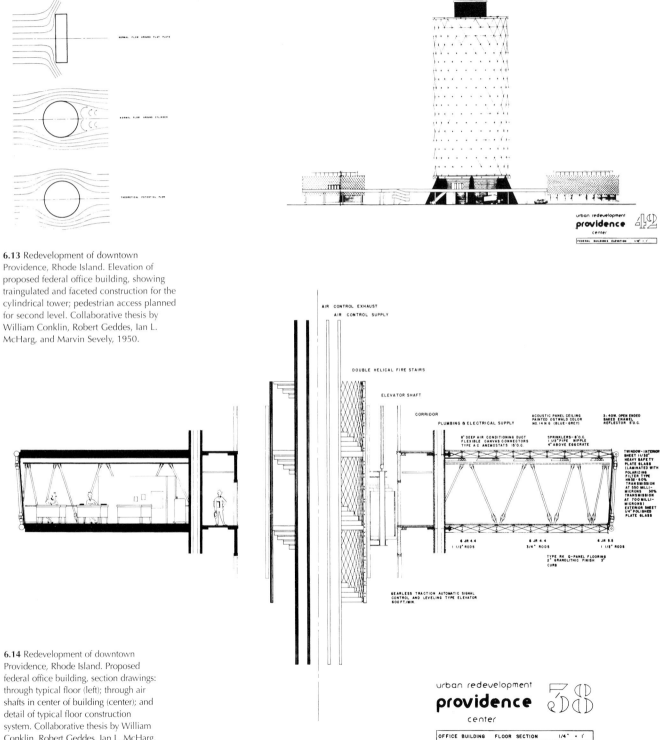

6.13 Redevelopment of downtown Providence, Rhode Island. Elevation of proposed federal office building, showing traingulated and faceted construction for the cylindrical tower; pedestrian access planned for second level. Collaborative thesis by William Conklin, Robert Geddes, Ian L. McHarg, and Marvin Sevely, 1950.

6.14 Redevelopment of downtown Providence, Rhode Island. Proposed federal office building, section drawings: through typical floor (left); through air shafts in center of building (center); and detail of typical floor construction system. Collaborative thesis by William Conklin, Robert Geddes, Ian L. McHarg, and Marvin Sevely, 1950.

6.15 Walter Gropius and master's class students, 1946. Clockwise: Professor Gropius, Harry Seidler, Ira Rakatansky, John C. Parkin, Norton Polivnik, Irving J. Maitin, Alvaro Ortega-Abondano, I. M. Pei, John "Chip" Harkness, two unidentitifed, and Royal McClure.

6.16 Nursery and kindergarten, Harry Seidler, 1945. Arch. 2d, master's class, taught by Walter Gropius and John Harkness. Perspective view.

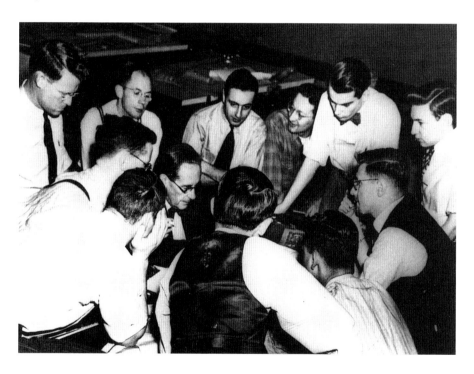

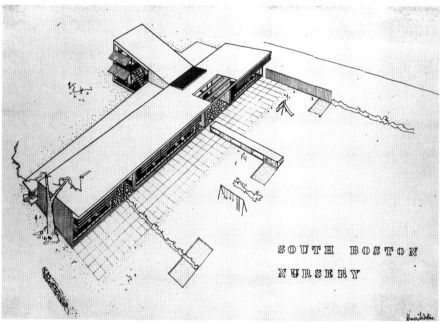

naturalism and romanticism, which persisted in general practice but were no longer appropriate. The only tradition beyond the Moorish design of the Middle Ages that had continuing validity, said McHarg, was that of the Orient, particularly Japan, but both of these traditions were rooted in specific social, cultural, and religious contexts. Informed by Tunnard's *Gardens in the Modern Landscape* (1948) and Mies van der Rohe's recently published appreciation of Frank Lloyd Wright, McHarg called attention to efforts to find a modern aesthetic and to establish objective limits over personal license. Citing Hudnut's *Architecture in the Spirit of Man* (his collected essays published in 1949), McHarg also noted that one contemporary search for principles of modern design pointed to functionalism, while another stressed that the modern landscape would arise from the same principles of economy and sociological needs that were affecting modern architecture.[18]

The direction that most appealed to McHarg, however, seemed to be within the rational development of the field of landscape architecture itself. Scientific research provided an increased knowledge of aquatic systems, plant materials, color and texture, along with knowledge and control of the microclimate. Manipulation of the microclimate and objective analysis of social conditions provided the means for a valid modern landscape architecture and a strong professional discipline. Here were the seeds of environmentalism and the emergence of the dominant path that landscape architec-

6.17 South Boston recreation center, Harry Seidler, 1945. Arch. 2d., master's class, Professor Gropius. Plan.

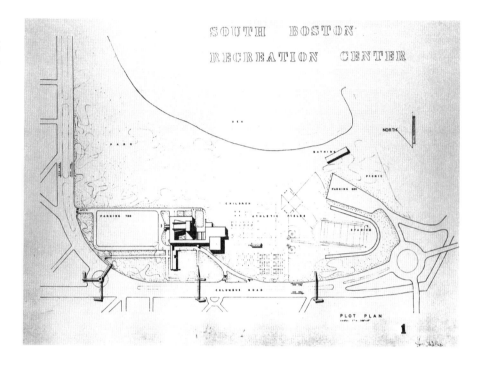

ture would follow; indeed, McHarg's own professional and academic life was spent in the advocacy of these goals on the broadest levels.[39]

The demonstration of these principles in the study of downtown Providence foreshadowed other trends as well. Gone were details of individual gardens; instead there were recommendations about vehicular and pedestrian circulation, parking lots and garages, and service routes to the city's civic center. Absent were parks and recreation facilities; plants and trees were used to control the climate by deflecting and absorbing heat, filtering the atmosphere, reducing glare, reducing air temperature through reduction of radiant temperature and evaporation, and reducing sound and wind. Water in pools, fountains, and cascades would provide the visual impression of coolness and would actually lower the temperature.

Landscape architecture thus forecast that it would take back the domain of the city—a domain it had possessed at the turn of century and from which city planning had evolved in America. At the same time, it carved a new analytical niche for itself that it would effectively pursue, perhaps with better results than parallel investigations in architecture and planning. Appropriate to the social and technological ambitions of the period, here was a landscape architecture that could be described in reports, developed in diagrammatic sketches, and prepared in engineering drawings. This architectural design did not display any visual acknowledgment that Providence is an

old, picturesque city by American standards. No renderers or makers of pictures need apply—history and heritage were irrelevant.

Gropius praised the students' work as a demonstration of his teamwork principle. But a close look at the relationship of the proposed buildings to the existing fabric of the city shows what Gropius seemed to overlook: the buildings are isolated objects, set back from the street's edge; they disrupt the scale of the urban fabric by juxtaposing big buildings next to small ones and leaving gaps of unarticulated space that have little civic use or meaning.

The work of students in Gropius's master's class also reflected modernism's social agenda. Harry Seidler's nursery and

kindergarten, designed in 1945, show the straightforward, practical approach required for economical construction (Figs. 6.15, 6.16). The exterior had projecting sun shades, and the interior included a mezzanine under the high part of the butterfly-shaped roof. To counter the abstract severity of the design, Seidler included a stone floor at the entry and a smattering of children's furnishings: a slide, swing and gym set, and a sandbox. Similar concerns for providing for community needs can be seen in Seidler's design for a recreation center in South Boston (Fig. 6.17). A parking lot with a capacity of 700 cars flanked the west side of the main complex of the building, which contained a large theater and other

6.18 Walk-up apartments, Harry Seidler, 1945. Arch. 2d., master's class, Professor Gropius. Model.

entertainment venues, while children's play areas, athletic fields, stadium, bathing pavilion, and picnic area were sited on the east side. For housing, Seidler limited his design of walk-up apartments to four floors and provided automobile parking by a series of attached, covered, parking garages, thereby controlling density (Fig. 6.18).

Such projects represented the results of a program that successfully fostered socially oriented and technologically expressive students who were duly inspired by the values Gropius espoused, often for the rest of their careers. The experience of Sam T. Hurst typified the generation that studied in the master's class in the late 1940s: he had heard of the Bauhaus while an undergraduate at the Georgia Institute of Technology; his studies were interrupted by service in World War II; and he arrived at Harvard in 1948, funded by the GI Bill, loans from Dean Hudnut, and a job at TAC. Hurst's comments on his training under Gropius synopsized the experience of his peers:

> In the Master's Class of sixteen we were made to feel that we were competent and dedicated and selected. We were expected to work and support each other. We were relieved of the anxiety of failure. Gropius never used the word Pedagogy or referred to the Bauhaus. He taught by question, pressing us to examine all issues in the widest range of possibility, to contribute out of our experience. He smoked a short cigar and carried a very short pencil and seldom drew anything. The clarity of his critique on aesthetic,

structural, and social grounds was brilliant. He was restrained in his criticism of other architects. Baited by our questions about Wright and Mies, he would only say, "Mies, he is a little naked." He spoke of principles, of collaboration, of the courage of commitment.[40]

Hurst took this message of principles, collaboration, and commitment with him to his subsequent teaching at Tulane and Georgia Tech, and to deanships at Auburn University and the University of Southern California.

Student Critiques

Gropius's call for commitment to principles and collaboration met with success both inside and outside the GSD. An indication that the war for the New Architecture had been won on Gropius's terms was seen in the complete identification of him with modern architecture. In 1947 the *Harvard Crimson*, the student newspaper, called him the "humbly proud Papa of a New Architecture which has tenaciously taken root to challenge traditionalist patterns." Joseph Hudnut went unmentioned; from the journalist's viewpoint, only Frank Lloyd Wright or Le Corbusier ranked ahead of Gropius, but whereas Wright's artistic triumph was seen as personal—his proposal for the ideal community of Broadacre City was overlooked—the article described Gropius, the "dreamer and masterbuilder," as having extended his vision to "the ideal of an organically-planned community, free from slums, smoke, and

6.19 Walter Gropius (center) with students from his master's class (*Harvard Alumni Bulletin*, 30 March, 1946, cover).

congestion, and their attendant social ills." Furthermore, his methods stressed "that an architect cannot be a sissy with a mere hand for sketching but must understand materials and productions systems as well." It was also noted that Gropius's philosophy was opposed by traditionalists: "To the older elements in the profession everything he stands for is still poison: these are men who are aware that the New Architecture steadily gains ground but who are doggedly wed to past formulas and the Roman column."[41]

This conclusion was one of many signals that modernist fervor had successfully misrepresented the past. The skills of drawing that rested on centuries of tradition were equated with effeminacy, and reliance on the vocabulary of the past was seen as an aping of classical forms and an implicit lack of concern with the demands and rational requirements of construction. Ironically, these criticisms least applied to the history of design at Harvard; its students in the old School of Architecture were highly skilled draftsmen, had experimented with a variety of vocabularies, including European modernist modes, well before the arrival of Gropius, and had experienced some of the most rigorous training available in structural analysis and materials. In a little over ten years, the history of design education at Harvard had been conveniently rewritten. The tone, however, accurately represented the bitter polarity of a position replete with moral self-righteousness.

The success of the revised curriculum and the influx of new students attracted the attention of the university, which used the rebirth of the design school as its lead story in a 1946 edition of the *Harvard Alumni Bulletin* (Fig. 6.19). The article confirmed the success of amalgamation and survival during the war and recounted the teaching of design at Harvard since the lectures of Charles Eliot Norton in 1874 and the near doubling of enrollment. The school's resources and facilities were impressive: a 110-foot-long drafting room; the most complete and best-equipped library of landscape architecture and regional planning in existence (assembled by Theodora Kimball Hubbard); an architecture library of 7,300 volumes, 25,000 documents and photographs, and 20,000 lantern slides; seminar room, exhibition galleries, offices, and studio shops. Of particular significance was the continued presence of women (though their numbers would diminish), veterans, married students, and foreign students. The Graduate School of Design had become a truly international institution bounded by neither New England nor the nation. The *Alumni Bulletin* quoted Hudnut's succinct explanation of the curriculum, its social goals and cultural interest, and the underlying desire to rise above technical service to put "some imprint of the human spirit upon its environment."[42]

The *Alumni Bulletin* illustrated the pursuit of modern architecture with groupings of models. Like the students, they too were international in locale and ranged from a museum for Shanghai by a Chinese student to an apartment building for Teheran by a Persian. In addition, the magazine cited planning studies for a shopping district in Hingham, Massachusetts, a cultural center for Concord, Massachusetts, a summer hotel for Atlantic City, New Jersey, and a master plan for Wayland, Massachusetts, based on projected population growth. These developments were all seen as emerging from Dean Hudnut's corner of the Yard.

Finally, to accentuate the success of the program, the *Alumni Bulletin* listed the prizes and awards garnered by the alumni and students of the Department of Architecture. The impressive list included winners of a dozen competitions, ranging from the selection of the architect for the Smithsonian Gallery of Art in 1939 to a competition for the design of a small plywood house in 1945. In summation, it reported that President Conant could claim that the GSD had "become the leading school of modern architecture on this continent and perhaps in the world."[43]

The exciting atmosphere at the GSD produced a vibrant camaraderie among students. Some of them felt a lack of broad representation through a student council; they decided to publish their own bulletin as a forum for discussion and as a chronicle of school events.[44] Their bulletin covered activities in the fall of 1947 and the previous summer, such as the Fête Charette (the annual costume party), as well as guest lecturers who reinforced the modernist ambiance, including Fernand Lèger, Lázló Moholy-Nagy, and Alexander Dorner (a former Bauhausler and then director of the Museum of the Rhode Island School of Design), plus an anthropologist, a psychiatrist, and the chief architect of the Tennessee Valley Authority. The students also expressed their awareness of attending "one of the foremost schools of design in the world."[45] As Henry Frost had pointed out to the students, "No matter how much we grunted and groaned about it, [the school] was looked up to by other schools all over the country to show the way to prove that modern design is on the right track."[46]

By the spring of 1948, a newly formed student council, chaired by Ian McHarg, had critical concerns. Particularly in landscape architecture, McHarg "concluded within two weeks that this curriculum would not engage the mind, far less challenge it. The faculty [as opposed to the students] was committed to the tradition of gardens for the rich. Their visions were small, as was their scale; they were without distinction, an anomaly at a great university. Yet it need not have been. The faculty was a product of the great Olmsted tradition. . . . This marvelous origin, however, had been largely abandoned, so that upon my appointment as chairman of the Student Council, a resolution of no confidence in the faculty of landscape architecture was passed and transmitted to President Conant."[47]

The student council utilized their bulletin to suggest changes in design instruction, grading, and promotion. Specifically, they wanted more instruction in design and called for the return of Marcel Breuer. Hudnut replied that he had repeatedly asked Breuer to return, to no avail, and that increases in salaries for more individual instruction were not possible.[48] He explained that with a fixed endowment, an increasing enrollment diminished the funds available on a per student basis; supplements to the endowment had not occurred because Hudnut apparently had an agreement with President Conant when he came to Harvard that he would not raise funds.[49]

The student bulletin extended its discussions beyond concerns about grading and the length of juries. The principles of social involvement derived from European modernist circles had begun to seep into students' questions about their own destiny at the school—and the outside world. Even the European craft ethos, admired in the early years of the Bauhaus, influenced the bulletin, which utilized block prints cut from wood or linoleum. The emphasis on technical problems of a structural or mechanical nature was satirized in an awkward dialogue called "The Way Beyond" in which McHarg criticized the standards used for determining promotion to the thesis as involving "safe solutions rather than experimental design."[50] Breuer had returned to give a lecture, which was praised as an example of obtaining personal insights into the philosophy of a creator, rather than learning specific techniques or methods about his works. Edward Larrabee Barnes, who had graduated in 1942 and had been working in Southern California, also returned to discuss design and construction of aluminum prefabricated houses.[51] His student reviewer disagreed with this proposal as a solution to low-cost housing, asserting that the houses in Levittown on Long Island, developed by the Levitt family beginning in 1946 and using on-site fabrication, were comparable in price and floor area, and included an attic. Although Barnes did not mention it, the Levitts' secret for achieving low costs was efficient organization of construction labor—a procedure learned from wartime military camps, not from the manipulations of the architectural design process.

Interest in issues outside the school was clear from the position taken by students in the burgeoning debate on regionalism versus the International Style. In a critique in 1947, Lewis Mumford irked modernists by asserting that the architecture of the San Francisco Bay Area constituted a "Bay Region style."[52] After listening to the ensuing debate at New York's Museum of Modern Art—which included Breuer's objections to having "redwood all over the place"—one student reviewer confirmed his own modernist allegiances in support of Breuer by countering that Mumford's claim was incorrect and that the Bay Region style was merely a "regional expression of the Modern Movement."[53]

International Acclaim

Despite continued questions from, and critiques by, the students, the GSD's program received confirmation and recognition from the outside world. By the late 1940s the three departments reached the acme of collaboration in the history of design education at Harvard; the extraordinary combination of dedicated teachers, dynamic students, and a shared sense of purpose made the core curriculum and collaborative studio one of the most effective innovations in design education in the century. Emulated by other professional schools, GSD became the model of modern design education. The school's impact was noted in *American Building News*, which pointed to Harvard as having influenced "a dozen schools in America, particularly in the field of teamwork . . . in active collaboration with other departments, such as Sociology, Public Administration, Psychology, and Biology."[54]

The success of the school reinforced Gropius's belief in his principles and further energized his efforts to incorporate them. Wanting to refresh students' understanding of his ideology, he had his views on education (reproduced from earlier statements) published in the students' bulletin in March 1948.[55] Lest anyone be unclear about his message and its origins, he included a block print of the Bauhaus building at Dessau.

Two years later, Hudnut's earlier lack of success in attempting to influence architectural policy in Washington, D.C., was vindicated when he was appointed to

President Truman's Commission on Fine Arts.[56] Here, along with modernist architect Pietro Belluschi, he continued his campaign to bring modern design to the nation's capital (Fig. 6.20).

Another kind of success could be seen in the collaboration that occurred between universities to deal with broad problems. Creating the kind of communication that William W. Wurster, dean of the School of Architecture at MIT, had sought in 1943, students and faculty from MIT, the GSD, and the School of Public Administration jointly organized a symposium to evaluate the principles that provided the basis of planning education in 1949.[57] Wurster moderated a session on the regional environment, and Hudnut one on the local environment. Regional issues concerned the use of a greenbelt as a buffer to development; decentralization into satellite cities as an imperative; and creating political boundaries to coincide with functional boundaries, or replacing the region for the state as a planning unit. Local issues outlined for discussion included defining a neighborhood as the smallest community with a maximum population of 5,000 people; making the elementary school and shopping center the neighborhood nucleus and locating them within walking distance of every home; locating the central workplace within walking distance of every home; providing each family with its own house on its own lot; and segregating uses by zoning.[58]

The final speaker, José Luis Sert, the Catalan architect who had moved to the United States in 1939, had recently taught at Yale, and was president of CIAM as of 1947, particularly disagreed with the idea that the workplace should be within walking distance of homes, and he argued against each house having its own lot in cities. Sert, with the help of Gropius and Hudnut, who wrote the introduction, had succeeded in having Harvard University publish *Can Our Cities Survive?* in 1942. The book had already become part of planning students' reading list.[59]

Gropius received international confirmation of his teaching at Harvard and his professional reemergence in America. In February 1950, *L'Architecture d'aujourd'hui* published a special issue on "Walter Gropius: The Spread of an Idea." Paul Rudolph, who had graduated from the master's class in 1947, selected the work of the school and provided a preface to the issue, while Sigfried Giedion wrote a short biography of Gropius, and Douglas Haskell, editor of *Architectural Forum*, expounded on Gropius's influence in America. A French writer, Michel Aime, identified the Harvard program as a model for other schools in the United States. Serge Chermayeff, a German-born pioneer in the modern movement who had practiced in England and emigrated to the United States in 1940, described an analogous attempt to create a new Bauhaus at the Institute of Design in Chicago. Finally, Gropius presented the Harvard program as a "Blueprint for an Architect's Training," which contained his clearest statement of ideology and description of the practical program to date.[60] As if this weren't an adequate testament, Chester Nagel

asserted that Gropius was the first architect-teacher to continually reconsider the modern expression of forms generated by the Industrial Revolution.

The philosophy of teamwork in the GSD was being applied to solve problems that reflected a host of modern building typologies that was spreading throughout America and to other parts of the modernizing world. In a collaboration among the architecture, landscape architecture, and regional planning departments, the students of Holmes Perkins, Bremer Pond, and Walter Bogner produced all the key generic elements of a shopping center, a major building type for post-war consumers.[61] Using a model to represent their scheme, they designed an "automotive" shopping center located fifteen to twenty miles outside Boston, which drew on a population of 40,000 people. The chief design challenge was to provide clear circulation and functional differentiation for different types of shops, with quick and easy access between stores and options for expansion. Parking within easy distance to the stores was needed for 5,000–6,000 cars—although the huge lots needed to accomplish this are conveniently absent from the model (Fig. 6.21).

The kind of community that would parallel such a shopping center would be a "Satellite City," a new township located, for instance, in a regional context east of Boston. The advanced students of the Departments of Architecture and Regional Planning, working under Wagner, Gropius, and John Harkness, presented the requisite activities for township life:

6.20 Presidential Commission on Fine Arts, 1950–54. Left to right: Pietro Belluschi, two unidentified, Joseph Hudnut, President Harry S. Truman, Edward F. Nield, Sr. (a modernist architect practicing in Shreveport, Louisiana), Elbert Peets, Felix W. de Weldon (the sculptor of the famed Iwo Jima memorial sculpture), H. P. Caemmerer.

community center, gas and electric lines, nursery, police, museum, hotel, high school, elementary school, recreation, and stadium. The size of the town was limited to what would be comfortable for pedestrians; the form of the town consisted of a cluster of amoeboid plans that had their evolution in the early 1940s in the work of Martin Wagner. A reaction to renovation both by lot and block, to sweeping square-mile rehabilitation, and to City Beautiful schemes, the township would be located along a superhighway and surrounded by farm belts (Fig. 6.22). A road would encircle each cluster and the roads to each cluster would end in a cul-de-sac. Speculation on property would be barred.

Individual students designed specific building types for satellite cities—and these, too, proliferated in the future. The modern cultural institution of the museum would become an international phenomenon, as exemplified in I. M. Pei's thesis, a Chinese museum in Shanghai (Figs. 6.23, 6.24). Gropius explained to the readers of *L'Architecture d'aujourd'hui* that "this design was highly prized by the Harvard Design faculty because we thought that here a modern architectural expression on a monumental level was reached."[62] With its interior courtyards and flat roofs, Pei's project bore a striking resemblance to Gropius and Breuer's competitive design of 1938 for the Wheaton College Art Center; perhaps the emulation of style in a movement that claimed to have no styles was inevitable (Fig. 6.25).

Another example, a "Living Art Museum" designed by Victor Lundy in 1948, provides an elegant solution to the challenge of aesthetically incorporating the various functions necessary to support a museum (Figs. 6.26, 6.27). Subtly incorporating both figural plan motifs of Le Corbusier and the open-plan gridded space of Mies van der Rohe, this design used a cof-

6.21 Model of shopping center, by students Robert Bergman, Amy Garber, Robert Geddes, Alford Griese, James Harris, Roscoe Jones, Peter Kitchell, Charles Mansfield, and Russell Myers. Students of Professors G. Holmes Perkins, Bremer Pond, and Walter F. Bogner. Collaboration between the Departments of Architecture and Regional Planning. As published in *L'Architecture d'aujourd'hui*, February 1950. Photo by Barre and Blau.

6.22 (opposite) "Satellite City," model plan for a township east of Boston, by advanced students under Professors Martin Wagner, Walter Gropius, and John Harkness. As published in *L'architecture d'aujourd'hui*, February 1950. Photos by Barre and Blau.

fered skylight laid in a checkerboard pattern in a flat roof. A lily pond adjacent to the museum's theater served as a sculpture garden and natural setting to soften the rectilinearity of the building mass.

Still other building types reflected the post-war need for buildings to support the leisure times that people could now enjoy again. Ulrich Franzen's thesis design for 1948, a summer hotel in Maine, showed a consideration of its site near a lake and an effort to investigate the structural possibilities of raising a building on columns to create a parking level while cantilevering wings from a central core. The aesthetics of the building with its flat roof (which overlooked the inevitability of heavy snow loads) and identical units opening to uniform terraces revealed the student's allegiance to International Style building—though designed for Maine, it could have fit in anywhere (Fig. 6.28).

Henry Cobb's thesis project was an amphibious skyscraper design that foreshadowed a building type relevant for crowded urban conditions (Figs. 6.29, 6.30). Conceived in 1949 as a waterfront redevelopment for Boston Harbor, Cobb's scheme consisted of eight towers located over the water on the ten-acre site of a former wharf. The towers were satellites to a centralized, circular parking building and were reached by ramps. Two building types were provided for the towers, along with variations in floor plans to accommodate a mix of apartments that ranged from studios to five bedrooms. Three hundred and thirty-six apartments provided space for an estimated density of 946 people. The tectonic expression of the towers

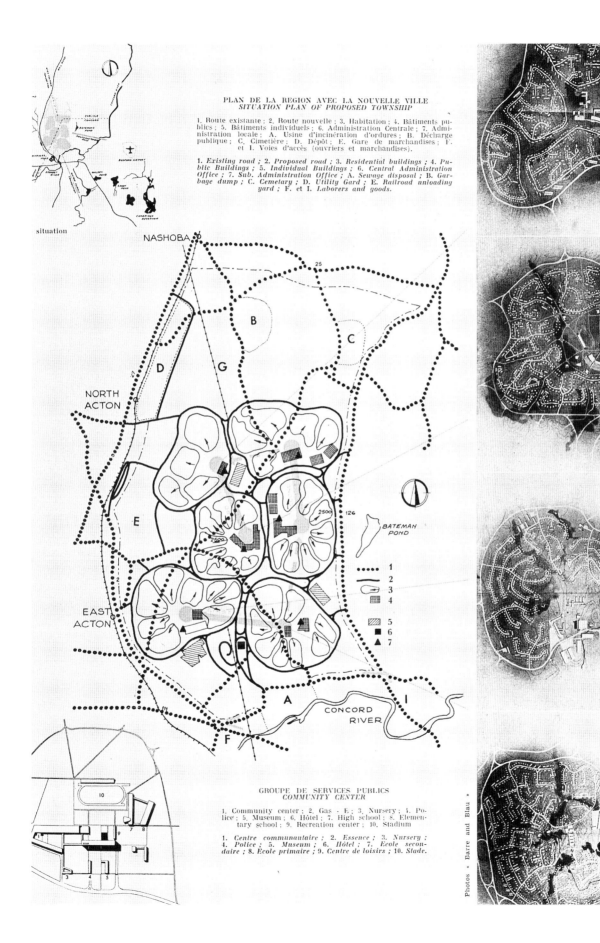

219

situation

PLAN DE LA RÉGION AVEC LA NOUVELLE VILLE
SITUATION PLAN OF PROPOSED TOWNSHIP

1. Route existante ; 2. Route nouvelle ; 3. Habitation ; 4. Bâtiments publics ; 5. Bâtiments individuels ; 6. Administration Centrale ; 7. Administration locale ; A. Usine d'incinération d'ordures ; B. Décharge publique ; C. Cimetière ; D. Dépôt ; E. Gare de marchandises ; F. et I. Voies d'accès (ouvriers et marchandises).

1. *Existing road* ; 2. *Proposed road* ; 3. *Residential buildings* ; 4. *Public Buildings* ; 5. *Individual Buildings* ; 6. *Central Administration Office* ; 7. *Sub. Administration Office* ; A. *Sewage disposal* ; B. *Garbage dump* ; C. *Cemetary* ; D. *Utility Gard* ; E. *Railroad unloading yard* ; F. et I. Laborers and goods.

NASHOBA

NORTH ACTON

EAST ACTON

BATEMAN POND

CONCORD RIVER

GROUPE DE SERVICES PUBLICS
COMMUNITY CENTER

1. Community center ; 2. Gas - E ; 3. Nursery ; 4. Police ; 5. Museum ; 6. Hôtel ; 7. High school ; 8. Elementary school ; 9. Recreation center ; 10. Stadium

1. *Centre communautaire* ; 2. *Essence* ; 3. *Nursery* ; 4. *Police* ; 5. *Museum* ; 6. *Hôtel* ; 7. *École secondaire* ; 8. *École primaire* ; 9. *Centre de loisirs* ; 10. *Stade.*

Photos « Barre and Blau »

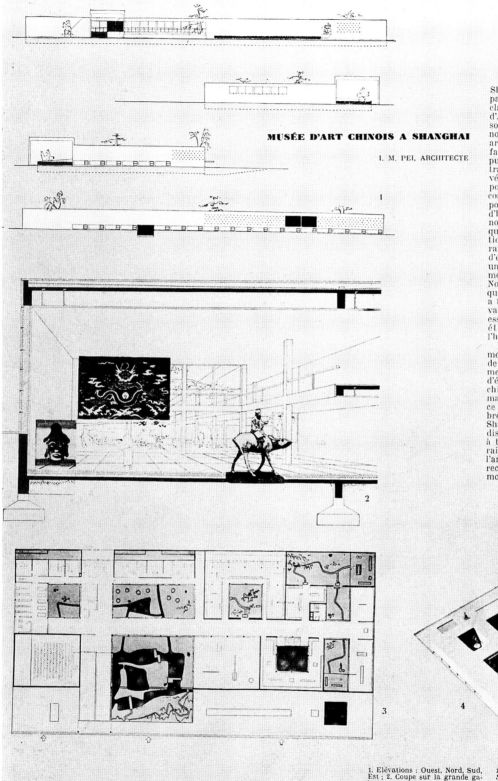

MUSÉE D'ART CHINOIS A SHANGHAI

I. M. PEI, ARCHITECTE

1

2

3

4

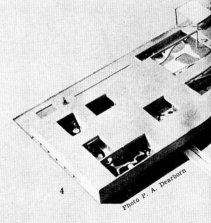

Photo P. A. Dearborn

Ce projet pour un musée à Shanghaï (Chine) fut établi par M. Jeoh Ming Pei dans la classe supérieure de l'Ecole d'Architecture de Harvard sous ma direction générale. Il nous montre clairement qu'un architecte de talent peut parfaitement continuer à s'appuyer sur les éléments de base traditionnels — dont il a pu vérifier la validité — sans pour cela renoncer à une conception moderne de la composition. Nous avons aujourd'hui suffisamment clarifié nos esprits pour reconnaître que le respect pour la tradition ne signifie pas la tolérance complaisante vis-à-vis d'éléments dus au hasard, ou une simple imitation de formes esthétiques révolues. Nous comprenons maintenant que la tradition architecturale a toujours signifié la préservation des caractéristiques essentielles qui résultent des éternelles habitudes de l'homme.

Lorsque M. Pei et moi-même discutâmes les problèmes de l'architecture chinoise, il me dit qu'il était soucieux d'éviter l'emploi de motifs chinois anciens, ajoutés d'une manière superficielle comme ce fut le cas pour de nombreux bâtiments publics à Shanghaï. Au cours de notre discussion, nous cherchâmes à trouver comment on pourrait exprimer le caractère de l'architecture chinoise sans recourir à l'imitation de tels motifs du passé.

WALTER GROPIUS.
(Cf. page 107)

1. Elévations : Ouest, Nord, Sud, Est ; 2. Coupe sur la grande galerie ; 3. Niveau inférieur ; 4. Maquette.

1. Elevations : West, North, South, East ; 2. Section through large gallery ; 3. Lower floor ; 4. Plot plan.

CHINESE ART MUSEUM IN SHANGHAI

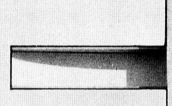

This project for a museum in Shangai, China, was designed by Mr. Ieoh Ming Pei in the Master class of Harvard's Department of Architecture under my general direction. It clearly illustrates that an able designer can very well hold on to basic traditional features—which he has found are still alive—without sacrificing a progressive conception of design. We have today sufficiently clarified our minds to know that respect for tradition does not mean complacent toleration of elements which have been a matter of fortuitous chance or a simple imitation of bygone esthetic forms. We have become aware that tradition in design has always meant the preservation of essential characteristics which have resulted from eternal habits of the people.

When Mr. Pei and I discussed the problems of Chinese architecture, he told me that he was anxious to avoid having Chinese motifs of former periods added to public buildings in a rather superficial way as was done for many public buildings in Shangai. In our discussion we tried then to find out how the character of Chinese architecture could be expressed without imitating such form motifs of former periods. We decided that the bare Chinese wall, so evident in various periods of Chinese architecture, and the small individual garden patio were two eternal features which are well understood by every Chinese living. Mr. Pei built up his scheme entirely on a variation of these two themes.

WALTER GROPIUS.
(Cf. page 107)

Photo by courtesy of « Progressive Architecture » –

(previous pages)
6.23, 6.24 Chinese art museum in Shanghai, I. M. Pei, 1946. Architecture master's thesis, as published in *L'architecture d'aujourd'hui*, February 1950.

6.25 (opposite) Competition entry, Wheaton College Art Center, Wheaton, Mass., Walter Gropius and Marcel Breuer, 1938. Second prize, as published in *L'architecture d'aujourd'hui*, February 1950. Photo by Paul Davis, Boston.

(following pages)
6.26, 6.27 A Museum of Living Art, Victor Lundy, 1948. Architecture master's thesis, model, as published in *L'architecture d'aujord'hui,* February 1950. Photo by Barre and Blau.

derived from their method of construction: four great concrete tubes, which contained services and acted as piers (or piles), were moored to the ocean and offered support for the floors of apartments. Relieved of the burden of carrying vertical loads, floor and wall elements could be light. The façades of the towers similarly became expressions of the rooms within the buildings.

Cobb's thesis represented his application of the rational lessons of the New Architecture: flexibility of plan, economy of construction, visual expression of technology, and independence from the surrounding building fabric. His living spaces were sensibly, logically, and handsomely conceived; any developer could see their potential. Yet, the drawings for the steel reinforcements of concrete revealed a latent interest in aesthetics overlaying rationality. Rather than having the hard quality of engineering drawing, or the precision of the engineer's calculations, the drawings were visual delights for designers who enjoyed the graphic qualities of their patterns. Cobb liked the way his designs looked more than he cared about their rational underpinnings.

From a public relations point of view, the publication of *L'Architecture d'aujourd'hui*'s special issue on Gropius's school represented a triumph of determination and the success of the collaborative idea. The praise bestowed on Gropius had a quality of devotional rapture matched only by the ardent followers of Frank Lloyd Wright—yet no two architects could have been further apart at this point in their careers: Wright viewed modern architecture as fundamentally organic, and Gropius saw it as func-

tional and social. For Gropius, the student projects, more than his own work, provided the greatest confirmation of the collaborative model executed in conditions that were meant to resemble the real world. By this time the GSD's original concept of collaboration—architects, landscape architects, and planners working towards a common goal—had melded into Gropius's vision of teamwork—architects working with other architects supported by other disciplines. Both were now interchangeable and both had become synonyms for the key to the success of modernism.

The predilections of students, however, did not always match the official positions and preferences of the faculty, or the image of the school that Gropius projected. Henry Cobb recalled that students in the late 1940s admired Le Corbusier's polemics about modern architecture and city planning, not Gropius's designs or his particular program.[63] Their interest was not so much in the formal structure of Le Corbusier's work but in his social programs and ideology. In fact, Le Corbusier was the single most important reference for Cobb and his friends at the GSD. His *Oeuvre complète* was a sensation and had a place on all the students' desks—but it was not discussed by the faculty. The New Architecture of modernism was, however, very influential in establishing the standards of graphic representation at Harvard during this period; surface treatments, monochromatic renderings, material selections, amoeboid landscape forms—all reflected the modernist sensibilities. The students intended to make technology aesthetic, reflecting the view

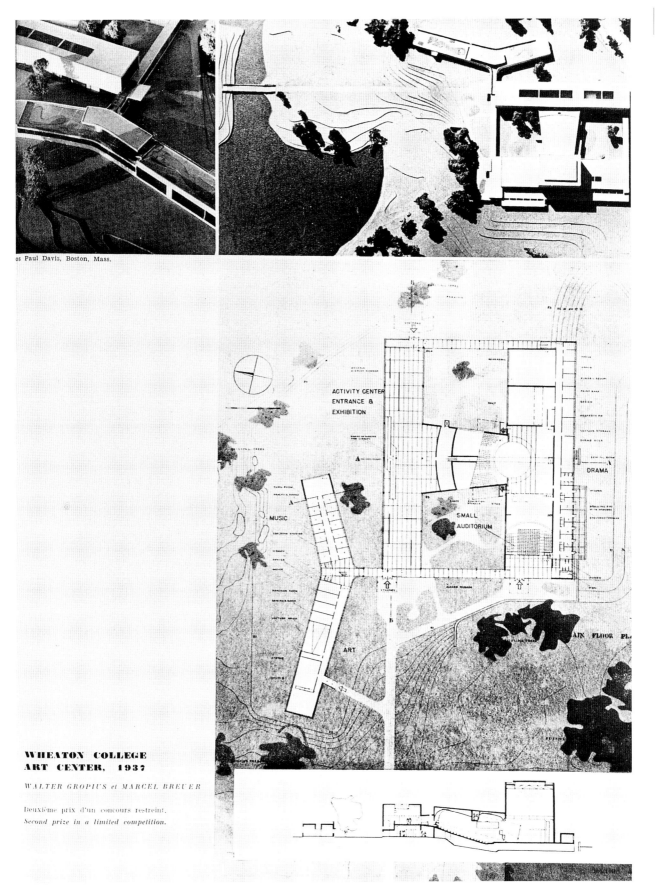

os Paul Davis, Boston, Mass.

ACTIVITY CENTER
ENTRANCE &
EXHIBITION

MUSIC

SMALL
AUDITORIUM

DRAMA

ART

MAIN FLOOR PLAN

WHEATON COLLEGE
ART CENTER, 1937

WALTER GROPIUS et MARCEL BREUER

Deuxième prix d'un concours restreint.
Second prize in a limited competition.

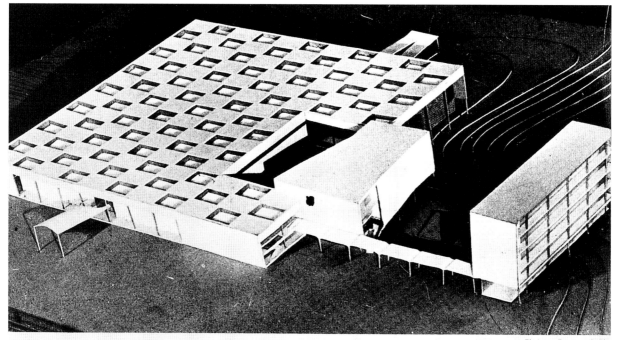

Photos « Barre and Blau

UN MUSÉE D'ART - A LIVING ART MUSEUM

PROJET DE VICTOR LUNDY. PROGRAMME ET CRITIQUE DE WALTER GROPIUS
ET WILLIAM LYMAN Jr.

Ce projet et celui de l'étudiant C. Elliot (voir p. 80) sont établis sur le même programme.

Extrait du programme proposé aux élèves : « Vous êtes chargés de projeter ce musée ainsi que le tracé des circulations adjacentes, l'aménagement du terrain, la construction de l'édifice, la construction du parking et de tous les services complémentaires nécessaires.

» Les exigences du programme sont réduites au minimum en vue de ne pas imposer de restrictions arbitraires aux projeteurs. Le programme donne quelques indications quant aux surfaces, mais elles ne doivent pas être considérées comme des limites rigides.

» Il vous appartient de juger si l'édifice doit être plus ou moins grand pour remplir la fonction à laquelle il est destiné. Vous êtes libres d'ajouter des surfaces, ou des volumes, ou des services, là où ils paraissent indispensables. Les directeurs de la Fondation sont votre client direct, mais il est très important que vous vous souveniez de ceci : les clients véritables, essentiels, sont les hommes, femmes et enfants de la ville qui feront dans ce musée une riche moisson d'enseignements et d'amour de l'Art, ou l'éviteront au contraire comme un monument mort, érigé à la seule gloire de l'architecte. *(Cf. page 107)*

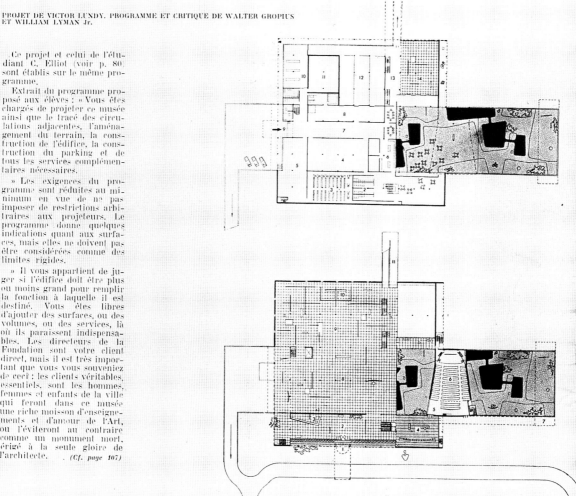

ELEVATIONS   OUEST

NORD

SUD

EST

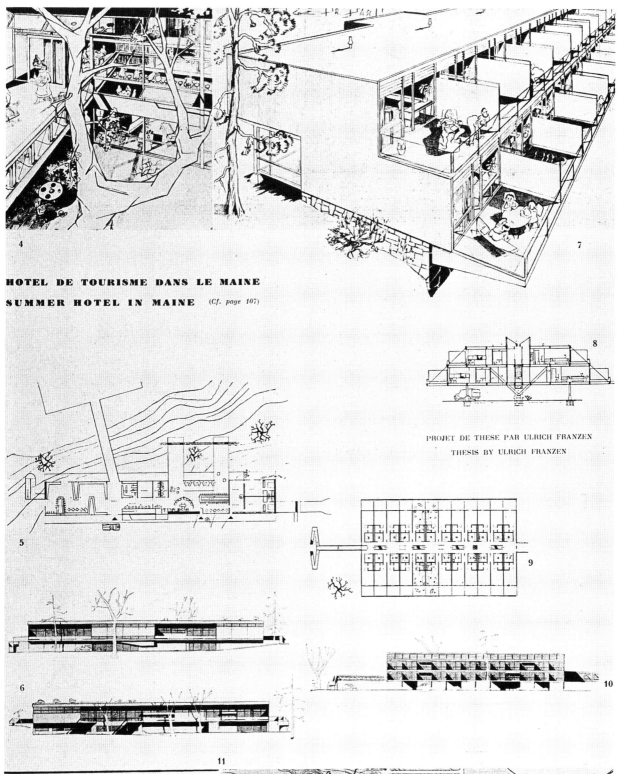

HOTEL DE TOURISME DANS LE MAINE

SUMMER HOTEL IN MAINE *(Cf. page 107)*

PROJET DE THESE PAR ULRICH FRANZEN

THESIS BY ULRICH FRANZEN

1, 2, 3. Plan, élévation et vue des pavillons de tourisme ; 4. Une vue de la terrasse de l'hôtel ; 5, 6. Plan et élévation du restaurant ; 7. Hôtel ; 8. Coupe ; 9. Plan du premier niveau ; 10. Elévation ; 11. Plan d'ensemble.

1, 2, 3. Plan, elevation and overall view ; 4. View of terrace ; 5, 6. Plan, elevation of restaurant ; 7. Hotel ; 8. Section ; 9. First floor plan ; 10. Elevation ; 11. Plot plan.

6.28 (opposite) Design for a tourist hotel in Maine, Ulrich Franzen, 1948. Architecture master's thesis, as published in *L'architecture d'aujourd'hui*, February 1950. Photo by Barr and Blau.

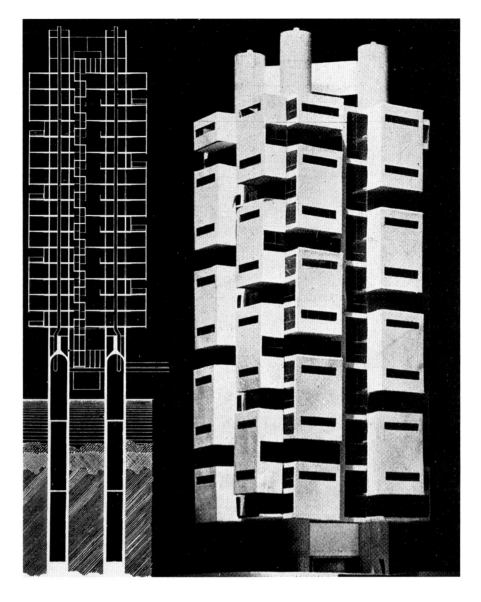

that the aesthetic liberation from historical forms brought by technology was as important as the technology itself. This view would soon direct students and professionals alike towards Mies, who in the 1950s was seen as having "the keys to the kingdom" as he demonstrated his aesthetic interpretations of technology, which updated the modern movement's interest in the machine as style. Cobb candidly admitted that image counted more; he and his peers saw the social programs, such as those proposed by Hugh Stubbins, resulting in back-to-back plumbing and nothing of consequence.

There was also another anomaly in the international presentation of the Harvard model and the acclaim it now received: Hudnut's role in the creation of the modernist program of collaborative education remained totally unrecognized, virtually invisible. The modern movement had always excised critics from within its own ranks, and Hudnut, though still dean, already had the anonymity that would cloak him the rest of his life. Hudnut's marginalization by Gropius is not surprising: in the midst of this public triumph, Hudnut had perceived a reductive quality in the modernist aesthetic of the New Architecture, warning that the grave risk now at hand was "the degradation of architecture into mere technology or business—a danger not clear to those very vocal persons who mistake air-conditioning for design." Gropius must have grimaced upon reading those last lines. Adding a poignantly humane note, Hudnut cautioned: "We have won the battle for modern architecture. We ought to act like victors, not run our swords through the dead body of the enemy."[64]

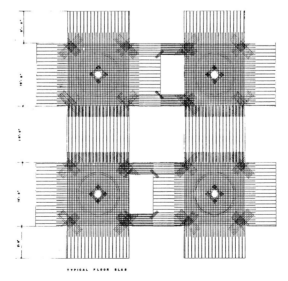

TYPICAL FLOOR SLAB

6.29 Waterfront redevelopment project, Boston Harbor, Henry N. Cobb, 1949. Architecture master's thesis, model and section, as published in *L'architecture d'aujourd'hui*, February 1950. Photo by Barr and Blau.

6.30 Waterfront redevelopment project, Boston Harbor, Henry N. Cobb, 1949. Architecture master's thesis, detail of steel in foundations.

"DECADENT DESIGN,"
1951–1953

Even as the collaborative dream at Harvard earned international acclaim, the undoing of the dream had already begun. Tensions between Gropius and Hudnut reflected serious philosophical and personal conflicts—conflicts around their differing views of modern architecture, the basic training of architects, and the role of history in that training. At the center of the conflict between them were two diverging visions of what modernism should mean, what it should represent, and how it should be manifested through physical design.

Breaches in Visions, Departure of Faculty

A signal factor in the mounting dissension between Hudnut and Gropius was Hudnut's criticism—one of the very first—of the International Style. The beginnings of his discontent with the results of the modernism he had championed in the 1930s emerged in his articles before the conclusion of the war. He wrote from his office in Hunt Hall, used as a retreat from his dean's office in Robinson Hall and called by the students "Hudnut's love nest" because of his affection for writing. Hudnut's explorations of the possibilities of developing housing during the doldrums of the war mixed humor with sharp criticism. He reacted to the rigidity of housing prototypes that modern architects were producing by recommending the lessons of history as sources of more hospitable solutions. For example, the design of windows that appear monotonous in housing

projects could be improved by using the kinds of proportion, spacing, and treatments found in some of the venerable buildings of Harvard Yard. According to Hudnut, the corner of the Yard containing Holworthy, Stoughton, and Hollis Halls was very much like a housing development itself, being built for people with little money for "frippery."[1] In addition, these buildings offered a tasteful sense of space and relationship, scale and rhythm. For Hudnut, windows represented the qualities that should be sought in residential architecture: "People live behind these windows, and the sense of life should and can be made to shine through them."[2]

The same vitriol that he had poured on the design for the Jefferson Memorial he began increasingly to heap onto the public housing schemes that were icons of modern architecture. He criticized these schemes as lacking relationship to the city fabric in which they were built, "like hospitals blown up to insane proportions, with ward after ward following in an endless march." In particular, he criticized housing schemes for not acknowledging the role of the street as "a theatre for a habit of life invented near the beginnings of social growth." Furthermore, he advised caution before accepting that "zigzags in a park"—the American translation of the German *Zeilenbau* row buildings—were "truly more appropriate to a habit of life . . . embedded in history." The challenge of housing projects raised, for Hudnut, a fundamental question: "How, without history, shall we hope for expression in architecture?"[3]

Hudnut's evolving critique of modern architecture and his call for a return to the lessons of history gathered momentum in 1945 when he coined the term "post-modern" in an article on domestic buildings published in *Architectural Record.*"[4] Although those who later used the term, starting in the 1970s, were unaware of his essay, Hudnut presaged their basic criticisms of modernism—identified with the International Style—by attacking it as a reductive functionalism that, at times, excised cultural, spiritual, and emotional identifications from design.

Arising out of their differences on the place of history in design education was another factor causing tension between Hudnut and Gropius: the dean's firm resistance to a revival of the Bauhaus at Harvard. Despite Gropius's efforts to gain appointments at Harvard for many of his former Bauhaus colleagues, only two of his candidates were approved—Breuer and Wagner—while suggestions for the appointments of artists Josef Albers and Naum Gabo were turned down.[5] Gropius's acceptance of American teachers of basic design came, however, with the expectation that they, too, would give a course resembling the *vorkurs* of the Bauhaus. But the quality and style of teaching of the basic design course by men like George LeBoutillier—appointed by Hudnut—never met Gropius's expectations. The proper teaching of the course became the focus of simmering conflict between Gropius and Hudnut.[6] And because LeBoutillier's appointment was as an instructor in architectural sciences

in Harvard College, Gropius was powerless to replace him.

Because of their disputes, neither wanted to retire before the other. At first it appeared that Gropius would have to go first, in 1952, when he reached age 70. Hudnut planned to undo Gropius's influence at the school and then retire himself. In particular, Hudnut wanted to restructure the curriculum, including abolishing the basic design course based on the Bauhaus. As a superficial compensation, Hudnut proposed making Gropius an emeritus professor.[7] Gropius, however, outfoxed Hudnut. When negotiating his appointment, Gropius had obtained a commitment from President Conant to the effect that retirement for extremely distinguished faculty could be extended beyond the normal deadline. Gropius, clearly a distinguished person, raised the exception, and Conant refused to back Hudnut.

The tensions between Hudnut and Gropius were augmented by retirements and departure of faculty in the GSD. During 1950–51 several veteran faculty retired: Bremer Pond, Martin Wagner, and Henry Frost (killed tragically a year later in an accident in the automobile given to him by the students of the school upon his retirement).[8] The most significant departure was that of G. Holmes Perkins, who, after his tenure at Harvard as Charles Dyer Norton Professor of Regional Planning from 1945 to 1951, left to become dean and chairman of the Department of Architecture in the Graduate School of Fine Arts at the University of Pennsylvania.

7.1 Joseph Hudnut, as pictured in *Time* magazine after his retirement, 1954.

There he sparked a renaissance: he moved architecture from undergraduate to graduate-level training, created a Ph.D. program, hired a vibrant faculty, and supported the teaching of Louis Kahn. Martin Meyerson, a former student and later colleague of Perkins, commented that the visions of interdepartmental collaboration Perkins had absorbed at Harvard under Hudnut and Gropius were carried out more fully at the University of Pennsylvania than at Harvard.[9] Perkins had witnessed the formulation of the principles, took part in their testing, and then actualized them in a less rancorous atmosphere. Perkins embodied the collaborative ideal, for example, when he appointed Blanche Lemco van Ginkel, his former student in planning at Harvard, to teach the introduction to architectural design at Penn. From the outset, designers at Penn learned the viewpoint of planners in their introduction to their profession.

Perkins also took planning faculty with him to Penn, and only two of four were replaced. William Wheaton, named associate professor, became chairman of the planning department; the chair of the Charles Dyer Norton Professorship went to Coleman Woodbury, a regional planner specializing in land economics. For the first time, both positions had not gone to the same person. An idealistic and gentle man, Woodbury witnessed the struggles of the school at the hands of Gropius and Hudnut and any prospect of growth or progress vanished. In reaction to the tense atmosphere and discord, he resigned after only two years.[10]

In the Department of Architecture some junior faculty left (including I. M. Pei and Chester Nagel); some were replaced, and others were assigned new administrative roles to compensate for the departures. Among the appointees were Norman Fletcher and Benjamin Thompson, both Yale graduates and among Gropius's young partners at TAC.[11] In the Department of Landscape Architecture, Lester A. Collins, who had been teaching since 1946, succeeded Pond; Hideo Sasaki, a graduate of the class of 1948, taught for two years and then departed (ten years later he would return to launch new initiatives in the Department of Landscape Architecture and the profession itself). Sasaki began his own firm, in 1953, as a means of putting into practice the principles of interdisciplinary collaboration between design and planning. Lastly, at the undergraduate level, Norman Newton followed Frost as chairman of the Department of Architectural Sciences.

The conflict between Hudnut and Gropius played itself out in the core curriculum in 1951–52. Changes in the teaching of engineering and mechanical systems represented an overall diminution in focus on building technology. Gropius's increasing focus on using the basic design course (Design 1) as his best opportunity for reinstalling the *vorkurs* of the Bauhaus was an implicit challenge to the importance of the other courses in the core. Though these courses remained for architects in the first year, electives, including history, were eliminated in the

program for the bachelor's degree in architecture. And landscape students were no longer required to take the full course in basic construction.[12]

Gropius finally succeeded in directly exposing students to Bauhaus design principles when he instituted a retooled version of Design 1 as "Design Fundamentals," funded by President Conant.[13] Hudnut hired Richard Filipowski, a teacher at the Institute of Design, or the "Chicago Bauhaus," for a two-year trial starting in the fall of 1950.[14] Hudnut implied his deep reservations to Filipowski by stating that the course was experimental and that it would be subject to his review—but assuring Filipowski of the faculty's support. To Gropius the appointment signified that abstract design would finally achieve the pivotal place he wanted for it, and he actually began setting up the workshop.[15] By the end of the 1951–52 school year, the student exhibition showed the results. The exhibition catalog, with a layout and typography typical of the Bauhaus aesthetics of graphic designer Herbert Bayer, explained that the work represented students' discovery of "the fundamental architectural elements of FUNCTION SPACE SCALE LIGHT COLOR."[16] The control of these elements created "FORM," and through further experiments led to the organization of space. Models promoted an understanding of building, while draftsmanship developed "organic" experimentation in line weights, texture, variation in speed of line, tonal value, and transparency—the modes of graphic expression developed, for instance, in Paul Klee's *Pedagogical Sketchbook*. Furthermore, insight into the "plastic/structural/spatial and visual" qualities of different materials was to be gained from the use of hand and power tools—a manual training directly borrowed from the *vorkurs*. Finally, in a gesture of direct attribution, the text of the catalog provided both its justification and its intellectual sources:

A DESIGN FUNDAMENTALS COURSE
SERVES AS A BRIDGE
CONNECTING
GENERAL EDUCATION
TO THE ART OF ARCHITECTURE

harvard's design fundamentals class
was developed here two years ago
by [Richard] FILIPOWSKI
BAGNALL was his assistant this year

it embraces the Bauhaus principles
    of GROPIUS
and demonstrates the belief
that a plastic concept of design
should integrate all forms of work.[17]

As Filipowski later recalled, "The risk [in giving the workshop] was great—the success, enormous."[18] Gropius was very pleased, and many of the faculty were highly enthusiastic. Hudnut, however, was appalled at the results of the experiment; the course embodied the abstract formalism in modern architecture—another sign of Gropius's success—that he had fought against and removing it became a central objective. One weakness in this course, however, became apparent: the workshop showed that,

despite the avowal that design "should integrate all forms of work," *how* to integrate landscape architecture and city planning remained unclear. Hudnut was not the only one unenthusiastic about embracing Bauhaus principles. When the *Harvard Alumni Bulletin* published the text description of Design Fundamentals, a Boston practitioner made fun of the jargon at the "Harvard Bauhaus."[19] Gropius's basic design course in its 1952 form symbolized the victory of Bauhaus ideology at the expense of the American system Hudnut had long sought to create. Its demand for students' time competed with that of the integrative collaborative course, Planning 1; it engendered jealousy among faculty members, who were increasingly unwilling to collaborate.

In May 1952, to alleviate conflicting demands on students' time and to prepare for the imminent change of administration that would occur with his retirement and that of Gropius, Hudnut called for a committee to consider discontinuing Filipowski's Design 1. He asked the committee to consider a complete restatement of operating principles, beginning with the basic premises of the school itself. The resulting report acknowledged that a proper balance between Design 1 and Planning 1 had been lost, that the courses competed for time, and that faculty exchange was dwindling—creating a "Chinese Wall."[20] The committee, headed by LeBoutillier, who represented the very approach Gropius rejected, proposed the major alterations to the curriculum that Hudnut sought as a corrective, including

increased flexibility of course scheduling. The original principle of the GSD—that all three departments share a common training—would be extended to include the first semester of the second year. Integration of this program would be ensured by implementing a faculty rotation in which the first-year instructors would teach the same students their courses in the second year.

The pivotal resolution was to combine aspects of the two major competitors—Design 1 and Planning 1—into a "super course" in the first year, Design A, which would be scheduled for thirty hours per week. In the first semester Design A would focus on shop and studio exercises involving elements of spatial organization, materials, texture, color, form—the visual language of form. These studies in the architectural expression of abstract elements were intended to lead to solutions of current social problems. In the second semester the course would focus on studies of building types, community analysis of social needs, preparation of programs to fulfill those needs, master plans, and neighborhood plans. In the third semester, the studies made in the previous semester would be used to make a neighborhood plan, with the design of a shopping center, elementary school, and housing; landscape architects and city planners would do detailed site plans during the housing phases. In effect, this sequence sought an ideal combination of formal studies, sociological analyses, and design centered on the community and its most social institutions: shopping center, the locus of commerce; elementary schools, the locus of education; and housing, the representation of mass shelter.

The faculty discussed the results of the report at a regular meeting.[21] Gropius stated, on the department's behalf, that Design A was generally favored as a means of ending the collision of the two first-year courses but expressed reservations about some minor details and how a system of rotation would be implemented. He suggested that rotation implied a dilution of the espoused principles of the design fundamentals by allowing inconsistency. The Department of Landscape Architecture, represented by Lester Collins, and the Department of City and Regional Planning, represented by William Wheaton, unanimously approved the proposals. Collins noted, though, that the plan would cut out a large proportion of courses in the undergraduate Department of Architectural Sciences. Norman Newton, director of the undergraduate program, agreed, but added that the GSD should devise its best possible program under the circumstances and that his program would adapt to the changes. The meeting concluded with an upbeat expression of collaborative spirit. This optimism was short-lived.

In June President Conant ordered a drastic reduction of the GSD's budget. To what degree the national recession affected the school remains unclear; in any case, its endowment from the Nelson Robinson, Jr., fund of $2.88 million in 1947 had dwindled by 1952 to produce insufficient income to run the school.[22]

The previous year Gropius's staff was cut from 13 to 10; he now lost three "aides" and a fourth was transferred. Gropius resigned on the grounds that the budget cut would require reorganization of the Department of Architecture, best left to his successor.[23] Undoubtedly the staff reductions placed a heavy teaching load on the sixty-nine-year-old Gropius, and the planned replacement of Design 1 with Design A hastened his departure. Because of the increasing disintegration of their association, Gropius may have considered that Hudnut had personal motivations for canceling appointments and courses. Privately, however, Hudnut and Gropius each conceded that the other had valid reasons for his actions and that each had to save face.[24] The public explanation for Gropius's departure centered on the fact that rampant inflation had reduced the school's income by half.

With the GSD unraveling, the architectural press took note and assessed the contributions of Gropius and Hudnut, and their conflicting stances towards modernism were made clear in polarizing appraisals. *Architectural Forum* identified Gropius as the man of the future and servant of collective effort: "[He] believes in anticipating the architectural needs of an industrialized civilization by making the architect the leader of a team embracing engineers, manufacturers, contractors." Hudnut, the sponsor of some of those same ideas, had, on the other hand, become the man of the past and champion of the isolated individualist: "Hudnut, critic and historian and once a strong

champion of modern architecture, recently grown increasingly squeamish about industrialism as such, pictures modern architects as mere technocrats, idealizes the individual architect as an individual artist, speaks with fond rotundity of his favorite Georgian age and architecture."[25]

Hudnut tried to reverse the trends that were undermining the core program; in August the school published the amended core course requirements.[26] Hudnut implemented the design course changes that had been in the planning stages: he jettisoned Gropius's Design 1 course based on the Bauhaus and its emphasis on formal, abstract principles. Instead, he proposed two courses: Design A, "Spatial and Structural Foundations: Design Laboratory," which dealt with basic spatial organization, color, materials, texture, as well as problems of social need; and Design B, "Community Analysis and Design," which resembled the original core course (Planning I) and would provide an introduction to the methods of city planners, architects, and landscape architects.[27] Taught by Newton, LeBoutillier, and Jean-Paul Carlhian, the latter course would begin with studies and sketches of building types and analyses that indicated the social needs of communities, followed by preparation of design programs for those needs and the design of a master plan and neighborhood plan. The content of other courses was shifted, reduced, and in some cases eliminated; graphics and projective drawing were returned to the curriculum, and a new course, "Community, Site, and Building Design," was added for the second year.

Public Scandal and Potential Closing

Ideological conflicts were paired with financial restraints, created by a debilitating period of inflation in the national economy in the early 1950s. Within three years of reaching its international apogee, the GSD became a shell. Hudnut assumed the role of acting chairman of the Department of Architecture for the academic year 1952–53. To fill the gap left by Gropius's sudden resignation, Hugh Stubbins managed the temporary arrangements for Gropius's master class, and four visiting critics from Europe and America gave design problems during the year (I. M. Pei, Gropius's former student, was the first critic). Nevertheless, Hudnut's victory was Pyrrhic: his efforts to revise the curriculum were too late and the changes were only temporary, until the next dean could enact his own program. The integrated first year was scuttled and the collaborative ideal was temporarily in shambles, the result of conflicting views of modernism.

The continuing departure of Hudnut's faculty members occurred in the midst of public revelations about the school's dismal condition.[28] The *Harvard Crimson* published a two-part editorial entitled "Decadent Design."[29] While labeling the events *decadent* was sensational, the paper sensibly called for the Harvard Corporation to quickly end two years of delib-

eration concerning appointment of a new dean. With new programs on hold until the appointment of a new dean to replace the soon-retiring Hudnut, the GSD had become, in the newspaper's view, "a skeleton of a school," not as a result of personal conflicts but because of financial strain from two sources. In part, the *Crimson* felt, inflation had caused Hudnut to slice away professors and courses to the extent that Gropius departed rather than work with what he considered an inadequate staff and budget. Some professors remained on a part-time basis, while others carried such heavy loads that they had little time for research or attention to individual students. The second source of strain came from Harvard College's refusal, the *Crimson* alleged, to help pay for instruction in the Department of Architectural Sciences. Although the college received tuition from the seventy-five students in the program, the School of Design still paid for their instruction. Apparently, the college would not pay for instruction it could not control.

The editorial recommended financial measures and the immediate appointment of a new dean. Recognizing that 90 percent of the GSD's endowment came from the Departments of Architecture and Landscape Architecture and that the Department of City and Regional Planning could claim only one endowed chair, the editorial suggested that the planning program be moved from Hunt Hall to the Littauer Center for Public Administration. This transfer would have placed city and regional planning totally in the domain of

the public administration school, despite the fact that planning culminated in a physical expression that required knowledge of design. A second suggested cost-cutting measure came from eliminating the expense of teaching undergraduates in Architectural Sciences. This savings of $12,000 would cover the deficit but deprive Harvard College students of a popular major and the School of Design of a specially trained entering class.

Rescuing the GSD's lost prominence lay, said the *Crimson*, in finding a new dean who could build research programs, raise funds, and secure "a faculty which will again pioneer in modern design." The ideal dean would combine a conservative, strong administrator, academic innovator, and fund-raiser with a fiery "long-haired designer." Two men had shared these responsibilities, but "A combination like this is easily inflammable. The brilliant academician may buck under the reins of a lesser-known dean, just as the Hudnut-Gropius arrangement flared up into an interdepartmental conflagration." The difficulties abounded in locating such a person. According to the editorial, "Gropius himself, though expected by the University to solicit gifts, was content to spend his time teaching and publicizing modern architecture." A new administrator, who could act as dean and departmental chairman, might solve the dilemma, but conditions had eroded to the point that "no new dean can merely step in and pull the school back together again with one decisive motion; its parts have drifted away, some irretrievably."[30]

At the same time that the newspaper publicly exposed weaknesses in the School of Design, the GSD received the most threatening news in its history. The president of the university called a meeting of the Faculty of Design in November 1952 to announce that the GSD was on the brink of insolvency and that temporary suspension of landscape architecture and city planning was recommended. No students would be accepted, pending receipt of new funds, effective January 1953.[31] In addition, President Conant recommended that the school's Visiting Committee coordinate the raising of endowment funds for the two suspended departments and that the new dean assume the functions of both Hudnut and Gropius. The Department of Architecture could continue operating because the Robinson Endowment allowed discretion in the allocation of funds to architecture or landscape architecture; architecture now got all the money. Furthermore, if landscape architecture and city planning were to resume, President Conant contemplated, perhaps they could reappear as a joint program. The situation was so extreme that some members of the Visiting Committee, who "were still disturbed over the shift from traditional design some fifteen years ago," questioned whether the GSD should continue at all.[32]

The Faculty of Design responded with shock to these announcements and suggested desperate measures to President Conant that might save their programs. Even the existence of the landscape architecture and regional planning library was

threatened, as it had been at the demise of the first School of City Planning in 1936 in the face of the Depression. President Conant reiterated that the library would be dissolved if no funds could be found to maintain it. One way of saving the most important planning library in the world was to start a cooperative program with the Department of Planning at MIT, but MIT preferred to maintain the small enrollment of about twenty-five students in its programs, which did not appear to warrant equally supporting a joint program. With respect to eliminating the Department of Architectural Sciences, Norman Newton, its chairman, pointed out that even if "Arch Sci" were eliminated from Harvard College, the GSD's budget would still need to meet the expenses for equivalent elective courses for its own graduate students.

Compounding the complexity of finding the most effective means and people to raise the endowment funds was the continued postponement of hiring a new dean. President Conant told the faculty that he personally would become involved in the search—as he had seventeen years earlier—in order to set the stage for the following year. In anticipation of the retirements of Hudnut and Gropius and given that the planning and landscape departments had only temporary heads, a group of alumni had already sent a list of possible candidates for the deanship to their fellow alumni in December 1951, including a synopsis of the GSD's recent history and current philosophy of education.[33]

A school whose students had received increasing recognition, a school that had a unique position in the academic world for collaborative training in the fields of architecture, landscape architecture, and city planning, now faced a future in which two of its three departments would close. The dream of Hudnut and Gropius appeared, at this moment, to have dissolved utterly—yet the scenario became more complex. In January 1953 President Conant reversed his proposal to cut off two branches of the school.[34] Instead, he suggested that the GSD proceed on a restricted budget, with limits placed on the number of students accepted into the landscape architecture and planning departments: fifty in architecture and a total of ten in the other two departments. Conant also recommended that the faculty consider the abolition of rigid requirements for the A.B. degree as a prerequisite, so that students who had three years of college could be admitted as "exceptional cases" (this echoed the temporary provision for the admission of war veterans to the GSD without a bachelor's degree during the mid-1940s) and that the school abolish the professional degree of bachelor of architecture, setting up a four-year master's program in the three departments. These proposals would allow a wider range of students to be considered for admission and reduce the total time required for the master's degree, a long-standing desire of President Conant, who believed that all education requirements were too long.

It was also a return to the earlier practice of granting only master's degrees in the Schools of Architecture, Landscape Architecture, and City Planning. Most significantly, the proposals would abolish the special status of the master's degree that had been created for Gropius. In effect, no longer would a master, in the tradition of the European *Meisterschule*, have such control over, or impact on, an advanced group of American and international students.

The Faculty of Design examined Conant's proposals in an informal committee, explored the requirements of staff and funding, and generally favored the plan. It noted, in particular, that the reduced time requirements put the GSD's curriculum in line with those at Yale and the University of Pennsylvania, thus putting Harvard on a more competitive basis. The four-year curriculum also was in line with the longstanding recommendations of accrediting and registration boards. In a subsequent faculty discussion, however, William Wheaton, chairman of the planning department, pointed out that the new curriculum would be disadvantageous to his department because it lengthened its curriculum to four years, when most other schools required less than three years for a master's in planning.

These proposals for a revised curriculum were occurring in the midst of negotiations to secure a new dean. Pending announcement of a selection, such proposals were premature. By one account, first choice for a dean was Oscar Niemeyer, the Brazilian architect in the lineage of Le Corbusier, who would, in three years, start designing the public

buildings of Brasília as an interpretation of the paradigm of the functional city. But Niemeyer's membership in the Communist Party made him an impossible choice in McCarthy-era America. Second choice for many was Ernesto Rogers, an Italian who also had been active in CIAM, but he declined the offer.[35] American candidates, none of them front-runners, included Robert Alexander, an architect and former chairman of the Los Angeles City Planning Commission; Carl L. Feiss, architect and planner in the redevelopment division of the Housing and Home Finance Agency; John M. Gaus, former GSD professor of regional planning and professor at Littauer; John A. Parker, head of the Department of Planning at the University of North Carolina; I. M. Pei, formerly of the GSD faculty and practicing in New York; G. Holmes Perkins, who had left Harvard to be the new dean of fine arts at the University of Pennsylvania; and William W. Wurster, former dean at MIT, then working on the West Coast. Finally, in early February 1953, the suspense was over: José Luis Sert, the fifty-one-year-old Spanish-born architect living in New York City and then-president of CIAM, was appointed the fourth dean of design at Harvard.[36]

Sert had worked briefly with Le Corbusier in the late 1920s, becoming one of his main disciples.[37] With the collapse of the Spanish republican government, he moved to the United States in 1939 and opened a practice, Town Planning Associates, that provided planning for Latin American cities; with his partner, Paul

Lester Wiener, he produced master plans for Brazil, Colombia, and two new communities in Venezuela. Sert had also designed private houses in the United States, the Spanish Pavilion at the Paris World Fair (1937), apartment housing, and schools in Barcelona, and was a professor of city planning at Yale 1944–45. At the time of his appointment at Harvard, he was on the Planning Committee of the Citizens' Housing and Planning Council of New York.

Gropius had recommended Sert because, among the candidates suggested by the alumni, Sert most clearly represented the modern movement in Europe and had the international perspective of an architect working on city planning problems.[38] Though the precise steps remain undetermined, Sert was appointed professor of architecture, dean of the Faculty of Design, and chairman of the Department of Architecture.

Although the university hoped Sert would begin his duties immediately, he did not take control until the fall of 1953. In the interim, dismissals and resignations in the face of the financial, emotional, and intellectual crises were ongoing. By February 1953 only eight regular faculty members and three adjunct instructors had received notification of their continued appointments.[39] Of these, only three would remain to teach the following year: Walter Bogner and Norman Newton were the only links to the history and traditions of the school.

According to *Architectural Forum*, the dean-designate "picked aides who gave

[the school] such a strong flavor of international modern design" that most of the faculty was resigning in protest.[40] Reported to be resigning in architecture were William L. Lyman, Jr., Charles Burchard, George T. LeBoutillier, Hugh A. Stubbins, with the return of Jean-Paul Carlhian uncertain. In planning, William Wheaton and Coleman Woodbury were leaving. In landscape architecture, Lester Collins resigned as chairman. In an effort to spare the GSD further embarrassment, Walter Bogner, acting dean and the only principal instructor remaining in the Department of Architecture, averred that all the resignations, with two exceptions, had been made prior to the appointment of the new dean.[41] According to Bogner, Charles Burchard and Hugh Stubbins were leaving to devote full time to their practices. Stubbins had been designated chairman of the Department of Architecture in 1953, before Sert's appointment; however, with Sert assuming both deanship and chairmanship, Stubbins's opportunities for a larger role in the school vanished.

Hudnut retired in the summer of 1953. He and his wife, Claire, moved to Maine, where he lectured at Colby College (Fig. 7.1).[42] In 1956 the Hudnuts returned to Dover, Massachusetts, and he lectured in architectural history at MIT until his final retirement in 1962, languishing in professional oblivion until his death in 1968. He left his collection of several thousand slides to MIT's library. His friend and beneficiary, Betty Deviney, recalled him as modest man with a marvelous sense of humor.[43] He kept no letters, jettisoned what he did not need, and left few personal records and only some of the publications written during his retirement—in which he addressed his long-term passions: teaching the history of architecture, civic design, and aesthetics in the teaching of design.[44]

Gropius returned to writing and a vigorous practice at TAC, and continued to exert a strong influence at Harvard (Fig. 7.2). Rather than recede, his professional practice entered its most prolific period, using the teamwork approach to design buildings around the world. Not only did his firm continue to serve as a training ground for many young Harvard graduates, but it retained close ties to the GSD, sending its practitioners to teach there. Honored and revered, Gropius's birthday was celebrated annually as a festive event at Robinson Hall until his death in 1969.

Sorting Through the Rubble

Understanding the collapse of such an extraordinary vision initially shared by Hudnut and Gropius requires consideration of the deeper forces operating beneath the more topical events. Strong institutions frequently confront the dilemmas of personnel and finances, survive, and even prosper. At Harvard, though, there were more fundamental tensions in play. By the 1950s, the domination of American design by European modernism had created the myth of the autonomous creation of the GSD, as if it had no forerunners in the American scene. The idea

that Gropius was its source gathered momentum and adherents over time. Students often subscribed to the myth because they believed they were part of a revolution.[45] They knew that they were at Harvard because of Gropius, yet they could not see that he was the emblem of a modernism that no longer distinguished between American and European approaches. He was respected as a teacher, yet his own work as an architect was ignored. Students at Harvard had emulated the work of Le Corbusier, Alvar Aalto, Frank Lloyd Wright, and even Mies van der Rohe more than Gropius's buildings. His polemic, not his architecture, made the school important.[46]

The power of Gropius's ideology of a democratic architecture rationalized by science, which was spread by his writings, his reputation, and the dispersal of his students as practitioners and teachers throughout the world, filled the public mind. Gropius's biographers (and colleagues) appraised him as a man who encouraged architects to take responsibility with respect to social problems and to acknowledge that the complexity of society required collaborative solutions. He was a man who "challenged each student to find within himself his own expression."[47]

Hudnut's long-term and consistent role in the development of the modernist agenda was quickly forgotten. After his death even his position as dean of the Harvard Graduate School of Design was not remembered; not only critics but even Harvard faculty wrote of Gropius as the dean. One exception was Robert C. Wein-

berg, a Harvard alumnus, who publicly defended Hudnut's title and role shortly after his death, while Gropius was still alive. To the *Harvard Alumni Bulletin*, which had stated that Sert had succeeded Gropius as dean, Weinberg responded: "Hudnut had been the first and only previous Dean of the School of Design, which Hudnut himself had created . . . out of the three separate schools of architecture, landscape architecture, and city planning. It was Hudnut who brought Gropius to Cambridge as a professor of architecture, and it was Gropius who did everything in his power to thwart the efforts of Hudnut to create a comprehensive curriculum in environmental design out of the three formerly separate schools, which Hudnut so noticeably achieved before he retired. And it was only through the fortunate resignation of Gropius in 1953 that Dean Sert was able to carry Dean Hudnut's great dream to its present state of fruition."[48] From this point of view, Hudnut had initiated the all-inclusive approach to the fields of design. The strength of Gropius's ideas and his involvement and identification with the school reinforced academic polemics and popular opinion.

Another force at work in the fashioning of history was the tension that inevitably arises from vastly differing temperaments. Hudnut was shy and expressed himself better in writing than in his lectures. In recalling Hudnut's lectures, Ian McHarg remembered him as "a small man with a lisp, audible only as far as the second row."[49] But outside the classroom Hudnut had a dry, finely tuned sense of humor.

7.3 Graduate Center, Harvard University, TAC, 1949. As pictured in *L'architecture d'aujourd'hui*, February 1950.

When asked why architects are good cooks, he replied that he had no answer but admitted that he was a pastry cook and specialized in making cakes: "My cakes have proportion, rhythm, and significant form; they are carved with miracles of frosting; and I write on them, in rococo letters of colored sugar, some beautiful sentiment such as 'Happy Birthday, Katherine.' I confess that my cakes aren't very good to eat—but what of that? When they get a little stale, they are put into the Metropolitan Museum (*not* the Museum of Modern Art), where they are exhibited in glass cases labeled 'Antique Cakes,' and people who go there and look at them have their taste in cakes prodigiously improved."[50]

While Hudnut could poke fun at himself and his profession, Gropius was seen as eternally serious and "always in control of himself" by many of his colleagues.[51] Kenneth Conant viewed Gropius as imperious and haughty, attitudes which he (and others) attributed to Gropius's Prussian ancestry: "Gropius was very arbitrary, and the faculty meetings could be sufficiently unpleasant when there was a difference of opinion between Hudnut, who was actually the Dean and responsible for the School, and Gropius, who was never more than the chairman of the Department of Architecture." Between Gropius and Hudnut, Conant saw that "there were divergences of policy. Gropius was really quite a big grump to handle on the faculty, and I don't know that there was jealousy, but Gropius, though only head of the Department, acted as if he were the

Dean and the center of world architecture. He was not a convenient or pleasant man as a faculty member."[52]

Beyond the personality conflicts was the friction between a famous professor of architecture whose reputation greatly surpassed that of his dean. In schools of design, the star architect, whether shy or extroverted, receives the public's attention; charismatic and larger than life, Gropius easily captured the attention of academia, the profession, and the public. Gropius had to have his own way. Hudnut, self-effacing, retreated to the shadows.[53] As Walter Creese recalled from his own experience as a graduate student and teaching fellow in the mid-1940s: "There can be little doubt that the prestige of Gropius at the time depended in some measure on his status as a political, rather than an architectural, icon. He manifested an early assertion of the political principle of internationalism, overcoming nationalism, nationalism being anathema of intellectuals at the time."[54] Gropius's burgeoning professional success only added to his stature and confidence, in contrast to Hudnut who had truly become a "paper architect."

The commission for the Harvard Graduate Center of 1949, designed by Gropius and his colleagues at TAC, constituted an official recognition of Gropius's status (Fig. 7.3).[55] Hudnut was instrumental in getting Gropius the job, but Gropius showed little appreciation for his efforts, providing yet another reason for Hudnut's resentment.[56] Gropius believed that he was creating an academic quadrangle

with variations on the theme of the Harvard residential colleges. The result was lackluster. In comparing the tautness of the 1926 design of the Bauhaus with the Harvard Graduate Center, architectural historian William Jordy noted the center's blandness and popularization. Furthermore, Jordy felt, rather than manifesting a healthy variety of design vision, the incongruity of the Harvard Graduate Center and later works, such as the American Embassy in Athens (1956) and the Pan American World Airways Building (1958), ultimately revealed a loss of "inner Imperative."[57] Nevertheless, Gropius and his partners had launched a highly successful international professional practice that was another vehicle inadvertently dwarfing Hudnut.

Gropius had personal charisma, and his skillful ability to promote an idea as simple as teamwork into a concept dispersed throughout the world garnered him tremendous success as an ideologue. His instrumental founding of the Bauhaus had already given him a place in history. Regardless of Hudnut's efforts to direct the school and propagate his own vision of American modernism, Gropius overshadowed Hudnut—and, in some ways, the entire school.

Part of the demise of the collaborative ideal stemmed from inherent problems in collaboration itself. The curriculum built around collaboration—a dream born at the beginning of the century and reformulated from the 1930s to the war's end—barely lasted five years, from 1945 to 1950, a brief existence. The pedagogical

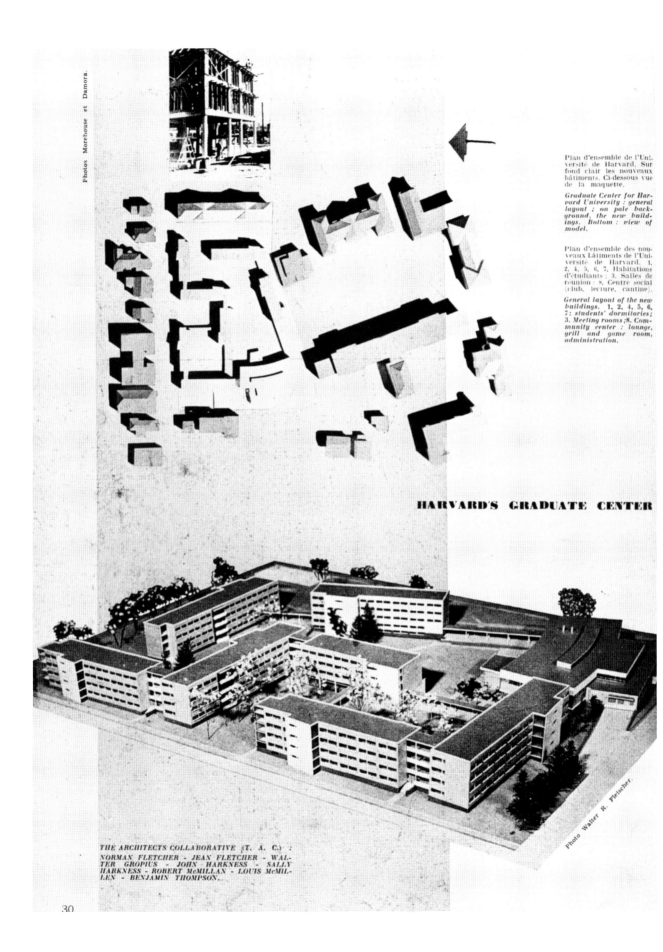

Photos Morehouse et Damora.

Plan d'ensemble de l'Université de Harvard. Sur fond clair les nouveaux bâtiments. Ci-dessous vue de la maquette.

Graduate Center for Harvard University : general layout ; on pale background, the new buildings. Bottom : view of model.

Plan d'ensemble des nouveaux bâtiments de l'Université de Harvard. 1, 2, 4, 5, 6, 7, Habitations d'étudiants ; 3, Salles de réunion ; 8, Centre social (club, lecture, cantine).

General layout of the new buildings. 1, 2, 4, 5, 6, 7: students' dormitories; 3. Meeting rooms ;8. Community center : lounge, grill and game room, administration.

HARVARD'S GRADUATE CENTER

Photo Walter R. Fletcher.

THE ARCHITECTS COLLABORATIVE (T. A. C.) : NORMAN FLETCHER - JEAN FLETCHER - WALTER GROPIUS - JOHN HARKNESS - SALLY HARKNESS - ROBERT McMILLAN - LOUIS McMILLEN - BENJAMIN THOMPSON.

program for a unified design education offered difficulties on a simply practical level: collaboration requires an enormous amount of time from both students and teachers. Teachers were reluctant either to demand more of their students' limited time in all-consuming courses or to give up their own time as pressures within their fields increased.

Gropius, furthermore, had a concept of teamwork that differed from the kind of collaboration that had evolved at Harvard over the preceding decades. For Gropius, the team consisted solely of architects or closely linked professionals, such as engineers. He did not accept the full democratic participation of professionals from disciplines that he saw as "outside" architecture—notably, landscape architecture and city and regional planning. Gropius's focus on teamwork for architects alone only exacerbated the imbalance among the design departments at Harvard—an imbalance so extreme that city and regional planning had already closed its doors once, during the GSD's first year, for lack of funds. Until the mid-1940s, planning had few resources with which to respond to the call of modernism. Landscape architecture, though open and functioning, often seemed lost in the collaborative effort. For example, when Gropius published the splendid results of his teamwork projects and his "Blueprint for an Architect's Education" in *L'Architecture d'aujourd'hui* in 1950, the collaborations were identified as occurring between architecture and city planning departments, with landscape architecture conspicuously missing.

Moreover, despite the determination of its proponents and beyond the external conflicts that hindered it, the success of collaboration was limited at other schools as well as Harvard. William Wurster, who left MIT to become dean of the College of Environmental Design at Berkeley with the goal of amalgamating landscape architecture, architecture, and planning, was unable to achieve what he had hoped.[58] Conversely, at the Illinois Institute of Technology (IIT) Mies van der Rohe brought in two colleagues from the Bauhaus and introduced a curriculum for architects only that followed a three-step process of design from a sequential study of materials and function to develop a creative synthesis resulting in "fullness and monumentality."[59] Freed from the burden of collaborating with other complex fields, Mies created a prescription that was easy to follow and allowed generations of his students, as well as practitioners elsewhere, to absorb the method. The glass curtain-wall office building that Mies developed using this process became the iconic image of the 1950s and 1960s—not the architectural designs of Gropius who stressed process over the creation of beautiful objects. In this sense Mies's Chicago Bauhaus at IIT triumphed over Gropius's Harvard Bauhaus, though Harvard was more prestigious and sent its graduates around the globe as teachers as well as practitioners to preach the Gropius pedagogical program. Achieving quality in the expression of "fullness and monumentality" was not, however, guaranteed, and imitation of the Miesian style

tended to produce uninspired glass boxes.

Still another factor complicating any collaborative effort was the growth of planning as an academic field and a profession. It expanded to include a widening variety of economic, demographic, and governmental issues—which, in turn, led to ties between planning and other disciplines, thereby diluting the field's ability to collaborate more closely in a school of design.

The situation with the field of landscape architecture was also problematic. European modernism did not provide a compelling model of professional reform for American landscape architects. With some exceptions, they did not identify with the European-inspired modern movement; they had their own modernism with roots in the philosophy of Olmsted, Eliot, and American progressivism. Their lack of identification with European modernists made them less than equal partners in the collaboration. At Harvard, though receptive to collaboration, the Department of Landscape Architecture did not provide significant ideological models, direction, or visual vocabulary for a modern landscape architecture of the 1940s. Many American landscape architects began finding the call to create solutions to the problems confronting a collective society more important than creating a compelling visual imagery that paralleled the abstract forms of the New Architecture. The social consciousness that animated students in architecture and planning was expressed in landscape architecture by a focus on the lingering projects of the New Deal— perhaps it was better to provide a park for a thousand than a garden for one.

American landscape architects had no new role models because the European modern movement had largely excluded landscape architecture; its focus (especially post-war) on providing minimal shelter for the dispossessed was more pressing. To paraphrase Jerzy Soltan, a collaborator of Le Corbusier who would later teach at Harvard, who could worry about roses when the forests were burning?[60] The traditions of *Gartenkunst* (garden art) and imperial design were on a separate path from that of the American landscape movement—as the young generation of landscape architecture teachers at Harvard, including Norman Newton and (briefly) Christopher Tunnard, knew.

The Role of Architectural History in Contemporary Education

Yet another problem contributing to the Hudnut-Gropius conflict was their view of the role of architectural history in contemporary culture and its relationship to education in general, and to the design arts in particular. During the period from the founding of the GSD in 1936 to the early 1950s, the role of architectural history changed in ways that we are only now beginning to understand. Many have asserted that modernists, personified by Gropius, rejected the importance of history; indeed, his former students continue to recall his opposition to it.[61] Critics of

this position assert that without historical knowledge, designers lose their ability to connect with their culture, which is what allows them to be able to identify, within physical form, the innate shapes and images that carry meaning for people. Modernism, therefore, was responsible for creating a cultural and spiritual void.

What happened to architectural history at Harvard, however, was far more complex. During World War II, a series of courses was taught on the history of cities. From 1942 to 1951 Hudnut taught the history of civic design (once with Christopher Tunnard), civic design and technology (with Martin Wagner), ancient, pre-industrial, and medieval civic design, and civic design in times of post-industrial Renaissance revolution. In these courses he tried to restore history to a more central place in education and society: history had the responsibility of providing the humanizing spirit missing in modern design. Decades later students still recalled these courses with great admiration.[62] According to Walter Creese, Hudnut seemed to have a kind of "civitas" idea of a community as a "polis."[63] The city provided the social arena of architecture.

In addition to their cultural, personal, and aesthetic differences was a core difference between Hudnut and Gropius: their visions of history itself. Hudnut's ideas, as expressed in his courses during the 1940s, focused more on the history of cities than on the issues of regional planning. Creese recalled that Hudnut "regarded historic cities as a deep well, a vast reference source, about the verities of

urban organic living. Hudnut and Gropius did have the common ambition of setting out new premises and principles. But Hudnut wanted to garner them from past *as well*." This respect for ideas from the past and even for people who were considered by modernists as "has beens" drove a wedge between the two.[64]

Commenting on the teaching of the history of architecture, Hudnut called for more than "data, visual expressions, and analytical knowledge" to reveal architecture as "distinct, separate, and firm in your imagination, occupying all of it; and through all of it idea and emotional content must be manifest." He urged teachers to bring to their students aesthetic experiences, new impressions, and observations even as he pressed his objections to "the facile orthodoxy of functionalism." For Hudnut, the study of architecture could not be reduced to practical issues alone— to seeing buildings as abstractions—but must include a perception of the human spirit for which architecture was the outward manifestation. Some sense of the spirit could be obtained by placing history's important architects in the middle of the creative event to reveal something of the personal nature of the endeavor.

This anthropocentric conception of the human struggle, conscious use of will, and individualism countered an emphasis on *zeitgeist*: "Following the lives of these great spirits the student may not so readily believe that architects are created by 'the Spirit of their Epoch,' or that architectural species evolve from their crude beginnings through variations imposed by biological law, or that excellent works of architecture can be invented by a collaborative committee." Hudnut felt increasingly strongly about the role of history, asserting that, "If I had my way every student should begin the study of the history of architecture on the day upon which he entered the school of architecture. He should continue that study, through widening horizons and kindling experience, during all of the five years of his curriculum, and that discipline should fling its radiance, like a gem, into every moment of his life."[65] In sum, Hudnut culminated his decades of deliberation by valuing the aesthetic experience of architecture over its technical production, by seeing its creation as an art directed by psychological circumstance, and by promoting it as a presentation of the human spirit. For Hudnut, an architecture of humanism superseded a dispirited architecture of collaborative effort. But if architecture were both an art and a science, balancing them was difficult.

Gropius's views on the role of architectural history were distinctly different—and critical, because they deeply affected generations of practitioners. His opposition to the role of history is popularly known, and he has been polemically presented as a man responsible for the historical ignorance of generations of students. This view of Gropius's influence contends that by disparaging the role of architectural history and discouraging its study, Gropius encouraged his students to lose contact with the historical legacies of their field. In turn, they carried these atti-tudes into their professional work and, since many Harvard graduates became teachers elsewhere, they transmitted this anti-historical position to several generations of students. Jean-Paul Carlhian recounted an anecdote that captures the essence of Gropius's approach to studying history. Gropius convened a departmental faculty meeting in response to the National Accreditation Board's threat that certification could be withheld because the department was deficient in history courses. Three semesters of history would be required, apparently, to satisfy the board. Gropius proposed medieval architecture as one course, because he believed that medieval guilds provided the traditions needed to restore the connections between society and design, as was apparent from his annual introductory lecture to beginning students.[66] In response to a recommendation for a course on Greek and Roman architecture, Gropius replied that the study of symmetrical architecture was unacceptable; as for Renaissance architecture, Gropius said, the design of façades—independent of interior plans—would not be taught at Harvard. He acquiesced to a course on modern architecture that would begin with the work of Henri van de Velde, Gropius's predecessor at the arts and crafts school in Weimar, forerunner of the Bauhaus; this choice implied a line of study characterized in Nikolaus Pevsner's *Pioneers of Modern Architecture* and Giedion's *Space, Time and Architecture*.[67]

According to this modernist account, then, the history of architecture would begin with ancient man, skip the classical world, focus on the Middle Ages, omit Renaissance, baroque, and neoclassical architecture, and begin the study of modern architecture along prescribed lines at the end of the nineteenth century. These propositions implied that continuity of tradition was valueless, symmetry equaled classicism, and that the design of façades as representational images or pure composition was irrelevant to the function of buildings.

Gropius's views were rooted in his own experience. After studying at a German gymnasium, he entered a technical school to study architecture, where most of the instruction involved copying the four orders of Greek columns. Despite the fact that his grand-uncle, the prominent Martin Gropius, and his father, Walther, had been architects and followers of the classicism of Carl Friedrich Schinkel, Gropius reacted with terror: "I was horrified. I was so terribly upset that I said to myself, 'No, I am not willing to do that. It had nothing to do with the training of a man so he knows something about building.' "[68]

The entire educational system was reprehensible to Gropius: "In Germany the whole method of training suppressed the individual. The sensitive creature suffers most." Indeed, the respect for individualism in America was precisely what allowed Gropius to succeed. His reaction to German education, combined with his manual difficulties in painting and drawing, caused Gropius to see a split between the representation of architecture and its

actualization, instead of seeing the former as part of the conceptual process and essential to a creative dialogue with construction. It also caused him to value conceptualization over a facility for visual presentation, which he reduced to "picture-making."[69]

Nevertheless, Gropius's deliberations on the study of history revealed an ideological position that was not absolutely against the study of architectural history. He advocated that the study of history take place later in professional education, after a student's initial training. Specifically, he recommended that history studies should start in the third year of training instead of the first "to avoid intimidation and imitation." Gropius observed that by confronting history too early in professional education, a student "is sometimes rather discouraged when he faces the old masters."[70]

While other architects in the 1950s, from Edward Durrell Stone to Louis Kahn, increasingly acknowledged the role of historical reference in their work, Gropius held firm on his position. Aware of opposition to his perspective, Gropius later fully developed his argument in a philosophical framework that presented his position with a brilliant reasonableness. He described the modern cultural context as one of visual illiteracy. Rapid change from local and national conditions to a domain of global interchange of experience, research, and goods obscured "former" values, creating a disorientation that caused art and architecture to be seen only as symbols of status and luxury. This

view superseded "the deeply-rooted, unselfconscious imagery of people who shared a common code and could be sure of response when any one of them raised his voice or hand in creative work." A new vision, however, would "propel tradition and continuity forward into the future." It required more than a study of the past; it also required the release of "creative energies that had been suppressed for generations." Gropius reasoned that creative energies should be released first and history postponed so as not to inhibit budding originality. At the Bauhaus, art history courses would have resulted in "instant emotional defiance" by students previously frustrated by the repression of their creative urges. At Harvard, Gropius's experience was that too early an exposure to art history, "when a student is pregnant with his own thoughts and works and has not yet felt a genuine curiosity for the works of the past, remains unassimilated, dead knowledge. . . . Sureness and experience come from being exposed to the realities of living and doing, not from seeing Pompeii." Being involved with the shaping forces of life resulted in a creative person, "his mind empty of prejudice and all non-essential considerations and . . . [in] a new state of innocence," who will pursue a new culture.[71]

Gropius's argument is vulnerable. Freeing the creative forces in an individual is a wonderful idea. But while it is logical, if scientifically unverified, to assert that imitation leads to dullness, why should studying history dull anyone's perceptions or creativity? Certainly experiencing human struggle, defeat, and achievement may increase the empathy required of the designer. But why couldn't a knowledge of Pompeii also increase that empathy and provide a sense of human continuity? Even in the twentieth century most major figures in the history of art and architecture, from Picasso to Jackson Pollock and Frank Lloyd Wright, appear to have worked *through* the history of their field. Gropius's view reflected the polemic of the early modern movement that equated history with slavish imitation of the past and with the social and political struggles that hindered cultural and social progress, ultimately leading to wars and human misery.

Gropius held fast to his view of America's industrial and factory production, which so impressed him on his first visit in 1928, while the American tradition of the "buildings in a landscape" bypassed him entirely. As Creese observed, Gropius ignored "the small but recent workers' model villages in New England by landscape architects around Cambridge, such as the Olmsteds, John Nolan, Arthur Comey, and Warren Manning."[72] He relentlessly called for serial production, universal systems, and industrial production at a time when America's industrial plants lay idle. He held rigidly to the precepts of the modern movement in the 1910s and 1920s, proudly extolling American democratic ideals but misunderstanding American history and tradition.

The basic architectural issues in this vision of European modernism included satisfying utilitarian function, pursuing social values, and maintaining a visual language of form. But does the satisfaction of utilitarian function simultaneously satisfy the complex emotional and psychological needs of people? Doubtful. The drive to inculcate social values through architecture has always been constrained by the social and political establishment that commissions and controls the field. The transmission of spiritual values is often beyond the capacity of educational institutions. In a truly free creative environment, would not the expression of individuals have a far greater range than in Gropius's tightly defined environment? Despite his admonitions against imitation of others' styles, Gropius's followers often sponsored an orthodoxy of style. Their principles produced a familiar family of forms while uninhibited, exploratory design moved to the background. Despite disavowals by its protagonists, modernism *did* have a style, as the visual language necessary for "literacy" produced one. Yet the style of modernism consisted of rules that were limited in their cultural application—rules that had no proof of universal validity and formed a closed system—ironically, not unlike the systems of style that Gropius and other modernists rejected. In valorizing self-control, is there not a risk that the controlling individual seeks to control the lives of others, regardless of espoused democratic ideals? Another irony is that deep within the stance of modernist realism was a utopian yearning for the past, when a collective vision understood a common language of signs and symbols. As at the Bauhaus, a communality, allegedly last seen in the Middle Ages, was called for, but the world had changed too much to make the vision viable. The instantaneous transfer of information and the constant transformation of images and symbols increasingly undermined the possibility of a cohesive and stationary set of social values.

Hudnut's position on the role of architectural history also was flawed. His assumption about where, and by whom, cultural courses should be taught only reinforced the modernists' skepticism about the role of architectural history as a tool in professional training. Hudnut provided one vehicle in his own courses in civic history, but the history of the buildings and evolution of modern architecture itself fell to Kenneth Conant—who played a pivotal though unintentional role in allowing Gropius's position to appear more valid than Hudnut's. Conant's courses, like Hudnut's, served two audiences, undergraduate and graduate, one for liberal arts students and the other for preprofessionals.[73] His long teaching career spanned the era of his own training at Harvard, when three full courses in the history of architecture were required, to his retirement in 1953, when three half-courses were taught. A gentleman of the old school, Conant felt no need to proselytize. He was not dogmatic in an era of dogmatism, and without fervor Conant could not make a case, as Hudnut was trying to do, for the relevancy of history to modernism. The combination of fervor and dogma succeeded in convincing students of the irrelevancy of history when

compared with the ethos of technological expression and social purpose. As the collaborative dream was increasingly disconnected from history, modernism's greatest strength and major weakness were concomitantly exposed.

The sense that something was missing in the curricula—in particular, the absence of history courses—had been addressed in 1948 when an elective in history was added, but it lasted only one year. With an increasing course load looming, students no longer had the time or opportunity to take advantage of the nourishment offered by "culture" courses in Harvard College, and the use of the elective courses to provide a humanistic background ceased. This reality points to the vulnerability in Hudnut's vision of when and how cultural courses should be taught. In the founding of the GSD he had assumed that not only history but also art and all other courses that provide the cultural context of design would be studied during the undergraduate years. The need for courses that responded to the complex problems of a modern technological society and for time limits on professional training allowed only the most pertinent and practical courses to be the subjects of graduate training. Hence came the justification for relegating history requirements to the undergraduate curriculum, as well as the traditional courses in drawing, watercolor, and the history of art and architecture.

If one believed that history and the cultivating experience that comes from the

study of art could be learned in undergraduate training, then the shift would have seemed to cause little concern. At Harvard the connections between the teaching of design and fine arts had been intimate and strong since 1875. This symbiosis had continued up to the arrival of the modernist program of the mid-1930s, whereupon the alliance between the Division of Fine Arts and the new Graduate School of Design proceeded to change radically over the next twenty years. On one hand, there was the perception that the fine arts program had become intellectually soft, replete with well-meaning dilettantes whose courses were more encyclopedic than insightful. In broader terms the university was, in policy, reluctant to offer nonacademic subjects, and, in particular, art and design. On the other hand, the Ruskinian tradition present at the founding of Harvard's Division of Fine Arts began to yield to scientific approaches and museology, reflecting the maturation of art historiography in general. The Germanic tradition of art historiography offered an approach to the study of art that allied the analysis of abstract, formal visual qualities with a method that appeared organized, rational, and scientific. Scientism had already gained a foothold as the Ruskinian legacy retired with its proponents. The teaching of drawing, painting, and sculpture—seen as applied arts and therefore suspect in the eyes of a university devoted to logic, science, and rationality—was replaced by the relatively young profession of the historiography of art. Although the Division of Fine Arts at Harvard had a tradition, from its beginnings in 1874, of teaching studio art, courses in applied art were now replaced by a discipline of historical study that appeared serious, scientific, orderly, and orthodox.[74]

With Arthur Pope's departure in 1948, seventy-five years of teaching studio courses in drawing and abstract design and methods of painting at the Fogg Museum virtually ended. Despite repeated efforts to find someone to teach studio courses, there was no long-term success and the Division of Fine Arts ultimately gave up this responsibility. Scientific analysis and deeper inquiries into creative processes replaced the listing of names, dates, and simplistic stylistic categories. For the sake of these advancements, the formerly unified teaching of history was split into history for art historians and history for design professionals. In reductive terms, the former was more academic and intellectual, the latter, more pragmatic. The theory of art replaced the practice of art.

Combined with the changes in art historiography, the end of applied art, and the demoted status of the history of architecture, the close alliance with the Division of Fine Arts, begun at the end of the nineteenth century, was replaced by a more informal collaboration, mutual respect, and the perception that art historians taught the history of architecture differently from the ways architects taught the history of architecture. John Coolidge, the architectural historian and director of the Fogg Museum who vigorously promoted modern art, described the relationship between the fine arts program and the GSD as one of "I mind my business, you mind yours, and we'll get along fine."[75]

The changing relationship between the Division of Fine Arts and the GSD critically affected the concept of collaborative education and undermined the premise that students could absorb the cultural foundation in college necessary for dealing with the complexities of modern problems. At Harvard students could no longer receive exposure to drawing and painting, which was stipulated as a prerequisite to professional training. Hudnut had hoped that the undergraduate Department of Architectural Sciences would provide pre-professional training. But the program's approach to design differed from the traditions of academic art; the focus was much narrower: the precepts of the Bauhaus and the teachings of Albers, Johannes Itten, Paul Klee, and László Moholy-Nagy, as well the analytical and critical thought of Konrad Fiedler and John Dewey.[76] Even the name "Architectural Sciences" implied that the department's program was based in scientific rigor and was analogous to other science departments that were central to the university. In the Department of Architectural Sciences the concept of cultural training was limited in scope, so that instead of learning about culture in its broadest senses, students received a filtered modernist culture. The result was that the students were trained as modernists without the benefit of either a strong historical background or a broad cultural comprehension in which to situate their modernist agendas.

The fundamental differences between Hudnut and Gropius had, at their center, the larger conflict between an American vision of modernism that began to lose its cohesion after the war, and a European vision that increasingly garnered international recognition. Hudnut fought for what had always been an American perspective, even if that perspective often had Europeans as its best proponents and even when Americans abandoned their own traditions in favor of it. Gropius, on the other hand, found in America a new voice and forum for the ideological programs that had emerged in Europe thirty years earlier. The American condition was essentially unself-conscious, the European, highly self-conscious.

Would an American modernism have resisted the inroads of European developments if neither Gropius nor Hudnut had been at Harvard? If Hudnut had never created the GSD? Without Hudnut, Gropius would not have had the articulated structure of a powerful university from which to operate. Without Gropius, Hudnut would not have had an articulate colleague capable of promoting the ideals of unity in both professional and educational realms. The power of the collaborative ideal originated in the unique confluence of circumstance, foreshadowed by the efforts of the founders in America at the turn of the century and paralleled by the efforts of European modernists.

A country spared two wars on its soil nevertheless endured a Depression that robbed its citizens of confidence in their own efforts. The resulting crisis of identity was resolved, at least in part, by the input of a European intellectual migration. From a broad perspective the cultural history of the twentieth century shows the immense dominance of European modernism around the globe. Yet, while European modernism in the design arts saw its greatest success in the era after World War I, American artists, like the abstract expressionists, made breaks that would leave European artists in their wake after World War II.

Holmes Perkins, who lived through and directed part of the new movement, characterized the demise of Hudnut and Gropius this way:

> What makes a tragedy is the great hero or heroes have come apart somewhere. . . . You had two people, great people who together had made Harvard the best architectural school in the country, unquestionably. It transformed architectural education across the country. The old way of looking at things was gone, there was a new, fresh breeze coming in. . . . There was a new vigor of drive for something different, better and more responsive to the current needs of the professional society as a whole in a different view of architecture. . . . It was a revolution, an absolute and extraordinarily successful revolution in a very short period of time. But like all revolutions, there comes a time when the leaders get old, and new people come up who maybe follow in this tradition, but make still further changes. This is as it should be. And the time really had come for the new.[77]

What defined "the new" remained to be answered. One thing was clear despite the difficulties of transition: mod-

ernism had arrived at Harvard to such an extent that any distinctions between American and European visions had vanished. The memory of American efforts was so distant and the embrace of European ideas embodied in Gropius and his colleagues so complete that no difference could be seen. For the next twenty years after the departure of Hudnut and Gropius, the GSD would be led by European-trained modernists. However, as Perkins correctly perceived, they would take the GSD in directions that differed from the ideals of Gropius: a sensibility that thrived in art and a broadened range of issues moved beyond the concept of teamwork and its emphasis on technology wedded to social issues. During the subsequent history of the GSD, the collaborative model of education as the project of modern design training would disappear for periods of time then reappear either in fragments or in some partial transformation of its original goals—but the collaborative ideal remained an important legacy even if its impact was subtle and its roots forgotten.

While the Graduate School of Design continued to produce successful practitioners and teachers in architecture, landscape architecture, and city planning, its role as a model of international and national significance had passed a summit by the end of the Hudnut-Gropius era. The GSD would create new programs in the field of design, and its curriculum would continue to be emulated, but the character and size of the school would change dramatically.

REVISIONS AND REACTIONS, 1953–1995

The End of American Modernism

The history of the Graduate School of Design and its relationship to the larger course of modernism since the end of the Hudnut-Gropius era in the early 1950s cannot be assessed yet from the perspective of critical history. Many events are too recent, many of their participants are still active professionals, and the story continues to evolve. To conclude, we will look instead at the reactions to modernism within the school and, to some degree, the larger reactions of society around it—which saw modernism revised, castigated, and then revived over the next fifty years. The varied fates of modernism would never have been imagined by its earlier proponents, whose ideological differences had been subsumed within a seemingly unified international movement by the 1950s. The International Style had become truly international, eliminating the distinction between American and European modernism.

The wholesale American adaptation of the International Style raises many questions. How could the American agenda to create modern architecture that valued both tradition and technological advances, as eloquently demonstrated in the Harvard student projects of the 1920s, so thoroughly disappear? Why did the collective effort to forge an American identity independent of European roots vanish upon the arrival of European modernists in the 1930s?

By the time Gropius, Wagner, Breuer, and many others arrived in the United States, the Great Depression had sapped American vitality. The validity of the search for an American identity became questionable in the face of the nation's fundamental economic insecurity. Ironically, the nation's economic dominance in the world marketplace never provided a fundamental cultural security. Hand in hand with these issues of identity was a new perception of history itself. In the face of the Depression, the traditional Western means of seeing the past as the model for the future became suspect. Following the past and anything associated with it—tradition, political conservatism, and values of the status quo—somehow had played a role in creating economic chaos, hardship, and suffering. The rejection of the past and the search for a new ideology of the future was a natural reaction to this failure—a view also embraced by radical European modernists at the beginning of the twentieth century. We have seen all of this played out within the design fields at Harvard: the early idealism of Herbert Langford Warren's programs, the increasing sophistication of American design under Harold Edgell, and the subsuming of the American vision as Hudnut was overshadowed by Gropius.

However, simultaneous with the triumph of the International Style in the 1950s were incipient reactions against it that would lead to a more inclusive pluralism, both inside and outside Harvard. Over the next fifty years the design professions continued to evolve as they absorbed new technologies. The reconsideration of the role of history in design—

8.1 Dean José Luis Sert with students and faculty on the steps of Robinson Hall, 1953. Left to right: G. K. Yeap, Robert Sperl, Fumihiko Maki, Arthur O'Connor, Harold L. Goyette, J. E. Adams, Stevenson Flemer, Dean Sert, Ned B. Wiederholt, and Professor Ronald Gourley.

which often appeared as the most suspect component in design education—continued. The embrace of disciplines outside the conventions of architecture, landscape architecture, and city planning, such as psychology and hermeneutics, gathered momentum in a rejection of the very tenets of modernism's functional approaches. These complex issues form the general outline explored here.

After the Hudnut-Gropius era came to an end at Harvard, a resurgence in the teaching of history was both a reply to the sense of "something missing" from orthodox modernism and a precursor to the developments of the 1970s. Though Hudnut's vision had faded, ironically his call for a humanized architecture, mediated through the study of history and cities, echoed in the emergence of postmodernism. Looking at this changing role of history is one way of seeing how we view ourselves and modernism's impact on our perceptions.

The collaborative ideal—Harvard's tool for enacting the modernist agenda—went through its own changes. In the

larger profession collaboration increasingly meant teamwork among groups of architects, or architects working with artists. As the scale of design projects increased, with buildings expanding in size to match the new scale of American corporations, architects were forced to work with landscape architects and to come to terms with city planners. At the GSD collaboration between the departments largely ended in the late 1950s, but the concept of collaborative education reverberated at other institutions, as former faculty and students fanned out to teach and practice. As noted earlier, Holmes Perkins brought the model to the University of Pennsylvania, where it proved highly successful; other graduates of the Hudnut-Gropius-era GSD went on to teaching and administrative positions at such widespread universities as North Carolina, Tulane, Illinois, Oregon, and UCLA. The full scope of the impact of the GSD's vision of collaboration both on the design professions and on design education is a story that is still waiting to be told.

During the 1950s, the fate of the GSD's modernist programs also became increasingly intertwined with the splintering and eventual dissolution of the largely European-based CIAM group: José Luis Sert, the GSD's new dean, was also the president of CIAM. Though CIAM's debates over the future of the modernist-functionalist ideal had consumed European designers through much of the 1940s and 1950s, it was Sert's arrival at the GSD that brought these ideas to a wider American audience of architects and planners. Sert's agenda at the GSD through the 1950s and 1960s was directly linked to the demise of the modernist ideal as expressed in the corruption of CIAM's tenets.

A New Dean: José Luis Sert

In the summer of 1953, the school that José Luis Sert would soon head as dean and chairman of architecture was, as we have seen, in disarray (Fig. 8.1). Before Sert could implement any ideological changes, many practical changes that were underway before his arrival needed attention. The university announced, for example, that in addition to continuing to train professionals who had received a cultural background in college, the GSD would emphasize "Design Research." Administrative changes would shorten the period of study: students with three years of college would be accepted in special cases in addition to those who had already graduated from college. The B.Arch. was eliminated, alleviating confusion about the relative status of B.Arch.

and M.Arch. graduates and bringing Harvard more in line with other universities.[1]

In a sudden and unexpected move, the university then announced that the GSD would combine the departments of landscape architecture and city and regional planning into one department. This consolidation was intended not only to ease the budget deficit but also to train planning students who would produce "public works of wide social value" and landscape architecture students who would develop "competence in large-scale design of outdoor space and the land underlying it."[2] In effect, this change ended the collaborative first-year program as Hudnut and Gropius had originally envisioned it, even as it ended the autonomy and blurred the identity of the two programs.

Accompanying these changes was the announcement of Sert's first round of new appointments. He assigned the chairmanship of the new combined department to Reginald R. Isaacs, an experienced Canadian-born architect and planner, who was appointed Charles Dyer Norton Professor of Regional Planning.[3] A member of Gropius's first master's class, Isaacs had graduated from the GSD in 1939, worked professionally as a planner and architect for public and private agencies, lectured at many schools, and written on housing, planning, and sociological subjects. Before coming to Harvard, he had been the director of the Michael Reese Hospital planning staff and consultant to the South Side Planning Board in Chicago, a position that involved large-scale planning on the South Side of the city. He had also served as a visiting lecturer on city planning and member of the Visiting Committee for the GSD. His interdisciplinary approach was reflected in his membership in the American Institute of Planners, the American Institute of Architects, and the American Sociological Society. Gropius later selected Isaacs as his official biographer. Isaacs retired from the GSD as an emeritus in 1978.

Serge I. Chermayeff was also appointed in the fall of 1954 (Fig. 8.2). Born in Russia, he had practiced as an architect and was a member of the MARS group in England before emigrating to the United States in 1940 and becoming active in CIAM.[4] In 1946 he began teaching at the Chicago Institute of Design where he instituted a curriculum based on the program of the Bauhaus. In 1951, when the Institute of Design merged with IIT, he moved to Boston to open a practice and serve as a visiting lecturer at MIT (1951–53).

Sert also named Naum Gabo, the Russian-born artist and leader of constructivism, as professor of design research. Gabo had the essential credentials of a European modernist: he had widely exhibited his constructivist art and scientific sculptures, lectured at the Bauhaus, and shown work (in 1926) with Theo van Doesburg's "Stijl" in New York City and in the Museum of Modern Art's "Cubism and Abstract Art" (in 1936). He spent the war in England, conducting research with Herbert Read intended to promote cooperation between artists and industry. He moved to the United States in 1946 and lectured at MIT and Black Mountain College in addition to his stint at Harvard. Though Gabo taught only for one year, his was the first appointment of an artist to the GSD since Hudnut had removed the artists of the Old Guard in the late 1930s.[5]

To teach city planning and to replenish the landscape architecture staff and curriculum, Sert appointed California-born Hideo Sasaki. A 1948 graduate of Harvard's landscape program, Sasaki had worked in the offices of Skidmore, Owings & Merrill in New York City and taught as an instructor in landscape architecture at the University of Illinois and at the GSD. He was professor from 1953 to 1970 and chairman of the Department of Landscape Architecture from 1958 to 1968. He left a considerable legacy through both his teaching and practice and the firms he founded that focused on corporate design and planning.[6] Huson Jackson and Ronald R. Gourley, both GSD architecture graduates, were appointed as design critics; they later became partners in Sert's firm in Cambridge. Jackson also taught at the Pratt Institute and Columbia University. Gourley started his teaching career at MIT, spent almost two decades at the GSD, then became dean of the University of Arizona's College of Architecture for ten years.[7] Joining them was Joseph Zalewski, an associate of Sert and former member of ATBAT (*Atelier des bâtisseurs*), an interdisciplinary research group formed by associates of Le Corbusier.[8]

8.2 Professor Serge I. Chermayeff and the "Patio House," 1956.

The new faculty and accompanying administrative changes were the first signs of a new agenda marking the beginnings of a revision of orthodox modernism. Both the agenda and the reactions that stimulated it were inseparable from developments in CIAM. In the 1940s students at the GSD, and Americans in general, were largely unaware of the existence of CIAM (though there were exceptions, like Blanche Lemco, a 1950 GSD city planning graduate who was an active CIAM member).[9] Criticism of the group centered on its neglect of its American constituency. In 1949 Bruno Zevi (the Italian GSD graduate who championed organic architecture for post-war Italy) accused the organization also for failing to cooperate with other international groups like UNESCO, and believed that CIAM was overly dominated by Le Corbusier, Gropius, and Giedion, excluding representatives of a humanistic, organic architecture that was emerging in Europe and America.[10] Even Gropius could see that CIAM's disconnection from American designers was disadvantageous to the organization's future, and in 1950 he submitted a list of American architects to Sert for inclusion in CIAM's membership.[11]

What Americans had missed, then, in the CIAM debates of the 1940s came to a head in the early 1950s and was brought to their attention with Sert's arrival in Boston. A crucial dissension between supporters of functionalism and the promoters of a revised functionalism (known as the New Empiricism) caused a split between the modernist status quo and its

vision of the Functional City and a more humanist vision of the future held by a new generation of designers. In 1950, CIAM was starting to splinter from within.

The criticism increased in intensity simultaneously with announcements of Sert's appointments in 1953. Young members who objected to the Functional City formed a group at the CIAM summer meeting in Aix-en-Provence. Led by Jacob Bakema, Aldo van Eyck, and Peter and Alison Smithson, the group questioned the principles of the modern movement itself. Though attendance at the meeting was large (five hundred members from thirty-one countries), the twenty-five-year-old CIAM began to disintegrate, despite the efforts of the older generation to hand over the organization to the younger ones.[12]

Sert's reply to the criticism, developed under the influence of Giedion and Le Corbusier, was an attempt to transcend the limits of functionalism by giving modernism a human face and making it meaningful for people at large. He argued for a middle ground—a position somewhere in between the founders of CIAM and its young radicals—that would allow a revision of modernism and ensure the CIAM's ongoing importance, with Harvard as the locus of these revisions.

When Sert arrived at Harvard in the fall of 1953, his agenda for humanizing the urban environment and countering the aridity of functionalism and visual discord was two-pronged: it called for a redirection of modernism's focus back to the human habitat of the city's core where most people lived, and a return to culture through the spiritualizing and edifying impact of art. But this return to culture did not equal a return to "culture courses." Sert's notion of culture was largely visual; no longer the domain of arts appreciation or connoisseurship, training in "visual culture" would require a grasp of the underlying abstract principles that affected design. For Sert, visual literacy was the key means of turning ugly, dysfunctional environments into beautiful, harmonious wholes.

After the new curriculum was developed in the spring of 1954, Sert prepared a memorandum to summarize the school's philosophy in which changes were made, he said, in response to a conscious desire "for a more complete knowledge of human needs." Students would take a not only revamped basic design course that included greater exposure to visual media but also the "History of the Visual Arts, Contemporary Architecture, and Urban Design," intended for architects, city planners, and landscape architects.[13] This revision signaled the official return of cultural studies to graduate training in design; artistic expression, at least as explored via design, and the study of history were again seen as humanizing factors in the evolution of modern architecture and city planning.

In practical terms, Sert needed faculty and resources to support these endeavors, and for these he turned largely to the friends and disciples of Le Corbusier. The creation of this new network of Corbusians would not have been possible without the intellectual and financial support of Nathan M. Pusey, who had been named Harvard's twenty-fourth president in 1953. Pusey, a scholar of classics, expressed his immediate support of the creative arts within a liberal arts education, and he became a close ally of Sert. Through Sert, Pusey supported creating a cultivated and sophisticated world of art and architecture and took seriously the role of architecture and visual arts in culture.

The effort to redress the undue emphasis on functionalism reverberated not only at the GSD but also at the undergraduate level. The *Harvard Crimson*, which had exposed the problems of the school during the Hudnut-Gropius impasse, applauded changes to the Department of Architectural Sciences that now instituted courses emphasizing the "art side of architecture."[14] These courses in freehand drawing, design fundamentals, and visual arts in history were the prerequisites for early admission to the master's programs at the GSD. Sert received much of the credit for this new focus on creativity and aesthetics. The changes marked the beginning of a new kind of study of the visual arts at Harvard, which Sert articulated in an address at an AIA symposium in Boston, "The Changing Philosophy of Architecture," in June 1954. He declared unequivocally: "Functionalism has been widely accepted as the guiding principle of all architectural work, but it has produced clichés of an appalling poverty. Today we need a new vocabulary, rich and flexible. Functionalism alone does not satisfy our needs."[15]

To manifest his vision, Sert brought major players in CIAM to Harvard in 1954–55. Foremost among the next round of appointees was Jacqueline Tyrwhitt, a member of CIAM since 1941 and assistant director of the MARS group since 1949, who retained connections to planning efforts in Britain (Fig. 8.3).[16] Tyrwhitt had assisted Giedion in preparing his book *Mechanization Takes Command*, was on the CIAM commission on urbanism in 1947, and was instrumental, with the support of Ernesto Rogers, in putting together the proceedings of the meeting and publishing them with revisions as *CIAM 8, The Heart of the City*.

Not only would the city become both subject and teacher, but the study of history would, once again, provide the cultural context for design. Sert called upon his friend Sigfried Giedion, the secretary-general of CIAM, to fill the gap left by the retirement of Kenneth Conant.[17] Absorbed in his research on the origins of art and architecture, Giedion was able to accept only a visiting professorship for one term in 1954, and parts of terms through the early 1960s; he lectured on ancient and modern architecture.[18]

Eduard F. Sekler, an Austrian architect and architectural historian who had come to Harvard as a Fulbright Fellow in the Fine Arts in 1954, was appointed visiting professor in 1955.[19] He and Giedion recommended the reinstatement of four terms of required history, which returned the study of history to its standing in the old School of Architecture (Fig. 8.4). Sekler soon assumed the task of teaching the major history courses at the GSD. He emphasized conditions of production and eventually expanded the scope of courses to include the use of the human scale, the history of the city, and the shaping of urban space. The study of the history of architecture paralleled the study of the history of landscape architecture, taught by Norman Newton. Despite fluctuations in the valuation of history in the landscape architecture program, it had never completely vanished.[20]

Implementing the return to a cultural perspective through an emphasis on the visual arts involved bringing back the design fundamentals course, with artists as instructors. To direct the design workshop in 1954–55, Sert invited Costantino Nivolo, a sculptor and close friend of Le Corbusier.[21] He was followed by the Italian sculptor Mirko Basaldella in 1957, who directed the design workshop until 1969.

To augment the new directions in the basic curriculum, Sert retained parts of the integrated first-year program but with a different emphasis. In 1950 the purpose of the unified program had been to acquaint students with the common bases of the design arts and to provide the basic techniques of the professions. In 1954 the purpose was to teach the techniques as well as to make students aware of the designer's role in addressing the needs of individuals and communities. Teamteaching became the principal form of instruction. Teachers in the introductory studio course, Environmental Design, included Isaacs, Sasaki, Paul Norton (who

8.3 Professor Jacqueline Tyrwhitt lecturing on the "New City" project, Urban Design studio, 1961.

8.4 Professors Eduard F. Sekler (left) and Sigfried Giedion during a seminar held at Robinson Hall, fall term 1960. Photo by Ueli Roth.

8.5 Exhibition in Robinson Hall of student work for the academic year 1953–54, June 1954.

8.6 Exhibition in Robinson Hall of student work for the academic year 1953–54, June 1954.

8.7 Student project for faculty housing, Harvard University, model. Fumihiko Maki, 1954. Arch. 2d, Professors Sert and Gourley.

taught planning), Tyrwhitt, and Chermayeff; Albert Szabo was appointed an instructor in design in 1954.[22] The resulting student work was displayed in the annual exhibitions held in the Great Space of Robinson Hall (Figs. 8.5, 8.6). Typical of the work done in the advanced studio was Fumihiko Maki's design for faculty housing (Fig. 8.7).[23]

The new design workshops and the return of history appeared to provide the elements for a new unification of the design arts. Not so. Despite Sert's sympathy for collaboration, his efforts to balance social and aesthetic considerations occurred at some expense to the actual unification of all design efforts. At the advanced level in architecture students had to choose among three different studio courses: monumental and large-scale buildings, civic design, or one whose subject was more exclusively technical (Figs. 8.8, 8.9). Under Gropius, the master's class had sought to deal with all three, as would occur in an office context.

Moreover, the practical implementation of Sert's program met with difficulties. Combining the funds of the landscape architecture and planning departments conflicted with endowment restrictions. Consequently, the experimental amalgamation of city planning and landscape architecture failed, and in 1956 the department split into two separate programs again. Isaacs headed the Department of City and Regional Planning and continued to emphasize the social role of planning. In his eyes the client of planning was the public; over

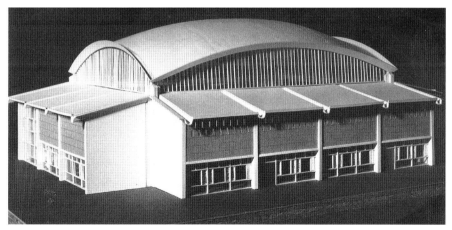

8.8 Student project for the redevelopment of Lowell, Massachusetts. Mark A. Biass and others, 1957. Arch. 2-3ab, collaborative problem, Professors Sert, Isaacs, Gourley, and Mr. Ortega.

8.9 Student project for Lowell Tech gymnasium, redevelopment of Lowell, Massachusetts. Norman L. Hoberman, 1957. Arch. 2-3ab, collaborative problem, Professors Sert, Isaacs, Gourley, and Mr. Ortega.

time, he pioneered the first investigations into participatory design. Walter L. Chambers, an expert in drainage, grading, and landscape construction, became chairman of the reconstituted Department of Landscape Architecture.[24] He was assisted by Charles W. Eliot II, who returned to teach in 1954 after several years of working in Washington, D.C., and as a planning consultant in private practice.[25]

In addition to dealing with flux in the planning and landscape architecture departments, Sert had to confront the fact that the symbiosis between art and architecture at Harvard had ceased long ago, with the only overlap occurring in history courses that were open to undergraduates. A former graduate student at the Fogg in 1954 recalled the attitude of the art historians there as "close-minded about the importance of artists: painters, sculptors, what have you. . . . The only space Harvard allocated for its one course on painting was one room on the third floor at the back of the Fogg."[26] These problems, however, concerned many people outside the Fogg, including President Pusey, who had avidly taken Fine Arts I as an undergraduate.[27] Aware that a similar course combining history, theory, and practice no longer existed, he appointed a committee to assess the situation of the arts. The committee's report, completed in 1956 and called the Brown Report after its chairman, ultimately resulted in the creation and implementation of new programs in the visual arts in the 1960s.[28]

In 1956, the National Architectural Accreditation Board found the GSD architecture program to be lacking in its integration of curriculum courses, leaving students unprepared for advanced work. Accreditation of the program was given conditionally for the next two years. This wake-up call prompted a temporary reinstatement of the B.Arch. degree along with the curriculum that led to it.

Other problems confronted Sert in 1957 with the increasing criticisms of CIAM's inability to implement its own propositions and to join other international efforts, particularly planning efforts in the United States. Most of the criticism came from the core group of dissidents that had formed at the 1953 CIAM. Now referred to as Team 10, they called for, in effect, a revision of the revision. Not only did they react against CIAM's entrenched efforts to create the Functional City, they also disparaged the middle ground Sert and Gideon represented, where art provided a humanizing force. Team 10's efforts were unequivocally directed toward the man in the street and reflected the rebellious attitudes that emerged from many corners in the 1960s.

Sert now set in motion events that would culminate in a conference held in April 1957 on "Urban and Housing Design," Harvard's first urban design conference.[29] At the meeting the future of CIAM was debated by its inner-circle members, with Giedion, Gropius, and Sert defending its validity but arguing for reorganization, and Jacob Bakema, representing the position of Team 10, claiming that

CIAM was finished. Though its founding precepts for making Functional Cities continued to ripple through the work of architects and planners around the world, and there were attempts at reorganization and a final meeting in the Netherlands two years later, CIAM essentially ceased to be effective in 1957, and Sert's presidency of the organization ended by default.

Team 10's presence was soon felt directly at Harvard with the appointment of Latvian-born Jerzy Soltan in 1959; he would become chairman of the architecture department in 1967.[30] One of Le Corbusier's two employees when the architect reopened his office in Paris in 1944 in anticipation of post-war commissions, Soltan worked with him until 1949. Le Corbusier's ideas and work had become the model for teachers and the guiding light for architects and urban designers (Fig. 8.10). An aestheticism that emulated the work of Le Corbusier and a common belief in the principles of CIAM established a Corbusian "line" at the GSD (Fig. 8.11). At Harvard Soltan retained personal allegiance to Le Corbusier, but he also aligned himself with Team 10 even as Team 10's members represented a different orientation from Sert's alignment with Le Corbusier and Gropius.[31]

In 1962 Sert hired another Team 10 member, Shadrach Woods, a former member of ATBAT.[32] The influence of Team 10 became even more evident when two GSD design instructors, Gerhard Kallmann and Michael McKinnell, won the prestigious commission for a new Boston city hall, a building that dramatically reflected Le Corbusier's La Tourette and the rough, exposed concrete of New Brutalism.[33]

A concerted effort was made on several fronts to fill the void left by the dissolution of CIAM, to address the broader issues raised by Team 10, and to confront the issues of the cities in crisis. In 1959 Harvard and MIT established the Joint Center for Urban Studies, which provided no programs for training designers. Martin Meyerson, appointed professor and named its first director, set up the program's offices in Hunt Hall.[34]

Harvard went further in addressing the crisis of the city by establishing a postgraduate interdepartmental urban design program, the first such academic program in America. Announced in January 1960 for the following academic year, the curriculum was elegantly simple: intensive studios on urban design and seminars on the factors that shape the city, and on the shaping of urban space, with at least two terms of study required in each area. [35] The program was open only to candidates who already had a degree from the GSD or equivalent training elsewhere.

Begun under the supervision of Sert, the urban design program was intended to involve all three departments in the school, and as such, was a surrogate for the collaborative agenda of the Hudnut-Gropius era—but with a focus on the city rather than on the individual building. Jacqueline Tyrwhitt, who remained a key figure in urban design and city planning at the GSD, gave a precise definition of the program in 1962: "The term *urban*

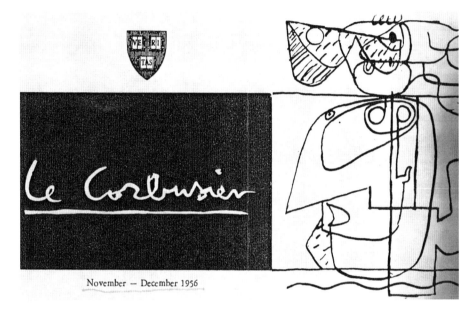

November – December 1956

8.10 Exhibit brochure for a showing of paintings and gouaches by Le Corbusier at the GSD, 1956.

8.11 Huson Jackson, student; Professors Serge Chermayeff and Jerzy Soltan, 1960 (left to right).

8.12 Student jury for the "New City" project, Urban Design studio, 1961. Foreground, left to right, Sigfried Giedion, José Luis Sert, Louis Kahn, and Willo von Moltke.

design is used at Harvard in quite a limited and specific sense to mean an area of interaction between the three professions of architecture, landscape architecture, and city planning, which are there housed together under the general umbrella of the Graduate School of Design."[36] With the appointment in 1963 of German-born Wilhelm von Moltke as its first director, the Department of Urban Design began to expand (Fig. 8.12).[37] Von Moltke, known as Willo, had received a degree from Gropius's master's class in 1942 and subsequently worked nationally and internationally as an urban designer and architect. Soltan also participated in the urban design program, and Sekler taught supporting history courses.

The founding of the urban design program accompanied an ideological reawakening of the social activism that had been present at the GSD in the 1940s. Its creation also added a fourth department to the school and signaled an increasing movement away from the unification of the design arts at a basic level. In a sense, the field of urban design sought to recapture for architects some of the ground that appeared to be lost to city planners as they pursued the means to influence the administration and organization of cities, and to integrate landscape architecture, which increasingly expanded its analytical tools for large-scale design. In accomplishing this aim, urban design had to define itself as different from other fields by showing it could give visual form to cities and regions in ways that planners and landscape architects could not (Figs.

8.13, 8.14). At first, the program could not grant its own degrees; its master's program was linked to preexisting degrees, producing the MAUD, Master of Architecture in Urban Design.

The results of the GSD's approach to urban design could be seen in Sert's own work in Cambridge, commissioned under the patronage of Nathan Pusey, during whose presidency Harvard's building space doubled. The firm of Sert, Gourley & Jackson designed several Harvard buildings in the 1960s, including Holyoke Center (1967), a major administrative building organized along a pedestrian core; Peabody Terrace (1964), multistoried residential towers for married students; and the Center for the Study of World Religions, a testament to post-CIAM concepts of community centers.

Within the GSD, however, integration of the teaching of landscape architecture into the urban design program proved problematic. Hideo Sasaki, who had succeeded Walter Chambers as chairman of Department of Landscape Architecture in 1958, inherited a department whose resources—in terms of staff, budget, and numbers of students—were seriously depleted.[38] Sasaki set about rebuilding the program and, through the often-unpaid assistance of his office staff, reconstructed the education of landscape architects with an initial emphasis on their roles as designers. Charles Ward Harris and Peter E. Walker joined the staff as instructors in 1958; each would successively chair the department.[39] In 1963 there was a brief return to collaborative

8.13 Student jury for the "New City" project, Urban Design studio, 1961. Foreground, left to right, Sigfried Giedion, José Luis Sert, Louis Kahn, and Willo von Moltke.

8.14 Martin Meyerson, critic, at the student jury for the "New City" project, Urban Design studio, 1961.

projects between landscape architecture and city and regional planning. Identified as "Regional Landscape Architecture Collaborative Studies," they continued for five years. Despite the effort, landscape architecture was moving away from architecture towards areas of research that expanded the field.

Modernism Splinters: Pluralism, Scientism, and Protest

The new focus of urban design, the stops and starts of collaborative efforts, and the lack of a unified overall approach to design education mirrored the fact that, by the early 1960s, modernism itself, as part of the larger cultural reaction, was splintering into pieces that both extended its original premises and reacted violently against them. A multiplicity of interests and directions characterized all the departments of the GSD and produced an intense ferment that mirrored the turbulence of American society. Among the many directions, the ideology pluralism dominated the 1960s. Pluralism—the acceptance of divergent values and multiple perspectives—attempted to redress the perception of modern architecture and urbanism as elitist, overly aesthetic, and disconnected from the lives of ordinary people. Jane Jacobs's *The Death and Life of Great American Cities* (1961) catalyzed popular sentiment about urban life and was widely read at Harvard, while Serge Chermayeff and Christopher Alexander's *Community and Privacy: Toward a New Architecture of Humanism*

(1963) attempted to use biological and sociological perspectives to examine the configurations that distinguish public and private realms. Robert Venturi's *Complexity and Contradiction in Architecture* (1966) took a wholly different tack by exposing the gulf between popular taste and the high-brow aestheticism of modernism. More than any other, Venturi's book allowed architects to embrace popular expression.

Pluralism now had a supporting literature. Team 10 exemplified the emerging pluralism, but pluralism encompassed much broader responses. One response was to emphasize the nonvisual determinants of form and to challenge valorizing aesthetics over questions of social meaning. These challenges occurred in the midst of attacks on the impact of modernism as seen in the urban renewal projects proliferating in America. Making beautiful buildings seemed irrelevant when it was obvious that political, social, and economic imperatives controlled the production of architecture and the shapes of cities. The radical politics of planner Chester Hartman catalyzed an awareness of the social considerations that could go into design and served as a bridge between architecture and planning issues.[40] His colleagues, William Wray Nash, Jr., and François Vigier, also made their students aware of social conditions as well as presenting city planning issues in a historical context and connecting political and social considerations to visual form.[41]

Increasingly the pluralists believed that the cognitive sciences could inform pro-

fessionals in the visual arts about the most fundamental processes by which the world is perceived. The scientific exploration of art and the psychology of perception could provide the methodologies and tools for dealing with the ever more complex technologies of modern life. Similarly, sociology appeared to hold great potential for the future of architecture.

This rise of scientism coincided with changes in technology and growing concerns about the environment. "Environmental studies," a relatively new concept previously limited to scientific analysis, was a response to an increased political awareness and to advanced research. At the GSD a new tool—the computer—was enlisted for research through the support of the Ford Foundation, which provided funds in 1965 for the creation of the Laboratory for Computer Graphics and Spatial Analysis. Howard Fisher was the laboratory's first director.

The landscape architecture department flourished under the rubric of scientific investigation, as staff and students embarked on explorations of large-scale domains that left the design of gardens in the dust. Under Sasaki, the department experienced a sensational if paradoxical rebirth. On one hand, it became increasingly less affiliated with other departments in the GSD (particularly urban design) and began to emphasize advanced and postprofessional research, which reduced the emphasis on basic training for students who had only a liberal arts education. On the other hand, the teaching became broader and more interdisciplinary, mirroring Sasaki's own office: team-teaching replaced the single instructor, new analytical methods for large-scale terrain analysis were taught, and the department consciously sought to promote environmental studies. Landscape architecture began to reclaim the territory absorbed by city and regional planning since the 1940s.

The new disciplines of computer graphics, geography, regional science, and systems analysis redefined the scope of landscape architecture and opened exciting and innovative fields of study. MIT graduate Carl Steinitz, among others, exposed students to the exciting technologies of remote sensing and computer mapping with various data sources.[42] In 1966 the Ford Foundation, recognizing the emerging concerns around the globe, funded a chair in resources and ecology as part of the new postprofessional Program for Advanced Environmental Studies (PAES) in the school's new Landscape Research Office, directed by Charles W. Harris.[43] The expanded scope of inquiry inevitably reduced the time students could spend on design per se. The emphasis on environmental issues appeared to be at odds with a design focus; the former was seen as strictly analytical and the latter as overly aesthetic—a tension that would continue. Sasaki's resignation as chairman of the Department of Landscape Architecture in 1968 to devote more time to his practice both mirrored and intensified this tension, further reducing the balance between design and analysis. The

new directions in landscape architecture seemed far more exciting than the predictable Corbusian aesthetics that still dominated the architecture studios.

The range of activities in the expanding fields started to make conditions crowded in Robinson and Hunt Halls. In its first capital campaign, the GSD began raising funds in 1964 for the PAES program and for a new building that would be named George Gund Hall after its major benefactor.[44]

The expanding focus on visual culture and the environment was seen in the creation of a new department in Harvard College, Visual and Environment Studies (VES) in 1968. In justifying its formation to the Harvard Faculty of Arts and Sciences, its proponents recalled the faculty's vote in 1938 to establish the Department of Architectural Sciences and suggested that, after thirty years of technological development and expansive urbanization, a change was in order.[45] The new undergraduate department occupied the Edward St. Vrain Carpenter Center for the Visual Arts, Le Corbusier's only building in North America, and a direct result of the Brown Report and Sert's efforts to give the visual arts a home at Harvard.[46] The inauguration of the Department of Visual and Environmental Studies marked the phasing out of the architectural sciences department, with its preprofessional studios oriented towards pragmatic architectural training. On one hand, the new major reflected the emphasis on visual literacy and the environment as a broad rubric of study for everything from archi-

tectural history to the psychology of perception. On the other hand, the program emphasized basic design, animation, film, graphic design, photography—all oriented towards analytical processes, not perceptually subjective ones.

By this time, the GSD, in Robinson Hall and Hunt Hall in Harvard Yard, and the VES, at the Carpenter Center across Quincy Street, were interconnected, with faculty holding joint appointments, and both undergraduates and graduates taking courses in all three locations. Art history was still taught in the Fogg Museum, and it still focused on scholarship, not the making of art. A polite distance existed between the faculties of fine arts and the GSD, based on mutual respect and a realization of the natural divergences between strictly scholarly work and professional training. The basic orientation of VES was not to train artists so much as to teach visual acuity, as could be seen in an early didactic exhibition, "Bauhaus—A Teaching Idea," in 1967. The prevalence of Bauhaus ideas was not surprising—Gropius, the Bauhaus's founder, still trekked across Harvard Yard for his annual birthday party at Robinson Hall and remained a much revered figure. But VES took on its own character—one that focused on preparing students for a broad range of careers that had little to do with the industrial orientation of the Bauhaus. Without realizing it, the founders of VES—Eduard Sekler, Albert Szabo (who also taught in the GSD), and their colleagues—were implementing the program that Hudnut had wanted. The basic design

8.15 Graphic for students' strike, 1969. Designed by Harvey Hacker, student.

principles originally used at the Bauhaus were expanded to include an emphasis on psychological and visual phenomena. From 1968 to 1974 Rudolf Arnheim taught the psychology of art; his *Art and Visual Perception* (1954, revised 1974) was a major text from the program's inception through the 1970s.[47] VES's broad scope included occasional courses by J. B. Jackson, pioneer in the study of American vernacular architecture and landscape, who taught from 1969 to 1977.[48]

The emphasis on visual phenomena and the image, however, appeared at odds with the mounting social activism in American culture. At Harvard, the national intensity of social consciousness culminated with the student strike of April 1969. Starting as part of the national student opposition to the Vietnam War, protesters occupied University Hall, Harvard's main administrative headquarters. When the police arrested the occupiers, the ensuing strike shut down the university, solidifying the politicization of students and faculty at the university and forcing emotional confrontations within the GSD concerning the role of design education in society. Robinson Hall became a headquarters for the production of graphics for the strike. In fact, the red fist, now a universal symbol of resistance, was designed there by GSD student Harvey Hacker and silk-screened onto posters and T-shirts in the basement of the hall (Fig. 8.15).[49]

Just as massive protests marked a nation in crisis, the strike marked a rupture in the idealistic premise of the GSD that joint efforts and commonality of purpose could ameliorate the conditions under which people live. Now the power of the design arts to change society was being questioned, and that questioning appeared to discourage designers even to attempt to serve society. In its simplest form, the critique of architecture's social efficacy asserted that the political structures in which the design fields operated dominated the efforts of the designer. For instance, an architect could design an orphanage to maximize the opportunities for its residents to interact with each other, but if the rules of the administration prevented that interaction, the designer's efforts were useless. Following from that assertion was a challenge to the validity—and value—of visual representation in its built form as well. If the structure of power determined the real uses of architecture, then what difference did the images of design make? In these terms, the traditions of drawing became peripheral, even irrelevant. Many saw architecture as an indulgence in aesthetics at the expense of political action and social need. The future of architecture appeared to lie almost solely in its connections to other disciplines—sociology, linguistics, and systems analysis.

Sert withdrew from the GSD during the student revolution and retired in 1969.[50] He continued his architectural practice and changed his name, in the late 1970s, to Josep Lluis to reflect his Catalan heritage. Maurice D. Kilbridge succeeded him as dean of the Faculty of Design and

professor of urban systems. Recruited from the Harvard Business School, Kilbridge's job was to stabilize the school and restore a sound financial footing.[51] These important changes occurred in the midst of the construction of Gund Hall, designed by the Australian John Andrews, a GSD alumnus and acclaimed architect. With a $7 million building budget, the building had seven levels, contained 170,000 square feet, and occupied a site of 300 by 90 feet.[52]

The Gund Hall Era

In fall 1972, after seventy years in Robinson and Hunt Halls on Harvard Yard, the Graduate School of Design moved to Gund Hall (Figs. 8.16–8.19). The school was facing serious challenges, both intellectual and fiscal. In Robinson Hall the GSD had been fractious, but it had nonetheless been a small, intimate school where people knew each other and shared an academic social life despite their perpetual arguments. The administration consisted of three or four staff members. The ambiance resembled that of an art school rather than a corporate office, and cooperation usually exceeded competition. That ambiance changed dramatically in the vast new spaces of Gund Hall.

The fundamental concept of the new building was that open "trays" of studios were a metaphor for the founding principle: the unification of the fields of design in one great intellectual space. Despite its legacy of functionalist and program-

matic design, however, Gund Hall functioned inefficiently in the midst of the national energy crisis of the early 1970s. Its open spaces and heating and air conditioning systems made it inordinately expensive to heat and cool. Kilbridge responded to the need for balanced books by increasing enrollment, which had been relatively stable since the beginning of the Sert era. Some programs now doubled within a year, resulting in dramatic increases in student population—particularly in the enrollment of city planners who did not require studio space—and increases in tuition.[53] Gund Hall had been designed to accommodate an increase in enrollment from 280 to about 340, but by 1977–78 it held 600 students, 100 full- and part-time faculty, and 50 staff members.[54]

Besides the financial strain, the departments of the GSD were largely separated in the new building. Each cultivated its own expertise, under the assumption that it was contributing to a larger, unified effort in an era of specialization. The core program had been eliminated, as had the collaborative studios, with rare exceptions. Collaboration had ceased not due to deliberate action but from neglect. The pressures of the moment, the separate crises of identity experienced by the departments, caused the community to forget the principle on which it had been formed.

Kilbridge sought to guide the school in the intellectual directions he thought best. In response to the call of Derek Bok, who had become president of the university in

8.16 Aerial view, future site
of Gund Hall on Harvard campus,
1967.

8.17 Gund Hall, Graduate School
of Design, model. John Andrews
with Anderson Baldwin, architects,
1967–69.

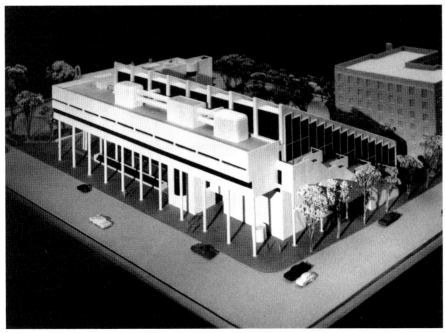

1971, to train individuals for public service, Kilbridge revised the planning curriculum by emphasizing political and institutional analysis, quantitative methods of economic and statistical analysis, and public finance and budgeting. The client destined for the planner was now federal, state, and local government.

The direction of the planning program affected the other programs as well, which began to respond to Kilbridge's interest in systems analysis and rational investigation. In architecture, there were attempts to focus on client needs, supported by programmatic analysis as design determinants. Paralleling the systems approach was the emergence of the first comprehensive course on the theory of architecture that integrated a sociohistorical approach with investigations of cognition. Formulated in the early 1970s by Alexander Tzonis, a Yale graduate and former assistant to Serge Chermayeff, the course comprised a two-part series that began with an introduction to the methodologies of design and progressed to an analysis of design programs and systems.[55]

Landscape architecture's expansion into other disciplines only mirrored the confusion in the profession itself and plunged the program into an extended identity crisis. Though analytical techniques became increasingly sophisticated, they appeared to conflict with design issues as the shaping influence of form and space. In January 1970, confusion and frustration about the program were voiced in discussions with the vis-

8.18 Gund Hall, Graduate School of Design, model. John Andrews with Anderson Baldwin, architects, 1967–69.

8.19 Gund Hall, Graduate School of Design, model of interior. John Andrews with Anderson Baldwin, architects, 1967–69.

iting accreditation team of the American Society of Landscape Architecture (ASLA). The team concluded that research courses conflicted with design, and that no resolution would be reached if the emphasis remained on environmental planning at the expense of training in landscape design. Five years later, on the seventy-fifth anniversary of the teaching of landscape architecture at Harvard, the ASLA criticized the program for still favoring resource analysis methods and detailed site design and called for stronger advanced design studio courses to reestablish the department's historic role of leadership in design. Though the split between design and analysis remained, it was reduced when Peter E. Walker became chairman in 1978. Utilizing his extensive professional experience, he emphasized design and brought artists and architects to the GSD to encourage collaboration between them and landscape architecture students.

While planners pursued policy, legislation issues, and economic forecasting, their work appeared to have no direct visual expression, and they no longer required desks in a studio. Their numbers swelled, yet their identity became increasingly problematic. By 1979 the situation reached a crisis that revolved around questions unanswered since the founding of city planning at Harvard seventy years earlier: What is the relationship of city and regional planning to the other fields of design? What should be the end product of planning: policy papers or physical plans? In what context is planning best taught: in a school of government, or in a school of design? The problems required outside mediation.

President Bok proposed moving the city and regional planning program from the Graduate School of Design to the John F. Kennedy School of Government (the new name, as of 1966, for the former Graduate School of Public Administration), a move that had been averted decades earlier.[56] The planning program's orientation was so thoroughly directed towards policy analysis of administration that Bok felt it should be aligned with the Kennedy School's master's program in public policy.[57] He also asked the GSD to establish a more physically oriented planning program, a request that implied the recruitment of faculty oriented more towards design than policy analysis. The move actualized a threat to the original idealistic purpose of the GSD. Unable to achieve integration, architecture and planning split apart. The Department of City and Regional Planning took the degree of master in city and regional planning, most of its faculty and students, and its tuition, and moved to the Kennedy School. Despite the struggles that had affected the departments of the Graduate School of Design and its predecessor schools from their very beginnings, this was the first time that a constituent program had actually withdrawn.

Kilbridge resigned the following year, after eleven years as dean. He had eliminated the physical design aspect of city

and regional planning training and replaced it with public policy.[58]

Upon Kilbridge's resignation Gerald M. McCue, chairman of the Department of Architecture, became the fourth dean of the Faculty of Design.[59] A successful practitioner comfortable in the corporate world, he confronted the departure of the planning program in the GSD by instituting new planning courses in the midst of a major expansion of the school's programs.[60] McCue immediately established a Department of Urban Planning and Design to replace the Department of City and Regional Planning. He fostered collaboration with the Kennedy School to assuage the hard feelings of the GSD planning faculty who had moved there. With the support of the city planners who had remained at the GSD—François Vigier, William Doebele, José A. Ibáñez-Gómez, and the newly arrived Peter G. Rowe—the school sought not only to recapture lost ground but also to reconceptualize the field of city planning.[61] Drawing in part on the legacy of the original urban design program, the issues traditionally identified as those of the city and region were now consistently identified as urban. Programs for study would proliferate to address the complexity of urban planning and design.

McCue's efforts and those of his faculty colleagues in the early 1980s coincided with the disappearance of the systems approach of scientism and the entrenchment of a multifaceted postmodernism. Already in the late 1970s postmodernism was addressing the alienation

between modernism and public taste, dissatisfaction with the design principles of the Functional City, and the burgeoning desire for the familiar and traditional. Using styles by choice was once again legitimate. Yet postmodernism not only attacked the myths of functionalism and the neglect of history, it also ridiculed the notion of a moral imperative in architecture to change society and the association of architecture with fields outside design. Postmodernism saw architecture not as a social art but as an autonomous field with its own language and syntax. This architectural autonomy paralleled the political autonomy that social critics deemed narcissism. The reconsideration of architecture's own history became the antidote to a "failure" of modernism. These efforts moved theorists, critics, and even some practitioners from the general conditions of postmodernism towards more specific emphasis on poststructuralist phenomena and the rise of theory as the locus of the new modernist "project."

Rather than extend the open acceptance of various values and positions inherent in pluralism, postmodernism tended to polarize the GSD into two camps: those who embraced history as a means of restoring architecture to cultural connections severed by modernists, and those who found expression in the development of building materials and technology. In the late 1970s students were taught that the only valid hope for design comprised architectural metaphors, in the form of buildings that represent narrative stories; the urban pattern of premodern European cities, as found in figure-ground studies of city plans; and symbolic gestures of archetypal forms such as pyramids, spirals, and classical architectural elements. Those interested in rational structure and technological development were portrayed as reactionaries still clinging to an outmoded and destructive functionalism. Scientism was no longer the answer but the enemy. The social agenda of modernism was ridiculed, while the goal of architecture became art, not revolution. But these polarized positions were extremes—and they were transitory.

After the rehabilitation of history as a "source" of an autonomous design language, architectural history once again took a back seat at Harvard. This time the sacrifice of a comprehensive sequence of history courses had occurred to make room not for more practical studies or more studio time but for less practical studies in the domain of critical theory. This shift in emphasis was part of a reductive attack on the role of history that claimed that any comprehensive view of history was Eurocentric, chauvinistic, and/or imperialistic. The experience of postmodernism, however, testified to the fact that eliminating or reducing students' exposure to history produced generations of designers whose lack of understanding of the past interfered with their ability to provide the sense of community that they wanted to create. Many sterile buildings of the 1950s and 1960s are testaments to a pursuit of rhetoric at the expense of historical sensibility.

Coming Full Circle

In July of 1992, Peter G. Rowe, professor of architecture and urban design and chairman of the Department of Urban Planning and Design, succeeded McCue as dean of the GSD. He moved the GSD forward in urban design, establishing a new postprofessional degree—the master's in urban planning program—which enrolled its first students in the fall of 1994. The efforts to reconcile the loss of the city planning program continued with an emphasis on urban design, when Alex Krieger, a graduate of the GSD and faculty member since 1984, became director of the new planning program.[62]

Rowe's goal was to position the GSD as a participant at a national and international level of visibility while retaining an emphasis on urban design by involving the school in professional practice, the allied fields of construction, development, and material technology; by engaging urban and social issues through liaisons with municipal and national government and direct community service; and by expanding linkages overseas, particularly with Asia, Latin America, and the Middle East.[63] By 1998, the school offered a total of seven degrees, three in urban design, and a Ph.D. degree. Gund Hall was originally designed to hold 500 students: in 1986 approximately 430 students worked in its studios; by the fall of 2000, there were 577 degree candidates.[64]

By the time of Rowe's appointment as dean, postmodernism in architecture had

trickled from the hands of its elite to middle-level practitioners. It was spurned by many of its former promoters with almost as much vehement criticism as they had heaped on modernism. Deconstruction, promulgated as the new alternative, proved to be merely another transitory style and lacked broad ideological applicability. As the century moved towards its end, it seemed that the only available path for the future of architecture lay in a return to modernism. Postmodern architects who had lambasted such ideas now became practitioners interested in technology, abstraction, and geometric form. The neomodernism of the 1990s superseded postmodernism. Images of the heroic modernism of the 1920s and 1930s suddenly proliferated, as did the exploration of building structure. The most viable remnants of postmodernism appeared in the designs of New Urbanism, whose proponents claimed that most Americans love the model of civic life that recalls the beginning of the nineteenth century.[65]

Despite the exuberance for neomodernism, the appearance of some extraordinary buildings in that idiom, and enthusiasm for the New Urbanism, there still existed an underlying anxiety about the absence of authenticity—and confidence—in training designers to construct the urban realm with all its individual buildings. In 1993 the GSD announced that it was considering providing its students with "an integrated introduction to the major design fields, including architecture, landscape, and urban design and planning."[66] Neil L. Rudenstine, who followed Bok as Harvard president in 1991, confirmed that the GSD was reviewing its curriculum.[67] In addition, recalling an issue central to the Bauhaus—the relationship of design to industrial production—Jorge S. Silvetti, the Nelson Robinson Professor of Architecture, announced a new design arts initiative to include industrial, interior, and decorative design in the curriculum. Mirroring Gropius's interest in total design, though deliberately avoiding any association with him, the initiative seeks an as yet undefined vehicle for integrating these fields in both design education and the profession.[68]

The idea of collaboration even seems interesting to the AIA, which conducted a conference on the subject in 1999. The chairman of the conference described the results as "one of the very few and very first analytical reports on the mechanics of the collaborative process."[69] But describing the event as unique implies no recognition of the previous history of collaborative efforts. The one-day experiment seems all the more misinformed in light of the fact that teams of collaborators comprised only architects. Connection to other disciplines was seen as needed but was nevertheless absent. The results appeared to resemble a community-based *charette*.

The apparent revalidation of modernism and the announcement of the GSD's interest in collaboration signal a philosophy that has come full circle, back to the founding principles of the GSD. But such a return is bound to be problematic,

for conditions are different on all fronts from the days of modernism's emergence. Neomodernism has neither the social agenda of modernism nor its moral fervor. The political, social, and economic conditions and agendas that stimulated American and European efforts to create their modern movements in the 1930s are so different now that reviving their forms appears a hollow gesture, a return to a style in an endless revival of styles. The desire to appropriate the model of the Bauhaus or the halcyon images of modern architecture tells more about the void of social purpose and meaning that surrounds these fields of design today than it addresses any viable training for new generations of designers. A call for an integrated training in design appears futile without recognition of underlying motivations and fractious agendas, without a grasp of the role collaborative teamwork once played.

The founders of design education at Harvard dealt with modernity from a perspective that was grounded in the principle of integrated training and collaborative effort. How valid is this idea of collaboration now? At the beginning of the twentieth century when the concepts of collaborative training began to emerge, Americans asked for buildings and cities that would give the country an identity. Architecture had a clear role in leading a quest for identity based on optimism, pride, and a belief in the benefits of good government. The young country was admired for its efficiency, independence, and strength. That optimism dimmed as the Depression undermined national confidence. Emerging from World War II, America encountered a different relationship with Europe, whose ambitions for designing the physical world somehow had endured the war and appeared more vibrant than American efforts. Without realizing that their national identity was changing, Americans generally still felt proud of their nation, even if they flinched at the rampant witch hunts of the McCarthy era. People identified with business as American business, industry as American production. Corporations were owned and run by Americans. Those perceptions would change from the mid-1950s, as corporations expanded beyond national borders to become multinational conglomerates, as the economy provided unprecedented wealth and technology, and the ease of travel and communication affected every level of American experience.

The issue of American national identity is no longer the issue it was a century ago. Rather, the issue is identity itself. Who are we in a world where multinational corporations and global capital flows have the power to undermine sovereign countries? We are indistinguishable from the sea around us, a sea of our own making. Technology has dissolved the cultural, political, and social boundaries so that we are constantly in touch with others and are pressed to separate ourselves from others. The antipathy that played out in the middle of the twentieth century between Europe and America no longer exists, as the differences seem increas-

ingly minimal. Europe and the rest of the world are Americanized, and America is constantly transformed by foreigners who are no longer foreign but current or future citizens.

The GSD's recent engagement of international and national issues tends to confirm the trend towards globalization, but what are the deeper motivations beneath such efforts? Are these efforts elitist and patronizing or altruistic and humanistic? Are there underlying moral and social imperatives reminiscent of modernist efforts, or is the goal one of global networking to promote institutional power and individual prestige? These are challenging questions. Whatever the answers, the trend towards globalization undeniably coexists with architecture's current interest in style, fashion, stardom, and its own packaging as a commodity.

The Graduate School of Design at Harvard is a microcosm of sorts, its saga raised to question what role, if any, collaboration can play in our future. When popes and monarchs ruled, they could demand collaboration from their artists and artisans in the making of buildings and cities. But democratic rule allows everyone a voice, so collaboration moves slowly and with conflict, and the dilemma of control remains. Who now controls the design of cities? Architects, planners, urban designers, or developers in conjunction with local government? Will new forms of professional collaboration in the design arts shape the human environment? Is there any possibility that the model of a unified design education, con-

ceived as a response to modern conditions, will allow students of these fields of design—the practitioners, teachers, and scholars of the future—to learn from one another? Must the architects, landscape architects, and urban planners of the future only follow the demands of the controlling forces around them, or can they take leading roles in shaping economic and social policies? The history of modernism at Harvard shows that the effort to foster collaboration among disciplines, though often tense and imperfectly actualized, can inspire generations of students and their teachers to grapple with issues of design not only to define themselves but also to humanize the world around them.

ABBREVIATIONS

In captions and text, course numbers are abbreviated with the following prefixes:

Arch.   Architecture
CP   City Planning
LA   Landscape Architecture

UNDERGRADUATE (BACHELOR'S) ABBREVIATIONS
B. Arch. Bachelor of Architecture
BLA   Bachelor of Landscape Architecture
M.Arch. Master of Architecture
MLA   Master of Landscape Architecture
MCP   Master of City Planning

In Notes, the following abbreviations are used:

HL   Houghton Library, Harvard University. Contains the Walter Gropius Papers, ms.131/storage.
HUA   General History collection, Harvard University Archives
HUG   Alumni Biography and Personal/Professional Papers of Faculty, Harvard University Archives
LL   Frances Loeb Library, Harvard Graduate School of Design, including Special Collections and ephemera in Vertical Files Collection
UAI   The Corporation, Official University Records, Harvard University Archives. The papers of Harvard's presidents are sealed for fifty years; contents of some documents were conveyed to the author by the University archivist and so indicated.
UAII   Board of Overseers, Official University Records, Harvard University Archives
UAV   Schools, Departments, and other offices, Official University Records, Harvard University Archives

AR   *Architectural Record*
JAE   *Journal of Architectural Education*
JSAH   *Journal of the Society of Architectural Historians*
LA   *Landscape Architecture*
NYT   *New York Times*

Official Register Official Register, Harvard University Graduate School of Design, and its predecessor schools. These contain the statements of purpose, course and faculty listings, and are cited by academic year. Unless otherwise noted, they are in the holdings of the Frances Loeb Library.

ALL   A. Lawrence Lowell
BWP   Bremer W. Pond
CWE   Charles W. Eliot
FLO   Frederick Law Olmsted
GHE   George Harold Edgell
GHP   George Holmes Perkins
HLW   Herbert Langford Warren
HVH   Henry V. Hubbard
JBC   James Bryant Conant
JH   Joseph Hudnut
JSP   James Sturgis Pray
KJC   Kenneth John Conant, interview with author, 3 March 1979
WC   Walter Creese, interviews with author, personal communication
WG   Walter Gropius

NOTES

Preface

1. The best overview on the education of architects up to the time of its publication is *The Architect, Chapters in the History of the Profession*, Spiro Kostof, ed. (New York: Oxford University Press, 1977). The essays, written by several scholars, include thorough bibliographies. For an essential overview of trends in architectural practice and the building industry, see Robert Gutman, *Architectural Practice: A Critical View* (Princeton: Princeton Architectural Press, 1988).

2. Reginald Isaacs, *Gropius, An Illustrated Biography of the Creator of the Bauhaus* (Boston: Bulfinch Press, 1991). The book is an abridgment of *Walter Gropius: Die Mensch und sein Werk*, 2 vols. (Berlin: Gebr. Mann Verlag GmbH & Co., 1983–84). See also Winfried Nerdinger, *Walter Gropius* (Berlin: Bauhaus-Archiv; Cambridge, Mass.: Busch-Reisinger Museum, Harvard University; Berlin: Gebr. Mann Verlag, 1986). This exhibition catalogue documents the drawings, prints, and photographs relevant for Gropius's architecture.

3. Paul L. Bentel, "Modernism and Professionalism in American Architecture,1919–1933", 2 vols. (Ph.D. dissertation, MIT, 1993).

4. Eric Mumford, *The CIAM Discourse on Urbanism, 1928–1960* (Cambridge, Mass.: MIT Press, 2000).

5. Recent publications by or about former faculty and graduates include monographs on Marcel Breuer, Garrett Eckbo, Ulrich Franzen, John M. Johansen, Philip Johnson, Fumihiko Maki, Ian McHarg, I. M. Pei, Paul Rudolph, Hideo Sasaki, Harry Seidler, José Luis Sert, John O. Simonds, Hugh Stubbins, and Anne Tyng.

6. Jill Pearlman's "Joseph Hudnut's Other Modernism at the 'Harvard Bauhaus,'" *JSAH* 56:4 (Dec. 1997): 452–477, confirms the proposition here of Hudnut's key role in the formation of a modernist ideology and the conflict that ensued with Gropius. It also provides invaluable insight into the intellectual basis of Hudnut's modernism. For a broad overview of the 1950s, see *Anxious Modernisms: Experimental Postwar Architectural Culture*, Sarah Williams Goldhagen and Rejean Légault, eds. (Cambridge, Mass.: MIT Press, 2000).

7. Melanie L. Simo, *The Coalescing of Different Forces and Ideas: A History of Landscape Architecture at Harvard, 1900–1999* (Cambridge, Mass.: Harvard Graduate School of Design, 2000).

Chapter One

1. For a concise prologue to the beginnings of the architecture of American modernism in the early decades of the twentieth century, see Marc Dessauce, "Contro lo Stile Internazionale: 'Shelter' e la stampa architettonica americana," *Casabella* 604 (1993): 46–53.

2. Ada Louise Huxtable, "Revamping of Architectural Education Being Pressed in Nation," NYT, 20 February 1966.

3. For an admittedly polemical treatment of Gropius at Harvard, see Klaus Herdeg, *The Decorated Diagram: Harvard Architecture and the Failure of the Bauhaus Legacy* (Cambridge, Mass.: MIT Press, 1983); reviewed by Richard Wesley, *JSAH*, 45:3 (September 1986), 310–311. For the widely read, popular treatment of the Gropius era at Harvard, see Tom Wolfe, *From Bauhaus to Our House: Why Architects Can't Get Out of the Box* (New York: Farrar, Straus, Giroux, 1981). It first appeared in two parts in *Harper's* (June and July 1981). For an irate reaction to Wolfe's book from a former Gropius student, see Chester Nagel, "Gropius Colleague Blasts Recent Best-seller on Modern Architecture," *The Daily Journal* (Denver), 27 January 1982. 85: 173; Ibid., "Book on Gropius a Monstrous Falsehood . . . ," *The Daily Journal* (Denver), 29 January 1982. 85: 175; Ibid., "On Gropius: 'Truth of the Informed Prevails,'" *The Daily Journal* (Denver), 4 February 1982. 85: 179; and, for comments on Nagels's articles, Max Price, "Architects Hammer Away at Tom Wolfe's 'Bauhaus,'" *Denver Post* (Housing Section), 7 February 1928, p. 2G.

4. See the author's "Towards a History of Teaching Architectural History: Herbert Langford Warren," *JAE* 33 (1983): 2–7; and "Tempering the École: Nathan Ricker at the University of Illinois, Langford Warren at Harvard, and their Followers," in Gwendolyn Wright, ed., *The History of History in American Schools of Architecture, 1865–1975* (Princeton: Princeton Architectural Press, 1990), 73–88.

5. For the first treatment of Gropius's coming to Harvard, see the author's "The Arrival of Walter Gropius in America: Transformations of a Radical Architect," *Walter Gropius e l'habitat del novecento*. Atti del Convegno Internazionale Roma, Goethe Institute 29–30 November 1983 (Rome: Effelle Edetrice, 1987), 48–66.

6. *The Harvard Guide* (Cambridge, Mass.: Harvard University Office of News and Public Affairs, 1998), 72. Sean Conlon [GSD Registrar's Office] to author, personal communication 4 December 2000.

Chapter Two

1. See William R. Ware, "On the Condition of Architecture and Architectural Education in the United States," Sessional Papers of the Royal Institute of British Architects (London, 1867), 85–86 in Caroline Shillaber, Massachusetts Institute of Technology School of Architecture and Planning, 1861–1961: A Hundred Year Chronicle (Cambridge, Mass.: MIT Press, 1963), 127, n. 4. For an introduction to Ware, see J. A. Chewning, "W. R. Ware at M.I.T. and Columbia," JAE 23:2 (November 1979): 25–28.

2. For the early architectural profession in America, see Mary N. Woods, *From Craft to Profession, The Practice of Architecture in Nineteenth-Century America* (Berkeley: University of California Press, 1999). For the history of Columbia University School of Architecture, see Richard Oliver, ed., *The Making of an Architect 1881–1981* (New York: Columbia University Press, 1981). For the evolution of the academy, see Nikolaus Pevsner, *Academies of Art Past and Present* (London: Cambridge University Press, 1940). Pevsner provides a preliminary account of the history of the architectural profession in *Kritische Berichte zür Kunstgeschichte*, 1930–1931, 97–122. For a summary of architectural education in America, see Turpin Bannis-

ter, *The Architect at Mid-Century* (New York: Reinhold, 1954), and Arthur C. Weatherhead, *The History of Collegiate Education in Architecture in the United States* (Ph.D. dissertation, Columbia University; Los Angeles: privately published, 1941).

3. Quoted in JH, "Education and Architecture," *AR* 92:4 (October 1942): 36. Bulfinch (1763–1844) designed, in addition to his serenely classical buildings in and around Boston, Harvard's Stoughton Hall in 1804, and University Hall, begun in 1813, which established the scale and coherence of the old Harvard Yard.

4. Weatherhead, *Collegiate Education*, 55–58. Dates on the founding of schools vary. The curriculum in architecture for the University of Illinois began in 1867; the school was operational by 1870 (WC). Matriculating from Illinois in March 1873, N. Clifford Rickert was the first graduate in the United States. MIT and Cornell graduated their first students in June 1873; Illinois graduated the first woman, Mary Page, in 1878 (WC). Harvard's own tabular list of early schools and their enrollments in 1899 included Tulane in New Orleans (1894) and McGill University in Montreal (1896). See UAI.5.150, Box 110, folder 142. Ts. with amendments.

5. See, for example, Ralph A. Cram, "A Case Against the École des Beaux Arts," *American Architect* 54 (26 December 1896): 107–108.

6. See Roula Geraniotis, "The University of Illinois and German Architectural Education," *JAE* 38:4 (Summer 1985): 15–21. For methods of teaching at the École, see Richard Chafee, "The Teaching of Architecture at the École des Beaux-Arts," in Arthur Drexler, ed., *The Architecture of the École des Beaux Arts* (New York: Museum of Modern Art, 1977), 61–109.

7. See Anthony Alofsin, "Herbert Langford Warren," American National Biography (Cary, N.C.: Oxford University Press and the American Council of Learned Societies, 1999); Id., "Tempering the École"; Id. "Towards a History of Teaching Architectural History."

8. Charles Allerton Coolidge, "Herbert Langford Warren (1857–1917)," *Proceedings of the American Academy of Arts and Sciences*, LXVII (1933): 691.

9. For the views of the architectural profession on education in this period, see "Report on Committee on Education, A.I.A.," *American Architect* 93 (11 March 1908): 86–89.

10. HLW, "Architectural Education at Harvard University," *Harvard Engineering Journal* 1:2 (1902): 78.

11. *Official Register of the Department of Architecture*, Cambridge, Mass.: Harvard University, 1902.

12. Morris H. Morgan, transl., *Vitruvius, the Ten Books of Architecture*, preface by Albert A. Howard (Cambridge, Mass.: Harvard University Press, 1914; reprint ed. New York: Dover, 1960).

13. HLW, *The Foundations of Classic Architecture*, introduction by Fiske Kimball (New York: Macmillan Press, 1919). For a contemporary appraisal of Warren, see Benjamin Baker, "Harvard Invitation Backed by the French Government," [1911]. HUG 300. Uncredited news clipping.

14. George H. Chase, "The Fine Arts, 1874–1929," in Samuel E. Morison, ed. *The Development of Harvard University Since the Inauguration of President Eliot 1869–1929* (Cambridge, Mass.: Harvard University Press, 1930), 130–131. For Norton's approach to studying art, see James Turner, *The Liberal Education of Charles Eliot Norton* (Baltimore: Johns Hopkins University Press, 1999).

15. *Official Register*, 1895, 7. For a description of the first year's program, see Harvard University, Lawrence Scientific School, Description of the Four Years Course in Architecture (Cambridge, Mass.: Harvard University, 1895). For a brief early account of the Harvard programs in architecture, landscape architecture, and city planning, see George H. Edgell, "The Schools of Architecture and Landscape Architecture, 1894–1929," in Morison, *Harvard University*, 443–450.

16. HLW to CWE, 27 January 1894. UAI.5. 150, Box 110, folder 142. For Americans trained at the École who headed schools, see Weatherhead, *Collegiate Education*, passim, 33–57.

17. For the Lawrence Scientific School, see Stephen Paschall Sharples, "The Lawrence Scientific School," *Proceedings of the Cambridge Historical Society* IV (1909), and Arthur Zaidenberg, "From Reforms to Professionalization: The Transition of Attitudes Toward Scientific Education in Harvard" (Ph.D. dissertation, University of California at Los Angeles, 1974). The author thanks J. A. Chewning for pointing out these publications.

18. Charles H. Moore to CWE, 27 January 1897. Eliot Papers. UAI.5.150, Box 115, folder 223.

19. For the Fogg Museum's early history, see Chase, "Fine Arts," 132, 133. Warren had also proposed that an architectural library be installed with books transferred from Gore Hall, the main University library (HLW to CWE, 2 April 1894, UAI.5.150, Box 110, folder 142). He also suggested that the upper portions of Dane Hall be remodeled for students of the Department of Architecture (HLW to CWE, 8 May 1897, UAI.5.150, Box 110, folder 142).

20. Bunting/Floyd, *Harvard Architecture*, 116.

21. For Robert S. Peabody (1845–1917) and his firm's work at Harvard, see Bunting/Floyd, *Harvard Architecture*, 126, 301. For Charles Eliot (1859–1897), see Charles William Eliot, *Charles Eliot, Landscape Architect* (Cambridge, Mass.: Harvard University Press, 1902, 1924; reprinted with introduction by Keith N. Morgan, Amherst: University of Massachusetts Press, 1999); and Norman T. Newton, *Design on the Land* (Cambridge, Mass., and London: Belknap Press of Harvard University, 1971), 318–336.

22. Eliot, Charles Eliot, 630.

23. Norman Newton, interview with the author, 19 November 1985.

24. FLO, Jr., to President Eliot, 16 August 1898, Eliot Papers, UAI.5.150, Box 109, folder 129. For Olmsted, see also Laura Wood Roper, FLO: *A Biography of Frederick Law Olmsted* (Baltimore: Johns Hopkins University Press, 1973). For Frederick Law Olmsted, Jr. (1870–1957), see Newton, *Design on the Land*, 389, 390.

25. See FLO, Jr., to President Eliot, 6 September 1898. Eliot Papers. UAI.5.150, Box 109, folder 129. The long ms. letter shows the great consideration and detail that Olmsted put into developing the program.

26. See Lawrence Scientific School, *Announcement of a Four Years' Progamme of Courses in Landscape Architecture* (Cambridge, Mass: Harvard University, March 1900).

27. The standards must have been high: eight students dropped out of Landscape Architecture I because of poor work or low marks. FLO, Jr., to CWE, 21 August 1903. Eliot Papers. UAI.5.150, Box 109, folder 129.

28. Arthur A. Shurcliff (1870–1957) started an independent practice in 1905 and became well known as the landscape designer of the gardens at Colonial Williamsburg. His son, Sidney N. Shurcliff (1906–1981) studied at Harvard College and in the School of Landscape Architecture, and joined his father's firm in the 1930s, which became Shurcliff, Merrill & Footit. LL. Special Collections Index.

29. *Official Register, 1902*, 5.

30. For Harvard's use of Gottfried Semper's analysis of classical proportions and Harvard's general approach to teaching architectural history, see Herbert Langford Warren, "The Study of Architectural History," *Architectural Quarterly of Harvard University* 1:2 (1912): 46.

31. For Warren's assessment of Roman architecture, see John Taylor Boyd, Jr., "Notes and Comments: Prof. H. Langford Warren," *AR* 42 (December 1917): 590. For the contents of Warren's teaching of medieval architecture, see KJC, AB 1915, "Notes Taken in FA4a, 1914–15," ms. HUC 8914.328.4.

32. For more on Charles Herbert Moore (1840–1930), see Frank Jewett Mather, Jr., *Charles Herbert Moore, Landscape Painter* (Princeton: Princeton University Press, 1957). Moore was adamantly pro-Gothic and anti-Renaissance because Renaissance styles lacked constructional logic. See his *The Development and Character of Gothic Architecture* (New York: MacMillan, 1890, 1899); and Ibid., *The Character of Renaissance Architecture* (New York and London: MacMillan, 1905).

33. Weatherhead, *Collegiate Education*, 47.

34. Ibid., 60, states that the four architects were appointed annually with each giving a major problem.

35. *Official Register 1902*, 5. The tone and style of the quotation is that of Langford Warren, who probably wrote most of the text for the first register of the offerings on architecture.

36. *Programme of Courses in Landscape Architecture*, 1900, 8, 9.

37. For Shaler, see Simo, *Landscape Architecture at Harvard*, 1.

38. Robinson made his initial gift on 26 June 1899; it was subsequently amended three times through March 1902 on 2 February 1901, 13 January 1902, and 18 March 1902. Kenneth John Conant stated that Robinson was a "traction magnate from Buffalo," his money coming from railroads. The source of the Robinson fortune, however, remains obscure, and judging from the absence of records, information, or even an obituary, it appears that Nelson Robinson chose the role of an extremely discreet and private person: "It is characteristic of Mr. Robinson that only after long persuasion was he even willing to allow the name of Robinson to be given to the building." The Robinsons' grief eased slowly; until at least four years after their son's death, the Robinsons continued to write to President Eliot on stationery edged with a black border of mourning. President Lowell's appraisal of the Robinson gift noted: "His father determined to create a memorial to him. It took the form of one of the most gracious, as well as generous, gifts which the University has ever received. . . ." ALL, Alumni in Architecture, 1st Report (1932), 4. Documents and letters between the Robinsons and President Eliot are in Harvard University Archives, UAI.5.150, Box 106, 1896–1903, folder 71.

39. *Programme of Courses in Landscape Architecture*, 23.

40. Charles Francis Adams II to CWE, 14 July 1899. Eliot Papers. UAI.5.140, Box 200. Nelson Robinson to CWE, 25 July 1899. Eliot Papers. UAI.5.140, Box 106, folder 71.

41. HLW to CWE, 5 July 1899. Eliot Papers. UAI.5.140, Box 110, folder 142.

42. For Warren's revisions of the building program, see HLW to CWE, 4 August 1899, Eliot Papers. UAI.5.140, Box 110, folder 142, his initial acceptance of McKim's sketches, Ibid., 21 October 1899.

43. HLW to CWE, 4 August 1899, Eliot Papers. UAI.5.140, Box 110, folder 142; Ibid., 21 October 1899; and Charles F. McKim to CWE, 31 October 1899, Eliot Papers. UAI.5.140.

44. Charles Eliot Norton, "A Criticism of Harvard Architecture Made to the Board of Overseers," [offprint], [March 1904], 359–362.

45. For James Sturgis Pray (1871–1929), see his *curriculum vitae* in [Harvard University Faculty of Architecture] Cambridge: the School, 1920, unpaginated biographical notes on KJC, et al., LL. See also the obituary, "James Sturgis Pray, Landscape Architect, February 26, 1871–February 22, 1929," *American Landscape Architect* 1:1 (July 1929): 16–17.

46. KJC, interview. Charles Wilson Killam (1871–1961) published only a portion of his textbook: *Architectural Construction, Part One*, Cambridge, Mass.: privately printed, 1947, revised 1950. See Reginald Isaacs et al, "Charles Wilson Killam—A Minute on His Life and Services" (1961), unpublished ts., 8. LL. See also George H. Edgell, "The Schools of Architecture and Landscape Architecture, 1894–1929" in Morison, *Harvard*, 445.

47. See Denman Waldo Ross, *Theory of Pure Design* (Boston: Houghton Mifflin, 1907); and J. M. Carpenter, *Color in Art: A Tribute to Arthur Pope* (Cambridge, Mass.: Fogg Art Museum, Harvard University, 1974), *passim*.

48. John Taylor Boyd, Jr., "Professor H. Langford Warren," *AR* 42:6 (December 1917): 590.

49. *Catalogue, Special Exhibition, Boston Architectural Club* (Boston, Mass.: The Club, 1897), 5–17 April 1897, Allston Hall, Grundmann Studio Building.

50. Warren, "Architectural Education." See also Herbert Langford Warren, "The Influence of France Upon American Architecture," paper read at the 33rd annual convention, AIA, Pittsburgh, Pa., 14 November 1899; reprinted in *American Architect* 66 (1899): 67–78.

51. For the incorporation of modern devices, technology, and even office organization, see Robert Bruegmann's *The Architects and the City: Holabird and Roche of Chicago, 1880–1918* (Chicago: University of Chicago Press, 1997).

52. For Wallace Sabine, see Hughes in Morison, *Harvard*, 432.

53. For "American Landscape and Architectural Design, 1850–1920," a collection from Harvard's Loeb Library of approximately 2,800 lantern slides, views of sites, estates, gardens, plans, maps, models, including work of landscape architects, including the Olmsted firm and Harvard instructors James Sturgis Pray and Bremer W. Pond, see the Web site http://memory.loc.gov/ammem/award97/mhsdhtml/aladhome.html.

54. See Hector James Hughes, "The Harvard Engineering School and Its Predecessors," in Morison, *Harvard*, 413–442. The complex changes at Harvard, spawned by a bequest of $1,000,000 from Gordon McKay to promote instruction in applied sciences included efforts to merge technical instruction with MIT. Earlier discussion of collaboration between Harvard's architecture program and MIT led nowhere. Langford Warren objected to earlier plans for a merger of the architecture schools of Harvard and MIT when they were proposed by Edmund Wheelwright in 1902 (HLW to CWE, 13 March 1902, UAI.5.150, Box 110, folder 142).

55. JSP to CE, 28 January 1909. UAI.5.150, Box 239, 1903–1909, folder, "James Sturgis Pray."

56. [JSP] to [CWE], 19 March 1908. UAI.5.150, Box 239, 1903–1909, folder, "James Sturgis Pray."

57. Quoted in John T. Bethell, *Harvard Observed, An Illustrated History of the University in the Twentieth Century* (Cambridge, Mass.: Harvard University Press, 1998), 45.

58. ALL to JSP, 20 June 1914, UAI.5.160, 1914–1917, folder 46, "Architecture, Department of, General Correspondence."

59. ALL to HLW, 8 July 1914, UAV322.7, Box 1.

60. JSP to ALL, 12 June 1916, UAI.5.160, 1914–1917, folder 46.

61. JSP to CE, 3 April 1908. UAI.5.150, Box 239, 1903–1909, folder, "James Sturgis Pray" FLO, Jr., to ALL, 20 October 1915, UAI.5.160, folder 46, "Architecture, Department of, General Correspondence."

62. Morison, *American People*, 811–817, 814 quoted.

63. By the late 1930s the profession recognized these sources as seen in the comments of the Visiting Committee in "Report of the Committee to Visit the School of City Planning," Report No. 51 in Report of the Committee to Visit Harvard College 1930–36, 259. UAII.10.7.3.

64. Newton, *Design on the Land*, 413–426. See also American Society of Landscape Architects Transactions, 1909–1921, 97.

65. John Nolen (1869–1937) studied from 1903 to 1904 at the Lawrence Scientific School, from 1903 to 1905 at the Bussey Institute, and from 1904 to 1905 in the Graduate School of Applied Science from which he received the degree of A.M. in Landscape Architecture in 1905. For Nolen, see Arthur Glass, "John Nolen and the Planning of New Towns: Three Case Studies" (Master's thesis, Cornell University, 1984); John L. Hancock, "John Nolen and the American City Planning Movement: A History of Culture, Change, and Community Response, 1900–1940" (Ph.D. dissertation, University of Pennsylvania, 1964); and Id., *John Nolen, Landscape Architect, Town, City, and Regional Planner: a Bibliographical Record of Achievement* (Ithaca, N.Y.: Program in Urban and Regional Studies, Cornell University, 1976).

66. For Bremer Whidden Pond (1884–1959), see E[duard] C[lark] W[hiting], "Necrology, Bremer Whidden Pond, June 23, 1884–September 2, 1959, A Biographical Minute," LA 50:1 (Autumn 1959): 47–48.

67. See S. D. Adshead, "The School of Civic Design at the Liverpool University," LA 1:3 (April 1911): 105–109. Adshead was the first director of the Liverpool program, the funds for which had come from wealthy industrialist W. H. Lever of Messrs. Lever Brothers, Port Sunlight (WC). See also The University of Liverpool, Faculty of Arts, School of Architecture. Department of Civic Design, Prospectus for the Session 1909–1910 (Liverpool: Liverpool University Press, 1909). Copies signed by Pray and Pond are in the Loeb Library.

68. "James Sturgis Pray, Landscape Architect, February 26, 1871–February 22, 1929," *American Landscape Architect* 1:1 (July 1929): 17. Landscape Architecture 10 was the basic course; Landscape Architecture 5 dealt with construction, Landscape Architecture 3 with design. For courses and their descriptions, see School of Landscape Architecture, Official Register (1909), 16.

69. Christiane Crasemann Collins kindly informed the author (14 April 1986) about material on Sitte, Pray, and the International City Planning Exhibition in Boston in the fall of 1910. Little is currently known of this exhibit, which was sponsored by a group called "Boston 1915." The old Museum of Fine Arts, site of the exhibition, was empty pending the move to the new building on the Fenway. Much later in 1917 Pray may also have met Camillo Sitte's son at the dedication of the Plymouth Rock monument. For Sitte's classic work, see *Der Städtebau nach seinen kunstlerischen Grundsatzen* (City planning according to artistic principles), Christiane Crasemann Collins and George R. Collins, transl. (New York: Random House, 1965).

70. Irwin J. McCrary's 1913 thesis in Landscape Architecture, "A Study in City Planning," was presented to the National Conference on City Planning. For the original drawing, see LL.

71. See Pray's curriculum vitae in [Harvard University Faculty of Architecture] Cambridge: the School, 1920, unpaginated biographical notes on KJC, et al., LL.

72. James Sturgis Pray and Theodora Kimball, *City Planning, a Comprehensive Analysis of the Subject Arranged for the Classification of Books, Plans, Photographs, Notes and Other Collected Materials, with Alphabetical Subject Index* (Cambridge: Harvard University Press, 1913).

73. Petition with initials "HLW" [1904]. ms. five leaves. UAI.5.150, Box 255, folder "Warren, Herbert Langford."

74. HLW to CWE, 12 February 1909, UAI.5.150, Box 255, folder "Warren, Herbert Langford." Warren's representation of the "undiluted French influence" was based in reality: the influx of French architects started with Despradelle at MIT in 1893 (following the 1892 death of Eugène Letang). Maurice Prevot was at Cornell University from 1904 to 1906 and was followed by Jean Hébrard from 1906 to 1911; Prevot went to Columbia University in 1907 and returned to France in 1914. Paul Cret taught at the University of Pennsylvania from 1903 to 1914 and returned in 1919; he taught there until 1937. While the French tradition waned in the 1920s, it persisted at Princeton where Jean Labatut, a former member of the Laloux atelier, was chief design critic in the School of Architecture from 1928 to 1967. Weatherhead, *Collegiate Education*, 90, 92, 100–101; see also Christine Yelavich, "Cret, Paul," *Macmillan Encyclopedia of Architects*, vol. 2 (New York: Free Press, 1982), 591.

75. KJC. On the appointment of John Sanford Humphreys (1875–1958), see also Carrère to [HLW], 15 December 1914. UAV 322.7, Box 2; George H. Edgell, *Alumni in Architecture of Harvard University. First Report*, 1932, Cambridge, Mass.: [Harvard University], 1932, 16; subsequently cited as Edgell, *Alumni*. See also UAV322.7, IIIa Box 2; Killam to Lowell, 24 March 1919, UAV322.7, Box 1.

76. ALL to E. J. A. Duquesne, 14 June 1910, Lowell Papers, 1909–1914, folder 66. Author translation. Duquesne had first become an official teacher upon his appointment to the jury in architecture at the École in 1906. In addition to his practice, he acted as auditor to the General Council for Public Buildings and National Palaces from 1902 to 1905. In 1908 he became architect for the machinery hall of the Franco-British Exposition in London, and was appointed architect to the French government for repair and restoration of the palace and gardens of Versailles and the Trianon. For biographical information, see "Duquesne, E. J. A." HUG 300, particularly "Eugene Duquesne Coming to Harvard," *Harvard Alumni Bulletin* (1911). See also Benjamin Baker, "Harvard Invitation Backed by the French Government," [1911]; ALL to E. J. A. Duquesne, 31 January 1910. UAI.5.160, 1909–1914, folder 66; HLW to ALL, 1 February 1910, Lowell Papers, 1909–1914, folder 66.

77. Jules Huret, *L'Amerique Moderne* (Paris: P. Lafitte & Co., 1911), v. 1, pl. 93. "Greek, Latin, and higher mathematics are taught at the same time as drawing and the fine arts." Author translation. Reference courtesy of Patricia May Sekler.

78. M. Baion to ALL, 8 March 1911, Lowell Papers, 1909–1914, folder 66, author translation. Baion, United States ambassador to France, enclosed a document from the French government dated 25 January 1911 and the decree, dated 15 February 1911. See Joseph Bedier to [HLW?], 17 November 1910, Lowell Papers, 1909–1914, folder 66; HLW to ALL, 23 August 1910, Lowell Papers, 1909–1914, folder 66.

79. ALL to Charles F. Doyle, 17 May 1911, Lowell Papers, 1909–1914, folder 66. A similar pageant was held when the new MIT wings were dedicated with Ralph Adams Cram presiding as Merlin (WC).

80. Benjamin Baker, "Harvard Invitation Backed by the French Government," [1911]. HUG 300, unidentified news clipping. See also E. J. A. Duquesne, "The Teaching of Architecture," *Architectural Quarterly of Harvard University* 1:3 (Sept. 1912): 73–83.

81. Lowell Papers, 1911–1914, Harvard University Archives. For the initiation of his study for Harvard Square, see E. J. A. Duquesne to ALL, 24 May 1912, Lowell Papers, 1909–1914, folder 66. For the pamphlet, see "The Future Development of Harvard Square and Its Neighborhood" in the Lowell Papers, 1911–1914. Only in 1922 did President Lowell form a committee to supervise the planning of the campus and create a working plan for Harvard's development for the next fifty to one hundred years (see Bunting/Floyd, *Harvard Architecture*, 151, 167, and 305, n. 4).

82. E. J. A. Duquesne to HLW, 5 August 1914; HLW to ALL, 6 August 1914, and ALL to HLW, 10 August 1914, Lowell Papers, 1909–1914, folder 66; and newspaper clippings for brief notices of Duquesne's resignation in biography file, "Duquesne, E. J. A.," HUG 300.

83. HLW to ALL, 10 February 1915, UAI.5.160, 1914–1917, folder 46.

84. John Galen Howard to HLW, 23 June 1914, UAV322.6, Subseries IIIa, Correspondence 1896–1962, Box 1. . UAI.5.160, 1914–1917, folder 46, "Architecture, Department of, General Correspondence."

85. Arthur Brown, Jr., to HLW, 28 July 1914,

UAV322.7 Subseries III, Correspondence 1896–1962, Box 1. "Extract," 30 September 1914, UAI.5.160, 1914–1917, folder 46, "Architecture, Department of, General Correspondence."

86. Arthur Brown, Jr., to HLW, UAV322.7, Subseries III, Correspondence 1896–1962, Box 1.

87. HLW to Arthur Brown, Jr., 14 December 1914, UAV322.7, Subseries III, Correspondence 1896–1962, Box 1. For the details of the maneuvering Harvard attempted in looking for a design professor, see the following series of correspondence: Chester Holmes Aldrich to Thomas W. Lamont, 7 December 1914; Thomas Hastings to Thomas W. Lamont, 15 December 1914; ALL to Thomas W. Lamont, 21 December 1914; Arthur Brown, Jr., to ALL, 5 January 1915; all UAI.5.160, 1914–1917, folder 46, "Architecture, Department of, General Correspondence" (Lamont was a Harvard Overseer from 1912–1925). See also Arthur Brown, Jr., to HLW, 31 July 1915, UAV322.7, Subseries III, Correspondence 1896–1962, Box 1.

88. "Report of the Committee to Visit the School of Architecture," No. 78 (1916). UAI.5.160, 1914–1917, folder 46, offprint, 315–318. The report was prepared in the spring of 1915, revised in March 1916, and submitted 5 May 1916 by Harry J. Carlson, Secretary of the Committee. Other members at the time were R. Clipston Sturgis (Harvard 1881), Charles K. Cummins, J. Harleston Parker, Henry Forbes Bigelow, and Robert P. Bellows.

89. Ibid., 316.

90. The Visiting Committee had raised two-thirds of Walker's salary for the three-year experiment. Walker, AB 1890, had begun to teach at the Fogg Museum in 1913 when supporters funded him to teach the first course on "Modern Art and Its Relation to the Art of Earlier Times." Ibid.

91. "Visiting Committee Report, 1916," 317. The committee also noted that students, who had received medals from the AIA (established in 1914 and first given at Harvard in 1915), showed all four years of their work for comparison at the convention of the AIA. The work from the

Carnegie Institute was specially noted for showing the "influence and value of a school where students in all branches of the Fine Arts work side by side" (Ibid., 318).

92. Boyd, "Warren," 588.

93. Edgell, "The Schools," 446.

Chapter 3

1. Bentel, "Modernism and Professionalism in American Architecture, 1919–1933."

2. George Harold Edgell and S. Fiske Kimball, *A History of Architecture* (New York: Harper and Brothers, 1918). See also Christy Anderson, "Writing the Architectural Survey," *JSAH* 58:3 (Sept. 1999): 350.

3. Chase, "The Fine Arts," 140.

4. *Twenty-Fifth Anniversary Report, Class of 1909* (Cambridge, Mass.: Harvard College, 1934), 185.

5. Alfred Panepinto to the author, 23 May 1986; John Coolidge interview with the author, 1986.

6. For a sketch of Haffner and illustrations of his student work, see William G. Perry, "French Comrades in America, II, Jean Jacques Haffner," *Pencil Points* 8, no. 2 (February 1927): 67–84; and Edgell, *Alumni*, 13–14. Haffner was as noted for his watercolors as for his architecture. He maintained a practice in France, and in America he designed an extension of the Ritz Hotel in Boston (Jean Paul Carlhian interview with the author, 5 September 1986), and a submission with Perry, Shaw, and Hepburn (predecessors of the Boston firm of Perry Dean Stahl & Rogers) for the Harvard Business School Competition.

7. *Official Register, 1926–27*, 32. By 1928, the course, which met on Saturday mornings in the lecture room, had become very informal and included discussions about the profession. Edward Aisner, interview with the author, 27 May 1986.

8. Panepinto to the author, 23 May 1986; Aisner interview.

9. Kenneth John Conant (1894–1984) received an AB from Harvard College, 1915, magna cum laude, entered the School of Architecture for one year from 1915 to 1916, and became a Rogers Fellow at the American Academy in Rome 1916–1917. He resumed his studies at Harvard in 1917, but enlisted in November 1917, went overseas in January 1918, served under General Douglas McArthur, and was wounded in action and returned home in January 1919. Conant received the M.Arch. degree in 1919.

After C. Howard Walker's resignation in 1922, Conant began teaching all three courses in the history sequence, assisting Chase and Edgell. Walter Creese retrospectively described Chase, Edgell, and Walker as "an unopposable triad—all as different as could be, but well-defined personalities. Chase was very neat and orderly, Edgell thorough, and Conant determined that you would see all. [They] were very good looking and natty dressers, with Conant giving the least variety, as he only wore dark blue ties and appeared to have only a Navy blue and a pearl grey suit." (WC) Conant also taught elementary architectural design under John Humphreys.

Conant became best known as an historian after receiving a Harvard Ph.D. in 1925; his best-known publications are *Carolingian and Romanesque Architecture 800–1200*, The Pelican History of Art, edited by Sir Nicholas Pevsner, vol. 213, which was first published in 1959 with a sixth edition appearing in 1979, and his pioneering work at Cluny, resulting in *Cluny—Les Eglises et la Maison du Chef d'Ordre* (1968). See John Coolidge, "Kenneth Conant and the Founding of the American Society of Architectural Historians," *JSAH* 43:3 (October 1984): 193–194.

10. Aisner interview.

11. Whitehead, *Collegiate Education*, 172–174.

12. Ibid., 174.

13. Perry, "French Comrades," 75.

14. Ibid., 76.

15. *Official Register, 1922–23.*

16. Aisner interview; Panepinto to the author, 23 May 1986.

17. Henry N. Cobb, interview with the author, 17 April 1986.

18. "A School of Americanization: All-Day Sketch," program notes for Architecture 4c, Thursday, October 2, 1930. LL.

19. Edgell, "Schools," 447.

20. Bernard Cohen, "Harvard and MIT: Where It All Began," *Planning* 47:3 (March 1981): 23.

21. Theodora Kimball, *Classified Selected List of References on City Planning* (Boston: National Conference of City Planning, 1915). It revised and expanded *City Planning: a Comprehensive Analysis* from 1913.

22. See *Official Register Landscape Architecture 1917–1918.*

23. Donald A. Krueckeberg, "The Story of the Planner's Journal, 1915–1980," *Journal of the American Planning Association* 46 (1980): 6.

24. For background developments in city planning, see "Report of the Committee to Visit the School of City Planning," Report No. 51 in *Report of the Committee to Visit Harvard College 1930–36*, 259 (UAII.10.7.3).

25. Newton, *Design on the Land*, 424. See also Cohen, "Harvard and MIT," 23; and, Krueckeberg, "Planner's Journal," 6.

26. Krueckeberg, "Planner's Journal," 5. For a synopsis of planning efforts and a general handbook for city planning of the period, see John Nolen, ed., *City Planning, A Series of Papers Presenting the Essential Elements of a City Plan*, National Municipal League Series (New York and London: D. Appleton and Company, 1916).

27. C. H. Williams, *The Housing Problem in America*, National Housing Conference 1916, 206.

28. Arthur Coleman Comey (1886–1954) attended Harvard College 1903–1907 and studied at the Bussey Institution 1905–1907. Upon graduation he initially began working as a landscape architect, first for the Lowell Park Commission, Dixon, Illinois, and then as superintendent of parks in Utica, New York. By 1911 he opened an independent practice as a consultant on city planning with offices in the Abbot Building in Harvard Square. From 1913 Comey operated as a member of the Massachusetts Homestead Commission; he was secretary of the Cambridge Housing Association, of which Harvard Professor of Social Ethics James Ford was president, and of which two members of the architecture faculty were members: Killam and Humphreys. For Comey, see Alofsin, "Comey, Arthur Coleman," *Macmillan Encyclopedia*, vol. 1, 443.

29. See Edward K. Span, *Designing Modern America: the Regional Planning Association of America and Its Members*, Urban Life and Urban Landscape Series (Columbus: Ohio State University Press, 1996).

30. See also JSP, "The Harvard School of Landscape Architecture," Harvard Alumni Bulletin (30 March 1922): 622–626.

31. For more on Charles William Eliot II (1899–1993, AB 1920, MLA 1923, Harvard), see *Who's Who in America, 1976–1977* (Chicago: Marquis), 912; an interview, "From the Backyard Garden to the Whole USA: a Conversation with Charles Eliot, 2nd" in Donald A. Krueckeberg, ed., *The American Planner* (New York: Methuen, 1983), 350; and for his initial appointment at Harvard, *Official Register School of Landscape Architecture 1922–1923*, 7.

32. *Official Register of the School of Landscape Architecture 1922–1923*, 9.

33. Ibid. 9, 10.

34. For details of the regular degree of Master of Landscape Architecture, see *Official Register School of Landscape Architecture 1928–1929*, 24, 28.

35. Lecturers included Alfred Bettman of Cincinnati, Frank Backus Williams (who later endowed a professorship), George B. Ford, Harland Bartholomew, Edward Bassett, James Ford, and Robert Whitten. Arthur A. Shurtleff came occasionally from his practice in Boston to speak to the landscape architects, included among whom was his son Sidney Shurtleff (later Shurcliff). See Shimoyama, "Speech," 3, 5.

36. *Examples of the Work of the Students in Architecture and Landscape Architecture in 1903–04, 1904–05 and 1905–06* (Cambridge, Mass.: The University, 1907). Between 1907 and 1921 no student work in architecture was published by the School. *The School of Architecture Harvard University* (Cambridge, Mass.: The University, 1921) summarized the interim improvements. Pray published a pamphlet, *School of Landscape Architecture,*

Harvard University, Exceptional Opportunities for Field Study: Examples of Landscape Design in the Vicinity of Boston (Cambridge, Mass.: The University, 1914). Intended to attract students by showing photographs of examples of gardens in the Boston area, it included no illustrations of student work. H. V. Hubbard and T. Kimball, *Landscape Architecture* (New York: Macmillan, 1917, 1931) gives, however, an indication of the kind of projects that were presented for students.

37. The award was announced in *Garden Club of America. Bulletin of the Eleventh Annual International Flower Show*, 16 (March 1924), p. 6; and subsequently illustrated in *House and Garden* 45 (May 1924): 180. On the use of the three-dimensional models in landscape architecture, see Carol Fulkerson, "Quarter Scale Landscape Models," *LA* 145 (July 1924): 257–264, 264 quoted.

38. "Two Prize-Winning War Memorial Designs," *The American City* 38:3 (March 1928): 143.

39. Henry James to HVH, 27 April 1928, UAV322.138, GSD Correspondence, Department of City and Regional Planning 1928–1957, PR-S Rockefeller Foundation, Folder III. James, a member of the organizational committee, later became a member of the Visiting Committee to the School of City and Regional Planning.

40. GHE to Frederic A. Delano, 30 April 1928, UAV322.138, GSD Correspondence, Department of City and Regional Planning, 1928–1957, PR-S Rockefeller Foundation, Folder III.

41. HVH to Dr. Edmund E. Day, 30 November 1928, UAV322.138, GSD Correspondence, Department of City and Regional Planning, 1928–1957, PR-S Rockefeller Foundation, Folder III.

42. GHE, "Schools," 449.

43. F. W. Honeywell to HVH, 29 May 1929, UAV322.138, GSD Correspondence, Department of City and Regional Planning, 1928–1957, PR-S Rockefeller Foundation, Folder III.

44. On the original funding of the School of City Planning, see Frederick J. Adams and Gerald Hodge, "City Planning Instruction in the United States: the Pioneering Days,

1900–1930," *Journal of the American Institute of Planners* 31:1 (February 1965): 43–51, 50 cited.

45. For the resumption of planning the program, see HVH to Dr. Edmund E. Day, 9 March 1929, UAV322.138, GSD Correspondence, Department of City and Regional Planning, 1928–1957, PR-S Rockefeller Foundation, Folder III.

46. Cohen, "Harvard and MIT," 23.

47. *Official Register, 1929–1930*, 49; Cohen, "Harvard and MIT," 24. Hubbard described an idealized and expanded curriculum for the program in a paper he presented in the City Planning Division of the Proceedings of American Society of Civil Engineers in 1929. See HVH, "City Planning Education for the Professional City Planner," *American Society of Civil Engineers, Proceedings* 55:10 (December 1929): 2527–2529. For the City Planning Visiting Committee's response to Hubbard's ideas, see Report No. 51 in *Report of the Committee to Visit Harvard College 1930–36*, 257, UAII.10.7.3.

48. See "Evansville Railroad Problem. Statement of Existing Conditions as Reported by the Consulting City Planner," n.d. [c. 1932], LL. A review of ten years of planning for the city, which included zoning plans made by Harland Bartholomew, was included in the railroad analyses.

49. Shigemaru Shimoyama, "Cabrillo, Port of Los Angeles," master's thesis, School of City Planning, Harvard University, 1930. LL.

50. HVH, "City Planning Education," 2527–2529, 2528 quoted.

51. John F. Cogswell, "What Spectacular Changes Would You See if You Returned to Boston 1000 Years from Today? And Would You Like it?" *Boston Sunday Post*, color feature section, 8 February 1931, 7, 10. For Hubbard's comments on city planning as a "synthetic profession" see HVH, "Professional Training for the Practice of City Planning, Paper for the discussion of the American City Planning Institute," 20 January 1930, typescript, LL.

52. By 1931 the *Harvard City Planning Studies* consisted of *Airports: Their Location Administration and Legal Basis*, vol. 1 (1930); *Building Height, Bulk and Form:*

How Zoning Can Be Used as a Protection Against Uneconomic Types of Buildings on High–Cost Land, vol. 2 (1931); and *Neighborhoods of Small Houses: Economic Density of Low Cost Housing in America and England,* vol. 3 (1931). In press was a fourth volume, "Urban Land Uses: Amounts of Lands Used and Needed for Variable Purposes by Typical American Cities—an Aid to Scientific Zoning Practice." In preparation was "Transition Zoning," vol. 5 (1933); *The Design of Residential Areas; Basic Considerations, Principles, and Methods,* vol. 6 (1934); and *Model Laws for Planning Cities, Counties, and States . . . ,* vol. 7 (1935).

53. Norman T. Newton, "Landscape Architecture at Harvard: A Brief History," unpublished ts., 14 February 1979, 424. LL.

54. GHE, "Schools," 450.

55. Charles W. Killam to Louis E. Lord (Secretary, Bureau of Appointments, Oberlin College), 10 December 1917. "School of Landscape Architecture of Harvard University," 1925, UAV322.7, Box 1, folder, "Dean Edgell Correspondence—Misc. 1925–34."

56. GHE to George B. Zug, 4 January 1925, UAV322.7, Box 2 (1a Edgell 1899–1939), folder, "Dean Edgell Correspondence, 1917–30: Misc., Academically Related." The McIntire School of Fine Arts had been established at the University of Virginia in 1918 and offered courses in art, architecture, and music that led to the degree of BS in Architecture. Fiske Kimball was the first professor of art and architecture and head of the department. He was succeeded by Joseph Hudnut who had previously been head of the Department of Architecture at Alabama Polytechnic Institute at Auburn, Alabama, from 1912 to 1916. Hudnut stayed at the McIntire School from 1923 to 1927 when he went to the School of Architecture at Columbia University. The Harvard-Virginia plan relied on courses in "culture"; training in elementary architectural design, construction, and freehand drawing would be given at Virginia, with advanced technical instruction given at Harvard, confirming Harvard's strong technical proficiency in the hands of Killam. The arrangement was perfected in 1925, and the training brought an M.Arch. degree from Harvard. The fate of the cooperative program, however, has not been confirmed. On Hudnut and the McIntire School, see Whitehead, *Collegiate Education,* 121, 129.

57. GHE to George Zug (Department of Modern Art, Dartmouth College), 18 February 1926, UAV322.7, Box 2 (1a Edgell 1899–1939), Folder "Dean Edgell Correspondence, 1917–30: Misc., Academically Related."

58. GHE to Ernest Langford, 25 November 1929, UAV322.7, Box 2 (1a Edgell 1899–1939), Folder "Dean Edgell Correspondence, 1917–30: Misc., Academically Related."

59. GHE to E. B. LaRoche (Agricultural and Mechanical College of Texas), 13 February 1924, UAV322.7, Box 2 (1a Edgell 1899–1939), folder, "Dean Edgell Correspondence, 1917–30: Misc., Academically Related."

60. See Herman Schneider, "New Cooperative Courses in Architecture and the Applied Fine Arts at the University of Cincinnati" (Reprint from the *American Architect and Architectural Review,* 16 January 1924, 4; cited in Whitehead, *Collegiate Education,* 134, n. 70). On the University of Cincinnati's program, which started in 1922, see Whitehead, *Collegiate Education,* 133, 134.

61. Ernest Pickering to GHE, 23 December 1930, with enclosure. UAV322.7, Box 1, folder, "Dean Edgell Correspondence, 1925–34." Pickering succeeded Herman Schneider as dean of the program.

62. Whitehead, *Collegiate Education,* 133.

63. See GHE, "Suggested Addition to Robinson Hall," *Harvard Alumni Bulletin* 33 (18 June 1931): 1138–1141; GHE, "School," in Morison, *Harvard,* 450.

64. Richard K. Webel, interview with the author, 22 October 1986. See also Garry R. Hildebrand, *Making a Landscape of Continuity: The Practice of Innocenti & Webel* (Cambridge, Mass.: Harvard University Graduate School of Design, 1997).

65. Thomas Adams, Letter to the Editor, "Town Planning. Teaching at the Universities," London Times 13 July 1929, n.p. (letter dated 9 July [1929]). Clipping, vertical files, LL.

66. See *Who's Who* (1952), 1672; *Planning and Civic Comment* 17:4 (December 1951): 6. For his views on professional interchange, see Howard K. Menhinick, "The Landscape Architect in the Role of City Planner," *LA* 42:4 (July 1952): 154–156.

67. GHE, "School," in Morison, *Harvard,* 450; Sally Symonds to Stewart Mitchell, 6 July 1928, "School of Landscape Architecture of Harvard University," 1925, UAV322.7. Box 1, folder, "Dean Edgell Correspondence—Misc. 1925–34." For the increase in library holdings, see GHE to Alice R. Felton, Metropolitan Museum of Art, 3 February 1926, "School of Landscape Architecture of Harvard University," 1925, UAV322.7, Box 1, folder, "Dean Edgell Correspondence—Misc. 1925–34."

68. GHE, "Suggested Addition to Robinson Hall," 1141.

69. Ibid.

70. Ibid.

71. "Cram Assails Harvard Plans for Robinson," *Boston Evening Transcript,* 23 June 1931, 17.

72. "Edgell Answers Cram's Criticism of Harvard Plan," *Boston Evening Transcript* (2 July 1931), 1, 6.

73. BWP, "The School of Landscape Architecture," in *Annual Reports to the President of the University, 1932–1933,* 168, 169. Ts; for efforts to abbreviate the program of study, see also *Official Register School of Landscape Architecture, 1931–1932,* 7, 14.

74. C. Raimond Johnson (School of Architecture, University of Southern California) to GHE, 6 April 1929, UAV322.7, Box 2 (1a Edgell 1899–1939), folder, "Dean Edgell Correspondence, 1917–30: Misc., Academically Related." The American Collegiate Schools of Architecture (ACSA) had canvassed 485 architects with questions that focused on courses applicable to business administration and professional training. Only half the respondents thought that students should spend research time in offices as a service to the profession. 99.4 percent concurred on the

need for the humanities. 76 percent favored more business courses; 70.6 percent applauded practical experience; and 68.6 percent saw the curricula as inadequate.

75. "Present Professions of Graduates of School of Architecture," 23 December 1925. "School of Landscape Architecture of Harvard University," 1925, UAV322.7, Box 1, folder, "Dean Edgell Correspondence—Misc. 1925–34."

76. *Official Register, 1930–31,* 16.

77. Aisner interview.

78. GHE, *Alumni,* 12.

79. GHE, "Address and Lectures," Edgell Papers, Harvard University Archives. HUG 4350.1c.

80. *Official Register, 1929–1930,* 12.

81. GHE to R. Clipston Sturgis, 2 May 1923, UAV322.7, Box 1, folder, "Fine Arts General." See also First Report of the Alumni in Architecture of Harvard University (Cambridge, Mass.: Harvard University, 1932), 72.

82. For Chambers's later career, see "School News," *LA* 49:1 (Autumn 1958): 52.

83. For the transition from Pray to Pond, see *Official Register School of Landscape Architecture,* 1929–30, 13, 26.

84. For the Country Estate tradition in America, see Keith N. Morgan, *Charles A. Platt, the Artist as Architect* (New York: Architectural History Foundation, 1985); Norman Newton, "100 Years of Landscape Architecture," *LA* 54 (July 1964): 262.

85. Shimoyama, "Speech," 3.

86. BWP, "Career of Landscape Architecture Needs Long Study & Experience. Well Grounded Knowledge of History, Fine Arts, Horticulture & Topography Involved in Profession That Caters Mainly to Well-Educated Clients," *Christian Science Monitor* (23 April 1930): n.p. Clipping files, LL.

87. *Official Register, 1930–1931,* 9.

88. Ibid., 12.

89. Ibid.

90. Kenneth Stowell, "The International Style," *Architectural Forum* 56 (March 1931): 253, cited in Bentel, "Modernism and Professionalism," 365.

91. Richard Bennett, interview with the author, 1986.

92. Francis S. Onderdonk, Jr., *The Ferro-concrete Style: Reinforced Concrete in Modern Architecture: with Four Hundred Illustrations of European and American Ferro-concrete Design* (New York: Architectural Book Publishing Co., 1928).

93. See Margret Kentgens-Craig, *The Bauhaus and America: First Contacts, 1919–1936* (Cambridge, Mass.: MIT Press, 1999), 68.

94. ALL to GHE, 4 November 1925, UAI.5.160, folder 127.

95. GHE to ALL, 5 November 1925, UAI.5.160, folder 127. My thanks to Rosemarie Haag Bletter for clarifying the possible nature of the exhibition (personal communication, 6 August 1986).

96. Kentgens-Craig, *The Bauhaus and America,* 72.

97. *The Harvard Society for Contemporary Art. 2nd Annual Report,* (Cambridge, Mass.: The Society, 1931). Lincoln Kirstein was an ex-officio executive of the Society and went to Germany in 1928 to see the work of Mies van der Rohe (WC).

98. Kentgens-Craig, *Bauhaus and America,* 73.

99. See Alfred Barr, Jr., Henry-Russell Hitchcock, Jr., Philip Johnson and Lewis Mumford, *Modern Architects* (New York: Museum of Modern Art and W. W. Norton, 1932); and Henry-Russell Hitchcock and Philip Johnson, *The International Style. Architecture Since 1922* (New York: W. W. Norton, 1932). For Forbes's and Sachs's era at the Fogg Museum, see Caroline A. Jones, *Modern Art at Harvard, The Formation of the Nineteenth- and Twentieth-Century Collections* (New York: Abbeville Press, 1985), 19–58.

100. See Henry-Russell Hitchcock, *The International Style* (New York and London: W. W. Norton, 1966), vii–xiii; WC.

101. For a discussion of the relationship of CIAM to America, see Eric Mumford, *The CIAM Discourse on Urbanism, 1928–1960* (Cambridge, Mass.: MIT Press, 2000).

102. See KJC, ed., *Modern Architecture, University Prints, Series GM* (Boston, Mass.: The University Prints, 1930); for Holabird & Roche, plate GM58, and for the work of Wright, plates GM71, GM80, GM81.

103. GHE to Jerome D. Greene, 16 October 1934, UAV322.7, Box 2. Edgell had contacted Wright as early as 1926 to obtain photographs of Wright's Imperial Hotel and a typical small country house for lectures he was preparing to give in Philadelphia (GHE to Frank Lloyd Wright, 3 February 1926, Frank Lloyd Wright Archives, Taliesin West, Scottsdale, Arizona).

104. Jerome D. Greene to GHE, 16 October 1934, UAV322.7, Box 2. Greene, the former secretary of the University and director of the tercentenary celebration, informed Edgell, "As for Frank Lloyd Wright I can see, as you suggest, that a good many eyebrows would be raised. As a frequent habitué of the Imperial Hotel in Tokyo I have suffered a good deal of torture at his hands, though I will confess that it has carried me through many earthquakes."

105. GHE to Jerome D. Green, 18 October 1934, UAV322.7, Box 2.

106. Panepinto to the author, 23 May 1986.

107. GHE, *The American Architecture of To-day* (New York and London: Charles Scribner's Sons, 1928), 3.

108. Edgell's selection of modern buildings appeared in his *University Prints Series GM103* (Boston: The University Prints, n.d.), compiled for Fine Arts 1d which covered for undergraduates everything from ancient art to modern architecture.

109. WC; GHE, *The American Architecture of To-day,* figs. 266, 277, 279.

110. KJC, *University Prints Series GM, Modern Architecture.*

111. G. Holmes Perkins, interview with the author, 17 October 1986.

112. GHP interview.

113. Conant's personal curriculum vitae lists for 1926 excavations at Chichen Itzá, Yucatán, with the Carnegie Institution of Washington, and Pueblo Bonito, New Mexico, with the National Geographic Society. LL.

114. Perkins interview. For the model project for Conant's history course, Landis Gores chose Bruno Taut's project for the Chicago Tribune Tower competition of 1922—the simplest solution to satisfy the requirement—whereas his fellow student, Bill Goulding, designed a model of Frank Lloyd Wright's Fallingwater (which was unveiled to acclaim in 1937) whose complicated forms caused Goulding to spend

more time on his history project than on his studio project. Gores interview.

115. GHE, *Reports to the President of the University 1932–33*, 161–167.

116. GHE, *Reports to the President of the University 1933–34*, 187–192.

117. BWP, "The School of Landscape Architecture," in *Annual Reports to the President of the University, 1932–1933*, 168, 169, 193, 198.

118. Ibid., 164.

119. Walter Francis Bogner (1899–1993) was born in Providence, Rhode Island, and was educated in Austria, before matriculating at Harvard's School of Architecture in 1923. At Harvard he was an instructor from 1929 to 1931, assistant professor 1935–1945, and professor of architecture 1945–1966, when he retired as professor emeritus. His long career demonstrated how an architect and teacher could make the transition from promulgating the methods of the Beaux-Arts to following the approach of Walter Gropius; his first course, taught in the Harvard summer school in 1929, was "Elements of Architectural Form—the Orders, Elementary Design," but he became a strong supporter of Gropius's approach. Bogner was one of the few faculty members who remained throughout the Hudnut-Gropius era.

120. GHE, *Reports to the President of the University 1933–34*, 190.

121. *Official Register 1933–34*, 17, 34.

122. BWP, *Reports to the President of the University 1933–34*, 189, 190.

123. BWP, Ibid., 198.

124. A tabulation of 52 men who had graduated from the School of Landscape Architecture since 1929 yields the following:

Professional office practice	8
Professional office assistants	11
Teaching, full or part-time	10
Government employment:	
Federal or state	19
Traveling fellowships, abroad	2
Business	1
Classification not known	1

LA 24:2 (January 1934): 112.

125. *Official Register School of Landscape Architecture, 1929–30*, 13.

126. *Official Register School of Landscape Architecture, 1934–35*.

127. HVH, *Report to the President of the University, The School of City Planning, 1932–33*, 174; HVH, *Report to the President of the University, The School of City Planning, 1933–34*, 199.

128. Ibid., 1932–33, 174, 176.

129. HVH, *Report to the President of the University, The School of City Planning, 1933–34*, 199.

130. "Report of the Committee to Visit the School of City Planning," Report No. 51, December 1934, in *Report of the Committee to Visit Harvard College 1930–36*, 257–261. UAII.10.7.3. (Before 1932, Harvard and MIT had the only two American planning programs; between 1932 and 1946, eight other universities established programs. Shillaber, MIT, 95.)

131. Ibid., 259.

132. Ibid., 257–261.

133. "Report of the Overseers' Committee to Visit the Schools of Architecture and Landscape Architecture," Report No. 56, submitted 13 May 1935, 287–300, 288 quoted.

134. Ibid.

135. Ibid., 289.

136. Columbia President Nicholas Murray Butler appointed a committee of five architects who made a thorough study of teaching conditions throughout the United States. It was published as "The Architects Committee Reports on Columbia's School of Architecture," *Architectural Forum* 62 (February 1935): 163. See Judith Oberlander, "History IV 1933–1935," in *Making of an Architect*, 120–122.

137. "Report of the Overseers' Committee to Visit the Schools of Architecture and Landscape Architecture," Report No. 56, submitted 13 May 1935, 297–299.

138. Panepinto to the author, 23 May 1986.

139. Ibid.

140. See "Report of the Committee to Visit the School of Architecture," Report No. 7 in *Reports of the Visiting Committee 1930–36*, 35–27 (UAII.10.7.3).

141. Ibid., 35.

142. GHE, *Reports to the President of the University 1933–34*, 190.

143. Ibid.

144. "Report of the Overseers' Committee to Visit the Schools of Architecture and Landscape Architecture," Report No. 56, submitted 13 May 1935, 300.

145. For James Bryant Conant's (1893–1978) work as a scientist, see G. B. Kistiakowsky, "J. B. Conant, 1883–1978," *Nature* 273 (29 June 1978): 793–795; as an educator, "ETS Mourns James B. Conant, Educational Activist," *ETS Developments*, 25, no. 2 (Summer 1978): n.p; and for a general synopsis, see Bethell, *Harvard Observed*, 114–146. For the origins of his ideas on reform in general education, see Conant's autobiography, *My Several Lives—Memoirs of a Social Inventor* (New York: Harper & Row, 1970), 363–373.

146. Conant, *My Several Lives*, 366, 370. The end product of Conant's studies was a report finished in the spring of 1943 and published as *General Education in a Free Society. Report of the Harvard Committee,* intro. by James B. Conant (Cambridge, Mass.: Harvard University Press, 1945[?]). Three fundamental areas of learning were defined—the humanities, the social sciences, and the natural sciences. Beginning with the Harvard College Class of 1955, students would be required to take at least one course—sweeping in scope and conception—in each of these areas and at least three courses outside the area of the student's concentration. This became the blueprint for undergraduate education at Harvard for the next forty years, only giving way to changes instituted in 1980.

147. Conant quoting his annual report to the University for 1941–1942 in *My Several Lives*, 368.

Chapter 4

1. "Report of the Student Council on the School of Architecture," ts., 18 pages. UAI.5.168, 1934–35, Box AP/AR, Architecture folder, Conant Papers.

2. Ibid., 14–15.

3. Henry A. Frost to JBC, 10 April 1935, UAI.5.168, Box AP/AR, folder, "Architecture, General," Conant Papers, 1934–35; Henry A. Frost to JBC, 2 May 1935, UAI.5.168, Box AP/AR, folder, "Architecture, Faculty Appointments," Conant Papers, 1934–35.

4. Henry A. Frost to JBC, 2 May 1935.

5. Ibid.

6. Ibid.

7. Jean-Jacques Haffner to JBC, 20 May 1935, Box AP/AR, folder, "Architecture, Faculty Appointments," Conant Papers, 1934–35.

8. Charles W. Killam to JBC, 21 May 1935, UAI.5.168, Box AP/AR, folder, "Architecture, Faculty Appointments," Conant Papers, 1934–35.

9. Ibid. Killam further explained that because of advocacy for an architect as dean, he had not signed the petition promoting Professor Hubbard. Nevertheless, he highly esteemed Hubbard and felt that "Professor Hubbard is the best man in the present faculty. . . . Hubbard has a wider reputation and wider context than any other member of the faculty. He is familiar with the organization of the University. He has sense. I believe he is the best man to appoint under the present financial conditions but not for a long term under normal conditions."

10. WC. See WC, *TVA's Public Planning: The Vision, The Reality* (Knoxville: University of Tennessee Press, 1990).

11. GHE to JBC, 5 March 1935, UAI.5.168, folder, "Architecture, Dean," Conant Papers, 1934–35.

12. See F. H. Bosworth, Jr., and Roy Childs Jones, *A Study of Architectural Schools* (New York: Charles Scribner's Sons for the Association of Collegiate Schools of Architecture, 1932). Bosworth was president of the ACSA 1925–1927, and Jones was president, 1934–1936.

13. Harold Bush-Brown to JBC, 10 March 1935, UAI.5.168, Box AP/AR, folder, "Architecture, Faculty Appointments," 1934–35. Harold Bush-Brown later wrote as a witness to the transition from traditional architecture to modernism; see Stanley Abercrombie, review of *Beaux Arts to Bauhaus and Beyond: an Architect's Perspective* by Harold Bush-Brown, *JSAH* 27 (December 1978): 45.

14. Grant LaFarge to Charles A. Coolidge, 31 January 1935, UAI.5.168, Box AP/AR, folder, Architecture, Faculty Appointments," Loeb Papers, 1934–35. For other recommendations sent to Coolidge, see Charles Butler to Charles A. Coolidge, 21 January 1935, UAI.5.168, Box AP/AR, folder, "Architecture, Faculty Appointments," Loeb Papers, 1934–35.

15. Harold Bush-Brown to JBC, 10 March 1935, UAI.5.168, Box AP/AR, folder, "Architecture, Faculty Appointments," 1934–35.

16. Ibid.

17. Western Union telegram, GHE to JBC, 13 March 1935. In addition to consulting in New York with Otto Teegen and Kenneth Stowell in mid-March 1935, Conant received other recommendations for the dean position including Eli Jacques Kahn, the prominent art deco architect in New York; C. Theodore Larson (Harvard School of Architecture '29) and his classmate Ralph Gulley, professor in the Department of Architecture at Rensselaer Polytechnic Institute; Richmond Harold Shreve of Shreve, Lamb and Harmon; and Ralph Walker, of McKenzie, Voorhees, Gmelin. Stowell thought that if Shreve were available, he would make an excellent dean. See JBC to GHE 23 March 1935, UAI.5.168, Box AP/AR, folder, "Architecture, Faculty Appointments," Conant Papers, 1934–35.

18. Fiske Kimball to JBC, 11 April 1935, UAI.5.168, Box AP/AR, folder, "Architecture, Faculty Appointments," Conant Papers 1934–35; G. Holmes Perkins, interview with the author, 17 October 1986. Early in May the proposal of Henry V. Hubbard was formalized and made public when a list of faculty from the Schools of Architecture, Landscape Architecture, and City Planning sent President Conant a petition in favor of making Hubbard dean of the combined faculties. The signers included Bremer Pond, Walter Chambers, Richard Webel, Herbert Langhorne, Henry Frost, Arthur Comey, Howard K. Menhenick, Kenneth Conant, Morley Williams, Walter Bogner, G. Holmes Perkins, John Nolen, Steven F. Hamblin, Aiden Lasalle Ripley, and Jean-Jacques Haffner. They stated that they had considered for a long time the possibilities for improving "instruction, collaboration and public service of the present three schools." Petition to President Conant, 8 May 1835, Box AP/AR, folder, "Faculty Appointments," UAI.5.168, Conant Papers, 1934–35.

For additional opinions of the candidates, see the following in UAI.5.168, Box AP/AR, folder, "Faculty Appointments," Conant Papers, 1934–35: HVH to JBC, 10 May 1935; HVH to JBC, 11 May 1935; A. B. Parson, class of '03, to Roger Lee, 10 May 1935; Roy Jones to GHE, 13 May 1935; John S. Humphreys to JBC, 15 May 1935; A. B. Parson to Roger Lee, 16 May 1935; Charles Killam to JBC, 21 May 1935; Walter Jessup, president of the Carnegie Foundation for the Advancement of Teaching, to Arnold B. Hall, 21 May 1935.

19. JBC to JH, Western Union telegram, 18 April 1935, UAI.5.168, Box CA/COL, folder, "Columbia," Conant Papers, 1934–35.

20. GHE to JBC [early April 1935], UAI.5.168, Box AP/AR, folder, "Architecture, Dean," Conant Papers, 1934–35; JBC to GHE, 27 April 1935, UAI.5.168, Box AP/AR, folder, "Architecture, Dean," Conant Papers, 1934–35.

21. JH to JBC, 20 April 1935, UAI.5.168, Box AP/AR, folder, "Architecture, Dean," Conant Papers, 1934–35. Hudnut's article was the "Gothick Universitie" reprinted from the *Columbia University Quarterly*, 26, no. 1 (March 1934), 1–10. He enclosed his "Report of the Dean of the School of Architecture for the Period Ending June 30, 1934," *Columbia University Bulletin of Information*, 35th series, no. 4 (New York: The University, 27 October 1934).

22. See JBC to Harold Bush-Brown, 2 May 1935, UAI.5.168, Box AP/AR, folder, "Architecture, Faculty Appointments," Conant Papers, 1934–35.

23. Ibid.

24. GHE to JBC, 9 May 1935, UAI.5.168, Box AP/AR, folder, "Architecture, Faculty Appointments," Conant Papers, 1934–35.

25. Harold Bush-Brown to JBC, 20 May 1935, UAI.5.168, Box AP/AR, folder, "Architecture, Faculty Appointments," Conant Papers, 1934–35.

26. JBC to JH, 7 June 1935, UAI.5.168, Box AP/AR, folder, "Architecture, Dean," Conant Papers, 1934–35.

27. JH to JBC, 8 June 1935, UAI.5.168, Box AP/AR, folder, "Architecture, Dean," Conant Papers, 1934–35.

28. Theodore K. Rohdenburg, *A History of the School of Architecture*, Columbia University (New York: Columbia University Press, 1954), 37.

29. For Hudnut's career, see "Letter of Biographical Information," 5 August 1913, for publication in the Harvard University Directory and other documents cited below in the Biographical file, Joseph F. Hudnut, HUG300. Subsequent references to HUG300 pertain to this note. Although some dates vary, see *Harvard Alumni Bulletin* 48 (March 30 1946): 481; "Harvard Portraits—55" *Harvard Alumni Bulletin* 52 (8 April 1950): 534. See also Jill Pearlman, "Joseph Hudnut's Other Modernism at the 'Harvard Bauhaus,' " *JSAH* 56:4 (Dec. 1997): 452–477.

30. Pearlman, "Hudnut's Other Modernism," 453–460.

31. WC, preface, *Modernism in America 1937–1941, A Catalogue and Exhibition of Four Architectural Competitions. Wheaton College, Goucher College, College of William and Mary, Smithsonian Institution*, James D. Kornwolf, ed. (Williamsburg, Va.: College of William and Mary, 1985), xi.

32. See obituaries, "Joseph Fairman Hudnut," *Boston Globe*, 19 January 1968, and *Boston Herald*, 17 January 1968, in HUG300.

33. JH, "The Education of an Architect," AR 69 (May 1931): 412.

34. Ibid., 413.

35. "New Dean, New Curriculum—Forum of Events," *Architectural Forum* 59 (October 1933): 37.

36. Obituary, "Joseph Fairman Hudnut," *New York Times*, 17 January 1968, in HUG300. See also the review of Hudnut's *Architecture and the Spirit of Man* (1949), in *The New Yorker*, 4 March 1950, in HUG300. For a discussion of Hudnut at Columbia University, see Rosemary Bletter, "Modernism Rears Its Head—the Twenties and Thirties," and Judith Oberlander, "History IV: 1933–1935," in Richard Oliver, ed., *The Making of an Architect* (New York: Rizzoli International Publications, 1981), 110–112, 119–126.

37. See "Hudnut to Head School of Architecture," *New York Herald Tribune*, 20 June 1935, in HUG300.

38. Rohdenburg, *Columbia*, 34–37.

39. "Columbia Changes Her Methods," *Architectural Forum* (February 1935), cited in Rolf Achilles, Kevin Harrington, Charlotte Myhrum, eds., *Mies van der Rohe: Architect as Educator* (Chicago: Mies van der Rohe Centennial Project, Illinois Institute of Techonology, 1986), 52.

40. Obituary, "James Fairman Hudnut," *Boston Globe*, 19 January 1968, in HUG300.

41. Obituary, "Joseph Fairman Hudnut," *Boston Herald*, 17 January 1968, in HUG300.

42. G. Holmes Perkins, interview with the author, 17 October 1986, Philadelphia, Pa.; Kenneth Conant reiterated the story of Hudnut's association with the perfume family (WC).

43. JH to JBC, 16 September 1935, UAI.5.168, Box 2, folder, "Architecture Budgets," and GHE to JBC, 28 March 1935, UAI.5.168, 1935, Box 2, folder, "School of Architecture," Conant Papers, 1935–36. Edgell had previously recommended the increases because "The young men, who are doing the heaviest work and supplying the imagination and constructive ideas, are receiving starvation wages. The older men are entrenched. This we probably cannot correct all at once. I should like, however, authority to raise Bogner's salary by a thousand dollars—even if it involves adding that sum to the deficit. We have as you know a generous surplus balance." (GHE to JBC, 20 March 1935, ibid.) For biographical information on Perkins, see *Alumni in Architecture*, 23, 103.

44. "Minutes of meeting held at Robinson Hall, 16 October, 1935, Faculty of Architecture," UAI.5.168, Box 2, folder, "School of Architecture," Conant Papers, 1935–36.

45. "Memorandum for President Conant in respect to the proposed changes in the curriculum in the School of Architecture," 28 October 1935, UAI.5.168, Box 2, folder, "School of Architecture," Conant Papers, 1935–36.

The degree programs and their duration are described in JH, Report to the President, Harvard Annual Reports, 1934–36, 229–230; and "Minutes of meeting of Faculty of Design," 6 January 1953 and 9 January 1953, folder, "GSD Faculty Meeting Minutes," UAV322.6. Harvard officially terminated the B.Arch. in 1970. Holders of the B.Arch. at that time could exchange their degree for the M.Arch.

46. JH to JBC, 25 November 1935, UAI.5.168, Box 2, folder, "School of Architecture," Conant Papers, 1935–36.

47. Henry James, graduate of Harvard College, 1899, and Harvard Law School, 1904, was also the biographer of President Eliot. Bethel, *Harvard*, 97; 311, n. 7.

48. JH to JBC, 4 December 1935, UAI.5.168, Box 2, folder, "School of Architecture," Conant Papers, 1935–36.

49. Henry James to JBC, 5 December 1935, UAI.5.168, Box 2, folder, "School of Architecture," Conant Papers, 1935–36.

50. Ibid.

51. JBC to Henry James, 7 December 1935, UAI.5.168, Box 2, folder, "School of Architecture," Conant Papers, 1935–36; JH to JBC, 10 December 1935, UAI.5.168, Box 2, folder, "School of Architecture," Conant Papers, 1935–36.

52. JH to JBC, 17 December 1935, UAI.5.168, Box 2, Folder "School of Architecture," Conant Papers, 1935–36, with enclosed resolutions, dated 16 December 1935. The Council of the Department of Architecture had voted for dual curricula on 23 October 1935.

53. Ibid. Hudnut's marginalia was "Savings—simplified administration—Independence—handicap school vs. Department Coop[eration] Bachelor's Degree, Master's Degree."

54. "Memorandum on the Proposed School of Design," 14 January 1936, UAI.5.168, Box 2, folder, "School of Architecture," Conant Papers, 1935–36.

55. Ibid.

56. Ibid.

57. JBC to Jerome D. Green, 5 February 1936, with enclosure, "Resolution Relating to the Establishment of the School of Design," UAI.5.168, Box 2, folder,

"School of Architecture," Conant Papers, 1935–36.

58. "Memorandum to the Corporation," J.W.L. [J. W. Lowes] 3 January 1936, UAI.5.168, Box 2, "Architecture, Landscape Architecture, Schools of," Conant Papers, 1935–36. See also JH, "Graduate School of Design," *Harvard Annual Reports 1934–36* (Cambridge, Mass.: Harvard University [1936]), 232.

59. GHE to W. G. Land, 25 May 1936, UAV319.322.7, Box 1, Records of the Office of the Dean, Subseries IA, Edgell, 1899–1934.

60. Ibid.

61. For a discussion of the Metropolitan Museum's collection of casts, see Calvin Tomkins, "The Art World. Gods and Heroes," *The New Yorker* (15 September 1986): 82–87.

62. The offer of a portrait of Charles G. Fall proved embarrassing because Fall's estate in Cohasset, Massachusetts, had been visited annually by classes in landscape architecture. See Stephen F. Hamblin to Emily B. Fall, 7 July 1937, and BP to Mrs. Charles G. [Emily] Fall, UAV322.7 GSD, Records of the Office of the Dean 1894–1980, Subseries III, Box 1, Faculty Correspondence and Records, Subseries IIIa 1896–1962, folder, "Fall, Charles G."

63. Hudnut recommended for reappointment: John Wilson as instructor in modeling; Charles A. Whittemore as lecturer on the mechanical planning of buildings; George Holmes Perkins as instructor in architecture, with an increased salary; Walter L. Chambers as instructor in landscape architecture; and Walter Bogner as instructor in summer school. For further details about salary negotiations see JH to Jerome D. Green, 6 March 1936; JH to JBC, 19 March 1936, UAI.5.168; Box 2, folder, "School of Architecture," Conant Papers, 1935–36.

64. Williams had been on the staff of the school for six years, teaching principles and practice of landscape construction. Pond had informed Hudnut that Williams's "work has not been of the same excellence as that of other members of the staff." (JH to Jerome D. Green, 6 March 1936, UAI.5.168, Box 2, folder,

"School of Architecture," Conant Papers, 1935–36). Langhorne's teaching had been more satisfactory, but his work had been affected by absence from illness. Langhorne's colleague, Richard Webel, recalled that he was a good designer. (Richard Webel, interview with the author; "Department of Landscape Architecture Newsletter," 5 December 1944).

65. Charles A. Coolidge to President Conant, 15 May 1936, UAI.5.168, Box COO/DEO, Conant Papers, 1935–36. Coolidge agreed with Murphy and thought "the ability to sketch in watercolor well gives the architect himself an added zest in his work." In sum, Coolidge communicated the essence of the issue to the president: that the transfer of the courses to Harvard College would be fine as long as the courses were well taught. Nevertheless, drawing courses in the College were phased out.

66. Jean-Jacques Haffner to JBC, 22 March 1936, copy of letter, UAI.5.168, Box 2, folder, "School of Architecture," Conant Papers, 1935–36.

67. The myth of Haffner's removal as a *retardataire* obstructionist has been repeated several times. See, for instance, Jacques Carlu's suggestions in Isabelle Gournay, "Architecture at the Fontainebleau School of Fine Arts 1923–1939," *JSAH* 45 (September 1986): 282–285.

68. JH, "Report to the President of the University, 1936–1937," 254.

69. Jean Jacques Haffner, *Compositions des Jardins* (Paris: Vincent, Fréal & Cie, 1931). Haffner worked on the book in Paris during his sabbatical starting the second half of 1931 (Edgell, *Alumni*, 14). From a student's point of view, "his interest in Landscape Architecture was evident only in his critiques of our site plans." Panepinto to the author, 23 May 1986. For Guevrekian's cubistic gardens, see Elisabeth Vitou, Dominique Deshoulieres, and Hubert Jeanneau, *Gabriel Guevrekian, 1900–1970 : une autre architecture moderne* (Paris: Connivences, 1987); Dorothée Imbert, "French Visions of the Modern Garden," *Gartenkunst* 7:2 (1995): 255–267. Haffner's landscape designs possibly influenced later in their careers

such designers as Thomas Church, who had graduated the School of Landscape Architecture in 1926. (GHP)

70. According to a former student, Alfred Panepinto, who met with him in Paris during World War II, Haffner was one of two people who knew where the masterpiece paintings of the Louvre were hidden. During the war, Haffner was commissioned by the government to design a French embassy for Madrid, but was frustrated because he could not visit the site (Panepinto to the author, 23 May 1986 and 6 June 1986).

71. JH to JBC, 17 April 1936, UAI.5.168, Box 2, folder, "School of Architecture," Conant Papers, 1935–36, with enclosure "Memorandum on Proposed Curriculum in Regional Planning," 28 January 1936.

72. JH, "Graduate School of Design," in *President's Report, 1935–36. Harvard Annual Reports, 1934–36* (Cambridge, Mass: Harvard University, [1936]), 229–240.

73. The Faculty of Arts and Sciences approved the new undergraduate major on 4 February 1936. The program's curriculum included courses in the history of art and architecture, drawing, the theory of design, and practical, or studio, courses in design, including architectural design, as well as required courses in physics, mathematics, economics, and history. As many undergraduates as graduate students were already taking courses in architecture so a large audience was assured (Ibid., 229). In the Department of Architecture, 51 graduate students were registered, and forty-seven undergraduates took courses in architecture that were open to them (Ibid., 232).

74. Ibid., 240.

75. Ibid., 238. Architecture had a total of 5,875 books, landscape architecture and regional planning, 14,010.

76. Katherine MacNamara, *Bibliography of Planning, 1928–1935. A Supplement to Manual of Planning Information by Theodora Kimball Hubbard and Katherine McNamara*. Vol X, Harvard Planning Studies (Cambridge, Mass.: Harvard University Press, 1936).

77. JH in *President's Report, 1935–36, Harvard Annual Reports, 1934–36*, 229–30.

78. Conant in Ibid., 6.

79. Ibid., 7.

80. Ibid., 23.

81. *Official Register of the Harvard Graduate School of Design 1936–37,* 5, 24.

82. GHP interview, 17 October 1986.

83. GHP interview.

84. For a biographical sketch of Oud (1890–1963), see Helen Searing, "Oud, J.J.P.," *Macmillan Encyclopedia*, vol. 3, 333–335.

85. Mardges Bacon, "Le Corbusier et l'Amérique: Première rencontre," in *Americanisme et modernité,* J.-L. Cohen and Hubert Damish, eds., (Paris, 1993); noted in E. Mumford, *CIAM Discourse,* 103 and n. 127.

86. Hudnut met with Gropius in August 1936 and returned to the United States the second week of September. Mary Therese Gain, "Theory and Practice in Architectural Education: The Harvard Curriculum, 1934–1956" (MA Thesis, Cornell University, 1977), 88.

87. E. Mumford, *CIAM Discourse,* 105.

88. Cited in Reginald Isaacs, s.v., "Gropius, Walter," *Macmillan Encyclopedia*, vol. #2, 253.

89. WC. See also WG, *Internationale Architektur, Bauhausbucher 1* (Munich: A. Langen, 1925).

90. Isaacs, *Gropius,* provides a detailed account of the events of Gropius's move from Germany to England.

91. JH to JBC, 21 September 1936, letter and memoranda, Conant Papers.

92. Sandra Honey, "Mies van der Rohe: Architect and Teacher in Germany," in *Mies van der Rohe: Architects as Educator* (Chicago: Illinois Institute of Technology, 1986), 45.

93. Alfred Barr, Jr., director of the Museum of Modern Art, had also previously brought messages from Hudnut to Mies as well as from the Museum. Barr had wanted Mies to be the architect for the new building of the Museum of Modern Art, but was unsuccessful in obtaining the commission for him. For Mies's offers to teach in America, see Rolf Achilles, Kevin Harrington, Charlotte Myhrum, eds., *Mies van der Rohe: Architect as Educator* (Chicago: Mies van der Rohe Centennial Project,

Illinois Institute of Techonology, 1986), 51–54.

94. Ibid., 52.

95. Gropius to Pierre Jay, 1 September 1936, document 40/265, Ms131/storage, Walter Gropius Papers, Houghton Library, Harvard University.

96. Pierre Jay to WG, 11 June 1931, Gropius Papers, HL cited in Gain, "Theory and Practice," 86. Jay also had advised Gropius in 1934 on a proposal from A. Lawrence Kocher, editor of *Architectural Record* to head a new school of architecture that Kocher and the architect Antonin Raymond planned to open on Long Island (WG to Pierre Jay, 20 June 1934, Gropius Papers, HL, cited in Gain, "Theory and Practice," 86). Jay suggested that pending the opening of the school, he would try to arrange with Hudnut, who was then dean at Columbia, for a position for Gropius pending the opening of the school on Long Island. This arrangement did not succeed, and the school never opened. Gropius had previously written to Douglas Haskell, impoverished and pleading for a job. Judith Oberlander, "History IV 1933–1935," in *Making of an Architect*, 125, n. 36.

97. WG to JH, 1 September 1936, Gropius Papers 40/265, HL.

98. JH to WG, 13 November 1936, Gropius Papers 40/253, HL.

99. For Mies at IIT and the Harvard episode, the indispensable study is Kevin Harrington's "Order, Space, Proportion—Mies's Curriculum at IIT," in *Mies van der Rohe, Architect as Educator,* 49–68. For an earlier, but less accurate account of Mies's consideration of Harvard, see Franz Schulze in "How Chicago Got Mies—and Harvard Didn't," *Inland Architect* 21 (May 1977): 23–24. Schulze asserts, without documentation, that Mies was Harvard's first choice. For a general study, see Alfred Swenson and Pao-Chi Chang. *Architectural Education at IIT, 1938–1978* (Chicago: Illinois Institute of Technology, 1980).

100. Harrington, *Mies,* 53.

101. "Memorandum on the appointment of Gropius," 24 November 1936, Conant Papers, conveyed by archivist. Killam's

name as the objector was deduced by the author.

102. HVH to JBC, 27 November 1936, Conant Papers, conveyed by archivist.

103. JH to WG, 28 November 1936, Gropius Papers 40/244, HL.

104. JH to WG, 8 December 1936, Gropius Papers 40/251, HL. As a token of their alliance Hudnut wrote the preface to the American edition of Gropius's *The New Architecture and the Bauhaus,* translated by P. Morton Shand (New York: Museum of Modern Art, 1937); introduction by Frank Pick (London: Faber & Faber, 1935). Hudnut's preface was eliminated from subsequent editions of the book, a reflection of the break between him and Gropius.

105. WG to JBC, telegram, 11 December 1936, received 12 December 1936; WG to JBC, 17 December 1936, Conant Papers, conveyed by archivist. The Harvard Board of Overseers approved Gropius's appointment on 1 January 1937 (Jerome D. Greene [Secretary of the Harvard Corporation] to WG, 14 January 1937, Gropius Papers 40/198, HL).

106. See Nerdinger, *Gropius.*

107. JH to WG, 18 March 1937, Gropius Papers 40/226, HL. Gropius's correspondence after 1936 is in the collections of the Houghton Library. His correspondence prior to 1936 is in the Bauhaus-Archiv Berlin. Both repositories have copies of the complementary letters for complete collections.

108. Alfred Barr, Jr., to JBC, 20 March 1937, Conant Papers, conveyed by archivist.

109. Leverett Saltonstall to JBC [n.d. 1937], Conant Papers, conveyed by archivist.

110. JH, *Report to the President of the University, 1936–1937,* 255.

111. William G. Dooley, "Gropius Brings Modernism to Harvard Post," *Boston Evening Transcript,* 25 January 1937, 28; and H. I. Brock, "A Modernist Scans Our Skyline: Gropius, German Architect Bound for Harvard Sees an Original Style Emerging in America," *NYT Magazine,* 11 April 1937, 12, 24.

112. Houghton mss. 40/205, 206 [1937]; WC.

113. JH to WG, 23 December 1936, Gropius Papers 40/248, HL. After Haffner's departure, Hudnut taught advanced design in the fall of 1936. Holmes Perkins assisted Hudnut, and they continued with the first studio problem in the spring of 1937. When Gropius arrived he took the second problem, also with Perkins as his assistant (GHP interview). Walter Bogner, who had studied in Austria, would also have been a logical choice to serve as Gropius's assistant since he spoke German and was enthusiastic about the arrival of Gropius.

114. JH to WG [n.d.], Houghton mss. 40/214, 215. Hudnut had written about Cram's work in "The Romantic Architecture of Morningside Heights," *Columbia University Quarterly* 22 (December 1930): 397–406; ibid., 23 (March 1931): 119–124.

115. JH to WG [n.d.], Gropius Papers 40/217X, HL.

116. JH to WG, 23 December 1938, Gropius Papers 40/208, HL.

117. WG, "The Development of the New Architecture," summary for the press of an address to the Boston Architectural Club, 14 April 1937 (Cambridge, Mass.: Harvard University, 1937).

118. Other lectures by Gropius also received criticism. See *The Octagon* (July 1937): 36, in Nerdinger, *Gropius*, 23, n. 126.

119. WG, "Education Toward Creative Design," *American Architect and Architecture* 150 (May 1937): 26, 27.

120. Ibid.

121. Ibid., 28.

122. Ibid. For the program of the preliminary course, or *Vorkurs*, at the Bauhaus see Marcel Franciscono, "The Founding of the Bauhaus in Weimar: Its Artistic Background and First Conception" (thesis, 2 vols., New York University, 1968); Id., *Walter Gropius and the Creation of the Bauhaus in Weimar: The Ideals and Artistic Theories of Its Founding Years* (Urbana, Ill.: University of Illinois Press, 1971). For the standard study of the Bauhaus, see also Hans Maria Wingler, *The Bauhaus: Weimar, Dessau, Berlin, Chicago* (Cambridge, Mass.: M.I.T. Press, 1979). See also Honey, "Mies van der Rohe: Architect and Teacher in Germany," *Mies van der Rohe: Architect as Educator*, 37–48.

123. WG, "Education Toward Creative Design," 29.

124. WG, "Architecture at Harvard University," *Architectural Record* 81 (May 1937): 10.

125. Both quotes this paragraph, Ibid., 11.

Chapter 5

1. JH, *Report to the President of the University, 1936–37*, 246–255.

2. *Official Register 1938–1939*, 38.

3. Martin Wagner (1885–1957) was born in Koenigsberg, Prussia, and received the degree of Dr. Ing. in City Planning from the Institute of Technology in Dresden in 1912 and the Technische Hochschule in Berlin in 1915. Wagner was chief city planner in several German cities from 1910 to 1916 and helped organize building cooperatives from 1920 to 1926. His built work is known mainly through the Britz Housing groups, such as the Horseshoe Housing (*Hufeiseniedlung*) of 1927–1928 that he designed with Bruno Taut. See JH, *Report to the President of the University, 1938–39*, 294; Francesco Dal Co and Manfredo Tafuri, *Modern Architecture* (New York: Harry N. Abrams, 1979), 186, 196; Reginald Isaacs, "Martin Wagner," *Macmillan Encyclopedia*, vol. IV, 356–35; and *Martin Wagner 1885–1957. Wohungsbau und Weldtstadtplanung: die Rationalisierung des Glücks*, exhibition catalog (Berlin: Akademie der Künste, 1985).

4. "A Fresh Approach to Housing," *Architectural Forum* 74 (February 1941): 86–90. Circular in plan, with apsidal sections, the designs are studies of conoidal room units, and recall the apsidal studies of Bruno Taut for Magdeburg in 1921–1922, and the Dymaxion house of Buckminster Fuller of 1927–30. For Taut's approach, see Franziska Bollerey and Kristiana Hartmann, "Bruno Taut. Von phantastischen Astheten zum asthetischen Sozial(ideal)-isten," in *Bruno Taut 1880–1935*, exhibition catalogue, Akademie Der Kunste (Berlin: Brueder Hartmann, 1980), 24–27.

5. For the complete description of Site and Shelter, see listings for summer courses for 1940 in "Announcement," folded into *Official Bulletin 1939–1940*.

6. For recommended courses for students concentrating in design in Harvard College, see *Official Bulletin 1936–1937*, 23.

7. Norman Newton, interview with the author, 19 November 1985.

8. *Official Bulletin 1939–1940*, 22–24. For a sample curriculum in architectural sciences, see ibid. and JH, *Report to the President of the University, 1938–1939*, 284–285, for detailed descriptions of the courses.

9. *Official Bulletin 1939–40*, 22–24.

10. [Eduard Sekler], "Statement to the Faculty of Arts and Sciences," 5 March 1968, n.p. Courtesy of Eduard Sekler.

11. Gores ms.

12. JH, *Report to the President of the University, 1938–39*, 246.

13. JH, *Report to the President of the University, 1937–1938*, 258.

14. JBC, *Report of the President to the Board of Overseers, 1937–1938*, 25, 26.

15. WC.

16. JH, *Report to the President of the University, 1936–37*, 248. A complete program was only made possible by offering a number of courses in alternate years. Henry Hubbard, chairman, Arthur Comey, associate professor, and Harold W. Lautner, a graduate in planning from the class of 1936, carried the bulk of the teaching load, with the assistance of Martin Wagner who taught during 1938–39. Wagner's courses on Housing and Site and Shelter became requirements that year along with the study of modern architecture (Fine Arts 7a²). Added to the curriculum was an additional design course in regional planning (Regional Planning 1a), and for the first time a choice of elective courses was instituted. The previously required course on Highway Engineering was offered as one of three possible electives. Other recommended choices included courses in economics, geography, and sociology. The requirement for the study of topographic surveying was eliminated.

17. JH, *Report to the President of the University, 1936–37*, 248.

18. JBC, *Report of the President to the Board of Overseers, 1937–1938*, 261; JH, quoting HVH, *Report to the President of the University 1938–1939*, 288.

19. JH, quoting HVH, *Report to the President of the University 1938–1939*, 294.

20. See Phoebe Cutler, *The Public Landscape of the New Deal* (New Haven: Yale University Press, 1986), on the shift between the Old and New Guards.

21. JH, *Report to the President of the University, 1936–37*, 255.

22. *Official Register 1944–45*. After his arrival at Harvard, Humphreys designed about a dozen houses, but when his work was discussed in 1932, it was noted, partly in jest, that he had done a good deal of architecture for which he no longer claimed responsibility (George H. Edgell, *Alumni in Architecture of Harvard University. First Report, 1932*, Cambridge, Mass.: [Harvard University], 1932, 16). On Humphreys, see UAV322.7, IIIa, Box 2; Killam to Lowell, 24 March 1919, UAV322.7, Box 1. On his appointment, see also Carrère to [Warren] 15 December 1914, UAV322.7, Box 2.

23. See JH, *Report to the President of the University, 1938–1939*, 289.

24. JH, *Report to the President of the University, 1937–38*, 266. In June 1937, Hudnut thought he had $5000 from the Carnegie Corporation to employ Breuer as a research associate for two years, but by the fall Hudnut had to fall back on funding from Harvard. The University's offer of $1250 for a three-month appointment, however, was inadequate, because Breuer was traveling with a British passport and needed at least a year's appointment to remain in the United States. Hudnut assured the University that Breuer's positive role in assisting Gropius would be shared by every member of the Faculty of Design. Hudnut subsequently recommended Breuer's appointment as associate professor for two years and eight months at a salary of $6000, starting on 1 January 1939. See JH to JBC, 29 October 1937, Conant Papers, conveyed by Harvard University archivist. See also [JH] to President and Fellows of Harvard University, 4 October 1937, Conant Papers, conveyed by Harvard University archivist. Memorandum JWL[owes] to JBC and correspondence, n.d. August 1938 to Jerome Greene, Secretary of the Harvard Corporation, Conant Papers, conveyed by Harvard University archivist; and JFH to JBC,

21 November 1938, Conant Papers, conveyed by Harvard University archivist. For a brief biography of Marcel Lajos Breuer (1902–1981), see Reginald R. Isaacs, "Breuer, Marcel," *Macmillan Encyclopedia*, vol. I, 286, 287. For an excellent summary of Breuer's career through the late 1940s, see Peter Blake, *Marcel Breuer: Architect and Designer* (New York: *Architectural Record* in collaboration with the Museum of Modern Art, 1949); for his houses, see Joachim Driller, *Marcel Breuer: die Wohnhäuser 1923–1973* (Stuttgart: Deutsche Verlags-Anstalt, 1998).

25. JH, *Report to the President of the University, 1937–38*, 260.

26. "Breuer Designs, Students Build, Hypothetic [sic] Ski Club in Austria," *AR* 84 (September 1938): 57.

27. See Nerdinger, *Gropius*, 29.

28. For Behrendt, see Reginald R. Isaacs, "Behrendt, Walter Curt," Macmillan Encyclopedia, vol. I, 164–165; and Walter Curt Behrendt, *Modern Building: Its Nature, Problems, and Forms* (New York: Harcourt, Brace, 1937).

29. Pearlman, "Joseph Hudnut's Other Modernism," 467, 469.

30. JH, *Report to the President of the University, 1938–1939*, 288. For Aalto, see Paul D. Pearson, "Alvar Aalto," *Macmillan Encyclopedia*, vol. I, 8, 9.

31. GHP interview.

32. Robert W. Christensen, Byron R. Hanke, Millard Humstone, A. E. Nakpil, and Oscar Sutermeister, "A General Policy and Method of Regulation of Accommodations for Automobile Travelers in the State of New Hampshire," [1939]; and idem., "Suggestions for Roadside Development Controls in the State of New Hampshire," Harvard Graduate School of Design, 3 May 1939, ts., LL. quoted "General Policy," 4.

33. For the broad context, see Donald Fleming and Bernard Bailyn, eds., *The Intellectual Migration; Europe and America, 1930–1960* (Cambridge, Mass.: Belknap Press of Harvard University Press, 1969).

34. JH, "Twilight of the Gods," *Magazine of Art* 30 (August 1937): 480–484, 522–524, 480 quoted. The article was given origi-

nally as a speech at the banquet of the twentieth-eight annual convention of the American Federation of Arts at Washington, D.C., 13 May 1937. See also Obituary, "Joseph Fairman Hudnut," January 17, 1968, NYT in HUG300.

35. JH, "Twilight of the Gods," 481.

36. For Pope's defense of the Memorial and Hudnut's rejoinder, see Pope, "In Defense of the Jefferson Memorial," reprint from *Magazine of Art*, and JH, "Classical Architecture Not Essential," *AR* 82 (August 1937): 54–55; and Id., "A Temple for Thomas Jefferson," *The New Republic* (22 March 1939), 190–191.

37. Ibid., *New Republic*, 190.

38. JH, "Architecture Discovers the Present," *The American Scholar* 7 (Winter 1938): 106–114; 109 quoted.

39. Ibid., 109.

40. Ibid., 114.

41. WC interview.

42. WC, Frederick Law Olmsted Lecture, 9 April 1986, GSD, Cambridge, Mass. For other projects to bring modern architecture to America, including the competition for Wheaton College which Gropius and Hudnut entered, and insights on this much neglected period, see James D. Kornwolf, ed., *Modernism in America 1937–1941*.

43. A. Conger Goodyear to JH, 9 April 1938; JH to A. Conger Goodyear, 20 June 1938. Private collection.

44. For Giedion (1888–1968), see Eduard F. Sekler, "Sigfried Giedion at Harvard University," in Elisabeth Blair MacDougall, ed., *The Architectural Historian in America* (Washington, D.C.: National Gallery of Art, 1990); Werner Oechslin, et al., *Sigfried Giedion 1888–1968: Der Entwurf einer modernen Tradition* (Zurich: Ammann, 1989); *Hommage à Giedion: Profile seiner Persönlichkeit* (Basel and Stutgart: Birkhäuser Verlag, 1971). For the comprehensive history of CIAM from its founding in 1928 to its closing in 1959, see Mumford, *CIAM Discourse*.

45. E. Mumford, *CIAM Discourse*, 123; Sekler, "Sigfried Giedion at Harvard University," 265–266.

46. Sigfried Giedion, *Space, Time and Architecture: The Growth of a New Tradition*

(Cambridge, Mass.: Harvard University Press, 1941; 5th ed., 1967). The popularity of the book reflects the waxing and waning of modernism itself: almost 65,000 copies were sold between 1941 and 1962, whereas sales dipped in the late 1980s to between 700 and 800 (Sekler, "Giedion at Harvard," 270). See also Joseph Rykwert, review of *Space, Time and Architecture: The Growth of a New Tradition* by Sigfried Giedion, *Harvard Design Magazine* (Fall 1998): 65–66.

47. KJC interview.

48. Ibid.

49. WC.

50. Gores, "Autobiography," chapter three, n.p.

51. WC.

52. KJC, *University Prints Series GM, Modern Architecture* (Cambridge, Mass.: University Prints, 19).

53. Bremer Pond, *Outline History of Landscape Architecture* (Fine Arts 1f), 2 vols. (Cambridge, Mass.: School of Landscape Architecture, [1936]), LL.

54. Ibid.

55. The author owes these observations about Haffner's and Guevrekian's garden designs to Melanie Simo, 23 October 1985. Though Haffner may have tried to make a bridge between the Beaux-Arts and modernism, his book was reviewed by Theodora Kimball and dismissed. See also Simo, *Landscape Architecture*, 26.

56. For overviews of the history of modern landscape architecture in America, including reprints of seminal articles of the late 1930s, see Marc Treib, ed., *Modern Landscape Architecture: A Critical Review* (Cambridge, Mass.: MIT Press, 1993), and Peter Walker and Melanie Simo, *Invisible Gardens, The Search for Modernism in the American Landscape* (Cambridge, Mass., and London: MIT Press, 1994). See also Dan Kiley and Jane Armidon, *Dan Kiley: the Complete Works of America's Landscape Designer* (Boston: Bulfinch Press, 1999).

57. Garrett Eckbo, "Pilgrim's Progress," reprinted in Treib, *Modern Landscape Architecture*, 208. See also Dorothée Imbert and Marc Treib, with afterword by Garrett Eckbo, *Garrett Eckbo: Modern*

Landscape for Living (Berkeley: University of California Press, 1997).

58. Garrett Eckbo, Daniel U. Kiley, and James C. Rose, "Landscape Design in the Urban Environment," *AR* (May 1939): 78–82; "Landscape Design in the Rural Environment," *AR* (August 1939): 83–86; and Ibid., *AR* (February 1940): 74.

59. James Rose, "Freedom in the Garden," *Pencil Points* (October 1938), reprinted in Treib, *Modern Landscape Architecture*, 68–70. For Rose's recollection of his student years at the GSD, see *Modern American Gardens—Designed by James Rose*, text by Marc Snow (New York: Reinhold, 1967), 17–25.

60. James Rose, "Why Not Try Science," *Pencil Points* (December 1939), reprinted in Treib, *Modern Landscape Architecture*, 76–77.

61. Garrett Eckbo, "Sculpture and Landscape Design," *Magazine of Art* (April 1938): 202. See also Id., "Small Gardens in the City," *Pencil Points* (September 1937): 573.

62. Garrett Eckbo, Daniel U. Kiley, and James C. Rose, "Landscape Design in the Urban Environment," reprinted in Treib, *Modern Landscape Architecture*, 82. For Kiley, see William S. Saunders, ed., *Daniel Urban Kiley, The Early Gardens* (New York: Princeton Architectural Press, 1999), and Kiley and Amidon, Dan Kiley: *The Complete Works of America's Master Landscape Architect.*

63. JH, *Report to the President of the University, 1938–1939,* 293.

64. Ibid. Christopher Tunnard (1910–1979) taught with Norman Newton in the summer session of 1942 a course on landscape design; Bremer Pond gave occasional lectures ("Summer School Pamphlet," 1942, LL). For Tunnard see *Who's Who in America*, 39th ed. vol. 2 (Chicago: Marquis, 1977), 3184; JH, *Report to the President of the University, 1938–1939*, 293); and Ralph Warburton, "Planner's Bio-Brief: Christopher Tunnard (1910–1979)," *Planning History Present* 4, no. 2 (1990).

65. For the MARS group, founded in February 1933 by Wells Coates, see Kenneth Frampton, *Modern Architecture: A Critical*

History (New York: Oxford University Press, 1980), 253, 271; Id., "MARS and Beyond: The British Contribution to Modern Architecture," *Architectural Association Quarterly* 2 (October 1970): 51–55; and E. Mumford, *CIAM Discourse*, passim, and especially, 77, 91–92, n. 65, 293.

66. Christopher Tunnard, *Gardens in the Modern Landscape* (London: The Architectural Press, 1938; 2nd ed., New York: Scribner, 1948). Much of the first edition appeared as a series of articles in the *Architectural Review* (London). See also Christopher Tunnard, "Modern Gardens for Modern Houses," *LA* 32 (January 1942): 57–64. Tunnard's later books included *The City of Man* (1953), *City Planning at Yale: A Selection of Papers and Projects* (1954), *American Skyline* (1955); with Vladimir Pushkarev, *Man-Made America: Chaos or Control?* (1963); *The Modern American City* (1968).

67. WC.

68. Lawrence Dame, *New England Comes Back*, introduction by Stewart H. Holbrook (New York: Random House, 1940), 229–230.

69. Ibid., 230.

70. Ibid.

71. Ibid., 213.

72. Ibid., 232.

73. JH to Frederick N. Clark, 16 November 1936, UAV322.282, Box 11, folder, F. N. Clark.

74. [Richard Elenhirt?] to WG, 2 November 1937, Gropius Papers 40/163, HL.

75. WG to Pierre Jay, 29 May 1937, Gropius Papers 40/255, HL.

76. JH to WG, 9 August 1938, Gropius Papers 40/210, 211, HL.

77. WG to JH, 9 June 1937, Gropius Papers 40/271X, HL.

78. "Bauhaus in Controversy," *New York Times*, 25 December 1938, in Nerdinger, *Gropius*, 23, n. 124.

79. Alfred Barr, Jr., to WG, 24 June 1955, Houghton ms, HL.

80. Alfred Barr to WG, 3 March 1939, cited in Nerdinger, *Gropius*, 23, n. 125.

81. "Wright and Gropius in Art Clash," *State Journal*, November 1937, cited in Nerdinger, Gropius, 23, n. 126. On Wright's attitude towards Gropius, see Edgar Tafel, *Years With Frank Lloyd Wright, Apprentice to Genius,* (New York: Dover, 1979), 66, 68.

82. Giedion, *Gropius,* 57; WC.

83. Ise Gropius, *History of the Gropius House* ([Lincoln, Mass.:] privately printed, 1977), 6, 20.

84. GHP interview and Giedion, *Gropius,* 234.

85. Schelp's explanatory comments were added to his 1938 student drawings as marginalia in 1986.

86. See "New Kensington Housing Project," *Architectural Forum* 81 (July 1944): 65–76.

87. For the response to the Torten housing, see Hans M. Wingler, *The Bauhaus,* 3d. rev. ed. (Cambridge, Mass.: MIT Press, 1978), 416.

88. I. Bayley, "New Kensington Saga," *TASK, a Magazine for Architects and Planners,* 5, 1944.

89. M. Goldwater, "What we Learned From the War," *TASK, a Magazine for Architects and Planners,* 5, 1944.

90. Abel Cutting to Harvard Board of Overseers, 11 July 1938, Conant Papers, conveyed by Harvard University archivist.

91. Jerome Greene to WG, 12 July 1938, Conant Papers, conveyed by Harvard University archivist.

92. WG to Jerome Greene, 13 July 1938, Conant Papers, conveyed by Harvard University archivist.

93. GHP interview.

94. Webel interview.

95. See Gores's obituary, Joan Cook, "Landis Gores, Architect, 71, Dies; Designer of Avant-Garde Houses," *NYT,* 20 March 1991, C19.

96. Landis Gores, "Seven Houses in Search of a Principle: An Architectural Autobiography with Pictures" ms. Chapter 3, 1. Quoted with permission of the author. Landis Gores (1920–1991) graduated Princeton University, 1939, and received his B.Arch. from the GSD in 1942 where he studied with Walter Gropius and Marcel Breuer. He was associated with Philip Johnson from 1946 until 1951.

97. Ibid.

98. John O. Simonds, *Landscape Architecture: The Shaping of Man's Natural Environ-*

ment (New York: F. W. Dodge Corp., 1961), 221.

99. Simonds, *Landscape,* 222. Dan Kiley, Simonds's colleague at Harvard, reported that an introductory course on music (Music 1) at Harvard was the most worthwhile course he took at the University (Symposium, GSD, September 1986).

100. Simonds, *Landscape,* 222.

101. For Bruno Zevi's views on his contemporary experience at Harvard, see "What We Did Not Learn," *GSD News* (Fall 1994): 41–42.

102. Simonds to Randolph Hester, 14 December 1984.

103. Seymour Howard to the author, 20 February 1986. Howard (M.Arch. 1939, GSD) taught as professor of architecture at Pratt Institute and in Marseilles, France, in addition to being an associate of Huson Jackson & Harold Edelman in New York.

104. Ibid.

105. See Gwendolyn Wright, *Building the American Dream: A Social History of Housing in America* (New York: Pantheon Books, 1981); idem, *Moralism and the Modern Home: Domestic Architecture and Cultural Conflict in Chicago 1873–1913* (Chicago: University of Chicago Press, 1980).

106. Nerdinger, *Gropius,* 272. The Frank House dates from 1939–40, and the design has been attributed to Breuer.

107. Seymour Howard to the author, 20 February 1986.

108. *Official Register,* April 23, 1940, 31–34. No *Official Register* of the GSD was published from 1941 to 1944, but courses were listed in the official catalogue of Harvard University.

109. *Graduate School of Design, Department of Regional Planning, Courses in City and Regional Planning* (Cambridge, Mass.: Harvard University, [c.1945]), 9. UAV322.138.5, GSD Dept. of City and Regional Planning, Administrative Correspondence (1907), 1945–1952.

110. Oliver, *Making of an Architect,* 144.

111. Josef Albers (1888–1976) became a major exponent of Bauhaus principles in America through his teaching, first at Black Mountain College and later at Yale. His course at Harvard was Theory and Prac-

tice of Design, Architectural Science S2a ("Summer School Announcement of 1941" folded into bound volumes of the *Official Register,* LL).

112. "Memorandum on Courses in the School of Design on the Three Term Basis," 26 April 1943, ts. folded into bound volumes of the *Official Register,* LL. Following previously announced reductions of 1940, the new program reduced the length of time required for the degree, and provided a trial run of the integrated first year. Consistent with university-wide changes, courses would be given year-round on a three-semester basis, in contrast to the usual two semesters and summer school for non-degree candidates. See also *Harvard Alumni Bulletin* (January–February 1987): 91.

113. "Memorandum on Courses in the School of Design on the Three Term Basis," 26 April 1943, 2. LL.

114. H. D. Langhorne, who had been removed from the faculty, wrote a letter of protest to the *Harvard Crimson,* 22 March 1940, HUG300.

115. Upon official retirement in 1941, Hubbard became an advisor to the Boston City Planning Board, worked in Washington with the National Capitol Park and Planning Commission, and maintained membership in the firm of the Olmsted Brothers (Office of the Chairman [Landscape Architecture Newsletter], 4 December 1944, 4 pp. ts. LL).

116. Hubbard, quoted in the *Fiftieth Anniversary Report of the Harvard Class of 1897* (1947—one year before Hubbard's death), 4.

117. GHP interview.

118. John M. Gaus, *The Education of Planners with Special Reference to the Graduate School of Design of Harvard University* (Cambridge, Mass.: GSD, 1943), 13,14. For Gaus's later views on planning education, see "Education for the Emerging Field of Regional Planning and Development," *Social Forces* 29 (March 1951): 229–237.

Lucius N. Littauer, class of 1878, provided the funds for a Faculty of Public Administration in 1936, the year of Harvard's Tercentenary. His purpose was to provide a better training than existed for men who intended to work in government and to address contemporary economic and administrative problems, but his gift was not large enough to pay for a new building and hire a separate faculty. The building, the Littauer Center for Public Administration, went up at the intersection of Massachusetts Avenue and Broadway, starting in May 1938; the faculty had to come from ranks of professors already at the University. Graham Allison, "KSG Celebrates Half Century of Public Leadership," *Harvard University Gazette* 81 (11 April 1986): 16.

119. Martin Meyerson, interview with the author, 21 August 1986. Martin Meyerson (1922– ; AB Columbia, 1942; MCP Harvard, 1949) returned to Harvard from 1957 to 1963, then continued an extremely distinguished career that has included two presidencies at the University of Pennsylvania and the State University of New York at Buffalo, the deanship of the College of Environmental Design at the University of California at Berkeley, and a brief chancellorship at Berkeley.

120. For Wurster's career, see Marc Treib, ed., *An Everyday Modernism, the Houses of William Wurster* (Berkeley: University of California Press, 1995). For Bauer, see Gwendolyn Wright, "Housing's Early Advocate," *Architecture* 89:4 (April 2000): 71, 151, a review of H. Peter Oberlander and Eva Newbrun, foreword by Martin Meyerson, *Houser: The Life and Work of Catherine Bauer, 1905–1964* (Vancouver: University of British Columbia Press, 1999).

121. Meyerson interview with the author. Meyerson, Wurster, and Bauer not only became friends, but formed a long–standing professional circle that connected the West Coast with the East: Meyerson succeeded Wurster as dean of the College of Environmental Design at Berkeley, where Bauer became Meyerson's associate dean.

122. WC, "Olmsted Lecture."

123. Eugenie L. Birch, *Macmillan Encyclopedia*, vol. IV, 451.

124. Office of the Chairman [Landscape Architecture Newsletter], 4 December 1944, 4 pp., ts. LL.

125. Newton, interview with the author, 19 November 1985.

126. Bremer Pond offered Newton the teaching position in landscape architecture at the GSD during the annual meeting of the American Society of Landscape Architects, which Newton was running in summer 1939. Newton visited Cambridge, met President Conant, and was delighted by Harvard. He commuted from his practice in New York until 1941 when Hudnut asked him to reside in Cambridge. (Norman Newton, interview with the author, 20 June 1986).

127. *Who's Who, 1977*, 3184; Office of the Chairman [Landscape Architecture Newsletter], 4 December 1944, 4 pp, ts. LL.

128. BWP to H. P. Hammond, 19 February 1943, in E. Lynn Miller, ed., *Landscape Architecture Retrospective 1943*, Norman T. Newton preface ([Pennsylvania State University]: North Central Section Pennsylvania Chapter American Society of Landscape Architects, 1975), 10. Hammond, Dean of Engineering at Pennsylvania State College, had solicited the opinion of Pond (via Hudnut) among other academics.

129. See Dorothy May Anderson, *Women, Design, and the Cambridge School* (West Lafayette, Ind.: PDA Publishers Corp., 1980). Bremer Pond taught at the Cambridge School until it was incorporated in 1924, and after joining the Board of Trustees he gave occasional instruction until the school was closed. For Pond's involvement with the Cambridge School of Architecture, see Whiting, "Necrology, Pond." Upon retiring as an emeritus in 1937, Charles Killam, the professor of architectural construction, taught in the Graduate School of Architecture and Landscape Architecture of Smith College until 1942 when the school was absorbed into the Graduate School of Design (Reginald Isaacs, et al., "Charles Wilson Killam—A Minute on his Life and Services," unpublished ts., 8 pp., 1961, LL). For the Cambridge School, see also Bremer Pond and Henry A. Frost, *The Cambridge School of Architecture and Landscape Design for Women. Bulletin No. 2,*

March 1917 (Cambridge: [the School], 1917), LL; Bremer Pond and Henry A. Frost, *Professional Instruction* ([Cambridge, Mass.: The Cambridge School of Architecture and Landscape Design for Women,] 1918), LL; "The Cambridge School of Architecture and Landscape Design for Women, Bulletin No. 9, The Summer School," 1923, LL; Doris Cole, *From Tipi to Skyscraper, a History of Women in Architecture* (Boston: i Press Inc., 1973), 78–105; and for former students, see the checklist of "The Cambridge School, Drawings and Photographs," exhibition held 29 October–14 November 1985, the Hilles Library Gallery, Radcliffe College, Cambridge, Mass. The exhibition was part of a larger exhibition, "A World of Gardens," organized by the Smith Alumnae College, 1984.

In 1932 the Cambridge School, located in a yellow colonial frame building at 53 Church Street, associated with Smith College in order to award M.Arch. and MLA degrees; the first degrees were awarded in 1934 to a group of earlier graduates of the Cambridge School. In 1938 the Cambridge School became a graduate school of Smith College, but remained so for only four years. For conditions prior to the amalgamation with Smith College, see Henry A. Frost and William R. Sear, *Women in Architecture and Landscape Architecture* (Northampton, Mass.: Smith College, [1928], 1931).

130. WC. Ruth V. Cook was born in Cambridge, Massachusetts. In 1911, she entered Radcliffe College to take special studies in Fine Arts and later graduated from the New School of Design in Boston with a specialization in interior decoration. For her career up to 1932, see Edgell, *Alumni*, 26.

The author is indebted to Christopher Hail of the Loeb Library whose typescript history (21 September 1981) of the library is the basis for factual material in this discussion.

131. The founding of the Society of Architectural Historians occurred in the Harvard Faculty club. See Marian C. Donnelly, *A History, Society of Architectural Histori-*

ans, 1940–1995 (Eugene: School of Architecture and Allied Arts at the University of Oregon, 1998); and *The Architectural Historian in America*, Elizabeth Blair McDougall, ed. (series, Studies in the History of Art, v. 35; Washington, D.C.: National Gallery of Art, 1990).

132. Theodora Kimball Hubbard died in 1935. McNamara had joined the staff of the landscape architecture and planning library in 1918. She and Ruth Cook continued as librarians of dual collections, despite the unification of the Graduate School of Design, until the libraries merged in 1956 when Cook retired. McNamara continued as librarian until her retirement in 1963. Caroline Shillaber, who had been assistant librarian from 1931 to 1951 and then at MIT to 1963, succeeded her as chief librarian until 1975. Angela Giral assumed the post from 1975 to 1981. Successive librarians include James Hodgson, Hinda Sklar, and Hugh Wilbourn.

133. Edgell, *Alumni*, 28–29.

134. Shillaber, *MIT*, 34. Even the crusty Charles Killam had early on observed a bias against the admission of women: President Lowell opposed allowing women to take even summer courses in the school. Charles Wilson Killam, ms. note of conversation with President Lowell, 9 April 1919, UAV322.7, Box 1.

135. *Official Register, 1940*, 41. See also supplement of summer school courses folded into the register.

136. Anderson, *The Cambridge School*, 151.

137. Henry A. Frost, [Letter] to the Editor, LA 32:3 (April 1942): 119.

138. See Dorothy May Anderson, "The Cambridge Connection: The Creation and Demise of a Smith Graduate School," *Smith Alumnae Quarterly* (Fall 1986): 22–26.

139. Office of the Chairman [Landscape Architecture Newsletter], 4 December 1944, LL.

140. "Report of the Committee to Visit the Graduate School of Design, No. 4," *Reports of the Committees to Visit Harvard College* 1943, 25–27. UAII36.3.

141. Ibid., 26.

142. For Wright at Harvard, see Anthony Alofsin, review of *The Architecture of Frank Lloyd Wright* by Neil Levine, Princeton University Press, 1996, in *Harvard Design Magazine* (Summer 1997): 76–77.

143. Two versions of the document exist: [JH], "Training the Architect at the Harvard School of Design, Exhibition in New York 1941," and "Outline for Exhibition in New York. Third Draft. February 4, 1941," UAV319.322.7. Records of the Office of the Dean, Subseries II, Box 25.

144. *Bauhaus, 1918–1928*, Herbert Bayer, Walter Gropius, Ise Gropius, eds. (New York: Museum of Modern Art, 1938).

145. JH, "Training the Architect," 2.

146. JH, "Outline for Exhibition in New York. Third Draft," 11.

147. Ibid., 24.

148. Ibid., 25.

149. *An Opinion on Architecture* [Cambridge, Mass.: N.P.] May 1941. Signers of the document (p. 16) were John B. Bayley, Arthur K. H. Cheang, William Joseph, John T. Moore, Jr., Warren H. Radford, Frank C. Treseder, Robert H. Rosenberg, Dahong Wang, T. J. Willo, and Bruno Zevi.

150. Ibid., 2.

151. Ibid.

152. Ibid., 5. See Frampton, *Modern Architecture*, 159.

153. Ibid., 8.

154. "Report of the Committee to Visit the Graduate School of Design, No. 4," *Reports of the Committees to Visit Harvard College 1943*, 25. HU36.3. The Visiting Committee met on 14 December 1942 and submitted its report on 12 April 1943.

155. Ibid. The GSD's budget for instruction included as of 10 December 1942: Architecture, $43,454; Landscape Architecture, $23,631; Regional Planning, $18,734; and in Harvard College $21,070.

156. "[GSD] Summer School Pamphlet, 1942," 7. LL.

157. Ibid., 10.

158. Cornelius Dalton, "Profile of a Dreamer Who Makes his Dreams Bloom into Reality," *Boston Herald*, 14 June 1942, B1.

159. Ibid.

160. Marcel Breuer to WG and subsequent replies, in Houghton mss. 48/107, 108, 109 (23 May 1941), HL.

161. Walter Gropius and Martin Wagner, "A Program for City Reconstruction," *Architectural Forum* 79 (July 1943): 75–82.

162. Seventy-seventh U.S. Congress. First Session of the House. *National Defense Migration*, XVII, 1941, 6949–6956.

163. For the report, see *The New City Pattern for the People and by the People* ([Cambridge, Mass.: n. p.], 1942), 95–116.

164. Martin Wagner to WG, 8 September, 1940, ms.131/storage, HL.

165. Ibid. Gropius's interest in mass production of housing began as early as 1909 when he was working under Behrens. Experiments in prefabrication included the Torten Housing near Dessau of 1926–29 where there was some use of prefabricated parts with major emphasis on the coordination of building processes. In his Weissenhof exhibition house, 1927, Gropius experimented with construction technology. At Hirsch, in 1931, for the Kupfer-und Messingwerke Gropius proposed a prefabricated copper house that Wagner included in his *Das Wachsende Haus*. See Giedion, *Gropius*, 74–78, 81.

166. Wilhelm von Moltke, interview with the author, 21 November 1980, Cambridge, Mass. See Gilbert Herbert, *The Dream of the Factory-Made House: Walter Gropius and Konrad Wachsman* (Cambridge, Mass.: MIT Press, 1984); Giedion, *Gropius*, 74–78; Wilhelm von Moltke, "Prefabricated Panels for Packaged Building," *AR* 93 (April 1943): 50–53; Nerdinger, *Gropius*, 312.

167. Giedion, *Gropius*, 76.

168. Willo von Moltke, interview with the author, 25 May 1986.

169. Giedion, *Gropius*, 77.

170. William Jordy, "The Aftermath of the Bauhaus: Gropius, Mies, Breuer," in Donald Fleming and Bernard Bailyn, *The Intellectual Migration: Europe and America 1930–1960* (Cambridge, Mass.: Belknap Press of Harvard University Press, 1969), 523.

171. "Summer School Pamphlet, 1942," 10.

172. Martin Wagner, "The Boston Contest," 2 vol. ms. [1944], Martin Wagner Papers, LL. For a short notice on the event, see "Boston Looks Ahead," *Architectural Forum* 82 (January 1945): 18, 22.

173. Nerdinger, *Gropius*, 286.

174. For Bogner's scheme, see lantern slide X146.2/h3, LL.

175. The program, "The Post-War Shelter for the Average Family," given from 1 February to 18 March 1943, was the third problem in Architecture 2d, LL.

176. Marcel Breuer, "A Redevelopment Problem (Boston South End), Problem V, Arch. 2c, 6 March 1944 to Wed. April 19," ts. program, LL.

177. JH, "Harvard University," in "Symposium: Philosophies Underlying the Teaching in our Schools of Architecture," *Octagon* 13, no. 2 (February 1941), 16.

178. JH, "Education and Architecture," *AR* 92:4 (October 1942): 36–37.

179. Ibid., 37.

180. Ibid.

181. Ibid., 38.

182. Ibid.

183. Ibid., 90.

Chapter 6

1. JH, "Forum," *AR* 83:5 (November 1945): 48.

2. *Official Register 1945–46.*

3. See "Graduate School of Design, Description of Courses Preparatory to the Professional Training in Architecture, Landscape Architecture, and City and Regional Planning," Cambridge, Mass.: Harvard University, n.d. [1945/46], UAV 322.138.5, GSE Department of City and Regional Planning, Administration and Correspondence (1907) 1945–52.

4. See Norman T. Newton, "Professional Training of Landscape Architects at Harvard," *LA* 39:4 (July 1949): 181–183.

5. By 1948–49, a full complement of bachelor's and master's degrees in all of the fields was reinstituted, including Master of City Planning (MCP) and Master of Regional Planning (MRP).

6. For the faculty roster, see *Official Register 1944–1945*, 27–28. Hugh A. Stubbins, Jr. (1912–), BA, Georgia Institute of Technology, saw his career at Harvard span from one major transition to the next: He was one of a handful of students trained in the traditional program, who successfully pursued the philosophy of Gropius and absorbed conceptions of scale, siting, and architectonic expression from Marcel Breuer. During his twelve-year teaching career at the GSD, Stubbins became associate professor in 1946 and was designated chairman of the Department of Architecture in 1953, the year of transition to the deanship of José Luis Sert and Stubbins's last year of teaching at Harvard. See Dianne M. Ludman, *Hugh Stubbins and His Associates: The First Fifty Years*, catalog for exhibition held at the GSD 30 September–17 October 1986 (Cambridge, Mass.: The Stubbins Associates in collaboration with Harvard University Graduate School of Design, 1986); Susan Strauss, "Stubbins, Hugh Asher, Jr.," *Macmillan Encyclopedia*, vol. IV, 146–147; and *Who's Who*, 41st ed. (1980–88), vol. 2, 3210.

7. Walter Chambers (BLA Ohio State University, 1929; MLA Harvard, 1932) was a trustee of the American Society of Landscape Architects and had been a vice president of the Boston Society of Landscape Architects until he resigned in 1943 due to a heavy workload.

8. Edward K. True (1915– ; S.B. Architectural Engineering MIT 1939) taught architectural engineering at the GSD for the next thirty-one years. He became professor of architecture in 1958 and taught until 1976. As a partner in the engineering firm of Souza and True, he collaborated in a professional capacity from 1959 on mainly with José Luis Sert, True's dean at the GSD. See *Who's Who*, 43d ed. (Chicago: Marquis, 1985), vol. 2, 3296.

Dean Peabody, Jr., (1888–1951) was a pioneer in the testing of concrete for building and wrote the standard text, *Design of Reinforced Concrete Structures*. After graduating from MIT he taught there for more than thirty-five years. He began teaching at Harvard as a visiting lecturer in 1946 and became professor of architecture in 1947. See "The Record Reports," *AR* 110 (September 1951): 246.

9. Charles H. Burchard (1914– ; B.Arch. MIT, 1938; M.Arch. GSD, 1940) taught at Harvard from 1946 to 1953. Burchard combined private practice with teaching, as did many graduates of the GSD, and spread the influence of the school when he became from 1964–1981 dean of the College of Architecture and Urban Studies at the Virginia Polytechnical Institute and State University. See *Who's Who*, 43d ed. (Chicago: Marquis, 1985), vol.1, 452.

10. For John C. Harkness (1916– ; AB 1938, B.Arch. 1941, M.Arch. 1941, Harvard) and the formation of TAC and its work, see *The Architects Collaborative Inc.* (Barcelona: Editorial Gustavo Gili, S.A., 1966).

11. Leonard J. Currie (M.Arch. Harvard, 1938) apprenticed with Gropius and Breuer, 1938–40. He returned to Harvard to teach from 1946 until 1951 during which time he also worked at TAC. He subsequently became professor and head of the Department of Architecture at the Virginia Polytechnical Institute from 1956 to 1962, thus preceding his Harvard College and former classmate, Charles Burchard. Currie was also dean of the College of Architecture and Art at University of Illinois from 1962 to 1972. See *Who's Who*, 43d ed., vol. 1, 730.

12. On Pei's early career, see "Pei, I. M." *Macmillan Encyclopedia*, vol. 3, 384–386. Chester E. Nagel (M.Arch. 1940, Harvard) worked at TAC and then set up his own office in 1958, which sought to carry on the concept of collaboration. Nagel returned to teaching and became an adjunct professor of architecture at the University of Colorado, Denver. See "Personalities," *Progressive Architecture* 42:6 (June 1961): 75.

13. Chester E. Nagel, "What's Wrong with the Institute?" *Journal of the A.I.A.* 7 (May 1947): 253.

14. "Personalities," *Progressive Architecture* 42:6 (June 1961): 75.

15. Jean Paul Carlhian (1919–), born in Paris, received the Bachelières Lettres, University of Paris, in 1936, and was made Architect Diplomé par le Gouvernement in 1948. At Harvard, upon conclusion of his planning degree he won the Wheelwright Traveling Fellowship. He taught at Harvard until 1955 and returned to teach as a visiting critic at the GSD and other schools of architecture. His practice centered at the Boston firm of Shepley, Bulfinch, Richardson and Abbott (*Who's Who*, 43d ed., vol. 1, 511)

16. JH, "What a Planner Has to Know. I," *Planning* 1946, Proceedings of the Annual Meeting Held in New York City 6–8 May 1946, American Society of Planning Officials (Chicago: ASPO, 1946), 157–163, 160 quoted. The speech was reprinted in JH, *Architecture and the Spirit of Man* (Cambridge, Mass.: Harvard University Press, 1949), 196–205.

17. Ibid., 162.

18. See JH, "Housing and the Democratic Process," *AR* (June 1943), reprinted in *Architecture and the Spirit of Man*, 278–288.

19. Martin D. Meyerson, "What a Planner Has to Know. III," in *Planning* 1946, Proceedings of the Annual Meeting Held in New York City 6–8 May 1946, American Society of Planning Officials (Chicago: ASPO, 1946), 167–172. At the time of his speech, Meyerson (MCP Harvard 1949) was associate planner of the Michael Reese Hospital Planning Staff in Chicago. He became president and university professor at the University of Pennsylvania.

20. Ibid., 170.

21. GHP interview.

22. Perkins hired Edward L. Ullman, a geographer interested in the location of cities and railroads, as assistant professor of regional planning. For Ullman's approach to planning issues, see Edward Ullman, "A Theory of Location for Cities," *American Journal of Sociology* 46:6 (May 1941): 853–864; and Id., "The Railroad Pattern of the United States," *The Geographical Review* 39:2 (April 1949): 242–256. Ullman later became professor of geography at the University of Washington.

    Perkins also hired William L. C. Wheaton who had extensive experience in the federal housing service, the Housing and Home Finance Agency. For his role, see *Journal of Housing* 5:9 (September 1948): 258; and Ibid. 20:9 (1963): 497.

23. For Perkins's planning program, see *Graduate School of Design, Department of Regional Planning, Courses in City and Regional Planning* (Cambridge, Mass.: Harvard University, 1945), UAV322. 138.5, GSD Dept. City and Regional Planning, Administrative Correspondence (1907) 1945–1952; 5 quoted.

24. GHP, "The Architect and City Planning," Technical Reference Guide No. 1, Department of Education and Research, *Bulletin of the American Institute of Architects* (March 1948): 17–20, including a comprehensive bibliography on city planning, compiled by Katherine McNamara, librarian, Department of Regional Planning, Harvard Graduate School of Design, 21–32.

25. *Regional Planning* 1945, 5.

26. Ibid.

27. See [William L. C. Wheaton], "Brief Biographical Information of 19 Planners," [1953] ts., LL; *Official Register 1948–1949*, LL. For other members of the Council of the Department of Regional Planning, see *Regional Planning* 1945, 3.

28. GHP interview.

29. The degree of Bachelor of City Planning required as a prerequisite an AB or SB degree. Six terms of study and an internship in a local, state, or national planning agency were required for the BCP; students who had concentrated in the appropriate program in Harvard College's Department of Architectural Sciences could receive advanced standing. For the degree of Master in City and Regional Planning, prerequisites included the BCP, a Master's degree in a social science, or their equivalent, and at least one of practical experience with a planning agency. Two terms of study were required for the degree. The Ph.D. in Regional Planning required a minimum of two years of additional study, one of which was spent in residency, a reading knowledge of French and German, general examinations, a thesis, and a final examination. A Ph.D. in technical research in architecture, landscape architecture, and city planning had been instituted in 1942. Advanced research for students pursuing the MCRP or the Ph.D. in Regional Planning was directed by Perkins, Bogner, and other members of the council.

30. GHP interview.

31. Catherine Bauer assumed the course in 1946–47 and lectured on housing through 1949 (*Official Register 1948–1949*).

32. "Report of the Committee to Visit the

Graduate School of Design, No. 4," *Reports of the Committees to Visit Harvard College 1946*, 25. HU36.

33. David A. Wallace to the author, 28 April 1986. Wallace (MCP 1950, Ph.D. Planning 1953, Harvard) was a student of Wagner, Holmes Perkins, and William H. C. Wheaton.

34. Norman Newton, "Professional Training of Landscape Architects at Harvard," *LA* 39:4 (July 1949): 181–183, 182 quoted.

35. Ibid., 183.

36. The group's thesis was submitted 18 November 1949 in satisfaction of the architects' Bachelor degree requirements, and McHarg's requirements for the Master of Landscape Architecture. LL.

37. "Collaborative Thesis Program," [June 1950] TS. in personal correspondence, William Conklin to Polly Price, 4 August 1987.

38. Christopher Tunnard, *Gardens in the Modern Landscape* (London: The Architectural Press, 1948), 12; and Mies van der Rohe, "An Appreciation of Frank Lloyd Wright," in Philip C. Johnson, *Mies Van der Rohe* (New York: The Museum of Modern Art, 1948), 195, cited in McHarg, "Thesis," D1–2. For Hudnut's essays, see JH, *Architecture and the Spirit of Man* (Cambridge, Mass.: Harvard University Press; and London: Geoffrey Cumberlege, Oxford University Press, 1949).

39. See Ian L. McHarg, *Design with Nature* (Garden City, N.Y.: American Museum of Natural History and the Natural History Press, 1969); *A Quest for Life: An Autobiography* (New York: John Wiley, 1996); and *Selections, 1998, To Heal the Earth: The Selected Writings of Ian L. McHarg* (Washington, D.C.: Island Press, 1998).

40. Sam T. Hurst, "Revelation, Reason, and Reaction: A Memoir on Gropius and the Bauhaus," prepared statement presented at the GSD 26 April 1997. My thanks to the author for providing a copy of his comments.

41. S.S.H., "Faculty Profile," *Harvard Crimson*, 25 April 1947, 4.

42. "The Yard and its Architecture," *Harvard Alumni Bulletin* 48:12 (1946): 478.

43. Ibid., 475.

44. Ibid. For Gropius's support of Dorner, see

Gropius, An Illustrated Biography, 239, 245.

45. "The Yard and its Architecture," 475.
46. "Harvard University, Department of Architecture, Bulletin," John Holabird, Henry Cobb, Ira Kessler, Claude Stoller, and Marvin Severly, eds. [no. 4], Cambridge, Mass., 1947–1948. LL.
47. McHarg, *Quest for Life*, excerpted in HGSD News (Winter/Summer 1996): 44–47, 44 quoted. McHarg's recollections of studying at Harvard from 1946 through 1950 were appreciative—his classmates were prodigious and mature—but trenchant. He claimed that he had to "teach at Pennsylvania for over thirty years to complete the education that Harvard so expensively denied" him (45).
48. "GSD Bulletin," Philip H. Dole, ed. 1:7 (March 1948), n.p. LL.
49. KJC to WC (WC).
50. "GSD Bulletin," Philip H. Dole, ed. 1:7 (March 1948), n.p. LL.
51. Edward Larabee Barnes (1915–) was born in Chicago, received his SB 1938 and M.Arch. 1942 from the GSD, and started his independent practice in New York in 1949.
52. See "The Sky Line," *The New Yorker*, 11 October 1947, and reports on the symposium "What Has Happened to Modern Architecture," held 11 February 1948, *Museum of Modern Art Bulletin* 35 (Spring 1948): 3. On the debates about regionalism, see Anthony Alofsin, Liane Lefaivre, and Alexander Tzonis, "Die Frage des Regionalismus," in *Für eine andere Architektur. Bauen mit der Natur in der Region* (Frankfurt am Main: Fisher Taschenbuch Verlag, 1981), vol. 1, 121–134.
53. "GSD Bulletin," Philip H. Dole, ed., 1:7 (March 1948). LL. The author signed his review RDT. Breuer's comments were noted by Walter Creese (WC).
54. *American Building* News, 485, clipping, LL.
55. WG, "Teaching the Arts of Design," January 1948, inserted into the "GSD Bulletin" 1:7 (13 March 1948). LL.
56. Hudnut received a Western Union telegram from the President's Office confirming his appointment and advising him to keep the information private for the time being. Matthew J. Connelly (Secretary to President Harry S. Truman) to JH, 16 February 1950, private collection.
57. Blanche Lemco and Elva Marshall, eds., *Symposium I. Debunk: A Critical Review of Accepted Planning Principles* (The Council for Planning Action, [1950]), transcript of the symposium held at Littauer Center, Harvard University, 7 May 1949. Blanche Lemco VanGinkle graduated Harvard MCP 1950. The symposium was a joint event of students and faculty from MIT and Harvard's Graduate School of Design and the School of Public Administration.
58. Speakers on regional issues were Hans Blumenfeld, Chief of Planning Analysis Division, Philadelphia Planning Commission; John M. Gaus; George K. Zipf, lecturer at Harvard and author of *Human Behavior and the Principle of Least Effort*; and Martin Wagner. Respondents to local issues were Catherine Bauer, author of *Modern Housing* and GSD lecturer; Paul and Percival Goodman, the brothers teaching at Columbia who had written *Commmunitas*; Sven Markelius, architect and chief city planner of Stockholm; and José Luis Sert.
59. For a brief biographical synopsis, see "Sert, Josep Lluis" (1902–1983), *Macmillan Encyclopedia*, vol. 4, 40–41; Paul Goldberger, "Josep L. Sert, 80, Architect, was Harvard Dean of Design," *New York Times* (17 March 1983); and the comprehensive study, Josep M. Rovira, *Jose Luis Sert 1901–1983* (Milan: Electa, 2000). For Sert's extensive involvement with CIAM, see E. Mumford, *CIAM Discourse*, passim. For José Luis Sert, *Can our Cities Survive?* (Cambridge, Mass.: Harvard University Press, 1942), see E. Mumford, *CIAM Discourse*, 116, 134.
60. *L'Architecture d'aujourd'hui* 20 (February 1950), special issue titled "Walter Gropius—The Spread of an Idea." Gropius's text, entitled "Blueprint for an Architect's Training," was the subject of an exhibition, "GSD Design Education: Gropius Era and Current Methods," curated by Margaret B. Reeve and held at the Graduate School of Design, 5–22 October 1982.
61. The students working on the collaborative problem were Robert Bergman, Amy Garber, Robert Geddes, Alford Griese, James Harris, Roscoe Jones, Peter Kitchell, Charles Mansfield, and Russell Myers. *L'Architecture d'aujourd'hui* 20 (February 1950): 84.
62. Ibid.
63. Henry Cobb, interview with the author, 6 April 1985.
64. "Harvard Portraits—55," *Harvard Alumni Bulletin* 52 (8 April 1950): 534.

Chapter 7

1. JH, "The Art in Housing," AR (January 1943) reprinted in JH, *Architecture and the Spirit of Man*, 265–277. The original article included sketches by Wilhelm von Moltke, who had graduated M.Arch. in 1942 from the masters class and who would return to teach urban design at the GSD. See also JH, "Love and Little Houses," *House and Garden* (May 1947): 76–77, 161–166; reprinted, idem, 120–132.
2. Ibid.
3. Id., "The Art in Housing," n.p. offprint. For the special case of expression of modern architecture in churches, see Joseph Hudnut, "Picture, Sentiment, and Symbol: Some Comments on Modern Church Architecture," AR (September 1944), reprinted in *Architecture and the Spirit of Man*, 69–79.
4. JH, "The Post-Modern House," AR (May 1945), reprinted in Lewis Mumford, *Roots of Contemporary Architecture* (New York: Reinhold, 1952), 306–315, 425–426.
5. Perkins, "Interview."
6. Jean Paul Carlhian, interview with the author, 5 September 1986.
7. Perkins, "Interview."
8. *Official Catalogue 1950–51*, vol. 47, 19.
9. Martin Meyerson, interview with the author, 21 August 1986.
10. Coleman Woodbury (1903–1994) held several important administrative positions at the National Association of Housing Officials and the National Housing Agency during the 1930s and 40s. In addition to the chairmanship, Woodbury became the Charles Dyer Norton Professor of Regional Planning. See [William L.C. Wheaton (?)], "Brief Biographical

Information on Nineteen Planners," ts. 14 January 1953, LL; and "Coleman Wood-bury," *Journal of Housing* 14:6 (June 1957): 190.

11. For Fletcher, see TAC 1945–1972, 322. For Thompson, see *Contemporary Architects* (1980), 814–816.

12. For proposed alterations to the core curriculum in 1951–52, see *Official Register 1951–1952*, corrected edition (Copy 2), 16, LL.

13. Pearlman, "Joseph Hudnut's Other Modernism," 469–474. For illustrations of typical work of Design Fundamentals course in 1951, see Figs. 13, 14, p. 473.

14. JH to Richard Filipowski, 20 June 1950. Courtesy of Richard Filipowski. Filipowski (1923–) was born in Poland, but emigrated to Canada age four with his family. He studied under László Moholy-Nagy at the Institute of Design 1942–46 and taught there after graduating, 1946–50. After his brief stint at Harvard, he pursued a career as an artist, designer, filmmaker, and educator, teaching in the Department of Architecture at MIT, 1953–89. Smithsonian Institution Research Information System, www.siris.si.edu, 30 July 2000; Richard Filipowski, interview with the author, 27 July 2000.

15. WG to Richard Filipowski, 3 July 1950. Courtesy of Richard Filipowksi.

16. The catalog's cover was a sheet of colored construction paper, with openings cut to reveal text on the following page, showcasing the typography. Exhibition catalog, "Design Fundamentals, Harvard University, 1952," Lucia Atwood, designer. UAV322.138, "GSD Correspondence and Papers of the Department of City and Regional Planning, 1928–57." Although primarily for graduate students, the Design Fundamentals course in the GSD was open to undergraduates as Architectural Sciences 201ab.

17. Ibid., n.p.

18. Richard Filipowski, interview with the author, 27 July 2000.

19. Gordon Allen, "Translate!," *Journal of the American Institute of Architects* 17:5 (May 1952): 236, commenting on the course description reprinted from the *Harvard Alumni Bulletin* (5 March 1952).

20. "A Beginning Curriculum for the Harvard Graduate School of Design. Report of a Committee to Study the First-Year Curriculum," George T. LeBoutillier, chairman, 20 May 1952. UAV322.6 GSD Faculty Meeting Minutes 1912–66. In addition to LeBoutillier, the other members of the committee were Charles Burchard (Architecture), Jean Paul Carlhian (Planning), Lester A. Collins (Landscape), and William L. C. Wheaton (Planning).

21. The following instructors attended the faculty meeting of 28 May: Hudnut, Gropius, Conant, Bogner, Woodbury, Chambers, Newton, Wheaton, True, LeBoutillier, Collins, Lyman, Sasaki, Filipowski, Hicken, Fletcher, and Bagnall. "Faculty of Design: Minutes of Meeting 28 May 1952," UAV 322.6 GSD Faculty Meeting Minutes 1912–66.

22. *Endowment Funds of Harvard University June 30, 1947* (Cambridge, Mass.: The University, 1947), 201.

23. Anon., "Walter Gropius," *American Building News* 202 (23 October 1952): 485; and "People . . . ," *Architectural Forum* 97:1 (July 1952): 59. Richard Filipowski, instructor in design, was reported to be transferring to MIT as an assistant professor; Norman C. Fletcher, assistant in architecture, was returning to The Architect's Collaborative to practice with Gropius and their associates.

24. Norman Newton, interview with the author, 19 November 1985.

25. *Architectural Forum* 97:1 (1952): 59.

26. "Changes in Course Offerings: An Amendment to the Pamphlet of the Harvard Graduate School of Design for 1950–51 (*Official Register of Harvard University*, XLVII, no. 19)" [August 1952], folded into *Official Register*, LL.

27. Ibid.

28. *Official Catalogue 1950–1951*, corrected for 1952–53 (copy 2), LL. Further departures included Stephen Hamblin, who retired without tenure or emeritus status, and Hideo Sasaki. Added to the faculty for the departures were Robert M. Becker, as instructor in Building Construction, and Perry L. Norton, instructor in City Planning.

29. "Decadent Design," *Harvard Crimson* (26 November 1952); "Decadent Design: II,"

30. "Decadent Design," ibid.

31. "Faculty of Design: Minutes of Meeting of 24 November 1952," 1–6. UAV322.6, Faculty Meeting Minutes, 1912–66. In attendance, in addition to President Conant, were Bogner, Woodbury, Chambers, Stubbins, Newton, Wheaton, True, LeBoutillier, Burchard, Collins, Lyman, Carlhian, with Hudnut and Kenneth Conant noted as absent.

32. Ibid., 4.

33. William J. Conklin, Louis P. Dolbeare, Robert L. Geddes, et al., "To the Alumni of the Graduate School of Design," 10 December 1951, ts, 5 pp. LL.

34. "Faculty of Design: Minutes of Meeting of 6 January 1953," UAV322.6 GSD Faculty Meeting Minutes, 1912–66.

35. Jerzy Soltan, interview with the author, 19 June 1986; reiterated in E. Mumford, *CIAM Discourse*, 238. The actual selection process and short list of nominees, however, remains unconfirmed by documentary evidence.

36. "A Dean for Design," *Harvard Alumni Bulletin* (7 February 1953), 2 pp, LL.

37. Isaacs, "Sert, Josep Lluis," *Macmillan Encyclopedia*, vol. 4, 40.

38. "Harvard University, School of Design, Announcement of Recent Changes," 1 July 1953, 3 pp. LL.

39. The following were listed as still having appointments: Walter F. Bogner, Charles H. Burchard, Jean Paul Carlhian, Walter L. Chambers, Norman T. Newton, Hugh A. Stubbins, Jr., and Edward True. The following had their yearly appointments renewed: Robert M. Becker, August L. Hesselschwerdt, and Philip B. Hicken. "Faculty of Design: Minutes of Meeting of 6 January 1953," UAV322.6, GSD Faculty Meeting Minutes, 1912–66. Kenneth Conant was scheduled for leave in 1953–54.

40. "People: Chermayeff and Isaacs Get Key Harvard Design Posts . . . ," *Architectural Forum* 98:5 (May 1953): 43, 46, 43 quoted.

41. Walter F. Bogner, "Harvard's Faculty" [letter to editor], *Architectural Forum* 99:1 (July 1953): 78.

ibid. (28 November 1952), n.p. clipping, LL.

295

42. At least one of Hudnut's years at Colby College was sponsored by a grant from the John Hay Whitney Foundation in New York, which provided funds for small liberal arts colleges to hire distinguished, retired scholars to supplement their faculty (private collection: clipping, n.p. *Time* magazine, 1954).

43. Elizabeth (Betty) Deviney, interview with the author 25 July 1993; and Elizabeth Deviney to the author, 27 April 1993.

44. Among the papers in Hudnut's archive are JH, foreword to *A Half Century of Architectural Education,* traveling exhibition of work of the alumni of the School of Architecture, George Institute of Technology, covering the years from 1910 through 1956, organized in recognition of the service and contributions to the School of Harold Bush-Brown and former directors (Atlanta: School of Architecture, Georgia Institute of Technology, 1956); Id., "Civic Design in the Renaissance," in *Student Publication of the School of Design, North Carolina State College, Raleigh, North Carolina* 7:1 (1957): 3–26, text of his lecture given at the school, November, 1956; Ibid., "On Teaching the History of Architecture," *JAE* 12:2 (summer 1957): 6–8; Id., "Aesthetics and Architecture," in *Proceedings of the Teachers' Seminar Held under the Auspices of the Joint ACSA-AIA Committee on the Teaching of Architecture,* Aspen, 1957: 5–9; Id., "The Anticipation of Order, *JAE* 13:2 (Autumn 1958): 21–25; Id., "Architect and Engineer," *Student Publication of the School of Design, North Carolina State College, Raleigh, North Carolina* 10:2 (n.d. [1961/62]): 29–35. Hudnut also kept the competition program for which he had been a juror: *Program for Franklin Delano Roosevelt Memorial Competition 1960* (Washington, D.C.: Frank Delano Roosevelt Memorial Commission, 1960).

45. Henry N. Cobb, interview with the author, 4 April 1986.

46. Ibid.

47. "Faculty of Design, A Memorial Minute, Walter Gropius 1883–1969," Reginald R. Isaacs, et al., *Harvard Gazette,* 24 October 1969; reprinted in *More Lives of Harvard Scholars,* collected and arranged by William Bentinck-Smith and Elizabeth Stouffer (Cambridge, Mass.: Harvard University, 1986), 147–153.

48. Robert C. Weinberg, "Dean Hudnut's Dream" [Letter to editor], *Harvard Alumni Bulletin* 70:8 (3 February 1968), 48. Weinberg was responding to the error printed in the *Bulletin* dated 11 November 1967, page 21. Weinberg (Harvard College Class of 1923, student at the School of Architecture, 1926–31) was former chairman of the GSD Alumni Council and communicated with Hudnut in 1936 as the new GSD was taking form. Christiane Crasemann Collins kindly pointed out the connection between Weinberg and Hudnut to the author.

49. Ian McHarg, *A Quest for Life,* excerpted in HGSD News (Winter/Spring 1996): 44.

50. JH to Mrs. Rudolph [Katherine] Stanley-Brown, 17 January 1936, UAV319.322.7, Records of the Office of the Dean, Subseries I B, Hudnut 1932–42, Box 5.

51. Perkins, "Interview"; and Isaacs, "Gropius— A Memorial Minute."

52. KJC, "Interview." Though he was fond of Gropius and Gropius very much supported him, Richard Filipowski made the same claim about Gropius's aloofness. He recalled Gropius in referring to his architect forebears, saying, "I am from the Prussian family" (Filipowski, interview with the author, 27 July 2000).

53. Perkins, "Interview."

54. WC, personal communication with the author, memo, 1 October 1999.

55. For projects and designs by TAC from 1946 up to 1949, see *The Architects Collaborative Inc. 1945–1972.* Barcelona: Editorial Gustavo Gili, S.A., 1966. See also Michiko Sakae, ed., *TAC: The Architects Collaborative: The Heritage of Walter Gropius. Process, Architecture,* no. 19 (Westfield, N.Y.: Eastview Editions, 1980).

56. Filipowski interview.

57. Jordy, "Aftermath," 521.

58. Meyerson interview.

59. Mies to Henry Heald, 10 December 1937, quoted in Harrington, "Order, Space, Proportion," 56. For Mies's German colleague in Chicago, see Kevin Harrington, ed., *In the Shadow of Mies: Ludwig Hilberseimer, Architect, Educator, and Urban Planner* (Chicago: Art Institute, 1988).

60. Soltan interview.

61. For typical polemic views of Gropius's attitudes towards history, see Herdeg, *Decorated Diagram,* and Wolfe, *From Bauhaus to Our House.*

62. Jean Paul Carlhian and Henry Cobb, interview with the author, 5 September 1986. Walter L. Shouse (director, Division of Planning and Zoning, Kentucky) to JH, 13 June 1963; Rodney E. Engelen to JH, 27 July 1964. Private collection.

63. WC interview.

64. WC, memo.

65. JH, "On the Teaching the History of Architecture," *JAE* 12:6 (Summer 1957), 6–8, 6 and 8, quoted. Hudnut's remarks are also discussed in Graeme McConchie, "Under Reconstruction: History in Architectural Education 1930s–1960s," *Proceedings of the Annual Meeting of SAHANZ* (Society of Architectural Historians of Australia and New Zealand) (Melbourne: The Society, 1998), 239–244.

66. Jean Paul Carlhian, interview with the author, 5 September 1986.

67. Cobb interview.

68. Cornelius Dalton, "Profile of a Dreamer Who Makes his Dreams Bloom into Reality," *Boston Herald,* 14 June 1942, B1.

69. Ibid.

70. "Walter Gropius—The Spread of an Idea," *L'Architecture d'aujourd'hui* 28 (February 1950). Special issue that contains Gropius's "Blueprint for an Architect's Education," 71–74.

71. WG, "When and How Should the Architect Study the Past," *Revue de l'Union Internationale des Architects,* no. 33 (1965): 31, 33, 35, 37; 35 and 37 quoted.

72. WC, memo.

73. KJC, interview with the author, 3 March 1979.

74. Courses in art, art history, and architectural history were jointly listed in the Division of Fine Arts and the predecessor schools of design. The definition of Fine Arts included theory and practice, that is, history of art, the theory of design, and applied study in the lessons of drawing and painting. Professors Paul Sachs and Edward W. Forbes ushered in a new emphasis in which the study of Fine Arts took place in the equivalent of a scientific laboratory and their goals became training not only teachers but also curators and museum directors for the rest of the country: Sachs had conducted work in the x-ray analysis of painting with the results that the university had the largest collection of shadow prints, and Forbes had begun new analytical approaches to art with his course, Methods and Process of Painting, which reflected his interest in the techniques of Italian primitives. See Caroline A. Jones, *Modern Art at Harvard: The Formation of the Nineteenth- and Twentieth-Century Collections of the Harvard University Art Museums* (New York: Abbeville Press; Cambridge: Harvard University Art Museums, 1985), 31–57, for the transformations of the pedagogical program at the Fogg Museum from 1915 to 1948.

To reinvigorate Fine Arts further and to support academic rationalism, the university sought new minds. In Germany it found Wilhelm Koehler, a specialist in medieval manuscripts whose appointment in 1935 paralleled Hudnut's. Koehler later became the first director of Dumbarton Oaks, the research center in Washington, D.C. Harvard's efforts to transform art history were strengthened by the appointment of a second German professor of art history, Jakob Rosenberg, an expert on Rembrandt who came to the Fogg Museum in 1939. Both Koehler and Rosenberg brought rigorous and scientific methods with them. John Rosenfeld, *Modern Art at Harvard*, 8. (Rosenfeld also erroneously states that Gropius was dean of the GSD.)

75. John Coolidge, interview with the author, 28 June 1986.

76. For a summary of the visual arts and the formation of the Department of Architectural Sciences at Harvard, see Eduard F. Sekler, "Introduction," –, 4–6.

77. GHP interview.

Chapter 8

1. Faculty of Design, Minutes of Meetings 6 January 1953 and 9 January 1953. Folder, GSD Faculty Meeting Minutes, UAV 322.6. Mary Therese Gain, "Theory and Practice in Architectural Education: The Harvard Curriculum, 1934–1956," M.A. thesis, Cornell University, 1977, 127, from Walter F. Bogner, "Report of Program and Degrees in Architecture," Files of the NAAB, Washington, D.C. The bachelor's degree, however, was again temporarily reinstated in 1956 and finally abolished in 1970.

2. Sert's appointment and the consolidation of the departments was also announced in Patrick J. Cusick, Luis P. Dolbaere, James D. Murphy, and Charles M. Zettek, letter to all alumni of the Graduate School of s

3. "Harvard University, School of Design, Announcement of Recent Changes," 1 July 1953, 3 pp. LL.

4. For additional material on Chermayeff, see "Harvard University, School of Design, Announcement of Recent Changes," 1 July 1953, 3 pp. LL. [curriculum vitae] "Serge Ivan Chermayeff," 28 May 1953, LL; E. Mumford, CIAM Discourse, 121–122, 208; and Richard Plunz, *Design and Public Good: Selected Writings 1930–1980 by Serge Chermayeff* (Cambridge, Mass.: MIT Press, 1982).

5. Naum Gabo (1890–1977) spent the war in England, working with Herbert Read to conduct design research intended to promote cooperation between artists and industry, he moved to the United States in 1946 and lectured at Harvard, MIT, and Black Mountain College in North Carolina. See "Harvard University, School of Design, Announcement of Recent Changes," 1 July 1953, 3 pp. LL. For Gabo, see also Martin Hammer and Christina Lodder, *Constructing Modernity* (New Haven: Yale University Press, 2000).

6. "Harvard University, School of Design, Announcement of Recent Changes," 1 July 1953, 3 pp. LL. See Melanie Simo, *Sasaki Associates: Integrated Environments* (Washington, D.C.; Cambridge, Mass.: Spacemaker Press, 1997); Id., Harvard Landscape, passim; and Anne Raver [obituary], "Hideo Sasaki, Influential Landscape Architect, Dies at 80," *NYT*, online edition, 25 September 2000.

7. Huson Jackson (1913–) (B.Arch. 1938, M.Arch. 1939, GSD) worked in the office of Charles Eames and operated a private practice in Boston (1940–42) and New York after 1944; he also taught at the Pratt Institute and Columbia University in New York.

Ronald R. Gourley (1919–1999) (M.Arch. 1948, GSD) started teaching at MIT in 1948. He worked in various architects' offices in California, Minnesota, and Massachusetts from 1936 to 1953 and was in private practice at the time of his initial appointment to the GSD. Gourley taught at the GSD until 1970, then for ten years was dean of the College of Architecture at the University of Arizona. [Obituary], *Harvard Magazine* (July–August 2000), 96.

8. E. Mumford, *CIAM Discourse*, 247. Joseph Zalewski taught at the GSD from 1953 to 1976.

9. Robert Geddes (M.Arch. 1950, GSD), for example, claimed GSD students were unaware of the CIAM in the postwar years. E. Mumford, *CIAM Discourse*, 323, n. 14. Geddes became co-founder of the firm Geddes Brecher Qualls Cunningham and the first dean of the Princeton University School of Architecture. For Geddes, see "Faculty News," *ACSA News* 29:2 (October 1999): 9.

10. Bruno Zevi, "Della cultura architettonica: Messaggio al Congrès International d'Architecture Moderne," *Metron* 51–52 (1949): 9–10 quoted and discussed; E. Mumford, *CIAM Discourse*, 198–199.

11. E. Mumford, *CIAM Discourse*, 204.

12. For the emergence of Team 10 and decline of CIAM, See E. Mumford, *CIAM Discourse*, 201–238.

13. [José Luis Sert] to President [Nathan Pusey], "Notes on the Graduate School of Design," UAV 319.322.1, Records of the Office of Dean, Suberies III.

14. R. L. Saxe, "Pusey Supports Design School's Revisions," *Harvard Crimson* 20 March 1954, 1, 4, with editorial dated 22 March 1954, 2.

15. "Contribution of José Luis Sert, Dean of the Harvard Graduate School of Design, to the A.I.A. Symposium on The Changing Philosophy of Architecture," Boston, held on June 16, 1954. 7 pp. Ts. LL. Quoted, 4.

16. E. Mumford, *CIAM Discourse,* 172, 202, 246, n. 192, 315.

17. Kenneth Conant stated that Dean Sert wanted to retain him as a teacher, but Conant opted for retirement after thirty-three years of teaching at Harvard, and went as a Fellow to Dumbarton Oaks in Washington, D.C. (KJC, interview with the author).

18. For Giedion (1888–1968) and his teaching, see Eduard F. Sekler, "Sigfried Giedion at Harvard University," in McDougall, *The Architectural Historian in America,* 265–273. For Giedion's turn to the origins of art and architecture, see his *The Eternal Present: A Contribution on Constancy and Change,* 2 vols. (New York: Bollingen Foundation; distributed by Pantheon Books, 1962–64), Bollingen series 35. A.W. Mellon lectures in the fine arts 6, pt. 1–2; and, posthumously, his *Architecture and the Phenomena of Transition; the Three Space Conceptions in Architecture* (Cambridge, Mass.: Harvard University Press, 1971).

19. Eduard F. Sekler (1920–) was born in Vienna, Austria, and studied and taught at its Technical University. He also studied at the London School of Planning and Regional Research, and received his Ph.D. from the Warburg Institute of London University in 1948. He was appointed visiting professor in 1954–55, was named professor of architecture at Harvard in 1960, and retired in 1992 as Osgood Hooker Professor of Visual Art, emeritus, but taught part time through 1999. Sekler was instrumental in establishing the Carpenter Center for the Visual Arts, served as coordinator of studies, 1962–64, was its first director in 1966–76, and from 1968 to 1970 was chairman of the Department of Visual and Environmental Studies, the program that superseded the Department of Architectural Sciences in Harvard College. Included among his writings is the definitive monograph on the architecture of Josef Hoffmann, *Josef Hoffmann, the Architectural Work* (Princeton: Princeton University Press, 1985). See US/ICOMOS Newsletter, 7:2 (February 1986): 5; interview with the author, 19 June 1986;

Who's Who in America, vol. 2, 5th ed., 4424.

For Sekler's contributions to teaching architectural history at Harvard, See Deborah Fausch's review of Alexander von Hoffman, ed., *Form, Modernism, and History in Honor of Eduard F. Sekler* (Cambridge: Mass.: 1996); and Wolfgang Böhm, ed., *Das Bauwerk und de Stadt: Aufsätze für Eduard F. Sekler/The Building and the Town: Essays for Eduard F. Sekler* (1994), in JSAH 57:4 (December 1998), 483–485.

20. See Simo, *History of Landscape Architecture,* 50.

21. For Nivola (1911–1988), see Grace Glueck [Obituary], "Costantino Nivola, 76, A Sculptor of Public and Small-Scale Works," *New York Times,* 6 May 1988, 11; and Richard Ingersoll, review of *Una piazza per un poeta,* by Salvatore Naitza, in *Design Book Review* 16 (Summer 1989): 48–49.

22. Albert Szabo (1925– ; M.Arch. 1952, GSD) studied at Brooklyn College, under Chermayeff at the Chicago Institute of Design, 1946–48, and was an apprentice to Marcel Breuer, 1947–48. He was chairman of Harvard's Department of Architectural Sciences 1964–68, and had administrative and teaching roles in the Department of Visual and Environment Studies at the Carpenter Center. He retired with emeritus status in 1986. For his professional activities and other academic research, see *Who's Who in America,* 43rd ed., 3208.

23. Maki was a graduate of Tokyo University who traveled to the United States where he obtained master's degrees from Cranbrook Academy and the GSD in 1954. Upon returning to Japan, Maki became a member of the Metabolism movement in Japan. See Herbert Muschamp, "Japanese Architect Wins the Pritzker Prize," *NYT,* 26 April 1993, B2.

24. Simo, *History of Landscape Architecture,* 47.

25. In an academic double entendre, in 1955 Eliot was named the Charles Eliot Professor of Landscape Architecture and Regional Planning, assuming a professorship in city and regional planning from

1959 through 1966, the year of his retirement as an emeritus professor.

26. John Hyland, interview with Lane Faison, "People of the Eye," *Newsletter of the College Art Association,* 23:4 (July 1998), 3. Faison, professor of art at Williams College (1936–76), studied at Harvard 1954–55 and became executive secretary of the Brown Committee at the request of Nicholas Brown.

27. Eduard F. Sekler and William Curtis, with contributions by Rudolph Arnheim, Barbara Norfleet, *Le Corbusier at Work: the Genesis of the Carpenter Center for the Visual Arts* (Cambridge, Mass. and London: Harvard University Press, 1978), 5.

28. Pusey requested that John Nicholas Brown, a member of Harvard's Board of Overseers, study the direction of fine arts at the University. For Pusey's receptivity to the role of the architect, See Nathan March Pusey, "The Needed New Man in Architecture" [AIA Purves Memorial Lecture] (Cambridge, Mass.: Harvard University 1966. LL).

29. E. Mumford, *CIAM Discourse,* 258.

30. Jerzy W. Soltan (1913–) received a Master of Engineering and Architecture from Warsaw Polytechnical Institute in 1948. Emigrating from Poland to the United States in 1958, he taught from 1959 to 1981 when he retired as Nelson Robinson, Jr., Professor of Architecture and Urban Design Emeritus. *Who's Who in America,* 40th ed., 1978–79, vol. 2, 3055; Mumford, *CIAM Discourse,* 156.

31. For a personal recollection of the period, see Jerzy Soltan, "A Letter to Eduard F. Sekler, Reminiscences of Post-war Modernism at CIAM and the GSD," in Alexander von Hoffman, ed., *Form, Modernism, and History* (1996), 95–98. See also Jola Sola, ed., *Jerzy Soltan* (Cambridge, Mass.: Harvard Graduate School of Design, 1995).

32. E. Mumford, *CIAM Discourse,* 159, 211. Woods's unexpected death in 1973 cut short his influence at the GSD.

33. Gerhard Kallmann (1915–) was born in Berlin and received his diploma from the Architectural Association School of Architecture, London. He taught at the GSD from 1963 to 1985 when he retired as an

emeritus professor. Noel Michael McKinnell (1935–) was born in Salford, England, and graduated from the University of Manchester. He began his practice with Gerhard Kallmann in 1962 in Boston and started teaching at the GSD in 1963. McKinnell was Nelson Robinson, Jr, Professor from 1983 to 1987 when he withdrew from teaching. For Kallmann, see *American Architects Directory*, 3d ed. (New York: Bowker, 1970), 470; for the works of their firm, Kallmann, McKinnell, Wood, see *Who's Who in America*, vol. 2, 5th ed., 3262.

34. Meyerson was appointed Frank Backus Williams Professor of City Planning and Urban Research. Now known as the Joint Center for Housing, it exists as a collaborative unit affiliated with the GSD and the Kennedy School of Government. Its programs of research, education, and public outreach deal with housing issues and how houses shape communities. (Source: http://www.gsd.harvard.edu/jcenter, 19 December 1998.)

35. [Announcement of Urban Design Program], poster, January 1960, 1 sheet, courtesy of Eduard Sekler.

36. Jaqueline Tyrwhitt, "Education for Urban Design," in *The Architect and the City: Papers from the AIA-ACSA Teacher Seminar, Cranbrook Academy of Art, June 11–22, 1962*, Marcus Whiffen, ed. (Cambridge, Mass.: MIT Press, 1966): 100.

37. Wilhelm von Moltke (1911–1987; M.Arch. 1942, GSD) studied at the Technische Hochschule in Berlin in 1937, left that year and began designing airports, community centers, housing, and schools in England and Sweden before coming to the United States in 1940. He arrived as an experienced architect to study in Gropius's master's class. He practiced with Marcel Breuer and Eero Saarinen before opening his own practice as a city planner. In 1964, he became professor of urban design at Harvard, continued developing the urban design curriculum, and retired in 1985. See *The Harvard Foundation for Advanced Study and Research Newsletter*, 15 May 1964, 7. LL.

38. Norman T. Newton, acting dean of the GSD, announced that Professor Walter L.

Chambers resigned August 1, 1958, after twenty-six years of teaching at Harvard to accept a position at the University of Michigan and directorship of the Nichols Arboretum. See "School News," *LA* 49:1 (Autumn 1958): 52.

39. Charles Ward Harris (1926–) received a BFA in landscape architecture and a BS in landscape operations from the University of Illinois in 1951, studied landscape at the GSD in 1952, and received a Master of Education from the Harvard Graduate School of Education in addition to working for several landscape firms and having his own practice. He was an assistant professor of landscape architecture at the GSD, 1958–60, resumed teaching, served as director of the Landscape Architecture Research Office, 1966–77, and was chairman of the Department of Landscape Architecture 1968–78. He retired in 1986. Interview with the author, 12 July 1986; see also Simo, *Harvard Landscape*, 38–39, 47–48, and passim. Peter Walker (1932–) (MLA 1957, GSD) taught from 1958 to 1987 and was chairman from 1978 to 1981. (See Simo, *Harvard Landscape*, 48, 70–73, and passim.)

40. Chester W. Hartman (AB 1957, Ph.D. 1959, Harvard) was an outspoken social activist at Harvard. He later became a Fellow at the Institute for Policy Studies, Washington, D.C. (*HGSD Alumni Directory*, 1986, 51).

41. William Wray Nash, Jr., (d. 1997; AB 1950, Harvard) was a professor of city and regional planning at the GSD from 1958 to 1971 and departmental chairman, 1964–68. He founded a planning consultancy with François Vigier, but later joined the faculty of Georgia State University, became dean of the College of Urban Life, retired in 1990 as Regents Professor, and was active in planning issues in Georgia. [Obituary], *Harvard Magazine* (May–June 1997): 760. François C. D. Vigier (B.Arch. 1955, MIT; MCP 1960, GSD; Ph.D. in City and Regional Planning 1967, GSD). He was first appointed to the Faculty of Design in 1962 and named Charles Dyer Norton Professor of Regional Planning in 1986. Vigier was chairman of the Department of City and

Regional Planning in 1969. From 1992 to 1998 he was chairman of the new Department of Urban Planning and Design. His professional partnership with William Nash spanned twenty-five years, including domestic planning projects and extensive work in developing countries, such as Egypt, Bahrain, Morocco, Tunisia, and Saudi Arabia. (Source of biographical material: http://www.gsd.harvard.edu, 7 July 2000.)

42. Carl Steinitz (M.Arch., 1961 and Ph.D. in City Planning, 1967, MIT) began teaching at Harvard in 1966 as an assistant professor associated with the Laboratory for Computer Graphics with a joint appointment in landscape architecture. During a long and productive career at the GSD, he was named the first Alexandra and Victory Wiley Professor of Landscape Architecture and Planning in 1986. For his work, see Simo, *Harvard Landscape*, 55–58, and passim.

43. Richard T. T. Forman succeeded Harris in 1984 and became professor of advanced environmental studies in landscape ecology. For Forman, see Simo, *Harvard Landscape*, 68, 83–84, and passim.

44. John L. Loeb, Harvard College 1924, an investment banker, Harvard overseer, and chairman of the fund-raising campaign, was also a major donor, providing $2 million. Additional gifts were received from the George Gund Foundation, the Gund family, GSD alumni/æ and friends, and the Office of Education of the U.S. Department of Health, Education, and Welfare. The overall funding goal was $11.6 million, which included $7 million not only for the building but also for new fellowships and new professorships. See John H. Fenton, "Harvard Honors School of Design Drive Leader," *New York Times*, 4 June 1968, n.p.

45. [Eduard Sekler], "Statement to the Faculty of Arts and Sciences," 5 March 1968, 4 pp ts. Courtesy of Eduard Sekler.

46. See A. Whitney Griswold, et al., *The Fine Arts and the University* (Toronto: Macmillan; New York: St. Martin's Press, 1965); *The Frank Gerstin Lectures, 1965: Carpenter Center for the Visual Arts, Tenth Anniversary*, introduction by Eduard F.

Sekler (Cambridge, Mass.: Carpenter Center, 1973).

47. Rudolf Arnheim (1904–) was born in Berlin. After retirement from the Carpenter Center as professor emeritus of the psychology of art, he continued to teach and write.

48. For J. B. Jackson at Harvard, see Simo, *Harvard Landscape*, 58–59, 62–64.

49. See "The Fist and Its Clencher," *Harvard Alumni Magazine* (July–August 1998), 80–81.

50. Sert had already resigned as chairman of the architecture department in 1964. In 1962 the National Architectural Accreditation Board had voiced a concern that Sert had so much responsibility as dean and chairman and designer instructor that his position should be divided (José Luis Sert to Nathan Marsh Pusey, UAV 319.322.7, Records of the of the Office of the Dean, Subseries IC Box 6). Despite subsequent discussion about hiring someone who could assist in fund-raising, Benjamin Thompson, a partner in TAC, was appointed from 1964 to 1966. Soltan became the chairman of the Department of Architecture from 1967 to 1973 and was succeeded by George Anselevicius (1973–75), Gerald McCue (1976–79), Henry N. Cobb (1980–85), José Rafael Moneo (1985–90), Mac Scoggin (1990–95), and Jorge S. Silvetti (1995–).

51. For Maurice D. Kilbridge's (1920–) agenda at the GSD, see "Dean's Column: The Ideal School, New Goals for the GSD," *HGSD News* (October 1975), 2 pp. LL; for his approach to urban issues, see Maurice D. Kilbridge, Robert P. O'Block, and Paul V. Teplitz, *Urban Analysis* (Boston: Division of Research, Graduate School of Business Administration, Harvard University, 1970); and for an example of urban planning policy analysis and administration, see his policy note, *Some Generalizations on Urbanization and Housing in Developing Countries* (Cambridge, Mass.: Department of City and Regional Planning, Harvard University, 1976).

52. John Andrews (M.Arch. 1958, GSD), an Australian working in Toronto, had been acclaimed for designing the University of Toronto's Scarborough College when his plans for Gund Hall were unveiled in 1968. ("Harvard Airs $7M Design School Plan," *Boston Herald Traveler,* 4 June 1968.) Scarborough College was seen at the time by critics as a megastructure; for the critical context, see Ada Louise Huxtable, "Don't Call it Kookie," *NYT,* 19 January 1969, Administrative Files, Gund Hall, GSD, LL.

53. In Landscape Architecture, the increased enrollment came from students who already had bachelor degrees, but no professional training. This allowed the resumption of much-needed first-year design courses and the return to offering a full three-year program which culminated in the granting of a Master's of Landscape Architecture.

54. "Harvard Airs $7M Design School Plan," *Boston Herald Traveler*, 4 June 1968, n.p.; *Official Register, 1978–1979,* 16.

55. Alexander Tzonis (1937– ; B.Arch. 1967, Yale) worked closely with Serge Chermayeff while at Yale. Tzonis taught at the GSD from 1967 to 1981. His first major publications were *The Shape of Community* (New York: Penguin, 1972) with Chermayeff; and *Towards a Non-oppressive Environment* (Cambridge, Mass.: MIT Press, 1972). Subsequent numerous publications included Liane Lefaivre as coauthor. Taking a taxonometric approach, they published *Classical Architecture* (Cambridge, Mass.: MIT Press, 1986). Tzonis transferred his analytic approach to the Technical University of Delft where he established in 1985 the Design Knowledge Systems Research Center in the School of Architecture. Its purpose is to offer a multidisciplinary research and an advanced education program to improve design methods and theory through better understanding of designing as a cognitive process embedded in social and cultural practice.

56. Susan K. Brown and Richard F. Strasser, "K-School and GSD Consider Public Policy Program Merger," *Harvard Crimson,* 28 November 1979, 1.

57. See "President Bok Proposes GSD and KSG Establish Three Joint Professorships in Planning," *HGSD News* 12:3 (January/February 1984): 2. For a summary of the conditions leading up to the transfer of planning to the Kennedy School, see François Vigier, "The New Master in Urban Planning Degree Program," *HGSD News* (Fall 1993): 33. The transfer fulfilled the suggestion of John Gaus, who in 1940 called for a division in planning education between physical design at the GSD and management training at the Graduate School of Public Administration, predecessor of Harvard's Kennedy School of Government.

58. Richard F. Strasser, "Kilbridge to Resign as Dean of GSD," *Harvard Crimson,* 4 June 1979, 1.

59. Gerald Mallon McCue (1928–) was born in Woodland, California. He completed undergraduate (1951) and graduate degrees (1952) at the University of California at Berkeley, and established an independent practice in the San Francisco area in 1954. His practice evolved through successive firms, each conducting work that included programming, master planning, and design for public, private, and corporate clients. In 1965, McCue was appointed professor of architecture and urban design at Berkeley and served as chairman of the department until 1970. He was appointed to the Harvard University Faculty of Design and named chairman of the department of architecture and associate dean in 1976. He served as dean of the Faculty of Design from 1980 to 1992. Until his retirement, he subsequently taught as professor of architecture and urban design and the John T. Dunlop Professor of Housing Studies, John F. Kennedy School of Government. His teaching focused on bridging the fields of architecture and landscape architecture, with emphasis on issues that affect planning and design in urban settings. See faculty biographies, http://www.ksg.harvard.edu, 14 December 1998; *American Architects Directory* 3rd ed. (New York: Bowker, 1970), 573.

60. The GSD expanded opportunities for post-professional study through the Master in Design Studies and Doctor of Design programs, which were established in 1986, and through the Ph.D. programs in architecture, landscape architecture, and urban planning. McCue created doctoral programs, although a doctoral program had long been available in the University, but rarely activated.

61. William A. Doebele began teaching at the GSD in 1958 and retired in 1997 as Frank Backus Williams Professor of Urban Planning and Design Emeritus. In addition to teaching and writing about legal issues and planning, he was founding curator of the Loeb Fellowship Program in Advanced Environmental Studies and retired in 1997. The program was another response to concern about the environment and turmoil in American cities in the late 1960s. Funded by John L. Loeb and based in the GSD, the fellowships allow post-professional independent study with access to all of Harvard's major schools. For a history of the program, see also Carter Wiseman, "A Fellows-Eye View of the Loeb Fellowship," 16 May 1997, Ts. José A. Ibáñez-Gómez graduated from Harvard College, AB, 1970, Master of Public Policy, 1972, Harvard University, and Ph.D., Kennedy School of Government, 1975. He started teaching at the GSD in 1975 and in 1984 was jointly appointed in the GSD and the Kennedy School for Government as the Derek C. Bok Professor of Public Policy and Urban Planning. At the GSD he taught courses on economics, infrastructure, and transportation planning. Formerly the Chairman of the Department of Urban Planning and Design (1984–88) and director of the Advanced Independent Study Programs (1992–95) at the Graduate School of Design, Gómez-Ibáñez was also Faculty Chair of the Master in Public Policy Program at the Kennedy School (1996–98). (Source: faculty biographies: http://www.gsd.harvard.edu, 30 July 2000)

62. Alex Krieger (MCP in Urban Design 1977, GSD) was formally appointed to the Faculty of Design in 1984, succeeding François Vigier as director of the Department of Urban Planning and Design in 1998. See "Alex Krieger, New Chairman of Department of Urban Planning and Design," *Harvard Design Magazine* (Summer 1998): 84.

63. Peter G. Rowe to the author, 1 April 1999.

64. AR 152 (November 1972): 101; *The Harvard Guide* (Cambridge, Mass.: Harvard University Office of News and Public Affairs, 1998), 72; and Sean Conlon, [GSD Registrar's Office] to author, personal communication, 4 December 2000.

65. Vincent Scully, "The American City in A.D. 2025," *Brookings Review* (Summer 2000); excerpted and reprinted in *Austin American Statesman*, 18 August 2000, A8.

66. *Harvard Magazine* 96 (November–December 1993): 78. The GSD's review of its first-year degree program paralleled a university-wide effort in all Harvard's professional schools.

67. "Rudenstine Report Outlines Priorities," in *Harvard College Gazette* (Winter 1994): 8.

68. Jorge S. Silvetti, "From the Guest Feature Editor," *Harvard Design Magazine* (Summer 1998): 3–5; and Peter G. Rowe, "The Design Arts Initiative," ibid., 84–85. Silvetti studied in Argentina, received his M.Arch. degree from Berkeley in 1969, and began teaching at Harvard in 1975. He was named Nelson Robinson, Jr., Professor of Architecture in 1990. For his professional work and publications, see biographical files, http://www.gsd.harvard.edu.

69. Frances Halsband, chair, Design Conference on Collaboration to Members of the Committee on Design (AIA), 16 June 2000 quoted in Wendy Feuer, "Observations on Collaborations," issued as offprint of *Places* 13:1, *Forum: AIA Committee on Design*, 4 pp.

APPENDIX:
CHRONOLOGY

1858 Frederick Law Olmsted, Sr., and Calvert Vaux win competition for design of Central Park in New York City.

1860 Frederick Law Olmsted, Sr., begins interdisciplinary practice of landscape architecture with allied professionals.

1868 William Ware establishes first university-based program in architecture in the United States at MIT.

Profession of landscape architecture established by designation of Olmsted and Vaux as landscape architects of Central Park.

1869 Charles William Eliot becomes twenty-first president of Harvard.

1874 Charles Eliot Norton includes the history of architecture in his courses on the fine arts.

1893 Herbert Langford Warren gives the first courses devoted exclusively to the history of architecture, with Greek and Roman traditions as focus.

1895 The undergraduate degree, SB, in architecture is established in the Lawrence Scientific School.

1897 Rotch Hall on Soldier's Field is used for classes in architecture.

1899 American Society of Landscape Architects is founded in New York City.

1900 President Eliot of Harvard, benefiting from a donor's gift, persuades Frederick Law Olmsted, Jr., to organize and head a four-year graduate program leading to the degree of SB in landscape architecture; established in Harvard's Lawrence Scientific School.

In memory of their son, Mr. and Mrs. Nelson Robinson provide funds for Robinson Hall, designed by McKim, Mead & White.

1901 Henry Vincent Hubbard, AB 1897, is the first student to be awarded the SB in landscape architecture.

1902 Nelson Robinson, Jr. Hall opens in Harvard Yard. Old Fogg Art Museum (Hunt Hall) continues to be used for classes.

1903 Charles Eliot Professorship in landscape architecture is created with Frederick Law Olmsted, Jr., as its first incumbent.

Herbert Langford Warren becomes Nelson Robinson, Jr., Professor of Architecture.

1906 Harvard establishes the Graduate School of Applied Science as a replacement for the Lawrence Scientific School, thereby creating graduate degrees. The programs in architecture and landscape architecture are moved to the new Graduate School of Applied Science as a division of the architecture curriculum.

1907 James Sturgis Pray becomes the second chairman of the landscape architecture program after Olmsted steps down. First master's degrees in architecture and landscape architecture are awarded.

1908 Landscape architecture becomes a separate department in the Graduate School of Applied Science.

1909 First U.S. course on city planning offered by Henry Vincent Hubbard, Frederick Law Olmsted, Jr., and James Sturgis Pray within the Department of Landscape Architecture.

Abbott Lawrence Lowell becomes Harvard's twenty-second president.

1914 An independent Faculty of Architecture is created to govern the Schools of Architecture and Landscape Architecture, which offer exclusively graduate degrees.

Langford Warren is named first dean of the Faculty of Architecture.

Eugene Joseph Armand Duquesne returns to France during World War I.

1915 James Sturgis Pray becomes the second Charles Eliot Professor of Landscape Architecture upon retirement of Frederick Law Olmsted, Jr.

1917 H. Langford Warren, founder of the School of Architecture, dies on June 27.

1922 George Harold Edgell appointed dean of the Faculty of Architecture, succeeding acting dean Charles Wilson Killam.

1923 The School of Landscape Architecture offers an option leading to a master's degree in city planning, the first such degree in the United States.

1928 Bremer W. Pond is appointed chairman of the School of Landscape Architecture.

The Committee on the Regional Plan of New York and Its Environs recommends formation of a professional school or institute devoted to city and regional planning.

1929 Harvard accepts a $240,000 grant from the Rockefeller Foundation to establish the School of City Planning, the first such graduate-level program in America, chaired by Henry Vincent Hubbard, professor of landscape architecture.

James Freeman Curtis, a graduate of Harvard Law School, donates $150,000 to establish a professorship in regional planning in memory of his friend, Charles Dyer Norton, a prominent civic leader and sponsor of regional plans in Chicago and New York.

1930 Bremer Whidden Pond is named as the third Charles Eliot Professor of Landscape Architecture after the death of James Sturgis Pray in February 1929.

1933 James Bryant Conant becomes twenty-third president of Harvard University.

1935 Joseph Hudnut assumes role as dean of the Faculty of Architecture and professor of architecture; Hudnut proposes the unification of the three schools into the Graduate School of Design.

1936 The Harvard Overseers approve a plan to unite the Schools of Architecture, Landscape Architecture, and City and Regional Planning into the Graduate School of Design under the guidance of the Faculty of Design, with Joseph Hudnut as dean and Bremer W. Pond as secretary.

Department of City and Regional Planning is closed 1936–37.

Architecture department offers the B.Arch. degree as a first professional degree and the M.Arch. as a postprofessional degree.

1937 Dean Hudnut brings Walter Gropius to Harvard as chairman of the Department of Architecture in the Graduate School of Design.

Instruction in planning resumes in the newly titled Department of Regional Planning.

Marcel Breuer appointed to the GSD faculty.

1938 Martin Wagner appointed as assistant professor of regional planning.

A new undergraduate program, the Department of Architectural Sciences, is established to train students at Harvard College in the history and principles of design.

1939 Norman T. Newton joins the Department of Landscape Architecture; residential problems in design are abandoned in favor of emphasis on public works.

1941 The Department of Regional Planning is closed again; no degrees are granted during the war, but a few courses are offered.

Paralleling the degree structure in architecture, the Department of Landscape Architecture adopts the BLA degree as the goal of the three-year curriculum for candidates holding the AB degree; BLA holders may then earn the MLA upon completion of an additional series of advanced special problems.

1942 Women are admitted as degree candidates.

The Faculty of Arts and Sciences is authorized, working jointly with the Faculty of Design, to grant doctoral degrees in architecture, landscape architecture, and city planning; the Ph.D. program remains largely inactive. The Departments of Architecture and Landscape Architecture later suspend indefinitely acceptance of Ph.D. candidates in their areas.

1943 For the duration of World War II, the Departments of Architecture and Landscape Architecture admit candidates for the B.Arch. and BLA who do not already hold the AB.

1945 The G. I. Bill encourages veterans to resume education and professional training.

The National Architectural Accreditation Board (NAAB), established in 1939 by the American Institute of Architects (AIA) with the Association of Collegiate Schools of Architecture (ACSA) and the National Council of Architectural Registration Boards (NCARB), begins evaluation of architectural schools.

1946 The GSD begins its collaborative program in which all first-year students in the school's three departments take the same large-scale studio course under an interdepartmental team of instruc-

tors; students also take specific courses in their respective departments.

1948 The GSD catalog for 1948–49 no longer lists curriculum leading to the BLA degree and restores the MLA.

1950 Lester A. Collins becomes chairman of the Department of Landscape Architecture, and Norman T. Newton is appointed secretary of the Faculty of Design, both upon the retirement of Bremer Pond, as Charles Eliot Professor of Landscape Architecture, after forty years of service.

1952 Walter Gropius retires as professor emeritus of architecture.

1953 End of the integrated first-year program and termination of professional bachelor's degree programs.

January: José Luis Sert is appointed dean-designate of the Faculty of Design and chairman of Department of Architecture; Lester Collins resigns and Norman T. Newton is appointed chairman of the Department of Landscape Architcture pending induction of the new dean.

June: Joseph Hudnut retires as professor emeritus of architecture.

September: Sert takes office as dean and combines landscape architecture with regional planning in one department under Reginald R. Isaacs as chairman.

Nathan Marsh Pusey appointed twenty-fourth president of Harvard.

1954 Charles W. Eliot II becomes the Charles Eliot Professor of Landscape Architecture.

1956 After three years of experimental combination with the Department of Regional Planning, the Department of Landscape Architecture resumes separate status under the chairmanship of

Walter L. Chambers; regional planning remains under Reginald Isaacs.

1957   Beginning developments in the field of urban design with formation of the Harvard Center for Urban Studies.

Martin Meyerson is named director and the first Frank Backus Williams Professor of City Planning and Urban Research.

1958   Hideo Sasaki is appointed chairman of the Department of Landscape Architecture, as Walter Chambers leaves for the University of Michigan.

1959   Harvard and MIT establish the Joint Center for Urban Studies (later changed to the Joint Center for Housing).

1960   An urban design program is established by Sert as an interdepartmental effort open only to candidates already holding a professional degree from the GSD; it is the first academic degree program in urban design in the United States. Upon completion of required courses, students would receive the respective degrees of M.Arch., MLA, or MCP in urban design.

1963   The Harvard Corporation elects Norman T. Newton the Charles Eliot Professor of Landscape Architecture.

Regional landscape architecture five-year collaborative studios are inaugurated with students from landscape architecture and regional planning.

1964   First capital fund-raising campaign supports the postprofessional Program for Advanced Environmental Studies (PAES), intended to accelerate experimental research, strengthen existing curricula, and erect new buildings to house the School of Design.

1965   Foundation funds establish a Laboratory for Computer Graphics and Spatial Analysis, with Howard T. Fisher as the first director.

1966   Charles W. Harris is named director of the new Landscape Architecture Research Office.

The Ford Foundation awards a grant to establish a new chair in resources and ecology as part of the PAES.

1967   Urban field source established.

1969   The Harvard strike.

Hideo Sasaki steps down as chairman of the Department of Landscape Architecture after ten years at that post; Charles W. Harris is appointed to succeed him.

Albert Fein, visiting professor in landscape architecture history, is named to direct a study of the profession of landscape architecture, co-sponsored by the ASLA/NCILA with a grant from the Ford Foundation.

1969   Dean Sert retires; Maurice D. Kilbridge is appointed dean of the Faculty of Design. Frederick E. Smith is appointed first PAES professor of resources and ecology.

1970   Visiting team for ASLA accreditation arrives. Discussion reveals confusion in present program and frustration about future of landscape architecture at Harvard.

Professor Sasaki resigns from the Faculty of Design.

Several grants from foundations are received, including one from the National Science Foundation, to support computerized procedures for land-use planning, and a Rockefeller grant for regional field service and further study of visual highway standards for the Department of Transportation.

Loeb Fellowship Program established to bring mid-career professionals to the GSD for independent study.
B.Arch. degree officially terminated; previous holders can exchange for M.Arch.

1971   Derek Bok becomes twenty-fifth president of Harvard.

1972–73 Gund Hall is completed as single facility for all design-related programs.

The needed first-year courses in design are resumed, allowing the Department of Landscape Architecture to reinstate its three-year program for MLA to holders of AB degrees.

1975   Landscape architecture at Harvard celebrates its seventy-fifth anniversary. Department again receives ASLA accreditation as a graduate program.

1978   Peter E. Walker is appointed chairman of the Department of Landscape Architecture, as Charles Harris steps down after ten years in the position.

1980   The Department of Regional Planning is transferred to the John F. Kennedy School of Government.

Dean Maurice D. Kilbridge resigns after serving eleven years.

Gerald M. McCue is appointed dean of the Faculty of Design.

Henry N. Cobb becomes chairman of the Department of Architecture.

1983   The Department of Urban Planning Design is established to focus study on the physical form of cities.

1985   Reorganization results in new Department of Urban Planning and Design with GSD.

Plans for expansion of degree programs (D.Des. and Ph.D.) announced. Second capital fund-raising campaign announced.

Laboratory for Construction Technology dedicated as a center for computer research and curriculum development in building technology.

CREDITS

1986 Fiftieth anniversary of the founding of the GSD and 350th anniversary of Harvard College.

Exhibition on history of the GSD held in Gund Hall.

Two postprofessional programs inaugurated: the master's of design studies and doctor of design.

1987 Unit for housing and urbanization established, later named the Center for Urban Development Studies.

1991 Neil I. Rudenstine named twenty-sixth president of Harvard.

1992 Peter G. Rowe appointed dean of the GSD.

1993 The GSD announces the possibility of an integrated introduction to the major design fields, including architecture, landscape architecture, and urban design and planning.

1994 First students enroll in master's program in urban planning.

1995 Centennial of architecture program at Harvard.

1997 Instructional Technology Group established to develop new uses of computer technology for educational initiatives.

1998 Jorge S. Silvetti announces design arts initiative.

1999 The Department of Landscape Architecture holds conference on interdisciplinary contributions of the 1990s.

2000 Centennial of the Department of Landscape Architecture marked with publication of its history.

Unless credited otherwise below, all figures are from the collections of Frances Loeb Library, Harvard Graduate School of Design and copyright President and Fellows of Harvard College. Permission to publish and quote from material in the Harvard Graduate School of Design's archives is gratefully acknowledged.

3.2, 3.4, 3.7, 3.11, 3.12, 3.14–3.16, 3.25, 3.41–3.44. Courtesy Alfred J. Panepinto

3.5. Courtesy Edwin J. Peterson

3.10, 3.17. Courtesy Edward J. Aisner

3.13. Courtesy Walter H. Kilham, Jr.

4.6. Wide-World Photos

4.7. Photo by K. K. Stowell

5.3, 5.4, 5.46, 5.47. Courtesy *Architectural Forum*

5.7. Courtesy *Architectural Record*

5.9, 5.40–5.42. Courtesy Hugh McK. Jones

5.10–5.17. Courtesy Robert A. Little

5.19–5.23, 5.34, 5.35. Courtesy Paul F. Schelp

5.26, 5.27. Courtesy Smithsonian Institution

5.28, 5.37–5.39. Courtesy John O. Simonds

5.44, 5.45, 6.21. Private collection

5.56, 5.57. Courtesy Philip Johnson and the Museum of Modern Art, New York

6.1, 6.19. *Harvard Alumni Bulletin*

6.11–6.14. Courtesy William J. Conklin

6.15–6.18. Courtesy Harry Seidler

6.21–6.29, 7.2, 7.3. Courtesy *Progressive Architecture*

6.30. Courtesy Henry N. Cobb

7.1. Courtesy Time-Life, Inc.

8.4, 8.10. Courtesy Eduard Sekler

8.11. Courtesy Peter Papesch

8.12–8.14. Harvard University News Office

INDEX